CONTEMPORARY FAMILIES AT THE NEXUS OF RESEARCH AND PRACTICE

Contemporary Families at the Nexus of Research and Practice integrates current research with clinical theory to establish the most up-to-date, evidence-supported treatment options for unique contemporary families. Each chapter begins with a case study and genogram. A research section that explains family experiences outlined in the case study follows. Finally, a treatment section presents clinical theory and provides an evidence-supported practice. Together, each chapter demonstrates how theory gets translated into practice. Family forms discussed include families of divorce, stepfamilies, families of addiction, impoverished families, families of incarceration, families of cyberbullying, and families of murder victims. Whether you're a professional or a student, this book will provide both relevant research findings and explicit instruction and case material to augment your practice.

Scott W. Browning, PhD, is a professor in the Department of Professional Psychology at Chestnut Hill College in Philadelphia. He is a noted authority on psychological treatment with stepfamilies, families of homicide, and families on the spectrum. He is the co-editor of *Contemporary Families* (Routledge, 2015).

Brad van Eeden-Moorefield, PhD, MSW, is an associate professor and director of the PhD Program in the Department of Family Science & Human Development at Montclair State University.

CONTEMPORARY FAMILIES AT THE NEXUS OF RESEARCH AND PRACTICE

Edited by
Scott W. Browning and
Brad van Eeden-Moorefield

Routledge
Taylor & Francis Group
NEW YORK AND LONDON

First published 2017
by Routledge
711 Third Avenue, New York, NY 10017

and by Routledge
2 Park Square, Milton Park, Abingdon, Oxon, OX14 4RN

Routledge is an imprint of the Taylor & Francis Group, an informa business

Library of Congress Cataloging-in-Publication Data
Names: Browning, Scott, editor. | Van Eeden-Moorefield, Brad, editor.
Title: Contemporary families at the nexus of research and practice / edited by Scott W. Browning and Brad van Eeden-Moorefield.
Description: New York, NY : Routledge, 2017. | Includes bibliographical references and index.
Identifiers: LCCN 2016051688 | ISBN 9781138950726 (hbk : alk. paper) | ISBN 9781138950733 (pbk : alk. paper) | ISBN 9781315668598 (ebk)
Subjects: LCSH: Families. | Families—Research.
Classification: LCC HQ519 .C68 2017 DDC 306.85—dc23
LC record available at https://lccn.loc.gov/2016051688

ISBN: 978-1-138-95072-6 (hbk)
ISBN: 978-1-138-95073-3 (pbk)
ISBN: 978-1-315-66859-8 (ebk)

Typeset in Times New Roman
by Apex CoVantage, LLC

Scott dedicates this book to Joanne; her brilliance, beauty, and compassion provide a foundation for his world.

Brad dedicates this book to his mother, Helen, partner, Andy, and fur baby, Sadie. He is grateful for their love, support, and inspiration.

CONTENTS

CONTRIBUTORS

Joyce A. Arditti, PhD, is professor of human development at Virginia Tech. She received her doctorate in family studies from the University of North Carolina at Greensboro. Her research interests include family disruption, parent-child relationships in vulnerable families, and public policy. Her scholarship is recognized nationally and abroad and she has published numerous empirical and review articles in therapy, human services, family studies, and criminal justice journals. She is the author of the book *Parental Incarceration and the Family: Psychological and Social Effects of Imprisonment on Children, Parents, and Caregivers*, published by New York University Press, for which she was the 2014 recipient of the Academy of Criminal Justice Sciences (ACJS) Outstanding Book Award, an honor awarded to a member of ACJS who has authored a book representing an extraordinary contribution in the field of criminal justice. Additionally, in August of 2016, Joyce was awarded the Alumni Award for Research Excellence by Virginia Tech for her significant research achievement in the area of parental incarceration. Joyce is also the editor of the recently released textbook *Family Problems: Stress, Risk, & Resilience*, published by John Wiley & Sons. Joyce served as the editor in chief of *Family Relations: The Interdisciplinary Journal of Applied Family Studies* from 2004 to 2009. She is a fellow of the National Council on Family Relations (NCFR), and is currently the research and policy brief editor for NCFR.

Catherine Bradshaw, PhD is a professor and the associate dean for Research and Faculty Development at the Curry School of Education at the University of Virginia (U.Va.); prior to her current appointment at U.Va., she was an associate professor and the associate chair of the Department of Mental Health at the Johns Hopkins Bloomberg School of Public Health. She holds a doctorate in developmental psychology from Cornell University and a master's of education in counseling and guidance from the University of Georgia. Her primary research interests focus on the development of aggressive behavior and school-based prevention. She collaborates on research projects examining bullying and school climate; the development of aggressive and problem behaviors; effects of exposure to violence, peer victimization, and environmental stress on children; and the design, evaluation, and implementation of evidence-based prevention programs in schools.

Sanford Braver, PhD, is professor of psychology at Arizona State University. Dr. Braver is a notable authority on divorce, has received over $10 million in funding for his work, has numerous publications, and has been featured in national media multiple times.

Scott W. Browning, PhD, ABPP, is a professor in the Department of Professional Psychology at Chestnut Hill College in Philadelphia. He is a noted authority on psychological treatment with stepfamilies, families of homicide, and families on the spectrum. As a scholar, teacher, and clinician, Scott has explored the intricacies of treating contemporary families, and has provided advanced training in the treatment of these diverse families to clinicians and graduate students, both nationally and abroad. He is the author of numerous chapters and articles on the topics of stepfamilies, empathy, codependency, strategic family therapy, and family therapy training practices. Scott is a diplomat in couple and family psychology and part of the clinical training team of the National Stepfamily Resource Center.

Lorig Charkoudian, PhD, is the executive director of the Community Mediation Center in Maryland. Her work includes developing partnerships with state agencies including the Department of Public Safety and Correctional Service, Maryland State Department of Education, Family Court Administration, and others, to bring collaborative conflict resolution to new and unique forums. Lorig serves as a trainer and provides technical assistance to the 18 community-based mediation programs serving Maryland, including mentorship for collaborative public policy facilitation. Lorig's research examines the impact of specific aspects of the mediation process on experiences for participants as well as broader cost-benefit analysis of community mediation. Community Mediation Maryland and Lorig have received national attention for the innovative work on prisoner reentry mediation.

Rachel M. Diamond, PhD, LMFT, is an assistant professor in the Marriage & Family Therapy Program at University of Saint Joseph, West Hartford, Connecticut. She provides mediation services at the Children's Law Center of Connecticut in the Families in Transition (FIT) Program. Dr. Diamond has a clinical and research interest in divorce and remarriage in couples and families.

Brad van Eeden-Moorefield, MSW, PhD, CFLE, is an associate professor in the Department of Family & Child Studies and director of the PhD Program in Family Studies at Montclair State University. His research includes a strong commitment to understanding and strengthening marginalized families, with his most recent work focused on stepfamilies headed by same-sex couples. Much of this research focuses on identifying how factors in the social world (e.g., stigma, stereotypes, policy) influence everyday family life and how both impact various indicators of individual (e.g., depression, happiness) and family well-being (stability), and has been featured in national media. Brad has provided training to various family and childcare practitioners and uses his previous clinical experiences to translate research into practice and practice into research.

John Hart is a fifth-year family science doctoral candidate from Gaithersburg, Maryland. He earned a B.A. in psychology with honors from the George Washington University. He also earned a M.S. in couple and family therapy at the University of Maryland. He is a licensed graduate marriage and family therapist currently working with couples and families in Columbia, Maryland. In addition, he is a graduate research assistant at the Maryland Center for Health Equity (M-CHE) at the University of Maryland, College Park, conducting research on racial health disparities. His primary research interests focus on the reentry experiences from prison of Black fathers and how they navigate back into their communities and families' lives, Black men's health, and the transition into adulthood for first- and second-generation African and Latino immigrant men.

Mary Beth Hays received her master of social work degree from the University of Pennsylvania. Ms. Hays has specialized in providing trauma-informed treatment to individuals exposed to interpersonal, family, and community violence for over 20 years with a special focus on co-victims of homicide. Mary Beth Hays is currently a program manager/community intervention specialist for the Healing Hurt People Program at a Level I trauma center located in Philadelphia.

Katherine M. Hertlein, PhD, is a professor and program director of the Marriage and Family Therapy Program at the University of Nevada, Las Vegas. She received her master's in marriage and family therapy from Purdue University Calumet and her doctorate in human development with a specialization in marriage and family therapy from Virginia Tech. She has published over 100 articles and book chapters and eight books. Dr. Hertlein also has produced the first theoretical model detailing the role of technology in couples and families. She has been a keynote speaker for several state conferences on technology and relationships and the recipient of numerous awards.

C. Wayne Jones, PhD, a child and family psychologist, is the founder and director of the Center for Family Based Training, an organization that promotes the implementation of evidence-informed systems-oriented approaches, such as eco-systemic structural family therapy (ESFT), to treating youth with severe emotional problems and their families. He has been the principal investigator of several major community-based federal research demonstration programs designed to improve the developmental outcomes of young children living in multi-stressed families, and has published numerous journal articles and book chapters on related topics. His book, *Setting the Stage for Change: In-Home Family Based Intervention*, is a treatment manual for therapists applying the ESFT model in intensive in-home programs, such as Pennsylvania's Family Based Mental Health program. Dr. Jones is also clinical associate professor of psychology in psychiatry at the University of Pennsylvania Perelman School of Medicine, where he is on the training faculty of the Center for Couples and Families.

Sara Smock Jordan, PhD, LMFT, is an associate professor in Texas Tech University's Marriage and Family Therapy Program. Sara's main research focus is on applying solution-focused brief therapy (SFBT) to a wide variety of clinical issues, including substance abuse. Recently, her work on applying SFBT with substance abusers has been recognized by SAMHSA as an evidence-based approach.

Mathis Kennington, PhD, is a licensed marriage and family therapist in Austin, Texas, specializing in couples therapy and men's sexual health. Dr. Kennington serves as the clinical director for the Austin Family Institute, where he trains and equips clinicians to provide accessible couple and family therapy to members of the Austin community. Dr. Kennington's dissertation research focused on how life outside prison shapes men's experiences of freedom. This work catalyzed his interest in promoting men's sexual and mental health, emotional intelligence, and relationship competence.

Krista Mehari, PhD, is a postdoctoral fellow at the Violence Prevention Initiative at the Children's Hospital of Philadelphia. She received her PhD in clinical psychology from Virginia Commonwealth University, where she conducted research in aggression, victimization, and cyberbullying at the Clark-Hill Institute for Positive Youth Development. Dr. Mehari completed her clinical internship at an acute inpatient psychiatric unit for children and adolescents, where she conducted group, family, and individual therapy. Currently, she conducts research and facilitates anti-bullying prevention programs in Philadelphia public schools. Dr. Mehari's interests are broadly in the area of violence prevention, and she has published in the areas of cyberbullying, contextual effects on adolescents' aggression and victimization experiences, and improving the ecological validity of violence prevention programs for urban youth.

Tamara Meixner is a doctoral student in clinical psychology at Ryerson University, Canada. Tamara's research interests surround maternal substance use and its impact on child and parenting outcomes. Throughout her graduate studies, she has assisted with the completion of a province-wide evaluation of addiction treatment programs designed to meet the needs of pregnant and parenting women with addictions.

Karen Milligan, PhD, C.Psych., is an assistant professor in the Department of Psychology at Ryerson University, Canada, and a registered psychologist. Karen's research is focused on maternal substance use and its impact on child and parenting outcomes. In addition to her clinical-developmental research, she has a special interest in community-based interventions and is currently completing a province-wide evaluation of addiction treatment programs designed to meet the needs of pregnant and parenting women with addictions.

Kay Pasley, EdD, was the Norejane Hendrickson Professor and Chair of Family and Child Sciences at Florida State University. She has published numerous articles, book chapters, edited volumes, and publications for the general public. Since 1977, much of her work focused on understanding the challenges of stepfamily life, including a focus on fathering after divorce and remarriage/repartnering. She is a former editor of *Family Relations*, a Fellow of the National Council on Family Relations, and a recipient of the 2012 Felix Berardo Mentoring Award. In addition, Kay serves on numerous editorial boards and is on the clinical training team associated with the National Stepfamily Resource Center.

Kevin Roy, PhD, is associate professor and director of graduate studies in the Department of Family Science at the University of Maryland College Park School of Public Health. His research focuses on the life course of young men on the margins of families and the workforce, as they transition into adulthood and fatherhood. Through participant observation and life history interviews, he explores the intersection of policy systems, such as welfare reform, community-based parenting programs, and incarceration, with caregiving and providing roles in kin networks. He has received funding for his research from NICHD, the W.T. Grant Foundation, and the National Poverty Center. Roy is a deputy editor for *Journal of Marriage and Family* and has published in this journal, as well as *Social Problems*, *American Journal of Community Psychology*, *Journal of Family Issues*, and *Family Relations*. His book *Nurturing Dads: Social Initiatives for Contemporary Fathering* in the ASA Rose Series was published by Russell Sage Foundation Press in 2012. He received a PhD in human development and social policy at Northwestern University in 1999.

Karina Sokol, PhD, is a professor in the Psychology Department at Glendale Community College in Glendale, Arizona, where she teaches introductory psychology, developmental psychology, statistics, and biopsychology. She received her B.S. and M.A. in psychology from Northern Arizona University and completed her PhD in developmental psychology from Arizona State University. Her research interests and publications have focused on the effects of divorce on children, specifically examining the links that parenting time has for child outcomes in divorced families.

Matt Stevenson, PhD, is a postdoctoral research fellow in developmental psychology at the Center for Human Growth and Development at the University of Michigan. He received his PhD in clinical psychology from Arizona State University in 2014. He is interested in the role of fathers in child development and developmental psychopathology. More specifically his research focuses on three main areas: (1) advancing foundational attachment theory as it relates to father-child relationships, (2) the unique impact of fathers on the development of children's self-regulation and social skills, and (3) the vulnerability of fathering and father-child relationships to marital conflict. Matt works with Dr. Volling on projects investigating fathering, attachment, marital conflict, and siblings.

Laura Tach, PhD, is an assistant professor of policy analysis and management at Cornell University. She received her PhD in sociology and social policy at Harvard University. Her mixed-methods research examines how public policy affects urban poverty and family life.

Amelia Usher, PhD, is a postdoctoral fellow in the Department of Psychology at Ryerson University, Canada. Amelia's research interests include community-based research and evaluation, addiction, mental health, and women and families. She is currently supporting a province-wide evaluation of addiction treatment programs designed to meet the needs of pregnant and parenting women with addictions.

Tracy Evian Waasdorp, PhD, holds dual appointments as research scientist at the Johns Hopkins Bloomberg School of Public Health and the Children's Hospital of Philadelphia. She earned a master's in counseling psychology from the University of Pennsylvania, her doctorate in human development and family studies from the University of Delaware, and completed her post-doctoral fellowship in prevention science at Johns Hopkins. Her research focuses on school-based bullying prevention and intervention, forms of aggression, bullying and peer victimization (e.g., relational aggression, cyberbullying, and bystander behaviors), coping with bullying, teachers' responses to bullying, parent-child relationships surrounding friendships and peer conflict, school connectedness, and the measurement of school safety and school climate.

Amy C. Wagner, PhD, LMFT, ABPP, is a staff therapist at the Family Institute at Northwestern University, Evanston, Illinois. She is coordinator of the Psychiatry Residents Program and a clinical lecturer in the Department of Psychology. For the past 30 years she has specialized in the clinical treatment of divorce and stepfamilies.

Ashley Peake Wellman received her PhD from the University of Florida in Criminology, Law and Society and is an associate professor at the University of Central Missouri. Her research focuses on violent offending and violent victimization. Her primary research focuses on the lived experiences of families left behind in an unsolved murder, often referred to as cold case homicide survivors. Additional work centers on the emotional, physical, and psychological tolls of sexual assault on its survivors, along with social reactions and interpretations of sexual assault. Dr. Wellman is dedicated to advocating for awareness and resources for victims of violence. Her work appears in several outlets including the *Journal of Death and Dying*, the *Journal of Family Studies*, and the *Journal of Loss and Trauma*. Thank you to Buddy and Reagan Wellman for your incredible love and support, and special thanks to the survivors of violence who trust me to be their voice for change.

PREFACE

In this book you will read two distinct writing styles: (1) research literature review and (2) clinical theory. Each of the seven primary chapters begin with a genogram and case study of an actual family treated by the clinical author(s), followed by a research section and, finally, clinical section. The family presented is central to each chapter. The case guided research scholars as they considered what research might be clinically relevant and included in the literature review, and was used by clinical scholars to detail clinical interventions. All potentially identifying information for each case was altered to protect confidentiality.

This book examines seven various contemporary family types. As one would expect, the research sections provide the reader with an empirical understanding of some of each family's experiences as well as some more general literature. Although these findings are hugely beneficial to placing each family type into a context that helps establish some level of understanding, one needs to avoid viewing these findings as establishing "fact." Slife (2003) challenges the social sciences to accept that findings proposing "truth" about human behavior or interpersonal relations are destined to be overstated. One reads such research with an understanding that the statistical operations used assume that findings represent a likely occurrence, rather than a certainty. The ongoing replication concern has only reinforced this truism. A common mistake is to treat research findings as "truth," rather than appreciate such findings as a likely possibility. Each researcher has attempted to identify how strong certain findings/patterns are as well as when some findings are novel yet hold promise.

Rather than bemoaning the presence of some uncertainty, social scientists should embrace the dictate of probability. Most researchers do respect the nuance involved in reporting findings. Researchers are careful to list exceptions and explain the variables held constant in order for each finding to have the best proportion of validity. However, the clinician has a narrow window in which to present relevant findings to her or his clients (usually in the service of psychoeducation). The presentation of research findings is timed so that clients (whether individual or family) reevaluate their allegiance to a particular belief. For example, discussing research with a stepfamily, a clinician might inform a stepfather (having been connected to this family for a year) that parenting "as if" he had raised this child is flawed. But if the clinician were to present this information with the necessary caveats and exceptions noted, the client would be uncertain as to what the clinician is actually saying.

When dealing with the media, researchers acknowledge frustration with the "sound bite." The sound bite is easily understood and, thus, highly appealing. In fact, many scholars find trying to convey information to reporters frustrating, and they often fear the final version of their information when it arrives on television or in print. However, conveying research information must be contextualized, or our science loses credibility. Clinicians generally do not take the same level of care in warning the public that research findings must be understood with an awareness of probability. Clinicians tend to see the big picture and present information in such a manner that the client might benefit from this material, even if there might be occasions that the information is not always accurate. Gelles (1982) referred to this phenomenon as the *Whozzle Effect*, and warned that clinicians were not disrespecting the research process, but rather did not fully appreciate the limitations of the original study.

Usually when research and practice are combined, it is research specifically aimed at supporting a specific intervention. Used in this way, the synergy between research and practice occurs. This book is referring to an earlier conception of this union. *The Boulder Model* advocated that training a psychologist must involve the interaction of practice and basic science. It may be the difficulty in coordinating this process that has led to the reduction of training programs explicitly embracing the scientist-practitioner model. However, Singer (1980) identified the concern by stating, "The practitioner who has not examined recent development in the research literature or who has not kept abreast of evaluation studies of various forms of treatment may well be violating the central ethic of the profession" (p. 372).

Although the reader should not expect an absolute fact about contemporary families, family science, sociology, and psychology (among others) have established remarkable knowledge about these families. Reading Sokol, Stevenson, and Braver's section, for example, one is struck by the extraordinary knowledge that exists regarding how children adjust to divorce, how custody reverberates throughout the system, and how divorce influences individuals' development, and these findings continue to give the reader confidence in understanding the general impact of divorce. In all the research sections, there is a great deal of knowledge directly applicable to the clinician. We have asked the research scholars and the clinical scholars to look for the research that is clinically relevant. We also went one step further and asked the clinical scholars to look through the research chapter for two reasons: (a) to find research findings that directly supported their clinical work, and (b) to identify pieces of specific psychoeducation that can be verbalized with clients. Often, clinicians simply skim the research since so much of that material is focused on methodology, not directly helpful to clinical practice. Accordingly, the research presented in this book is more similar to a literature review and focuses most on that which is clinically relevant. Clinicians will be pleased with the clinical sections, obviously.

Alternatively, researchers also will find merit in clinical theory, especially in those sections' abilities to generate ideas for future research. Admittedly, clinical theorists say things that cannot always be supported by specific research, but expertise in treating families provides questions that researchers will find critical in determining future projects. If these two factions of the field are not, to some extent, synergistic, what purpose do they serve in isolation? To begin, the opening chapter examines the state of evidence-based treatment as it applies to complex families. From there, in reading this book, both researchers and clinicians will find that the closer alliance of research and practice serves both groups well. We hope to see more actions related to such *bridging* between research and clinical practice in the future.

References

Gelles, R. J. (1982). Violence in the family: A review of research in the seventies. *Journal of Marriage and the Family*, *42*, 873–885. doi: 10.2307/351830

Singer, J. L. (1980). The scientific basis of psychotherapeutic practice: A question of values and ethics. *Psychotherapy: Theory, Research and Practice*, *17*, 372–383.

Slife, B.D. (2004). Theoretical challenges to therapy practice and research: The constraint of naturalism. In M. Lambert (Ed.), *Handbook of psychotherapy and behavior change* (pp. 44–83). New York: Wiley.

ACKNOWLEDGEMENTS

This project represents the next step in a much longer journey stemming from our shared commitment to bridging research and practice, especially for those families often considered among the more vulnerable. Stated another way, our primary goal is to support and strengthen families, and we see bridging research and practice as a particularly impactful way to do this. From our experience, we have come to see great value in the myriad ways research can inform and direct clinical practice, from assessment to intervention and through the identification of ways in which clinical systems and practices can be improved. We equally value the use of clinical experiences to inform new and needed research questions. In many ways, clinicians see family processes unfold, contextual shifts that impact families, patterns across families with whom they work, and so much more. Such intimate knowledge, depth of understanding, and insight into nuances absolutely are things that excite much research and spur new studies. Unfortunately, various barriers and a lack of perceived shared interests often impede collaboration. There are too many lost opportunities—opportunities that could lead to better science and practice, thereby stronger and healthier families.

This volume is meant to be both a stand-alone text and a companion to Browning and Pasley (2015) with the intent of seizing on some new opportunities. We are grateful to Kay Pasley for facilitating our introduction and collaboration on this endeavor, and Brad is grateful to Scott for both his openness to bring him on board as well as for the friendship that developed along the way. Kay's friendship and collegiality humbles both of us, and we wish nothing but joy and relaxation for her retirement. Scott wishes to thank Brad for his tireless work, positive attitude, and wonderful ideas. Also, Scott wishes to thank Rachel Hull. Rachel read, edited, and generated terrific ideas that greatly influenced the quality of this book. We also wish to thank the tremendous scholars who contributed to this book and really worked to create their own bridges between research and practice. Their expertise, dedication, and interdisciplinary perspectives merged to produce tangible, insightful knowledge and evidence-supported practices that we believe will prove useful in treating families and inspiring new research questions. Finally, we are indebted to the staff at Routledge Press, especially Elizabeth Graber, who believed in this work and provided their guidance and expertise throughout the process.

References

Browning, S., & Pasley, B.K. (2015). *Contemporary families: Translating research into practice*. New York, NY: Routledge.

1

INTRODUCTION

Scott W. Browning and Brad van Eeden-Moorefield

Across a variety of fields, the relationship between research and practice is often complementary but not integrated. Since the early 1980s there has been a call for increased collaboration between research and clinical scholars (Singer, 1980). Both those discussing individual treatment and systemic therapies have articulated a vision in which therapy is best situated on the solid foundation of research (Lebow, 1988). Vivian et al. (2012) emphasized researchers must inform clinicians of evidence and clinicians must communicate to researchers their observations. Some journals explicitly include this in their mission statements, and some scholars actively engage in both practices. However, integration still rarely occurs. Those who engage in both often state it is like tapping into "both sides" of their brains. Stricker and Keisner (1985) articulated this idea by suggesting that the thought-process involved in research is analytical whereas the clinician highlights a creative integration.

Following the many voices that have suggested the integration of research and practice is worthwhile, the challenge remains to establish a format that bridges both perspectives and provides mutual benefit. Too often, exchanges between researchers and clinicians are unsatisfying for one or both. An ongoing and mutually beneficial exchange is extremely rare, and when this occurs it likely was facilitated, at least in part, by an ability to coalesce around a single mutual goal. We speculate the goal of *helping others* (why most of us go into the related fields) is a powerful unifying force that can bridge research and practice. Achieving commitment to doing so may be the more difficult task, given often-competing job demands and roles. Even when researchers graciously provide findings that assist clinicians in forming a foundation for their work, these researchers often feel that clinicians cherry-pick only the findings that support their clinical hunches (Ganong & Coleman, 1986). At the same time, we do observe (anecdotally) that newer generations of research and clinical scholars seem more interested in building bridges.

The current book continues the method established by Browning and Pasley (2015) in *Contemporary Families: Translating Research into Practice.* Although the family types examined here are new and the method of integration slightly revised, the primary process remains. In order to create a central unifying focus, a case study guided the work of both research and clinical scholars. The term *research scholars* is used to refer to those authors who are established experts in their subfields, whereas *clinical scholars* is used to refer to those authors who are established experts for whom the merging of clinical theory and practice represents their professional identity. In some cases, scholars have some expertise across both areas. It is hoped that a wide range of those interested in both the research findings and clinical practice with families will find this book captivating, informative, and useful. Case studies and genograms in this volume have been moved to the front of each integrated chapter. These are followed by a research and a clinical section that, together, use evidence to inform practice.

Creating a Verifiable Clinical Practice With a Diverse Population

Although the argument has been made (Browning & Pasley, 2015) that relying entirely on evidence-based practice (EBP) is too narrow and prescribed given the great variation in contemporary families, it would be naïve to ignore the benefits of culling useful interventions. No specific EBP is designed for the families discussed in this volume; however, each practice offers a coherent and supported approach to treating a clearly delineated population. If one were to separate EBPs into two categories, they could be labeled "diagnostic-centered" and "systemic." The diagnostic-centered therapies address an individual and the specific diagnosis (e.g., anxiety) that the treatment is designed to ameliorate. Systemic treatments seek to improve family functioning, but can focus on problems that may be individual (such as an adolescent's drug abuse). Both general categories rely on an understanding of the population in question, some component of *Common Factors* (e.g., empathy, alliance, and goal setting), and a specific intervention. We acknowledge these treatment recipes (treatments delineated in specific steps) do assist clinicians. However, they do not form a complete treatment.

An example of a "gold standard" EBP from the diagnosis-centered treatment is dialectical behavior therapy (Linehan & Dexter-Mazza, 2008). Following the recipe reveals that the primary features of borderline personality disorder are defined so that the practitioner can tailor the approach, thus avoiding mistakes that occur when these symptoms are poorly understood. The approach combines an understanding of emotional regulation, interpersonal systems, cognitive behavioral therapy (CBT), and strategic interventions. Next, the common factors of alliance, goal setting, and safety are added to create a sophisticated and effective approach.

A "gold standard" systemic approach, such as emotionally focused therapy (EFT; Johnson, 2004), creates a clear delineation of the way attachment needs are presented in couple interactions. Johnson's approach addresses the rigid, constricted interactional patterns that lead to attacks, withdrawal, and disassociation—common problems in distressed couples. Thus, EFT assists people in identifying the pattern such that they can curtail attacks on each other. The goal of this approach is to increase safety and security so that couples can again trust each other. These interventions solidify this work by pushing the clinician to remain steadfastly present in the emotional experience of the couples' attachment needs.

This brief summary is not intended to lessen the importance of these approaches; rather, it is profoundly useful to examine the steps that make these targeted approaches effective. By understanding these treatments, practitioners can increase their therapeutic effectiveness regardless of the clinical diversity they face. It is in this process that the integration of research and practice is particularly useful, especially when the clinical target is more complex. Certainly, a *contemporary family* (e.g., a family of homicide) may have members that greatly benefit from a targeted EBP. For example, a family may arrive for treatment following the murder of a 22-year-old son. The mother's recent agoraphobia may be best addressed partially with exposure-based cognitive therapy.

Make no mistake, when one can find a specific EBP tailored to the presenting problem, it is always worth understanding how that approach is effective. However, when the complexity of the case demands a more variegated procedure, one shifts from EBP to ESP (evidence-supported practice), such as the approaches described in this volume. One could argue that the ESP approach to creating practice models is ideally suited to cases with a high level of complexity, and we believe that today's families exhibit such a level. What makes an ESP distinct is that by using the research-supported common factors of psychotherapy and relying on the extant research literature describing the specific needs of particular families, therapy can both benefit from the traditional EBP approaches and extend to properly address the complexity.

Social psychologists have suggested researchers are participant-observers in their research. Beyond the idea that true objectivity in psychological research is elusive, psychological concepts are ephemeral. In some instances objectivity may not even be desired. As Stricker and Keisner (1985) stated, clinicians made "dubious assumptions . . . that research represents an objective approval to understanding human activity whereas clinical inquiry is based on a subjective model" (p. 10). Connecting research and practice relies on assisting clinicians to see the "objectivity" of their work, and for researchers to recognize the subjectivity of their work. Stated another way, bridging this gap requires we break down the underlying erroneous dichotomy of objective-subjective and see the gray space between.

Given this understanding about research and therapy, it is useful to understand further the relationship between EBP (evidence-based practice) and ESP (evidence-supported practice).

All approaches that fall within this spectrum (see Figure 1.1) have adherents who prefer one model over the other. Evidence-based practice receives the

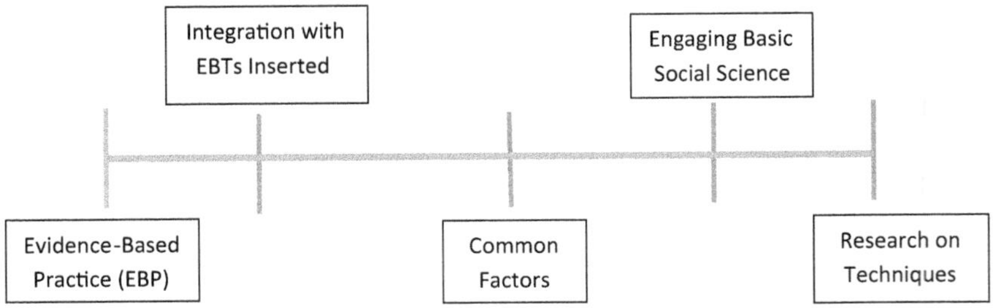

Figure 1.1 Spectrum of Therapeutic Outcome Validation

greatest respect from insurance companies and government-sponsored grants. However, legions of scholars, practitioners, and agencies recognize the importance of widening the range of treatment options given the complexity of the human condition. Most approaches considered ESPs combine two or more of the categories in Figure 1.1. In other words, many practicing therapists utilize one evidence-based treatment (EBT), but for many clients they have preferred techniques, or they emphasize common factors. Such integration is increasingly common in the United States, whereas some countries (e.g., Italy) tend to encourage clinicians to adhere to a single theoretical approach. In addition to simple integration (combining two approaches), some models are bringing multiple pieces together by including some aspects of specific EBT approaches with other components not formally validated.

Research into specific clinical techniques suggests that reliance on these techniques may be less useful than people suspect. Specific treatments independently account for (at most) 10% of positive treatment outcomes (Castonguay & Beutler, 2006). Given the "close to 150 different models to treatment that are effective" (p. 632), it is sensible to approach successful therapeutic outcome as a thoughtful integration of specific techniques, a positive therapeutic alliance, and client factors. Further, in a recent review of meta-analyses, it was reaffirmed that most active psychotherapeutic treatments produce approximately the same outcome (Luborsky et al., 2002). In a meta-analytic review of treatment component studies, Ahn and Wampold (2001) found that treatment with a specific intervention was no more effective than treatment without the specific intervention component. At a minimum, the importance of factors common to all therapies such as the therapeutic relationship, client/therapist factors, and the placebo effect must be respected in both research and practice.

This book represents a focused attempt to establish a class of clinical approaches supported by basic social science research. Nonclinical research or basic research is "directed at the understanding of people, rather than the means of intervening with them" (Cohen, 1979, p. 7). The question becomes, "Exactly how is research informing practice?" This is a critical issue because an unskilled clinician could slip into the ESP umbrella within this category. Therefore, it is incumbent upon the clinician who is using these approaches to be conversant with the relevant research. This is a critical caveat, "the relevant research," since most clinicians, even at the doctoral level, drift rapidly away from reading research after graduating. Even those who enjoyed research tend to drop down to reading a couple studies a month (Cohen, 1979). Further, clinicians admit to a significant preference for consulting with colleagues when bewildered by a case rather than looking to the extant literature for answers.

For this interaction of research and practice to succeed, clinicians need to update their knowledge as the science reveals new material, but also, researchers must point out information that appears clinically relevant. Keeping researchers interested in clinical scholarship is more difficult. Except for those researchers who engage in clinical practice, researchers are not even advised to examine the clinical literature. Clinical scholars could improve their exchange by articulating questions that researchers could pursue.

Seven Contemporary Families

The family types considered in this volume have no single commonality. They are defined rather by the fact that they fall outside the increasingly rare delineation of "typical families." The same determination was made in selecting the family types examined in *Contemporary Families: Translating Research into Practice* (Browning & Pasley, 2015). In that volume the families studied were: (1) families of adoption; (2) families of autism; (3) interracial families; (4) grandparent-headed families; (5) foster families; (6) LGBTQ families; and (7) families of chronic illness. This volume selected seven different families: (1) families of divorce; (2) stepfamilies; (3) "fragile families"; (4) families of addiction; (5) families of homicide; (6) families post-imprisonment; and (7) cyberbullied families. In addition to being complex systems, each of these family types has certain impediments that affect clinical progress when they seek treatment.

Divorced families predominantly exist within a context of conflict. In a divorce, at least one partner is seeking to end the current status quo of the family. There is virtually always someone left hurt and angry. Because these families also lead to a new residence for certain members, issues of familial connection, affection, finance, and communication are invariably raised. This is a potentially difficult population because permission for treatment may be withheld by parents who are angry at a former spouse. A parent (with shared legal custody) cannot bring his or her own child to treatment without the other parent's permission. This type of behavior is usually justified by anger and hurt. Therapists can intervene and attempt to present a position in which the child will benefit, but numerous reasons may be used to justify not allowing a child in treatment.

Stepfamilies are distinct from first-union families, yet by outside appearances can look identical, and that perceptual appearance is one of the challenges for these families. The stepfamily should not be considered the same as a first-union family, and this error often sabotages treatment when the clinician is naïve to these differences. The stepfamily consists of some people who barely know each other, yet are living in intimate proximity and often vying for reassurance of connection with old and new stepfamily members. The stepfamily often is surprised by the emotional volatility within the home shortly after the union, whether that be marriage or cohabitation.

The *"Fragile Family"* is an amorphous system. It has few consistencies, even in defining the unit, except for the fact that these families are poor and chaotic. The greatest impediment to treating the fragile family is the chaos itself. A clinician often is stymied in trying to intervene when sudden disruptions derail treatment. Clinical needs are often secondary to more basic needs such as food, shelter, and possible imprisonment, and the list goes on. Invariably, someone in the system is usually traumatized, meaning that emotional triggers are everywhere, and they are powerful. So, a clinician needs to teach and treat trauma on top of creating stability. The fortune of these families changes quickly, and their vulnerability is astonishing. Session to session reveals that these families are living with the sword of Damocles hanging over them. Housing is often uncertain, addiction is highly common, and few members are getting significant emotional support because the chaos is too great.

Families of addiction, in which at least one member is suffering from an addiction, often result in members feeling silenced. Reactions to the effect of drugs or alcohol, or even sexual addiction, often are exhibited in either screaming battles or paralyzing silence. Due to the myriad of problems that often accompany addiction, family members are trying to keep the peace in the family, but avoiding the inevitable conflicts that often percolate just under the surface. Therefore, these families often present as "stuck" and unable to envision how to proceed.

The *Family of homicide* has predictable commonalities, in most cases. Due to this family archetype being formed by familial trauma, family members are generally overwhelmed and have reduced functioning. However, reactions among people can be highly varied. Therefore, the therapy proposed by Hays and Browning (this volume) combines trauma-focused treatment with an understanding of both the accompanying legal issues and complicated grief. Alongside the treatment of trauma, the family's readjustment is supported with a variety of contextual and play therapy interventions.

The *Post-imprisonment family* is an under-served family type. For various reasons, family therapy has done a poor job of creating effective interventions for this population. These family systems are so complex that therapists must have some outside support. Therapy services may have to be linked to parole or offer some form of reward for participation. But, if a clinician increases participation, positive results occur. Datchi, Barretti, and Thompson

(2016) highlight three important components for improved family functioning in post-imprisonment families. Datchi et al. (2016) emphasized the need for family connections to be preserved and kept relevant during incarceration, as well as the importance of maintaining one's family role identity during imprisonment. Finally, prisons, communities, and family members must collaborate and work together in the common goal of improving success of prisoner reentry. Shamblen, Arnold, McKiernan, Collins, and Strader (2012) implemented a program emphasizing improved communication for couples in which one member was recently released from prison. They found that couples who received the intervention reported more harmonious relations directly following the interventions at three-month follow-up.

The therapeutic agenda is clear: stabilize and calm the family system. Diffuse physiological arousal (DPA), which is typically referred to as the fight or flight response, has been found to directly correlate with intra-couple tension (Gottman & Gottman, 2015). The clinician must link the couple together and arrange contact with extended family with whom the returning prisoner has a tolerable relationship. But regardless how one gets there, the end goal is that the family can tolerate disruption of any type. These families are often so close to crisis that a minor thing pushes them into chaos. Without an active extended family or a community (religion, sports, hobbies, psychoeducation, or cultural pursuits), it is almost impossible to hold the family together. As Monica McGoldrick (personal communication) suggested, "A therapist should have to justify not inviting in a brother." She was absolutely right, and research bears this out; familial relationships usually increase stability. This sounds reasonable in theory, but in practice, the post-prison family is still considered one of the most difficult to treat. Often these families border on volatile chaos. Without a systems perspective, recidivism will never be reduced (Sexton, 2016).

The *Cyberbullied Family* is the least examined of the families in this volume. Usually the person targeted by cyberbullying is a teenager, and the process of landing into a morass in the social networking universe is a modern phenomenon. In a sense, these families are so diverse that to try to examine them as a typology is difficult. However, what they do have in common is that they are a family in which one member feels particularly disempowered, and this person is often too ashamed to utilize the resources within her or his home.

The Importance of the Genogram

A genogram delineates all potentially involved family members, their familial relationship, and the interactional quality between central figures. Those most central to the family are the ones likely to be involved in therapy, or at least invited to participate at some point. However, by including all family members in the genogram the clinician is aware of all who may play a role in the family. Such a family map can be overwhelmingly complex, but we believe it is the best way to get to know a family and to identify various patterns and sites for intervention. Attempting to grasp the complexity of a stepfamily without a genogram is difficult (see Chapter 3). In this genogram the remarried couple has a solid marriage, but the tension between stepmother and one stepdaughter is destabilizing.

Unfortunately, the genogram has been underused in case presentations. It suffered greatly with the advent of the computer-based genogram programs. The computer-based programs include two critical flaws also related to the genogram's underuse. First, programs that exist are unnecessarily complex. The second mistake is the multiple colors utilized in the computer-based programs. Since hand-drawn genograms are created quickly during the clinical family interview with a simple pencil or pen, a useful genogram needs to be monotone.

As mentioned, specific interventions may flow directly from the genogram. Depending on the symbol used to represent the interactional status, specific questions and interventions may follow. A cordial relationship between two people generates the question about whether or not the relationship can be improved, or is a cordial relationship the best one can expect between these two people? The clinician may even wonder if an intervention is necessary to keep the relationship from becoming distant. Every symbol raises specific questions. In order for this system to be effective, there should be an inflexible basic legend, as can be seen at the end of this chapter. All the genograms within this volume follow our legend so that the most salient relationships are automatically understood (see Figure 1.2). (Importantly, we ask clinical scholars to create more streamlined genograms for the purposes of this text.) If desired, an author may always add one or two narrative qualifiers in any genogram. The genogram has its structural lines that define legal and familial ties (marriage, divorce, death, adoption, etc.) and the interactional lines that are always between any two people on the genogram. Interactional lines may evolve as therapy progresses. In other words, a therapist may find that showing a genogram is useful in explaining and getting buy-in for an intervention. If a family member feels the initial interactional lines do not accurately portray the relationship (e.g., "I wouldn't say my Dad and I are distant"), then one graciously alters the line to represent the client's view. In addition, when clinical progress is made, the interaction line is changed to reflect that more positive relationship.

The cutoff (—| |—) is a powerful symbol. While a cutoff between two people may be inevitable, a clinician should always assess if that relational separation might be repaired. This is not to imply that all cutoffs are bad—on the contrary, some are protective—but many represent a reaction that is too great for whatever trespass initiated this action. When a clinician can bring two people together and repair this bond (ending the cutoff), significant relational progress can occur. Of course, such an intervention must be based on the desire of at least one person to address this relational loss.

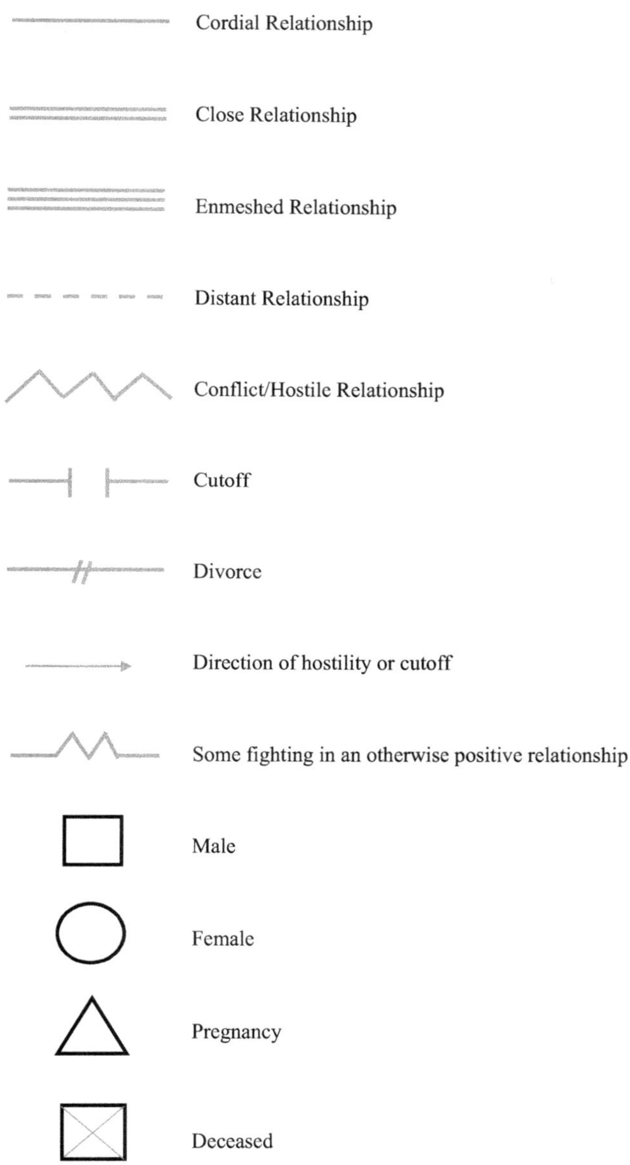

Figure 1.2 Genogram Legend

Conflict ( ) is a common symbol for families seeking treatment. However, this is a symbol that must be conveyed accurately. The conflict may occur rarely between two people who otherwise are close ( ) or represent the totality of the relationship ( ). It may even be directional; in other words, if the conflict primarily involves an adolescent screaming at her parent, while the parent does not mutually engage, the symbol would reflect that interactional style ( ). Seeing conflict, the clinician is challenged to determine some critical issues in order to best treat the conflict. Some areas of relevance are: Is the conflict around a single topic? Are there exceptions when the conflict is less? Is the conflict deep-seated or more situational? Can those in conflict tolerate moving toward improvement?

Distance ( ) is common in many families. The reason may not be traumatic. Sometimes distance occurs due to one intense miscommunication. The clinician therefore needs to determine if this distance from a particular person is mutual. Being mutual does not mean that treatment might not help, but it does influence motivation for change. The best clinical approach is to gently question if one person is saddened by this distance. If so, engage that person with the questions, even if it is not your initial client. In other words, with the proper permissions, one can reach out to family members who are not part of the initial conceptions of the cause.

Enmeshed ( ) is the most culturally sensitive symbol. Certain cultures are far more likely to have interactional enmeshment. Often those close bonds are healthy. However, every culture has a level of psychological enmeshment that is unhealthy. Used correctly, this concept refers to one's ability to be an individual. One can be extremely close to a loved one and still be able to act freely in situations away from the significant other. Alternatively, unhealthy enmeshment means that all aspects of one's life are still influenced, no matter how subtly, by close relatives. Therefore, the clinician needs to assess if this enmeshment between two people is psychologically damaging to one or both persons. Once it is determined if the enmeshment should be addressed, the clinician may benefit from these questions: Does this pattern create a "weaker" member? What purpose does the enmeshment serve? Is it mutually desired or unidirectional? And finally, did the enmeshment evolve out of a specific need at a certain time, and if so, has that need changed? For example, a single mother and her intellectually disabled daughter may have both benefited from being enmeshed at one point in their lives due to external and internal challenges that meant survival. Their survival was dependent on a symbiotic existence; thus, at a certain point, enmeshment would be both practical and effective.

Genograms are not given credit by most quantitative scholars because there are no numbers, no Likert scale, and they are not feasible to use when large samples are needed. The genogram forms a narrative/graphic tool useful for accurately delineating the relationship quality across a family and is more useful in qualitative research settings. We believe that while therapists primarily use the genogram, researchers too may find information conveyed in a genogram useful for generating research questions. In fact, many studies would find genograms a particularly helpful data collection tool, and we encourage such use.

Putting It All Together

Agency administrators are under a great deal of pressure, some from funding sources, to show that the majority of their staff therapists are making progress with their clinical cases (more often than not). An evidence-supported approach to treatment is valid. Thus, each therapist can follow a similar path toward creating his or her own approach. Everyone has created their own approach, but due to the fact that it is usually not conscious, people do not credit themselves in that way. And usually this integration is not written out, it is simply in the clinical methodology that each clinician employs.

Milton Erickson suggested that to be truly effective a clinician must create a separate approach for each client (Haley, 1973). Although this idea is impractical, the truth imbedded in the assumption that all cases demand some variation. The only way to shift therapy enough to handle a wide variety of family cases is to utilize a form of integration. It is not that integration is better, necessarily, but it is more able to garner research support. In order to create an integrated approach, the clinician must follow specific steps:

1. Determine an accurate diagnosis, of either significant individually based or family concerns.
    a. If an individual condition can be addressed with an EBT, it is advised to proceed with implementing, or referring just for that diagnosis. This respect for a specific goal will increase alliance.
2. Establish the systemic pattern, in the words of Sexton and Alexander (2004) "the function." Begin to share and refine the systemic pattern so that everyone agrees that the pattern described is accurate. When one is completely accurate, most people do not resent hearing their role described, as long as the positive connotations are included with the negative aspects of the pattern. This is well articulated by the contextual therapists (Nagy, Goldenthal) in their discussion of partiality.
3. Clarify how one achieves the common factors. One can read the lists of common factors and determine which clinical interventions are closest to her or his natural approach. Once a list has been embraced, document how you achieve this with your clients and use examples.
4. Use the research literature. It is easy now; just a simple Web search and legitimate journals are available, or go to the Substance Abuse and Mental Health Services Administration (SAMHSA).
    a. Find five research findings that are directly related to your clinical work. Either the finding supports your specific interventions, or

the research is useful to share with the family in order for them to normalize their situation.

5. Determine a clinical theorist who has articulated an approach, and incorporate the aspects of that model that appeal to you.
6. Continue to attend continuing education and supervision and cite that experience in your file.
7. Assess your therapy. Use one of the ongoing assessment systems, such as the Outcome Rating Scale (Miller et al., 2003, p. 100), and always assess the results of treatment at termination.

In essence, we are suggesting a return to Stricker's local clinical scientist model (Stricker & Trierweiler, 1995). Some updates have been made, but George Stricker was prescient to the problem that would occur due to the vast diversity of clinical issues. Thus, while EBTs will always be an important part of any treatment, for family cases, the approaches have to be more flexible. If one examines multisystemic therapy (MST) and functional family therapy (FFT), and emotion-focused therapy (EFT), there is a step-wise system, but these steps are not necessarily in specific order; rather, they involve creating a framework with specific premises and goals that need to be met in order to achieve treatment goals.

So, if the clinical readers of this book wish to convey that they are achieving the ESP level of validation for the therapy, four specific steps are necessary.

1. Find the EBT that addresses some specific aspect of the case. Visit SAMHSA's National Registry of Evidence-based Programs and Practices (NREPP) to view 396 current interventions at nrepp.samhsa.gov.
2. Read and make notes on the research chapter.
3. Be aware of at least one scholarly theoretical understanding of the direction of treatment.
4. Use some basic assessment tool (at least the SRS [Session Rating Scale]; Duncan et al., 2003).

References

Ahn, H., & Wampold, B. E. (2001). Where oh where are the specific ingredients? A meta-analysis of component studies in counseling and psychotherapy. *Journal of Counseling Psychology*, *48*(3), 251–257. doi: 10.1037//0022-0167.48.3.251

Browning, S., & Pasley, B.K. (2015). *Contemporary families: Translating research into practice*. New York, NY: Routledge.

Castonguay, L. G., & Beutler, L. E. (2006). Principles of therapeutic change: A task force on participants, relationships, and techniques factors. *Journal of Clinical Psychology*, *62*(6), 631–638. doi: 10.1002/jcip.20256

Cohen, L. H. (1979). The research readership and information source reliance of clinical psychologists. *Professional Psychology*, *10*(6), 780–785. doi: 10.1037/0735-7028.10.6.780

Datchi, C.C., Barretti, L.M., & Thompson, C.M. (2016). Family services in adult detention centers: Systemic principles for prisoner reentry. *Couple and Family Psychology: Research and Practice*, *5*(2), 89–104. doi: 10.1037/cfp0000057

Duncan, B. L., Miller, S. D., Sparks, J. A., Claud, D. A., Reynolds, L. R., Brown, J., & Johnson, L. D. (2003). The session rating scale: Preliminary psychometric properties of a "working" alliance measure. *Journal of Brief Therapy*, *3*(1), 3–12.

Ganong, L. H., & Coleman, M. (1986). A comparison of clinical and empirical literature on children in stepfamilies. *Journal of Marriage and the Family*, *48*, 309–318.

Gottman, J.S., & Gottman, J.M. (2015). *10 principles for doing effective couples therapy*. New York, NY: W.W. Norton & Company, Inc.

Haley, J. (1973). *Uncommon therapy: The psychiatric techniques of Milton H. Erickson MD*. New York, NY: W. W. Norton & Company, Inc.

Johnson, S. (2004). *Creating connection: The practice of emotionally focused couple's therapy*. New York: Brunner Routledge.

Lebow, J. (1988). Research into practice/practice into research. *Journal of Family Psychology*, *1*(3), 337. doi: 10.1037/h0084979

Linehan, M. M., & Dexter-Mazza, E. T. (2008). Dialectical behavior therapy for borderline personality disorder. In D. Barlow (Ed.), *Clinical handbook of psychological disorders* (pp. 365–420). New York, NY: Guilford Press.

Luborsky, L., Rosenthal, R., Diguer, L., Andrusyna, T. P., Berman, J. S., Levitt, J. T., Seligman, D. A., & Krause, E. D. (2002). The dodo bird verdict is alive and well—mostly. *Clinical Psychology: Science and Practice*, *9*(1), 2–12.

Miller, S. D., Duncan, B. L., Brown, J., Sparks, J. A., & Claud, D. A. (2003). The outcome rating scale: A preliminary study of the reliability, validity, and feasibility of a brief visual analog measure. *Journal of Brief Therapy*, *2*(2), 91–100.

Sexton, T. L. (2016). Incarceration as a family affair: Thinking beyond the individual. *Couple and Family Psychology: Research and Practice*, *5*, 61–64.

Sexton, T. L., & Alexander, J. F. (2004). *Functional family therapy clinical training manual*. Baltimore, MD: Annie E. Casey Foundation.

Shamblen, S.R., Arnold, B.B., McKiernan, P., Collins, D.A., & Strader, T.N. (2012). Applying the Creating Lasting Family Connections Marriage Enhancement Program to marriages affected by prison reentry. *Family Process*, *52*(3), 477–498. doi: 10.1111/famp.12003

Singer, J. L. (1980). The scientific basis of psychotherapeutic practice: A question of values and ethics. *Psychotherapy: Theory, Research and Practice*, *17*, 372–383.

Stricker, G., & Keisner, R. H. (1985). The relationship between research and practice. In G. Stricker & R. H. Keisner (Eds.), *From research to clinical practice* (pp. 3–14). New York: Plenum Press.

Stricker, G., & Trierweiler, S.J. (1995). The local clinical scientist: A bridge between science and practice. *American Psychologist*, *50*(12), 995–1002. doi: 10.1037/1931-3918.S.1.37

Vivian, D., Hershenberg, R., Teachman, B. A., Drabick, D. A. G., Goldfried, M. R., & Wolfe, B. (2012). A translational model of research-practice integration. *Psychotherapy*, *49*(2), 143–151. doi: 10.1037/a0027925

2

FAMILIES AND DIVORCE

Case Study

Amy C. Wagner and Rachel M. Diamond

Anne and Doug, a Caucasian couple in their early 40s, have been married for fifteen years. Anne is from a prominent Protestant family, while Doug grew up in a traditional Irish Catholic family. While Anne remains very close to her mother, Doug is distant from his family, who live across the country, and he considers his father to be an alcoholic. They have two children, 7-year-old Sean and 12-year-old Kenzie.

The couple have felt more like "roommates" for years and have not slept together. Instead, Doug has slept with Sean on an extra bed in his room when he was not traveling for work. Meanwhile, Anne and Kenzie developed a close relationship, in which Kenzie was often in the role of the "little mother." Anne and Doug blamed each other for their enormous financial stress. He was angry about her overspending and refusal to work full-time. She resented his unsuccessful attempts at start-up technology companies, and that because of these failed ventures her parents paid for Sean and Kenzie's private school and extracurricular activities. Additionally, Anne suspected that Doug had been unfaithful the last few years when he went away on long business trips that resulted in limited contact with her and the children. Anne began to suspect Doug avoided coming home.

As the children were exposed to more of the parents' mounting tension, Kenzie assumed more caretaking responsibilities of Sean, as she perceived her mother as unable to manage all the tasks of the household. However, Sean became more defiant, particularly when Doug went out of town. Kenzie's attempts to parent Sean at these times often resulted in even greater difficulties for the family, as the children would get into conflict with one another. As a result, Doug belittled Anne for not being able to handle the household while he was away, and Anne felt hopeless in the current living situation.

Eventually, tensions came to a head after Anne found emails on Doug's computer from a female colleague that indicated they had been having an affair. She told Doug she wanted a divorce. He knew his family would disapprove and, consequently, refused to initiate filing. Therefore, Anne sought out an attorney and filed for the divorce. The legal process created more conflict between the couple, but they used collaborative attorneys and were formally divorced within a year.

As the legal process progressed, Anne and Doug sat down with their children and told them that they would be getting a divorce and selling the house. Among the first questions the children asked were "*Who are we going to live with?*" and "*Where are we going to live?*" Unfortunately, Anne and Doug had only a vague plan. With Anne working part-time in retail and Doug working as an IT consultant, neither could independently afford to stay in their current house. Thus, the immediate plan was for Anne and the children to move in with her widowed mother, who lived nearby, and for Doug to rent an apartment temporarily. Because of Doug's work schedule, the informal plan was for the children to primarily live with Anne and her mother while staying with Doug every other weekend and having the occasional after-school dinners with him when he was in town.

A few months after they moved out, difficulties in the family were apparent. One weekend when the children were at Doug's apartment, Kenzie borrowed his cell phone to call Anne. On the phone she saw text messages from the woman he had been seeing. Kenzie became very upset and immediately called her mom to tell her all about her dad's girlfriend. In this conversation she told Anne that she couldn't believe her dad already had a girlfriend and blamed him for the divorce. Meanwhile, Sean was having a difficult time adjusting to not seeing his dad daily. The days following a visit proved to be particularly difficult for him; despite Anne and his grandmother's encouragement to get ready for school, he cried and refused to get out of bed. These behaviors were not only disruptive for Sean, but also for the rest of the family. While Anne would try to talk calmly with him at first, eventually she would lose her temper with him for "being so difficult." Anne's mother, worried about how Anne was holding up with the separation, sought to comfort her. Additionally, Kenzie would become angry at Sean for upsetting their mother and would lash out at him as well. Finally, both the children's teachers sent letters home reporting a decline in their school performance.

Presently, Doug and Anne are struggling to help their children deal with the many rapid changes that are happening, and each blames the other for the current situation. Because the children spend the majority of the time with Anne, Doug believes it must be Anne's anger over his extramarital relationship and "bad parenting" that is causing the children's problems. Anne believes Doug's inconsistent presence and attention toward his girlfriend rather than the children must be causing them to struggle to adjust. Both also blame one another for talking negatively about the other in front of the children. Anne believes that if she were to take full custody, the issues with the children would be resolved and her life would be easier. Doug believes the opposite; if Anne would make it easier for him to spend more time with the children, they would have an easier time adjusting. They have sought family therapy at the suggestion of their attorneys in hopes of finding ways to adjust to life during this transition.

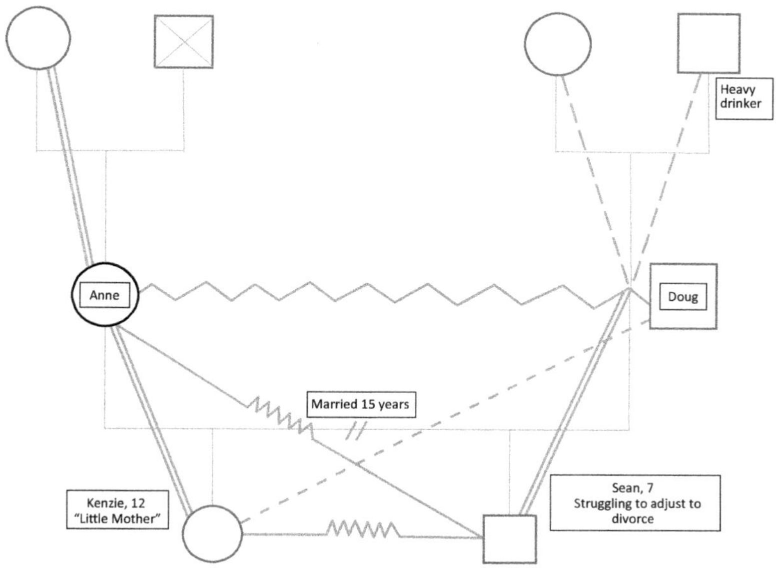

Figure 2.1 Divorced Family Genogram: Anne and Doug

Families of Divorce

A Research Perspective

Karina R. Sokol, Matthew M. Stevenson, and Sanford L. Braver

Families have changed over the past century, with two first-married heterosexual adults who have children younger than 18 years of age at home (i.e., the traditional U.S. benchmark family) now the minority family structure (US Census Bureau, 2015). More and more families are diversifying in terms of both structures and transitions, often with implications for family functioning. One such transition is divorce. When America was founded in the 18th century, divorce was remarkably atypical; in the entire 72-year history of the Plymouth colony, less than 10 divorces took place (Riley, 1991). The divorce rate gradually rose over the next couple of centuries, but began to swiftly increase throughout the 1970s and 1980s. The rate peaked at 5.3 per 1,000 people in 1981. Since that time, the divorce rate has gradually drifted downward where it reached 3.6 for every 1,000 people in 2005 (Stevenson & Wolfers, 2007). However, this decline applies only to college-educated couples (Amato, 2010), and today the divorce rate is 20% higher for African-American couples (Bramlett & Mosher, 2002).

Divorce, per se, is neither good nor bad in all cases; its impact is highly variable based on the specific circumstances for each case. Yet, for the majority of families, it is a life-defining event that changes both the organization and operation of the family (Braver & Lamb, 2012)—almost every routine and dynamic of the family requires reorganization and change. For Anne and Doug, their marital dissolution seems to have led to a large amount of tension and a number of questions regarding how best to parent their two children, Kenzie and Sean.

Research Questions with Clinical Significance

This case raises a number of questions regarding the well-being of children as well as potential suggestions for decisions that either the parents or the court could make during this transition:

1. Over time, what is the typical pattern of adjustment for children post-divorce?

2. What factors best predict child adjustment to the marital dissolution?
3. How should parenting time be allocated between both parents?
4. How do transitions such as moving or changing schools influence a child's adjustment, and how can these sometimes necessary transitions be mitigated?
5. How can social media/electronic communication influence coparenting and/or promote access and involvement from a nonresidential parent?
6. What is the role of mental health professionals in helping families through these transitions and in the court process?

Custody

One key task for divorcing parents is to come to a decision, either on their own or through the court system, about custody and parenting time. It is key to understand the differences between many terms used in the court system regarding who has the authority to make decisions on behalf of the child(ren) and where and with whom the children will spend their time. *Legal custody* refers to the decision-making authority one or both parents have regarding their child(ren). *Sole legal custody* allows for one parent to have the exclusive rights to make decisions regarding medical care, religion, education, and so forth, whereas *joint legal custody* affords both parents decision-making power in these areas. Additionally, *physical custody* refers to where and with whom the child lives. With respect to *sole physical custody*, children live primarily with one parent (the residential or custodial parent) and have "visitation time" with the other (nonresidential or noncustodial parent) during weekends, holidays, and vacations. Alternatively, *joint physical custody* (also called *shared parenting*) has children living with both parents, although importantly, not necessarily equal amounts of time (50/50; Stevenson, Braver, Ellman, & Votruba, 2012). Time splits are commonly 30/70, with mothers regularly getting more time with children (Kelly, 2007; Venohr & Kaunelis, 2008). Parents can come to this decision together, and often do. However, if they cannot reach agreement, the court gets involved, requiring interventions such as settlement conferences (Fabricius, Braver, Diaz, & Velez, 2010), parent education programs (Braver, Salem, Pearson, & DeLusé, 1996; Pollet & Lombreglia, 2008), and/or mediation (Kelly, 2004). Depending on the jurisdiction and the conclusions of the specific judge, one or more of these approaches might be imposed.

When courts have to make decisions regarding custody, the most common legal standard is the *Best Interest of the Child standard* (*BIS*; Ellman et al., 2010). The formal statement of most states requires courts to consider the following when making a decision: (1) a parent's wishes regarding custody; (2) a child's wishes regarding custody; (3) relationships between children, their siblings, their parents, and any other person who may considerably affect the child's best interests; (4) the child's adjustment to his or her home, school, and community; and (5) the physical and mental health of all involved. In practice, most courts give greatest weight to judgments about each of the parent's "fitness," about how each parent relates to and has provided caregiving to the child, and whether parents can work together collaboratively (Stevenson et al., 2012).

Ongoing Adjustment Among Children

In the aforementioned case, it seems that Kenzie and Sean are having some difficulty adjusting to their parents' divorce (i.e., emotional outbursts, declining academic performance). These are common occurrences for children experiencing parental divorce according to over two decades of research using large-scale, longitudinal data sets. On average, findings suggest that children experience better psychological, social, academic, and physical health outcomes when raised in two-parent families compared to those children raised in divorced families, separated families, or never-married single parent households (e.g., Amato, 2000; Clarke-Stewart & Brentano, 2006; McLanahan & Sandefur, 1994). However, differences between these groups are quite small and the variability within groups is quite large, such that some children from divorced families are faring better than some children from married families. In fact, only 20%–35% of children in divorced families may be classified as having adjustment problems compared to 12%–15% of children in married families (Braver & Lamb, 2012). The majority of individuals in post-divorce families may be described as adjusting normally, if not better than average, as young adults, although it is common for them to experience some psychological pain throughout the divorce period and shortly thereafter (Emery, 1998; Hetherington & Kelly, 2002; Laumann-Billings & Emery, 2000; Schwartz & Finley, 2005). As such, although Kenzie and Sean's behavior may seem troubling, it is fairly typical following parental divorce, especially earlier in the divorce process. If their stressful situation can be mitigated, their future adjustment will most likely normalize as they progress throughout their childhood and adolescence.

Factors That Predict Child Adjustment

There are numerous factors that are important for post-divorce adjustment. For this family, the key issues seem to be the relationship between Anne and Doug, the relationship between both children and each parent, and the amount of time (both in person and otherwise) Anne and Doug each have parenting their children. Here, we focus on these three factors, which are also consistently identified by research as key to ongoing adjustment among children.

Interparental Relationship

Parental conflict is linked to a wide variety of childhood adjustment difficulties such as externalizing behavior (e.g., aggression, delinquency, and conduct disorder), internalizing behavior (e.g., depression and anxiety), and physical health problems (Fabricius & Luecken, 2007; Grych & Fincham, 1990; Troxel & Matthews, 2004). It is common for parental conflict to develop or worsen during the separation and divorce processes, and often it continues for some time thereafter (Lamb, 2012). The relationship between parents is thought to be the most vital mediator of childhood outcomes and is key in determining how children fare both short- and long-term, regardless of family type (Buehler, Lange, & Franck, 2007; Cummings & Davies, 2002; Cummings, George, McCoy, & Davies, 2012; El-Sheikh, Buckhalt, Mize, & Acebo, 2006). For divorcing/divorced families, conflicted interparental relationships that focus on child-centered issues (e.g., custody, parenting time, child support) may be even more detrimental than in married families. Additionally, children in divorcing families are undergoing a number of life stressors during that time and may have fewer resources available for support (Hetherington & Stanley-Hagen, 1999).

Alternatively, cooperative parenting or coparenting appears to greatly benefit children with divorced parents. Successful coparenting, in which parents demonstrate mutual respect, allows for enhanced communication regarding the children and is linked to several benefits. For example, children with cooperative parents tend to function quite well and display improved psychological functioning, lower levels of externalizing and internalizing problems, and improved academic performance compared to children with non-cooperative parents (Buchanan, Maccoby, & Dornbusch, 1991; Hetherington, Bridges, & Insabella, 1998).

Taken together, research would suggest the lack of coparenting and presence of conflict and tension between Doug and Anne is harmful to Kenzie and Sean. It is not surprising that both children are suffering psychologically from this divorce, as their parents continue to increase the stress the children are experiencing by talking negatively about each other in front of the children and disagreeing about key issues such as custody and parenting time. This conflict may actually be more damaging to children than the divorce itself, whereas an improving coparenting relationship could help mitigate these adjustment difficulties.

Role of Parents

There may be different loyalties and dynamics that alter a child's impression of and reaction to the divorce. In this case, Kenzie seemingly sides with Anne and assigns all the responsibility for the divorce to Doug. The relationship between mother and daughter was exceptionally close before the divorce and has remained so after. Kenzie has not only sided with Anne when it comes to problems with Doug, but also in response to Sean's behavior. As Kenzie has taken on a motherly role during this period, she has lost patience with Sean when she feels that he is upsetting Anne. Sean, on the other hand, seems to miss the relationship he had with his father. His emotional reactions following time with his father are indicative of a disruption that he feels in the relationship. His reaction draws out a negative response from Anne that only exacerbates Sean's situation.

Parent-Child Relationship

As seen above, the parent-child relationship can serve as a source for both risk and resilience, especially during stressful times in the family such as during a divorce. Davies and Cummings (1994) described the mechanism by which this may occur as emotional security. The conflicted and stressful parent-child relationship can lead children to feel emotionally insecure and disrupt children's emotional regulation. Internal regulation aids in calming the physiological stress response system, and dysregulation of such a system can promote pathophysiology for both the brain and body, resulting in psychological and physical health troubles. Thus, the parent-child relationship is key in protecting against negative outcomes following divorce. To further complicate things, interparental conflict may lead to a worse parent-child relationship, as mothers may be more rejecting and less warm and fathers may withdraw from parenting or increase their intrusive interactions with their children (Davies & Cummings, 1994; Grych, 2005). Cases in which parents experience difficulties adjusting to divorce themselves, financial instability, and/or when parents have begun dating or remarried are related to an increased likelihood that the quality of their parenting may diminish (Amato, 2000; Hetherington, 1999; Kelly, 2000; Pruett, Williams, Insabella, & Little, 2003; Simons, Lin, Gordon, Conger, & Lorenz, 1999; Wallerstein & Kelly, 1980).

If parents are to promote resilience for children post-divorce, the parent-child relationship must remain warm and supportive (Amato & Fowler, 2002; Buchanan, Maccoby, & Dornbusch, 1996; Hetherington, 1999; Martinez & Forgatch, 2002; Simons et al., 1999). Parents should monitor their children's activities, remain involved in their (extra)curricular endeavors, and provide authoritative discipline. To put it briefly, the better relationship a child has with his or her parents, the better the child will adjust to divorce.

The most at-risk relationship post-divorce is the father-child relationship given fathers often become the nonresidential parent (Stevenson et al., 2012). As such, the involvement fathers have with their children often is limited, thereby hindering the continued development of a father-child relationship. Previous research has shown that children do best academically and psychologically when their noncustodial parent is actively involved in their lives. Nonresidential father involvement can protect children from negative post-divorce outcomes such as school dropouts and school failure (Nord, Brimhall, & West, 1997).

Parenting Time

One source of conflict between Anne and Doug concerns parenting time. While Anne wants Doug to have no parenting time, Doug wants to split parenting time with Anne. Almost two decades ago, Lamb, Sternberg, and Thompson (1997) observed that "to maintain high-quality relationships with their children, parents need to have sufficiently extensive and regular interactions with them" (p. 400). Quality parenting needs time and involvement in a child's life to occur. Thus, it is important that parents be integral parts of their children's lives. Even as children grow older, parents should know teachers and friends, happenings at school, and be aware of daily ups and downs in their children's lives. This would be quite difficult without regular and extensive involvement with their children in a variety of contexts.

The ideal situation post-divorce would be for children to have the opportunity to interact with both parents frequently in a variety of contexts, including overnight periods (Kelly & Lamb, 2000; Lamb, 2002; Lamb & Kelly, 2009). Activities during these periods promote trust and strengthen parent-child attachments and need to be considered when making decisions about parenting time post-divorce. One might label time spent caring, playing, and interacting with a child as *quality* time. And, it has been well established that quality time with fathers following parental divorce is important for later healthy adjustment (Amato & Gilbreth, 1999; Dunn, Cheng, O'Connor, & Bridges, 2004; Hetherington et al., 1998; Simons et al., 1996).

For the past 20 years, researchers have explored the idea of parenting time relating to children's functioning after the divorce, especially with reference to quality and quantity. There appears to be a positive relationship between the amount of contact a father has with his child(ren) and children's well-being such that more time leads to better parent-child relationships (Buchanan et al., 1996; Whiteside & Becker, 2000). Fabricius and colleagues have found in multiple studies that up to 50% parenting time for fathers results in better outcomes for children and adolescents experiencing parental divorce (Fabricius, 2003; Fabricius & Luecken, 2007; Fabricius, Sokol, Diaz, & Braver, 2012). Specifically, as children gain time in their father's care, their relationship with him increases and peaks at that 50% point. In other words, children that spend half of their time with their father post-divorce are likely to have better adjustment than children who spend less time with their father (e.g., every other weekend). Moreover, increasing father's parenting time does not put the mother-child relationship at risk. Thus, the most beneficial arrangement of time to promote both healthy and strong father-child and mother-child relationships would be to share parenting time 50/50.

There has been some hesitation by researchers in coming to this same 50/50 conclusion when there is high parent conflict. The thought process is that more contact with the nonresidential parent would expose children to more interparental conflict, and since it is well established that exposure to parent conflict predicts a host of negative outcomes for children, researchers might pause when making statements concerning equally sharing parenting time in these situations. At the same time, there have been mixed findings, with some studies concluding that more parenting time in the face of high levels of interparental conflict is harmful, at least for some children (Amato & Rezac, 1994; Hetherington, Cox, & Cox, 1982; Johnston, Kline, & Tschann, 1989), and other studies finding that more parenting time for fathers in high-conflict families was either not related to children's adjustment or improved children's well-being (Buchanan et al., 1996; Fabricius & Luecken, 2007; Healy, Malley, & Stewart, 1990; Kurdek, 1986).

Recently, this question has been examined in depth by Fabricius et al. (2012). A 2005–2006 data set collected by two of the authors asked college students who had experienced parental divorce during their childhood to report on their previous parenting time arrangements, interparental conflict, and current well-being. This allowed researchers to examine long-term relationships between parenting time and adjustment in both high- and low-conflict families. As has been found, parenting time was associated with both better father-child relationships and better outcomes in low-conflict families. For those individuals in high-conflict families, the same relationship between parenting time and outcomes was found such that even in the face of high interparental conflict, individuals with more time with their fathers had better relationships with him and, in turn, did better during the transition to adulthood. Therefore, even though Anne and Doug are currently experiencing high levels of conflict, a 50/50 split in parenting time may still benefit Kenzie and Sean.

Transitions Post-Divorce

As is common for children adapting to divorce, Kenzie and Sean are experiencing some difficulty with transitions relating to the divorce. For this family, neither parent was financially able to live in the house alone, so the children currently live with Anne in her mother's house and Doug rents an apartment nearby. The children have to adjust to new living arrangements and transitions between them. Anne and Doug have not set clear schedules for parenting time, so this creates some unpredictability for Kenzie and Sean about when and how often they will see their father. Kenzie and Sean have also shown declines in school performance. Financial constraints may mean that Anne and Doug have less money available to afford private lessons/tutoring, toys, books, home computers, and other goods that improve Sean and Kenzie's likelihood of success at school.

Research suggests that transitions following divorce are hard for children (Sandler, Wolchik, & Braver, 1988; Sandler, Wolchik, Braver, & Fogas, 1987; Wolchik et al., 2000). Economic hardship may mean less access to activities and goods, leading to more behavioral problems, and this is more prominent in sole custody situations (Amato, 1993, 2000). Further, children can experience decreases in standard of living, moving, changing schools, losing pets, loss of friends, and loss of contact with other family members such as grandparents (Lamb, 2012). Research shows that frequent moving, often associated with a lower income of a single parent, is associated with increased emotional and behavioral problems (Ellwood & Stolberg, 1993). Additionally, the relocation of one parent following separation has been associated with negative outcomes for children such as being more concerned about financial support, more hostility in children's interpersonal relations, more distress related to the divorce, perceived worse physical and emotional health, and lower general life satisfaction (Braver, Ellman, & Fabricius, 2003).

The above negative effects can be mitigated with parental support, and there are several empirically based programs (this is not a comprehensive list) that teach parents skills to help children navigate transitions following divorce such as: Parenting Through Change (PTC; Stolberg & Mahler, 1994), the New Beginnings Program (NBP; Wolchik et al., 1993), and Dads for Life for nonresident parents (DFL; Braver, Griffin, & Cookston, 2005). There also are programs for children: Children of Divorce Intervention Program (CODIP; Pedro-Carroll & Cowen, 1985), Children's Support Group (CSG; Stolberg & Garrison, 1985), and Kids in Divorce Situations (KIDS; Pelleboer-Gunnink, Van der Valk, Branje, Van Doorn, & Dekovic, 2015).

Social Media/Electronic Communication Influences

There have been rapid and vast technological changes for this generation of children. Smartphones, computers, and tablets have enabled easy contact with parents via phone calls, texting, emails, video chats, and a variety of social media applications such as Facebook and Twitter. The effects of technology on families going through a divorce has not been well studied.

"Virtual visitation" is increasingly considered cutting edge in family law, with some families going as far as to ask the judge to prescribe virtual visitation rights and schedules (Shefts, 2002). In essence, technology has enabled increased modes of communication, and, like any form of communication, parents can choose to use it in positive or negative ways. Thus, frequent texting or video chats could be used to enhance the emotional bond between a noncustodial parent and child, but it could also be used to say negative things about the other parent, foment conflict, and make the children feel more stuck in the middle. The age of a child is important because at young ages a child may not be sophisticated enough to use a computer or tablet whereas at older ages (adolescence) it may be difficult to enforce any parameters of virtual visitation as children become more autonomous and spend more time away from the house. The use of virtual visitation requires Internet and may require a computer or some installation, so questions arise as to who should bear the cost of equipment. Additionally, it would be easier for one parent to sabotage electronic communications than physical visits through control of technology, Internet passwords, and mobile phone plans.

Family research has not kept up with the rapid advances of technology, and there are limited empirical studies from which to draw. Generally, virtual parent-child contact when parents and children are separated is useful for maintaining parent-child contact, but only when the parent and child both perceive the time they spent in person as positive (Hofer, Souder, Kennedy, Fullman, & Hurd, 2009). It is not clear whether virtual contact could help to repair a negative parent-child relationship. Research indicates that parents who were separated from their child for short times favored using video chats and reported higher satisfaction when using technology (Thompson, 2005). During virtual visits parents tend to focus on the importance of day-to-day interactions whereas children focus more on the eventual reunification with a parent (Yarosh & Abowd, 2011). The use of parent-child virtual contact in intact families has not been related to aspects of the parent-child relationship (Lee, 2009), but several small studies indicate that parents and children view virtual visits positively (Saini, Mishna, Barnes, & Polak, 2013). Technological difficulties were a source of frustration for both parents and children in the above study, but parents felt closer to their children through the use of virtual visits. Children preferred face-to-face contact whenever possible (Saini et al., 2013). However, some worry that the ability to use virtual visits as time spent with children may diminish the overall face-to-face time with a nonresident parent.

Role of Mental Health Professionals

Given that Anne and Doug appear to be undergoing a transformation with respect to child custody and visitation, and that they have ongoing conflict and their visitation schedule is informal, they would benefit from the involvement of one or more mental health professionals in the divorce process. Impressively, they have already begun family therapy—good! Most couples ultimately come to a custody agreement on their own, but in about 2%–10% of cases a judge decides child custody. Anne and Doug would benefit from seeking out a professional mediator. A mediator provides a neutral third party to help create a more formalized parenting plan to both reduce parental conflict and to provide the children with consistency. Many states require a couple to attempt mediation prior to receiving judicial resolution (Braver & O'Connell, 1998). There is general agreement that a negotiated or mediated settlement is better for children than judicial custody contests that can often promote long-lasting and deleterious parental conflict (Pruett & Jackson, 1999). In about 5%–10% of divorces a custody evaluator, usually a psychologist, is hired by the parents to assess the family and make nonbinding custody recommendations (Stevenson et al., 2012). Often the evaluator makes recommendations to the family first and later to a court if an agreement is not reached (Gould & Martindale, 2007). Importantly, custody evaluators work separately from any ongoing family therapy; the same person would not conduct both, and these processes are independent tasks.

However, the scientific basis of custody evaluations remains debated (Bow & Quinnell, 2004; Kelly & Ramsey, 2009). Several courts offer (or mandate) the option that ex-couples attend universal parent education programs for divorcing parents (Fabricius et al., 2010). Many programs report that they target reducing children's exposure to conflict, improving parenting skills, and decreasing legal complaints (Braver et al., 1996). There are also several empirically based programs, as mentioned in the Transitions Post-Divorce section, that are more in depth, lasting several weeks, and ones that target either parents or children or both. Many of these programs have long-term follow-up data that suggest they are effective at helping children adjust to the divorce by significantly decreasing psychological disorders by as much as 37% compared to controls, and increasing academic success in as many as 35% of cases, depending on the program (Pedro-Carroll & Cowen, 1985; Wolchik et al., 2009).

Summary

Each family's situation is distinct, and each family has different needs to be met post-divorce. For Anne, Doug, Kenzie, and Sean, there are many questions in determining adjustment to the divorce and decisions that either the parents or the court will need to make. Needless to say, any choices that the family makes need to keep in mind the children's best interests. Family therapy should focus on strengthening the parent-child relationships and reducing interparental conflict. Further, each parent should have parenting time with the children to facilitate the relationships between each parent and the children. Anne and Doug should work to maximize the use of virtual visitation from a noncustodial parent. Research suggests both the parents and children would benefit from engaging in supportive, relationship-building interactions. Knowing that Kenzie and Sean will have a difficult period adapting to new transitions, the family may consider involving other professionals to help the children navigate divorce transitions, provide consistency, and reduce family conflict.

References

Amato, P. R. (1993). Children's adjustment to divorce: Theories, hypotheses, and empirical support. *Journal of Marriage and the Family*, *55*, 23–38. doi: 10.2307/352954

Amato, P. R. (2000). The consequences of divorce for adults and children. *Journal of Marriage and the Family*, *62*, 1269–1287. doi: 10.1111/j.1741-3737.2000.01269.x

Amato, P. R. (2010). Research on divorce: Continuing trends and new developments. *Journal of Marriage and Family*, *72*, 650–666. doi: 10.1111/j.1741-3737.2010.00723.x

Amato, P. R., & Fowler, F. (2002). Parenting practices, child adjustment, and family diversity. *Journal of Marriage and Family*, *64*, 703–716. doi: 10.1111/j.17413737.2002.00703.x

Amato, P. R., & Gilbreth, J. G. (1999). Nonresident fathers and children's well-being: A meta-analysis. *Journal of Marriage and the Family*, *61*, 557–573. doi: 10.1111/j.1741-3737.2006.00274.x

Amato, P. R., & Rezac, S. (1994). Contact with residential parents, inter-parental conflict, and children's behavior. *Journal of Family Issues*, *15*, 191–207. doi: 10.1177/0192513X94015002003

Bow, J. N., & Quinnell, F. A. (2004). Child custody evaluations: Critique of child custody evaluations by the legal profession. *Family Court Review*, *42*, 115–127.
Bramlett, M. D., & Mosher, W. D. (2002). Cohabitation, marriage, divorce, and remarriage in the United States. *Vital Health Statistics*, *23*, 1–32.
Braver, S. L., Ellman, I. M., & Fabricius, W. V. (2003). Relocation of children after divorce and children's best interests: New evidence and legal considerations. *Journal of Family Psychology*, *17*(2), 206–219. doi: 10.1037/0893-3200.17.2.206
Braver, S. L., Griffin, W. A., & Cookston, J. T. (2005). Prevention programs for divorced nonresident fathers. *Family Court Review*, *43*, 81–96. doi: 10.1111/j.1744 1617.2005.00009.x
Braver, S. L., & Lamb, M. E. (2012). Marital dissolution. In G. W. Peterson & K. R. Bush (Eds.), *Handbook of marriage and the family* (2nd ed., pp. 487–516). New York, NY: Springer Publishing Co. doi: 10.1007/978-1-4614-3987-5_21
Braver, S. L., & O'Connell, D. (1998). *Divorced dads: Shattering the myths*. New York: Tarcher/Putnam. doi: 10.1111/j.174-1617.1999.tb00550.x
Braver, S. L., Salem, P., Pearson, J., & Delusé, S. R. (1996). The content of divorce education programs: Results of a survey. *Family & Conciliation Courts Review*, *34*, 41–59. doi: 10.1111/j.174-1617.1996.tb00399.x
Buchanan, C. M., Maccoby, E. E., & Dornbusch, S. M. (1991). Caught between parents: Adolescents' experience in divorced homes. *Child Development*, *62*, 1008–1029. doi: 10.1111/j.1467–8624.1991.tb01586.x
Buchanan, C. M., Maccoby, E. E., & Dornbusch, S. M. (1996). *Adolescents after divorce*. Cambridge, MA: Harvard University Press. doi: 10.2307/2655650
Buehler, C., Lange, G., & Franck, L. (2007). Adolescents' cognitive and emotional responses to marital hostility. *Child Development*, *78*, 775–789. doi: 10.1111/j.1467 8624.2007.01032.x
Clarke-Stewart, A., & Brentano, C. (2006). *Divorce: Causes and consequences*. New Haven, CT: Yale University Press. doi: 10.1080/01926180902945988
Cummings, E. M., & Davies, P. T. (2002). Effects of marital conflict on children: Recent advances and emerging themes in process-oriented research. *Journal of Child Psychology and Psychiatry*, *43*(1), 31–63. doi: 10.1111/1469-7610.00003
Cummings, E. M., George, M. W., McCoy, K. P., & Davies, P. T. (2012). Interparental conflict in kindergarten and adolescent adjustment: Prospective investigation of emotional security as an explanatory mechanism. *Child Development*, *83*(5), 1703–1715. doi: 10.1111/j.1467-8624.2012.01807.x
Davies, P. T., & Cummings, E. M. (1994). Marital conflict and child adjustment: An emotional security hypothesis. *Psychological Bulletin*, *116*, 387–411. doi: 10.1037/00332909.116.3.387
Dunn, J., Cheng, H., O'Connor, T. G., & Bridges, L. (2004). Children's perspectives on their relationships with their nonresident fathers: Influences, outcomes and implications. *Journal of Child Psychology and Psychiatry*, *45*, 553–566. doi: 10.0000/j.14697610.2004.00245.x
Ellman, I. M., Kurtz, P. M., Weithorn, L. A., Bix, B. H., Czapanskiy, K., & Eichner, M. (2010). *Family law: Cases, text, problems* (5th ed.). New Providence, NJ and San Francisco, CA: LexisNexis.
Ellwood, M. S., & Stolberg, A. L. (1993). The effects of family composition, family health, parenting behavior and environmental stress on children's divorce adjustment. *Journal of Child and Family Studies*, *2*, 23–36. doi: 10.1007/BF01321298

El-Sheikh, M., Buckhalt, J. A., Mize, J., & Acebo, C. (2006). Marital conflict and disruption of children's sleep. *Child Development*, *77*, 31–43. doi: 10.1111/j.14678624.2006.00854.x

Emery, R. E. (1998). *Marriage, divorce, and children's adjustment* (2nd ed.). Thousand Oaks, CA: Sage Publications.

Fabricius, W. V. (2003). Listening to children of divorce: New findings that diverge from Wallerstein, Lewis, and Blakeslee. *Family Relations*, *52*, 385–396. doi: 10.1111/j.1741-3729.2003.00385.x

Fabricius, W. V., Braver, S. L., Diaz, P., & Velez, C. E. (2010). Custody and parenting time: Links to family relationships and well-being after divorce. In Michael E. Lamb (Ed.), *Role of the father in child development* (5th ed., pp. 245–289). Hoboken, NJ: John Wiley & Sons.

Fabricius, W. V., & Luecken, L. J. (2007). Postdivorce living arrangements, parent conflict, and long-term physical health correlates for children of divorce. *Journal of Family Psychology*, *21*, 195–205. doi: 10.1037/0893-3200.21.2.195

Fabricius, W. V., Sokol, K. R., Diaz, P., & Braver, S. L. (2012). Parenting time, parent-child relationships and children's health. In K. Kuehnle & L. Drozd (Eds.), *Parenting plan evaluations: Applied research for the family court* (pp. 188–213). New York, NY: Oxford University Press.

Gould, J. W., & Martindale, D. A. (2007). *The art and science of child custody evaluations*. New York, NY: Guilford Press. doi: 10.1111/j.174-1617.2000.tb00581.x

Grych, J. H. (2005). Interparental conflict as a risk factor for child maladjustment: Implications for the development of prevention programs. *Family Court Review*, *43*(1), 97–108. doi: 10.1111/j.1744-1617.2005.00010.x

Grych, J. H., & Fincham, F. D. (1990). Marital conflict and children's adjustment: A cognitive-contextual framework. *Psychological Bulletin*, *108*, 267–290. doi: 10.1037/0033-2909.108.2.267

Healy, J. M., Malley, J. E., & Stewart, A. J. (1990). Children and their fathers after parental separation. *American Journal of Orthopsychiatry*, *60*, 531–543. doi: 10.1037/h0079201

Hetherington, E. M. (Ed.). (1999). Should we stay together for the sake of the children? In E. M. Hetherington (Ed.), *Coping with divorce, single parenting, and remarriage* (pp. 93–116). Mahwah, NJ: Lawrence Erlbaum Associates, Inc. doi: 10.1177/0907568203010002008

Hetherington, E. M., Bridges, M., & Insabella, G. M. (1998). What matters? What does not? Five perspectives on the association between marital transitions and children's adjustment. *American Psychologist*, *53*, 167–184. doi: 10.1037/0003-066X.53.2.167

Hetherington, E. M., Cox, M., & Cox, R. (1982). Effects of divorce on parents and children. In M. E. Lamb (Ed.), *Nontraditional families* (pp. 223–288). Hillsdale, NJ: Lawrence Erlbaum Associates, Inc. doi: 10.1016/S0002-7138(09)60052-2

Hetherington, E. M., & Kelly, J. (2002). *For better or for worse: Divorce reconsidered.* New York, NY: W. W. Norton & Company, Inc. doi: 10.2143/INT.8.2.2004434

Hetherington, E. M., & Stanley-Hagen, M. (1999). The adjustment of children with divorced parents: A risk and resiliency perspective. *Journal of Child Psychology and Psychiatry*, *20*(1), 129–140. doi: 10.1111/1469-7610.00427

Hofer, B. K., Souder, C., Kennedy, E. K., Fullman, N., & Hurd, K. (2009). The electronic tether. In I. Garey (Ed.), *Who's watching? Daily practices of surveillance among contemporary families* (pp. 277–294). Nashville, TN: Vanderbilt University Press.

Johnston, J. R., Kline, M., & Tschann, J. M. (1989). Ongoing postdivorce conflict: Effects on children of joint custody and frequent access. *American Journal of Orthopsychiatry*, *59*, 576–592. doi: 10.1111/j.1939-0025.1989.tb02748.x

Kelly, J. B. (2000). Children's adjustment in conflicted marriage and divorce: A decade review of research. *Journal of the American Academy of Child Psychiatry*, *39*, 963–973. doi: 10.1097/00004583-200008000-00007

Kelly, J. B. (2004). Family mediation research: Is there empirical support for the field? *Conflict Resolution Quarterly*, *22*, 3–35. doi: 10.1002/crq.90

Kelly, J. B. (2007). Children's living arrangements following separation and divorce: Insights from empirical and clinical research. *Family Process*, *46*, 35–52. doi: 10.1111/j.1545-5300.2006.00190.x

Kelly, J. B., & Lamb, M. E. (2000). Using child development research to make appropriate custody and access decisions for young children. *Family and Conciliation Courts Review*, *38*, 297–311. doi: 10.1111/j.174-1617.2000.tb00577.x

Kelly, R. F., & Ramsey, S. H. (2009). Child custody evaluations: The need for systems-level outcome assessments. *Family Court Review*, *47*, 286–303. doi: 10.1111/j.1744-1617.2009.01255.x

Kurdek, L. A. (1986). Custodial mothers' perceptions of visitation and payment of child support by noncustodial fathers in families with low and high levels of preseparation interparent conflict. *Journal of Applied Developmental Psychology*, *7*(4), 307–323. doi: 10.1016/0193-373(86)90002-X

Lamb, M. E. (2002). Placing children's interests first: Developmentally appropriate parenting plans. *The Virginia Journal of Social Policy and the Law*, *10*, 98–119.

Lamb, M. E. (2012). Critical analysis of research on parenting plans and children's well-being. In K. Kuehnle & L. Drozd (Eds.), *Parenting plan evaluations: Applied research for the family court*. New York, NY: Oxford University Press.

Lamb, M. E., & Kelly, J. B. (2009). Improving the quality of parent-child contact in separating families with infants and young children: Empirical research foundations. In R. M. Galatzer-Levy, L. Kraus, & J. Galatzer-Levy (Eds.), *The scientific basis of child custody decisions* (2nd ed., pp. 187–214). Hoboken, NJ: John Wiley & Sons.

Lamb, M. E., Sternberg, K. J., & Thompson, R. A. (1997). The effects of divorce and custody arrangements on children's behavior, development, and adjustment. *Family and Conciliation Courts Review*, *35*, 393–404. doi: 10.1111/j.1741617.1997.tb00482.x

Laumann-Billings, L., & Emery, R. E. (2000). Distress among young adults in divorced families. *Journal of Family Psychology*, *14*, 671–687. doi: 10.1037/08933200.14.4.671

Lee, S. J. (2009). Online communication and adolescent social ties: Who benefits more from Internet use? *Journal of Computer-Mediated Communication*, *14*, 509–531.

Martinez, C. R., Jr., & Forgatch, M. S. (2002). Adjusting to change: Linking family structure transitions with parenting and boys' adjustment. *Journal of Family Psychology*, *16*, 107–117. doi: 10.1037/0893-3200.16.2.107

McLanahan, S. S., & Sandefur, G. (1994). *Growing up with a single parent: What hurts, what helps*. Cambridge, MA: Harvard University Press. doi: 10.1002/pam.4050150116

Nord, C. W., Brimhall, D., & West, J. (1997). *Fathers' involvement in their children's school*. Washington, DC: National Center for Education Statistics.

Pedro-Carroll, J. L., & Cowen, E. L. (1985). The children of divorce intervention program: An investigation of the efficacy of a school-based prevention program. *Journal of Consulting and Clinical Psychology*, *53*, 603–611. doi: 10.1037/0022-006X.53.5.603

Pelleboer-Gunnink, H. A., Van der Valk, I. E., Branje, S. J. T., Van Doorn, M. D., & Dekovic, M. (2015). Effectiveness and moderators of the prevention intervention KIDS in divorce situations: A randomized control trial. *Journal of Family Psychology, 29*, 799–805. doi: 10.1037/fam0000107

Pollet, S. L., & Lombreglia, M. (2008). A nationwide survey of mandatory parent education. *Family Court Review, 46*, 375–394. doi: 10.1111/j.1744-1617.2008.00207.x

Pruett, M. K., & Jackson, T. D. (1999). The lawyer's role during the divorce process: Perceptions of parents, their young children, and their attorneys. *Family Law Quarterly, 33*, 283–310.

Pruett, M. K., Williams, T. Y., Insabella, G., & Little, T. D. (2003). Family and legal indicators of child adjustment to divorce among families with young children. *Journal of Family Psychology, 17*, 169–180. doi: 10.1037/0893-3200.17.2.169

Riley, G. (1991). *Divorce: An American tradition*. New York: Oxford University Press.

Saini, M., Mishna, F., Barnes, J., & Polak, S. (2013). Parenting online: An exploration of virtual parenting time in the context of separation and divorce. *Journal of Child Custody, 10*, 120–140. doi: 10.1080/15379418.2013.796265

Sandler, I. N., Wolchik, S. A., & Braver, S. L. (1988). The stressors of children's postdivorce environments. In S. Wolchik & P. Karoly (Eds.), *Children of divorce: Empirical perspectives on adjustment* (pp. 231–245). New York, NY: Gardner.

Sandler, I. N., Wolchik, S. A., Braver, S. L., & Fogas, B. (1987). Significant events of children of divorce: Toward the assessment of a risky situation. In S. M. Auerbach & A. Stolberg (Eds.), *Crisis intervention with children and families* (pp. 589–598). New York: Hemisphere.

Schwartz, S. J., & Finley, G. E. (2005). Divorce-related variables as predictors of young adults' retrospective fathering reports. *Journal of Divorce & Remarriage, 44*, 145–163. doi: 10.1300/J087v44n01_08

Shefts, K. R. (2002). Virtual visitation: The next generation of options for parent-child communication. *Family Law Quarterly, 36*, 303–327.

Simons, R. L., & Associates. (1996). *Understanding differences between divorced and intact families*. Thousand Oaks, CA: Sage Publications.

Simons, R. L., Lin, K. H., Gordon, L. C., Conger, R. D., & Lorenz, F. O. (1999). Explaining the higher incidence of adjustment problems among children of divorce compared with those in two-parent families. *Journal of Marriage and the Family, 61*, 1020–1033. doi: 10.2307/354021

Stevenson, B., & Wolfers, J. (2007). Marriage and divorce: Changes and their driving forces. *National Bureau of Economic Research Working Papers*. Retrieved from: http://www.nber.org/papers/w12944.pdf. doi: 10.3386/w12944

Stevenson, M. M., Braver, S. L., Ellman, I. M., & Votruba, A. M. (2012). Fathers, divorce, and child custody. In N. J. Cabrera & C. S. Tamis-LeMonda (Eds.), *Handbook of father involvement: Multidisciplinary perspectives* (2nd ed., pp. 379–396). New York: Routledge. doi: 10.4324/9780203101414.ch21

Stolberg, A. L., & Garrison, K. M. (1985). Evaluating a primary prevention program for children of divorce. *American Journal of Community Psychology, 13*, 111–124. doi: 10.1007/BF00905724

Stolberg, A. L., & Mahler, J. (1994). Enhancing treatment gains in a school-based intervention for children of divorce through skill training, parental involvement, and transfer procedures. *Journal of Consulting and Clinical Psychology, 62*, 147–156. doi: 10.1037/0022-006X.62.1.147

Thompson, B. (2005). Life support: A system of care for military families. *Zero to Three, 25*, 49–55.

Troxel, W. M., & Matthews, K. A. (2004). What are the costs of marital conflict and dissolution to children's physical health? *Clinical Child and Family Psychology Review, 7*, 29–57. doi: 10.1023/B:CCFP.0000020191.73542.b0

U.S. Census Bureau. (August 18, 2015). *American families and living arrangements: 2014*. Retrieved from: http://www.census.gov/hhes/families/

Venohr, J. C., & Kaunelis, R. (2008). *Arizona child support guidelines review: Analysis of case file data*. Denver: Center for Policy Research.

Wallerstein, J., & Kelly, J. (1980). *Surviving the breakup: How children and parents cope with divorce*. New York, NY: Basic Books.

Whiteside, M. F., & Becker, B. J. (2000). Parental factors and the younger child's post divorce adjustment: A meta-analysis with implications for parenting arrangements. *Journal of Family Psychology, 14*, 5–26. doi: 10.1037/0893-3200.14.1.5

Wolchik, S. A., Sandler, I. N., Jones, S., Gonzales, N., Doyle, K., Winslow, E. et al. (2009). The New Beginnings Program for divorcing and separating families: Moving from efficacy to effectiveness. *Family Court Review, 47*, 416–435. doi: 10.1111/j.1744-1617.2009.01265.x

Wolchik, S. A., West, S. G., Sandler, I. N., Tein, J. Y., Coatsworth, D., Lengua, L. et al. (2000). An experimental evaluation of theory-based mother and mother-child programs for children of divorce. *Journal of Consulting and Clinical Psychology, 68*, 843–856. doi: 10.1037/0022-006X.68.5.843

Wolchik, S. A., West, S. G., Westover, S., Sandler, I. N., Martin, A., Lustig, J. et al. (1993). The children of divorce parenting intervention: Outcome evaluation of an empirically-based program. *American Journal of Community Psychology, 21*, 293–331. doi: 10.1007/BF00941505

Yarosh, S., & Abowd, G. D. (2011, May). Mediated parent-child contact in work-separated families. In *Proceedings of the SIGCHI Conference on Human Factors in Computing Systems* (pp. 1185–1194). doi: 10.1111/j.1083-6101.2009.01451.x

Therapy With Divorcing Families

Amy C. Wagner and Rachel M. Diamond

One of the most challenging constraints facing clinicians who work with families experiencing the multiple demands of divorce is slowing down the process so family members have time to adjust to the inevitable and often rapid transitions that occur. While legal/court proceedings may move slowly for many, the transitions in the family's life often do not follow the same timeline. For example, a family may need to move out of their home into new, smaller residences, or a parent may quickly begin dating. Consequently, rapid transitions will need to be addressed by clinicians working with divorcing/divorced families.

Before initiating the process of divorce, one or both parents likely struggled with the decision for many months or years. Typically only upon beginning the separation process do parents inform their children. For many children, day one of the divorce starts when they are told of the decision. Children's lives are often destabilized on many levels as they experience multiple losses (e.g., relationships, homes, friends, school, neighborhood, extended family, economic security). Parents may also be overwhelmed by the emotional and legal process involved in ending a marriage, oftentimes making it difficult for them to provide support for their children's emotional needs. It follows that one of the most important goals of therapy is to provide the family with stability in a time of change, while encouraging flexibility and adaptability. In this chapter we present a therapeutic model for addressing common issues facing divorcing families, such as Anne and Doug Miller and their children.

Conceptualizing Divorce: A Process Perspective

Divorce and the subsequent transitions and reorganization of family structure that follow have become a normative experience in our society. The most commonly accepted theoretical model of divorce supports a process perspective that proposes marital dissolution is not a single, discrete event. Instead, it is an ongoing couple and familial process that increases relational conflict and emotional instability and ultimately involves the loss of the intact family that once existed. Certainly, families can benefit from some professional support in the divorce process to navigate these transitions over time. By understanding the rapid changes that often occur when one or both partners begin the process of marital dissolution, therapists can directly respond to the impact on family dynamics. Further, therapists can assist families in understanding the challenges of divorce by helping normalize their struggles and make a series of interconnected necessary adjustments.

Importantly, clinicians must understand that clients will enter treatment at any point across this transitional continuum (i.e., marital dissolution), so their needs can vary greatly. This can be true even within the parental unit, as less than 10% of divorcing partners report the divorce as being a "mutual decision" (Braver, Whitley, & Ng, 1993). One or both parents may come to therapy contemplating divorce and wanting to better understand the potential impact on their children, often seeking advice about telling their children about their decision to divorce and help supporting them in this transition. Others may seek therapy during the divorce process if their children exhibit signs of anxiety, depression, or disruptive behavior. After the legal divorce, parents pursue treatment if they see their children struggling to adjust to changes in family structure, a new school, or community.

In the case of the Millers, they sought family therapy at the suggestion of the parents' attorneys, precipitated by the family's continuing difficulties adjusting. While families attempt to adjust to a post-divorce family structure, oftentimes their attempted solutions evolve into problems, as they are unable to adapt to a single parent or binuclear family (Ahrons & Rodgers, 1987). The following section details the therapeutic framework used when working with the Miller family, as well as a blueprint for treatment when working with families seeking treatment for issues related to divorce.

Integrative Problem-Centered Metaframeworks: IPCM

Our approach to working with divorced families is based on the integrative problem-centered metaframeworks (IPCM) model developed over 20 years at the Family Institute at Northwestern University (Russell, Pinsof, Breunilin, & Lebow, 2016). This problem-centered integrative approach is based on common factors found across a multitude of family systems theories. Utilizing a strengths-based perspective (Braver, Hipke, Ellman, & Sandler, 2004), clients are viewed as having the ability to solve their own problems, but are somehow constrained from presently doing so. Therapy proceeds in a cost-effective fashion, moving from more direct, systemic, and behaviorally focused intervention in the "here and now" to those interventions that are more indirect, internally focused, and historic in origin. That is, therapy focuses on current interpersonal constraints (e.g., current communication patterns between parents) before those that are more embedded in historic individual experiences or internally driven (e.g., communication patterns in the family or origin). The therapist uses empirically informed strategies and techniques to intervene and collaboratively achieve an adaptive solution to the presenting problem, based on hypotheses about where constraints exist in the system. Drawing from many psychotherapy models to transcend and replace the specific theories of problem formation and maintenance, the IPCM model identifies eight domains of human functioning that prevent problem solving: sequences, organization, development, mind, culture, gender, biology, and spirituality. Constraints can exist on many interconnected levels across the biopsychosocial spectrum and interact in a web of human experience. "IPCM hypothesizes that the clients' capacity to implement the adaptive solution sequence as an alternative to the presenting problem sequences is blocked by the Web of Constraints" (Breunlin, Pinsof, Russell, & Lebow, 2011a, p. 302). The ultimate goal of therapy is to empower individuals and families to solve their own problems by identifying alternative adaptive sequences and lifting constraints. Common constraints for families of divorce involve organization, sequences, development, and cultural and gender-based belief systems for the individual as well as family and larger systems within which they are embedded.

Organization

Based on general systems theory, a family system is organized in a defined structure in which each part functions recursively in relation to the whole. These subsystems (e.g., parental, sibling, parent-child) interact with, and, in turn, are influenced by others within the nuclear family as well as larger systems within which the family exists (e.g., extended family, community, society). This interaction between multilevel variables creates a web of mutual influence with each system contributing differentially to any relational process (Breunlin et al., 2011a).

In the case of the Miller family, the post-divorce organization of the family system was constraining the ability of the family to function successfully in several ways. Coparenting was ineffective; subsequently, there was no clear or unified leadership in the family. Doug and Anne were unable to transition from spouses into the role of collaborative coparents. Consequently, Kenzie was positioned in a role not suitable for her in that it included taking on parenting responsibilities for Sean. As Sean's relationship with his mother became more conflictual and distant, the loss of contact with his father was further distressing to him. Kenzie's relationship with her mother can be characterized as very close (i.e., enmeshed), and with Kenzie's parentified role came diffuse boundaries between herself and her mother. The boundaries in the family are reciprocal; that is, as Kenzie's boundaries with her mother were weakened, her boundaries with her father became rigid as she distanced herself from her father and blamed him for the divorce. Sean's relationship with his mother became more conflictual.

Due to financial constraints, the family moved out of their home to new residences. Thus, the children lost their family home and needed to adjust to living in new homes with new organizational systems (i.e., Anne and her mother in one home and Doug in the other). Additionally, Anne's mother became overinvolved in her relationship with the children. Her mother's well-intended efforts to be supportive undermined Anne's effectiveness, thus contributing to her children's view of her as less competent. As Anne was perceived as less capable, Kenzie's parentified role increased. Highly permeable boundaries between mothers and daughters appear to be a pattern of family organization spanning two generations, as this pattern is isomorphic to the relationship between Anne and her mother; in both dyads Anne is seen as less than competent as a parent.

Sequences

The term "sequences" is used to describe the systemic patterns of interaction that exist within the family system. Some patterns of functioning may have predated the divorce or were adaptive at some previous time but are no longer functional for the family. In treatment, the focus is on problem sequences, which involve the "interwoven tapestries of behavior, emotion, and cognition" (Breunlin et al., 2011a, p. 301). Alternative adaptive solutions to problem sequences emerge from a collaborative exploration between the family and the therapist (Russell, Pinsof, Breunlin, & Lebow, 2016). The therapist and the Miller family co-constructed the following problem sequence that occurs in Anne's home with the children the mornings following parenting time with his dad: Sean misses his dad, cries, and does not get out of bed; Anne and Grandma encourage Sean to get up; he continues to cry; Anne continues to be encouraging until she loses patience and yells due to mounting concerns about the children being late for school; Grandma shifts attention to comfort Anne; Kenzie lashes out at Sean for upsetting their mother and causing her to be tardy. Thus, in this family the problem sequences around Sean's difficulty leaving for school following visits with his dad are both influenced by, and influence, the constraints of the system within which they are embedded.

Problem sequences are often reported by family members, and they can also be evidenced in session. For example, the therapist may observe Kenzie acting like a parent by directing Sean to take off his coat or sit up straight. By commenting on this behavior ("*It looks like Kenzie is trying to be helpful to you, Anne, by acting as another parent to Sean*") and helping Anne to interrupt this sequence ("*However, it is important for her to see you are in charge of her and her brother so she doesn't have to take on this responsibility, so what can you do now to give her that message?*"), the therapist helps the client(s) work to implement adaptive sequences as an alternative to the problem sequences.

Development

Understanding the competencies required for adjustment to divorce for each individual, subsystem, and the larger system as a whole is necessary when crafting appropriate interventions. Clinicians need to consider the developmental needs of different children and initiate interventions based on chronological and/or developmental age. For example, a therapist may include family play therapy techniques in order to engage children in the therapeutic process, as younger family members may not be able to express themselves in traditional "talk therapy." Additionally, some topics may be inappropriate to discuss when children are present, such as parenting or issues related to parenting time. The therapist should instead have sessions, as needed, with the parent(s) alone in such instances, especially if issues arise around parenting differences or conflicts. Such "parenting" sessions may involve one parent, both parents separately, or both parents together—a decision the therapist must make while considering the family's current relationship with the legal system.

Developmental transitions for children typically create oscillation in the sense that children develop older and newer developmental competencies. In healthy systems this normal process diminishes over time once a new level of functioning is achieved. However, when development becomes constrained or disrupted, which often happens during the divorce process, these oscillations continue or even intensify dysfunction. This was seen in the Miller family through Kenzie's behaviors. Kenzie's behavior oscillated between acting older than her age (e.g., behaviors of a parentified child) and behaving in ways in which she acted as a younger child (e.g., sleeping with her mother at night).

In addition to individual development, family development is disrupted during the divorce process. Understanding what the needs are for each family member and how each individual is impacted by the dissolution of the family unit is important in relation to individual developmental tasks. Since Kenzie is in the preadolescent stage of development, it is expected that she would become more involved with peers outside the family system. However, her role throughout the divorce process as her brother's "other mother" may pull her back into her family unit and constrain her development of healthy peer relations. For Sean, his heightened separation anxiety related to the divorce may also interfere with his individual emotional growth. Developmental demands for individuals may be in conflict within the current unstable state of the larger family system.

Culture

Identity is derived, in part, by the beliefs and practices one draws from a particular system's location in a set of biosociocultural contexts that define typical behavior and experience (Pinsof, 1995). Contexts specify normative beliefs—in the case of the Millers, beliefs about divorce. For example, despite Doug's unhappiness in the marriage and infidelity, his cultural and religious views on divorce led him to refuse filing. Across all levels of the psychosocial system, issues of cultural fit or compatibility can generate constraint (Breunlin et al., 2011a). Anne, alternatively, did not experience similar cultural and religious constraint impacting the decision to divorce. However, her family culture, with few emotional boundaries between herself and her mother, made it difficult for her to feel competent as a single parent.

Gender

Although gender is linked to culture, it is distinct and should be examined separately due to its importance to human relationships. That is, therapists should take into consideration gender roles, power, beliefs, and expectations. When thinking about divorce there are several gender-related issues to take into consideration.

Divorce Initiation

The majority (about two-thirds) of divorce initiators are female (Ahrons & Rodgers, 1987; Baum, 2003; Braver et al., 1993; Pettit & Bloom, 1984). It is thought that women tend to experience the stress of marital breakdown earlier in the process of dissolution than men and that periods of stress are highest for women before the decision to divorce is made; whereas stress is highest for men post-divorce (Baum, 2003; Braver & O'Connell, 1998).

Post-Divorce Adjustment

When understanding the post-divorce adjustment process, gender considerations also exist. In addition to men mourning later, Baum (2003) details the differences in what men and women mourn post-divorce. Men mourn the loss of their children and their home and family life more than the loss of a spouse. Women, in contrast, are more prone to mourn the loss of the marital relationship. This difference is understandable when considering that custody arrangements typically favor women (Fabricius, Braver, Diaz, & Velez, 2010; Kelly, 2007; Venohr & Kaunelis, 2008). As was seen in the Miller family, while the family could not afford either parent to remain in the family home, the children resided with Anne the majority of the time, while Doug saw the children on a schedule that was less frequent and less consistent. Additionally, men are more likely to express their adjustment in ways that are deemed socially acceptable (e.g., increased work/activity, somatization, and/or self-medication), rather than expressing feelings directly through words or emotions like women (Baum, 2003).

The Therapy Process

Beginning Therapy

Prior to beginning any treatment with children and their parents, it is essential to clarify legal agreements about seeking therapy. It is our belief that unless both parents consent to family therapy, it will not be successful. Before seeing a child we first meet with the parents to obtain consent/assent and review a therapeutic contract. We make it clear that it will not be our role to determine custody arrangements, but that we will act as a facilitator for the family in reaching their goals. We believe it is best practice to separate the legal and therapeutic issues and to maintain a positive alliance with *both* parents to act in the best interest of their children. The need for a therapist to utilize multidirectional partiality (i.e., not acting as a judge but a person with enough empathy to connect with each family member) is of particular importance with divorcing parents since the parents often attempt to make the therapist *their* ally (Greenberg, Gould, Gould-Saltman, & Stahl, 2003).

Working with families of divorce necessarily requires clear structure within the therapeutic setting because there is often a lack of organization during periods of conflict or transition with a resulting sense of uncertainty or chaos. Additionally, families of divorce may be actively involved in the legal system (e.g., attorneys, guardian ad litem, etc.). Thus, at the start therapists should review a therapy contract with parents that, in addition to the typical information that is covered at the start of treatment, will review the following information: who will participate in treatment; who will be responsible for therapy fees; and with whom the therapist can and will communicate and how often. Channels of communication are clarified concerning what information will be discussed with the direct and indirect system; that is, both those who are directly involved in therapy (e.g., children and parents) and those who are not directly in session, but can influence therapy (e.g., legal system and school) are specified. Clear expectations need to be established around confidentiality for parents and children. It is best that the therapist decides what information to share with each parent in order to facilitate harmony and cooperation, yet avoid triangulation between parents. It should be clear that the therapist will not withhold any important information about the children from the other parent. Further, the therapist should request that any email communication received from one parent should have the other parent copied onto it. Since children participate in sessions with both parents, children are told they can share whatever they want with the other parent, but that parents should respect their child's wish to not discuss what happened in a session with the other parent. In this way therapy models an organizational system where the child is not caught in the middle. In our experience, these measures are also put into place to create a therapeutic space whereby members of a family can feel safer. That is, structure creates a sense of safety for clients (*and the therapist!*). Because there are established, agreed upon rules that govern the process, the treatment is more predictable and ultimately more successful.

Meeting With the Necessary Subsystems: Working With Parents

In our approach to family treatment we always begin by meeting with the parents, or with each parent alone if they are not able or willing to meet together, to discuss their concerns about their children. In this way we are developing a solid treatment alliance and we are also establishing an appropriate boundary highlighting an organizational structure where the adults in the family engage in competent and cooperative leadership. While the IPCM model begins treatment with the largest family system, we believe that in divorcing families this is contraindicated; there is often a high degree of emotional reactivity and conflict between divorcing parents. Our experience is that meeting with parents alone first prevents children from being further exposed to any continued conflict and allows us to stabilize the system and co-create a safe therapeutic space.

Therapeutically, we take a collaborative, nonjudgmental approach. The therapist's first task is to co-construct a conversation in order to come to a mutual understanding of why the family is seeking treatment and what the goals are for therapy. This task involves defining the problem sequences that are causing distress in the family and may take some time, as parents often have and convey different understandings. With Anne and Doug, they reported that their attorneys recognized the difficulties they were having coparenting and their children's difficulties adjusting to the divorce. It was difficult for Anne and Doug to identify a specific problem sequence causing distress, as each had different and linear views of the problem. That is, Anne identified the problem as being Doug's inconsistent presence and attention toward his girlfriend rather than the children as the source of the children's struggle. Doug identified Anne's anger over his extramarital relationship and "bad parenting" as the source of the problem. Clients often have difficulty stepping back to take a systemic view and see the problem sequences, especially having difficulty seeing their role. Therefore, it is the therapist's job to collaboratively explore how the sequence is developed in a way in which a single person is not responsible for behavior, but all members of the system contribute to and maintain the problem through repetitive and recursive pathways. We convey that this will be an "action" oriented therapy, focused on replacing constraining cognitive, emotional, or behavioral patterns with adaptive solutions to address areas where the family is "stuck" in the divorce process. The focus of our conversation is exploring the times when the problem does not occur or is less prevalent. We are curious about what keeps them from acting in a way that may solve the problem.

During the "*What brings you here and what would you like to work on in therapy?*" conversation, parents often have difficulty focusing on child-related concerns and talk about their own feelings toward their ex-spouse or the divorce process instead. In order to facilitate the development of a positive therapeutic alliance with both parents, it is important to hear their divorce narrative and understand each family's unique story. Part of this narrative also includes understanding the timeline for the family and the degree and speed of change that has occurred for the system within the process of the separation and divorce. Within this narrative, the therapist should listen for the impact of individual cultural, religious, or gender-related beliefs and the meaning of the divorce for each parent. Listening to the Millers' divorce narrative, the therapist learned that the separation and divorce occurred quickly and with minimal preparation. There was little planning in the way of creating a clear structure or schedule for the children. Unfortunately, Anne and Doug did not have enough time to center themselves emotionally and, therefore, were not attuned or responsive to the children's emotional needs.

After acknowledging their emotional experience and validating each parent's divorce narrative, the therapist must clearly establish that the purpose of family therapy for divorced parents is to find a way to act together in the best interest of their children. Initially this involves psychoeducation about what typically predicts positive adjustment for children and the family as a whole. (These factors are detailed in the research section of this chapter.) The therapist emphasizes the need to find ways to let go of the negative emotions associated with the ex-spouse and divorce experience, as continued parental conflict has been linked to a wide variety of childhood adjustment difficulties (Fabricius & Luecken, 2007; Grych & Fincham, 1990; Troxel & Matthews, 2004). If it becomes evident that parents' own emotional instability is interfering with their ability to focus on the children's needs, recommendations for individual work with another therapist or a divorce support group may be warranted.

Parents are given a clear message that they will need to establish a functional working coparent relationship in order to best help their children adjust. Before any work with the children, work with the parental subsystem to establish healthy communication and decision making may be indicated. Although most parents who divorce may not get along or may dislike one another, we ask them to aim for a position of neutrality. We urge them to try to separate their feelings about their ex-spouse as a partner from those of a parent. Establishing a regular method of communication specific to child-related issues is often helpful to parents. We also find it helpful to understand the constraints that keep parents from being able to work together. In the case of Anne and Doug, we would pose the question "*What keeps you from . . .*" [focusing on the children, being on the same page, etc.] in order to see what gets in the way of adaptive problem solving. This question serves two functions: (1) the therapist is provided with helpful information to understand problems that exist in the current method of functioning, and (2) the question leads the parents into a conversation that often demonstrates the problem sequence that is enacted outside of session. In both instances, the therapist is able to assist clients in implementing more adaptive solutions as an alternative to the problem sequence(s). It is important to note, if a therapist recognizes that parents are unable to successfully engage with one another without the presence of high-conflict arguments, therapists can help establish a "parallel parenting" plan. This type of arrangement involves coparenting by means of disengaging from one another, without disengagement from the child(ren), and having limited contact with one another, particularly in situations that tend to stimulate disrespect and conflict. This plan may be long or short term; with the passage of time the level of conflict can lessen between parents to better allow them to cooperatively coparent with higher levels of engagement and communication.

At times families are so stuck in recriminations and defensiveness that little progress can be made by the therapist without a court appointment as a parenting coordinator. This allows therapists more legal power to create a parenting plan to promote desirable changes (Coates, 2015).

Meeting With the Necessary Subsystems: Parent-Child(ren) Sessions

Once the parental subsystem is stabilized sufficiently to establish shared goals for therapy, the next step is to meet with each parent and their child(ren). We believe having the family meet together as the original unit is contraindicated, except in unusual circumstances or after a substantial time has passed since the divorce. By structuring therapy in this way we are facilitating their functioning in their new and different family form, as a binuclear rather than nuclear family. An initial task in parent-child(ren) sessions is to talk about why they are coming to family therapy and their treatment goals. Much like the parents needed a place to be validated for the difficult transitional process, so do the children. In the process of setting goals, children need their voice to be heard and need to understand what is expected of them in therapy. In the case of Sean and Kenzie, the therapist helped the children understand that the therapist's job was to help everyone in the family get along better and for the children to adjust to living with their mom and dad separately. Most children do not want their parents to divorce unless there is a high degree of overt conflict. It is typical for children to express they are unhappy or that it is difficult for them. This expression might be overt (e.g., a child says she does not like living in two homes), or it may be less so (e.g., a child may engage in school refusal, as seen by Sean on the days following parenting time with Doug). Acknowledging children's feelings is vital; it should also be acknowledged that it is common for them to feel this way and, over time, most children whose parents divorce are able to feel happy again.

Once children understand their place in therapy, the family can set goals for treatment. These may be different for each of the binuclear family groups. For the Miller family the goals for therapy were to (1) develop a more clear and stable schedule for parenting time (*Organization*); (2) help each of the family members adjust to the new roles and responsibilities within the new family structure (*Organization, Development, Culture, Gender*); and (3) develop healthier patterns of communication that facilitate effective coparenting, which allows for children to express themselves while parents demonstrate attunement and responsiveness to their emotional and developmental needs (*Development, Sequences, Culture, Gender*).

Establishing Clear Organization

When the Miller family came to therapy, physical separation had already happened. The children were splitting their time between their parents' temporary households and were in the process of (albeit unsuccessfully) developing new routines. This is often the most "dramatic and stunning of occurrences throughout the divorce process" (Everett & Volgy, 1991, p. 515). The separation begins the process of accepting the reality of the divorce for the children, and often the rest of the extended family as well.

Based on the IPCM model, initial interventions use strategies and techniques that primarily target behavioral sequences. Generally, these are interpersonal and focus on how people behave with each other, but also may target meaning and emotions (Breunlin, Pinsof, Russell, & Lebow, 2011b; Russell et al., 2016). Common tasks on which these interventions focus early in therapy are often around establishing clearer organization. Indeed, clear boundaries, schedules, rules, and expectations are the focus. These may be different in each household, but should be similar enough around important issues like bedtime or expectations about homework and school performance. Stabilizing each household and helping children understand changes in family structure and relationships allows them to better process the situation, and predictability helps them feel safe. In addition, by allowing a space for children and parents to talk about these changes as a result of the divorce, children can feel safer to raise concerns. Some dislikes may involve a simple solution, such as making sure a child has certain possessions in both homes so the child does not have to bring items back and forth or ever be without; other concerns may not have an easy remedy, such as a child not wanting to move out of the family home.

Typical issues for children in divorced families include the transitions between households. Most children report feeling afraid, uncertain, or a lack of control. Practically, this involves the logistics of understanding who will pick them up or where they will be staying and having their needed possessions. With the Miller family, the therapist worked with the parents to establish a more formal, structured arrangement for parenting time. The occasional after-school dinner with Doug was formalized into Doug picking the children up from school on Tuesdays and Thursdays. On these nights they would do homework, make dinner and eat together, and then Doug would take them to Anne's house to get ready for bed. Initially, Anne had concerns about increasing Doug's parenting time during the week, as she reported that she was the parent who had to deal with Sean's meltdowns before school the following day and would just as soon prefer that Doug's parenting time during the week be removed altogether. The therapist discussed with the parents how Sean's behavior might be a method of communicating missing his father and feeling out of control with the uncertainty of the current schedule. The therapist asked the parents to discuss how they could handle this situation differently. The parents agreed to try out this new schedule to see if it alleviated some of the organizational difficulties and Sean's behaviors. They also agreed that Sean could text Doug in the morning after he woke up for school if he missed him and Doug would send him a message back to let Sean know he was thinking of him too, as a way to demonstrate emotional support. In a short time, as the children began to trust that this schedule was predictable and stable, there was a decrease in Sean's acting out. This adaptive solution had a systemic effect on improving relationships between family members in Anne's household as well.

Additionally, practical organizational solutions can be helpful to families in which children live in two homes. Examples include children having duplicates of items whenever possible. However, if a child has an item that is sentimental (e.g., a favorite stuffed animal), parents should assist the child in being able to bring the item from home to home to facilitate the ease of transition and increase the level of emotional comfort. An item of sentiment for Sean was his father's baseball card collection, given to him just before the divorce. They were symbolic for Sean and helped him feel connected to his father when he was not physically. When the importance of this item was acknowledged, arrangements were made to ensure Sean had the item when at Anne's house.

Finally, in divorced families children often move together as a subsystem between households. That is, typically Kenzie and Sean would spend their time together at Anne or Doug's homes, but they rarely had the opportunity to spend one-on-one time with either parent. This was particularly true for Doug, as he did not have another caregiver to assist with parental responsibilities. It can be vital that parents and children have the opportunity to have one-on-one time, particularly if a parent has solo caregiving responsibilities in the home. Special accommodations may need to be made for this by the other parent or by an extended family member, which the therapist can help facilitate.

Redefining Roles

Transitioning to being a family of divorce involves redefining parenting roles as two single, rather than married, parents. Often parents are overwhelmed by the multiple responsibilities for their children's well-being that were previously shared. It may be difficult to negotiate differences between households for both children and parents. Change can be scary and overwhelming, especially with uncertainty about the future. It is helpful for therapists to normalize this process for family members as a "learning curve" with achievable goals. Parents and children need to redefine and renegotiate their relationships as binuclear families, rather than a nuclear family. For parents, it is important to establish new physical and emotional boundaries that maintain a coparenting partnership. Discussions and action-oriented interventions can occur within sessions where anxiety is better managed and relational skill-building and modeling can occur. For example, Anne's mother was invited in for a session to work on establishing roles in the family. In session, Anne, her mother, and the children role-played how to work together when Sean is feeling sad about missing his father, evaluating and adapting their roles in the process. Anne practiced, with the guidance of the therapist, supporting her son without the assistance of her mother or daughter; thus, freeing both to assume their own respective roles within the family.

Furthermore, within the IPCM model the therapist moves deeper to also focus on meaning and emotion that increases client awareness about how they are constrained by maladaptive cognitive and emotional sequences. In the Miller family, this included conversations that facilitated mourning the loss of the original family. The therapist helped family members explore and share their feelings and beliefs about the divorce and the meaning it had to each of them. This helped to increase empathy and validate each person's experience. Through this process the therapist can facilitate the definition and acceptance of each member's role within a binuclear family structure.

Developing Healthier Communication

Common tasks in therapy sessions are often around establishing healthier patterns of communication. One common negative occurrence in families of divorce is that the children get "stuck in the middle" between parents. This is especially common in divorce cases with ongoing custody litigation and conflict. Often, the children remain stuck between parents who express anger to the children or leverage them against the other parent. This can blind the parent to seeing the emotional needs of the child and the anxiety created in the face of the ever-changing family structure. Parents are told early, and often, that they should not put children in the middle between themselves and their ex-spouse. Further, children should not be asked to take sides, as they should be given the message that they are allowed to love both parents. They are children; they are not buffers, mediators, or messengers. Communication, instead, should go directly between ex-spouses, and anger should be expressed in more appropriate ways. Anne and Doug agreed to these guidelines and to use a software program designed to assist parents of divorce with scheduling and communication (e.g., Our Family Wizard) to better navigate child-related concerns or issues. If they could not settle these differences themselves, they agreed to discuss them with the therapist.

For the Millers, there had been a pattern for years of Kenzie serving as a supportive resource for her mother, rather than the other way around. Thus, many of Kenzie's emotional needs had been ignored. In addition to the interventions directed at targeting Kenzie's role (as detailed in the section above), she and her brother were allowed the opportunity to communicate their feelings about the divorce to their parents. Children should be allowed to express their feelings, as they may feel scared, lonely, and confused during this time of rapid transition. Often parents may be too caught up in their own turmoil from the divorce to tend to their children's emotional needs. In family therapy, the therapist helps children identify and label emotions and helps parents to respond empathetically. Parents may need to first be educated about how to be clear and responsive to their children's emotions, as well as answer any questions and fears that surface. When working with children it can be useful to use art or play materials, as they often do not have the emotional vocabulary to describe their experience. For example, Kenzie and Sean were asked to depict worries since the divorce in varying sized "worry balloons" on a sheet of paper with three empty balloons of increasing size. They were told to put their small worries in the small balloon, medium-sized worries in the medium-sized balloon, and their biggest worries in the largest balloon. When processing the activity, a shared concern by both children was a fear that they would need to move again, highlighting their discomfort with the unpredictability of their living situation. Hearing this information reinforced earlier goals for Anne and Doug of creating and maintaining a predictable, structured schedule for the children. Further, in parent-child sessions Anne and Doug listened to the children's concerns and the emotions associated with them, validated them, and continued to work toward creating solutions.

While parents and children may not be in the same household, we advocate for children to have one opportunity each day to communicate with the other parent at a prearranged, scheduled time. While in the past there may have been a number of barriers to discuss regarding the logistics of maintaining communication between parents and children, technology is changing the face of parent-child communication in families of divorce. Virtual visitation laws are a new, growing phenomenon, and since 2004 several states have enacted laws allowing courts to order virtual visitation in parenting order plans. Technology can be useful in facilitating this connection, from simpler technologies such as cell phones and standard electronic communications (e.g., email, texts, and instant messaging) to more advanced technologies that allow for video (e.g., webcams, video conferencing, etc.) as well as social media and photo-sharing sites. Although there are definite benefits that can be drawn, limits need to be established as well. Saini, Mishna, Barnes, and Polak (2013) provide guidelines for developmentally appropriate virtual parent-child contact: Doug and Anne arranged virtual visitation times for Sean, being that he is school-aged (7 years old), whereas Kenzie had independent ability to use virtual platforms of communication, such as email, Skype, and phone, and could be more involved in scheduling the virtual visitation times due to her older age (preadolescence; 12 years old). However, because Kenzie had seen text messages not intended for her on her father's phone, a conversation about clear boundaries when utilizing communication devices was established.

Conclusion

It is important for therapists to take a systemic view and approach to cases of divorce and the challenges of what is often rapid change that occurs for these contemporary families. Indeed, therapists need to consider the needs of all members of the family, as well as the systemic influences that are recursively affecting each individual and the family system as a whole. The IPCM model offers clinicians a blueprint for identifying constraints and developing an intervention plan with divorcing families. Divorce is often a challenging, difficult, and painful process for both children and their parents. We believe that therapists who view this as a transitional process can better help their clients let go of the original family that was and move toward embracing their new and different family form. Despite the loss of the family that once was, divorce provides an opportunity for growth and the development of flexibility and resiliency in response to change in a rapidly changing world.

References

Ahrons, C. R., & Rodgers, R. H. (1987). *Divorced families: Meeting the challenge of divorce and remarriage*. New York, NY: W. W. Norton & Company, Inc.

Baum, N. (2003). The male way of mourning divorce: When, what, and how. *Clinical Social Work Journal, 31*, 37–50. doi: 10.1023/A:1021462517875

Braver, S. L., Hipke, K. N., Ellman, I. M., & Sandler, I. N. (2004). Strengths-building public policy for children of divorce. In K. I. Maton, C. J. Schellenbach, B. J. Leadbeater, & A. L. Solarz (Eds.), *Investing in children, families and communities: Strengths-based research and policy* (pp. 53–72). Washington, DC: American Psychological Association.

Braver, S. L., Whitley, M., & Ng, C. (1993). Who divorced whom? Methodological and theoretical issues. *Journal of Divorce & Remarriage, 20*, 1–19. doi: 10.1300/J087v20n01_01

Breunlin, D. C., Pinsof, W., Russell, W. P., & Lebow, J. (2011a). Integrative problem-centered metaframeworks therapy I: Core concepts and hypothesizing. *Family Process, 50*, 293–313. doi: 10.1111/j.1545-5300.2011.01362.x

Breunlin, D. C., Pinsof, W., Russell, W. P., & Lebow, J. (2011b). Integrative problem-centered metafameworks therapy II: Planning, conversing, and reading feedback. *Family Process, 50*, 314–336. doi: 10.1111/j.1545-5300.2011.01361.x

Coates, C. A. (2015). The parenting coordinator as peacemaker and peacebuilder. *Family Court Review, 53*(3), 398–406.

Everett, C. A., & Volgy, S. S. (1991). Treating divorce in family-therapy practice. In A. S. Gurman & D. P. Kniskern (Eds.), *Handbook of family therapy* (Vol. 2, pp. 508–524). New York, NY: Brunner/Mazel, Inc.

Greenberg, L. R., Gould, J. W., Gould-Saltman, D. J., & Stahl, P. M. (2003). Is the child's therapist part of the problem? What judges, attorneys, and mental health professionals need to know about court-related treatment for children. *Family Law Quarterly, 37*(2), 241–271.

Pettit, E., & Bloom, B. (1984). Whose decision was it? The effects of initiator status on adjustment to marital disruption. *Journal of Marriage and the Family, 46*, 587–595.

Pinsof, W. M. (1995). *Integrative problem-centered therapy: A synthesis of family, individual, and biological therapies*. New York, NY: HarperCollins Publishing.

Russell, W., Pinsof, W., Breunilin, D., & Lebow, J. (2016). Integrative problem centered metaframeworks (IPCM) therapy. In T. Sexton & J. Lebow (Eds.), *Handbook of family therapy* (pp. 530–543). New York, NY: Brunner/Mazel, Inc.

Saini, M., Mishna, F., Barnes, J., & Polak, S. (2013). Parenting online: An exploration of virtual parenting time in the context of separation and divorce. *Journal of Child Custody, 10*, 120–140. http://dx.doi.org/10.1080/15379418.2013.796265

3

STEPFAMILIES

Case Study

Scott W. Browning

Carolyn and her husband, Brian (see Figure 3.1), have been married three years after a period of dating for about a year and a half, both brought children into their remarriage, and all children experienced an uneventful first meeting. Carolyn is divorced, whereas Brian is widowed. The main presenting problem is the ongoing tension between Carolyn and her stepdaughter, Hope. Carolyn also reports that she feels more distant from her biological daughter, Maria. This distance was precipitated when Maria started to date a man approximately four years older. Although not central, Brian casually mentioned that he is not sure if he and his daughters, Hope and Melanie, have mourned Christine's death. Christine was the biological mother to Melanie, and the adoptive mother to Hope. Carolyn and Maria identify as Italian/Irish American. Brian and Melanie are from English descent, and Hope was adopted from Korea. Hope was informed at an early age of her adoption and was given appropriate support by both Brian and Christine while growing up. Hope and Melanie see themselves as sisters. Hope would like to visit Korea someday and is curious, but does not feel her heritage or adoption status are a major part of her life. All family members identify as either Catholic or Presbyterian, but rarely attend church.

Carolyn conveys her position as trying to win Hope over, yet feels pushed away. She and Melanie get along, but Melanie is described as either "very passive" or "mildly depressed." Brian is concerned that it is depression related to the death of her mother. Anthony, Maria's nonresident father, is perceived to be reasonable and still connected to his daughter. Carolyn and Anthony have tense, minimal contact, but not volatile. Brian appears to be passive. While he clearly loves his family he is distracted and overly involved with work. He appears fully committed to therapy, but seems a bit oblivious to the importance of his role in the stepfamily. While his love for Christine was attractive to Carolyn at first, she finds his regular discussion of Christine somewhat off-putting. Most of the hostility in the family seems to generate from Hope, who has loud disagreements with both Carolyn and Maria. Hope loved Christine dearly. While Hope denies that issues regarding her adoption are directly involved in her anger, she did mention that Carolyn is now her "third mother." Due to where they live, Hope primarily associates with European-Americans, but she does have one Korean friend.

The other prominent emotional issue is the palpable dysthymia evident in both Brian and Melanie. Their relatively low affect is overshadowed by the emotional intensity between Hope and both Maria and Carolyn. While Carolyn initiated the request for therapy based on the volatility in the home and her waning relationship with her biological daughter, as the intake progressed, the relationship between Brian and Carolyn became more of a concern.

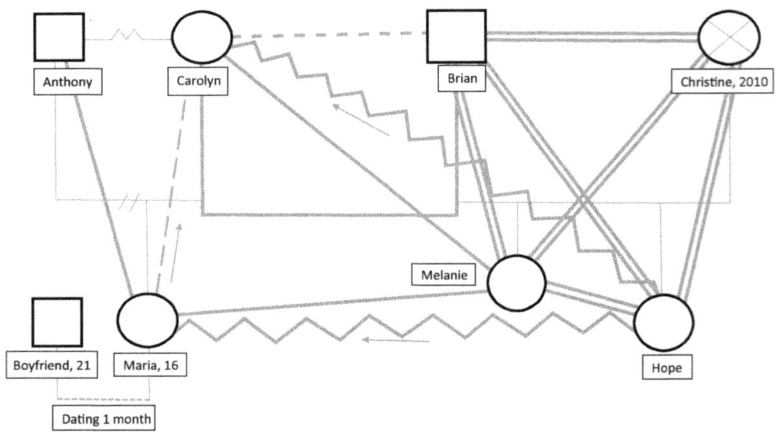

Figure 3.1 Stepfamily Genogram: Carolyn and Brian

An Empirical Look at Contemporary Stepfamilies

Kay Pasley and Brad van Eeden-Moorefield

Research on stepfamilies has a long and rich history, much of which has been summarized by notable scholars (e.g., Coleman & Ganong, 1990; Coleman, Ganong, & Fine, 2000; Sweeney, 2010; van Eeden-Moorefield & Pasley, 2012). Most reviews (and research) commonly were limited to traditionally defined stepfamilies—couples wherein the current marriage represents a remarriage for at least one of the adults, and at least one adult had children from a prior union. Scholars now are more inclusive in the way they define stepfamilies, recognizing the diverse pathways through which they are formed. No longer is divorce or death of a spouse the typical pathway to stepfamily life. Instead, couples can create a stepfamily through any number of legal (marriage) or non-legal (e.g., cohabitation, living apart together) structures. For example, some couples form stepfamilies by entering committed partnerships, which later dissolve, and they go onto repartner through marriage (i.e., legal stepfamilies) or cohabitation (i.e., non-legal stepfamilies); these repartnerships are stepfamilies when children from prior unions are involved (Sweeney, 2010; van Eeden-Moorefield & Pasley, 2012). It is also noteworthy that we now recognize stepfamilies headed by either same-sex or different-sex couples. This chapter provides a brief synthesis of the extant literature on stepfamilies headed by different-sex couples, paying special attention to that which is most clinically relevant in general and to Carolyn and Brian's stepfamily more specifically.

Prevalence and Demography of Stepfamilies

The U.S. Census and other common national surveys (e.g., American Community Survey [ACS], Current Population Reports [CPR]) often are used to estimate the prevalence of stepfamilies; however, estimates vary across data sources (for a discussion, see Kreider & Lofquist, 2014). Both the Census and ACS determine prevalence only by noting children under 18 years of age who are related to the designated householder by biological or legal means, such as birth, marriage, or adoption. However, CPR references children in the household by type of relationship to both coresident parents, and as such, the resulting estimates are higher. Unfortunately, these data generally exclude stepfamilies in which (a) stepchildren live elsewhere (nonresident) and (b) both resident and nonresident children are 18 years and older. Taken together, the prevalence of stepfamilies is consistently underestimated.

Best Estimates of Prevalence

Estimates suggest remarriage rates have dropped steadily since the 1990s, with some leveling off in the past eight years (Kreider, 2007; Payne, 2015). Using 2001 data, estimates show that 30.2% of all marriages were a remarriage for at least one of the partners (Kreider, 2005), and data from the 2008–2013 ACS suggests a total of 27.9 in 1000 adults available to remarry in 2014 did so, with men more likely (39.7) than women (Payne, 2015). These estimates are down from earlier estimates (50.2 in 1000 adults) likely due to increases in cohabitation (Cherlin, 2010). Of the 30% of all marriages, 17% were remarriages for only one partner and 13% were remarriages for both (Kreider, 2007). About 65% of remarriages form stepfamilies, with either stepfather-only or stepfather-stepmother families being the most common; stepmother-only families are the least common. Data from the 2006 and 2013 National Survey of Family Growth (NSFG) suggest unions (cohabiting and marital) among women create stepfamilies at the following rates: 24% of first, 65% of second, and 74% of third unions (Guzzo, 2016). Data further suggest that when a woman's first union (cohabiting or marriage) creates a stepfamily, 55% are stepmother-only, 29% are stepfather-only, and 17% are stepmother-stepfather households. Among women entering second unions, 17% are stepmother-only, 41% are stepfather-only, and 42% are stepmother-stepfather households, and this is almost the same for third unions (Guzzo, 2016). Further, non-legal stepfamilies are increasingly common among unmarried couples. Again, all of these are underestimates.

A more valuable picture comes from estimates addressing children's living arrangements. We know that fewer children today live with two parents, and that more children live with an unmarried or previously married parent (Kreider & Elliott, 2009). From a recent report using 2010 data (Kreider & Lofquist, 2014), we also know that about 10% of children live in a household with a stepparent; this includes 4.3% of children under 18 and 5.7% of children 18 years and older. These estimates of children living with a stepparent also show that about 37% are 12–17 years old, and another 33% are 18 years and older, and many are younger than 12 (23.5% are 6–11 and 6.8% are under 6). We do not know how many of these stepparents also have children living elsewhere, but it is likely that half of stepfathers do, because of the continued preference for maternal custody of minor children.

Other evidence shows that remarriages end more frequently than first marriages (e.g., Sweeney, 2010), and steprelationships formed through cohabitation are highly unstable (Xu, Hudspeth, & Bartokowski, 2006). In the past, remarriages (4.5 years) ended more quickly than first marriage (8 years), but data show that 50% of those who divorce following a first marriage or a remarriage do so within 8 years (Kreider, 2005).

Demographic Characteristics of Stepfamilies

Studies commonly show that the majority of children in legal stepfamilies are White (61%), with 21% Hispanic and 12.5% African-American compared to households where only biological children reside (55.5% White, 22.5% Hispanic, and 13.3% African-American; Kreider & Lofquist, 2014). Women who enter a first union, through marriage or cohabitation, that forms a stepfamily are more likely to be Black (57%) compared to Hispanic (26%) or White (18%), and this trend continues but weakens when women enter a second union that forms a stepfamily (Black, 84%; Hispanic, 78%; White 58%; Guzzo, 2016). Generally, women living in the western United States and men in the southern United States are most likely to remarry, whereas women and men living in the northeast are least likely to remarry (Payne, 2015).

Compared to children living with two biological parents, children in stepfamilies are more likely to be foreign born (6% vs. 3%), have at least one disability (6% vs. 4.6%), and are less likely to live in poverty (16.2% vs. 21%; Kreider & Lofquist, 2014). Interestingly, there is more racial diversity among members of stepfamilies than members of biological families as evident in racial differences between adults and children (12.6% in stepfamilies and 7.1% in bio-families). Further, data from this same report shows that stepchildren reside in families with more members, higher income, and with adults who have less education. These adults are also more likely to report having prior cohabitation experiences (Guzzo, 2016; Sweeney, 2010).

Little is known about stepfamilies formed through cohabitation, except that the adults are more likely to be younger, Black or Hispanic, and have lower incomes, both parents in the labor force, and children from prior partnerships (Guzzo, 2016; Kreider & Lofquist, 2014). The children are also likely to be younger (Kreider & Lofquist, 2014). Importantly, much of the cohabitation literature suggests that such unions are unstable (50% lasting up to 14 months), most common among those with a high school diploma or less, and are less likely to end in marriage or remarriage (Cherlin, 2010).

Collectively, this demographic information suggests therapists are likely to see stepfamilies with adolescents or older stepchildren, and face issues related to greater racial and ethnic diversity and fewer resources, especially resources related to the needs of developing adolescents and preparing them for independence or launching children and concerns over their need for continuing support. Further, among those in cohabiting stepfamilies, who may be easily missed by therapists, issues related to parenting of younger children (those under 12 years), the lack of resources to meet needs, and concerns over relationship stability may surface. Those with adolescent children may be more hopeful, as they "can see the light at the end of the tunnel" with anticipation of an end to childrearing, whereas cohabiting stepfamilies must anticipate more years of parenting and childrearing, thereby likely increasing stress and conflict.

Inherent Stress in Stepfamily Life

In 1987, Pasley and Ihinger-Tallman conceptualized the stress associated with stepfamily life as having three primary sources: merging different family histories, dealing with differences in resource distribution, and loyalty conflicts. In later work, Pasley added competing developmental needs as another source of stress. These and other scholars (see Amato, 2000, stress-adjustment perspective) determined that much of the stress experienced occurred early in the formation of the stepfamily, as members attempted to clarify expectations about roles, rules, and boundaries, and match them within their lived experiences. Typically, stepfamilies who reach the developmental milestone of the 5-year mark are considered largely successful in that they have settled in to a fairly functional set of roles and responsibilities with clearer boundaries. It is at this point that the likelihood of dissolution reduces (Michaels, 2006).

Effects of family transitions and stress are not limited to the experiences within a family—other transitions also complicate the process of adjustment to stepfamily life (Gosselin & David, 2007; van Eeden-Moorefield & Pasley, 2012). For example, repartnering often results in changes in residence and neighborhoods—schools/workplaces, friendship groups, and activities change. When stepfamilies are able to weather the challenges inherent in these multiple internal and external family transitions and establish workable roles and rules, much of the associated stress can be reduced. However, as is evident in the higher rates of dissolution among stepfamilies (Cherlin, 2010; Kreider & Lofquist, 2014), many are unable to accomplish this. Given Carolyn and Brian have been married three years and dating a little more, research would expect them to still be in the process of transition especially with regard to developing rules, roles, and boundaries. Accordingly, research suggests this as a site for clinical assessment of such factors that could help identify needed interventions to assist with transition-related stressors.

The Couple Relationship

The couple relationship serves as the unifying force in stepfamilies, connecting others in the family system, and is an important predictor of stepfamily functioning. Accordingly, assessing the couple's relational health can provide critical insight into the health of the larger stepfamily. Implicit in this is the couple's unique family position and role. Typically in first-union families the couple relationship is forged before adults transition into parenthood.

These couples are afforded the benefits of focusing solely on getting to know one another and creating their relationship. For couples with children from prior unions, this is not the case. These couples must navigate the development of a new relationship in the context of at least one adult parenting existing children from a prior union, and at least one adult figuring out how to become a stepparent and get to know a new child, often with an ex-partner closely watching. Essentially, there is a steep learning curve of shared experience. Such unique challenges often create feelings of frustration and conflict, of being an outsider and at a loss for how to promote cohesion within the stepfamily, all reinforced by the legal view of stepparents as legal strangers (Mason, Harrison-Jay, Svare, & Wolfinger, 2002). In a longitudinal study of women in stepfamilies, van Eeden-Moorefield and Pasley (2008) found that as fairness decreased and conflict increased, relationship quality declined over time and eventually predicted couple instability, including redivorce (van Eeden-Moorefield & Pasley, 2008). Clearly, couple adjustment requires time and patience, strong communication and problem-solving skills, and empathy, especially when conflict arises over differences.

Unfortunately, compared to research on the effects of stepfamily life on children, much less is known about such relational dynamics among couples (Sweeney, 2010; van Eeden-Moorefield & Pasley, 2012). In fact, research on how couples navigate the aforementioned unique challenges and develop successful relationships is quite limited. We do know that cohabitation is the typical path, especially for men (Cherlin, 2010; Sweeney, 2010). For some this leads to remarriage, and for others it does not. Research on remarried couples shows that those with more secure attachment styles reported higher levels of commitment, and this can enhance adjustment and stability (Ehrenberg, Robertson, & Pringle, 2012). Jensen, Lombardi, and Larson (2015) found that the negative impact of more anxious and avoidant attachment styles on common stepfamily issues is reduced when the couple perceives higher relationship quality. Accordingly, what is going on in the couple's relationship plays an important role in influencing the larger system directly, as well as serving as a possible conduit through which individual characteristics can influence the stepfamily system.

Some research shows that couples enter into stepfamilies with multiple concerns (e.g., about stepparenting, children's well-being and management, coparenting, stepparent-stepchild relationships). However, less than half of couples discuss these concerns thoroughly prior to remarriage (Cartwright, 2010), and uncertainty about one's relationship is linked with topic avoidance (Wilder, 2012). Still, Cartwright (2010) found that discussing the decision to cohabit or remarry with children and giving children the opportunity to talk about their concerns and feelings was linked with children's higher stepfamily acceptance. Thus, having discussions about important matters, rather than avoiding them, and including children in important decisions may facilitate adjustment. Again, for couples in first unions these typically are not concerns, and many couples assume their relationships and stepfamilies with work similarly to first unions.

Regarding other relationship processes, couples who report higher levels of adjustment also report lower levels of negative affect (DeLongis, Capreol, Holtzman, O'Brien, & Campbell, 2004), and there is some evidence that less marital conflict and more withdrawal from conflict (e.g., men concede more; Halford, Nicholson, & Sanders, 2007; Hobart, 1991) are common. For Brian and Carolyn we see some concerning negative affect, and this should be relevant for the treating therapist. Clearly, couples have more opportunities for conflict with the complexity of their relationships with children, stepchildren, and coparenting with former spouses and their new partners, when present. As such, is it not surprising that couples report more open expressions of anger, irritation, and criticism during conflict. However, these potentially negative behaviors appear to be diminished by other demonstrations of spousal support, inclusion (Ganong, Coleman, Jamison, & Feistman, 2015), and use of affirming communication strategies (Bray & Kelly, 1998; Pace, Shafer, Jensen, & Larson, 2015), such as respect and acceptance (Michaels, 2006).

The influence of former spouses/partners on the couple relationship has been the focus of some research. Unresolved issues and poor interactions with former spouses is linked negatively with both satisfaction and stability of the new relationship. However, the strength of this link diminishes when couples put forth more effort, are more committed to the repartnership (Pace et al., 2015; Shafer, Jensen, Pace, & Larson, 2013), and work together to parent effectively within the new stepfamily (Favez, Widmer, Doan, & Tissot, 2015). There is some research support for the importance of positive coparental communication, as it is associated with higher marital satisfaction (Pace et al., 2015). Additionally, there is related research identifying the characteristics associated with more effective communication in stepfamilies (Shrodt, 2006). These characteristics include more involvement, flexibility, and expressiveness (both positive and negative), and less dissention and avoidance. Collectively, these characteristics are linked with reports of more positive, closer, and more cohesive relationships.

Generally, couple research in stepfamilies finds that relationship quality and stability are strongly linked, such that relationships of poorer quality are more likely to dissolve (Stewart, 2005; van Eeden-Moorefield & Pasley, 2008); in fact, relationship quality is a stronger predictor of stability in stepcouples than among couples in first unions. There is also evidence that the stepfamily complexity is associated with more dramatic declines in relationship quality and stability, such that those in simple stepfamilies (children from a prior union of only one adult) experience less decline than those in more complex stepfamilies (his/her or his/her/ours combinations; Slattery, Bruce, Halford, & Nicholson, 2011). Such findings suggest that children complicate the adjustment process and may serve as a source of relationship dissatisfaction for these couples. In fact, newer research suggests that therapists are likely to see more complex stepfamilies because the number and nature of the relationships both within the household and across households creates more opportunity for problems to emerge.

Parenting and Stepparenting in Stepfamilies

Parents and stepparents face considerable challenges in childrearing. In fact, there is a good deal of research that shows parents in stepfamilies experience more stress in general and are challenged by loyalty conflicts and/or feeling torn between meeting the needs of their children and those of a new partner. Stepparents often struggle with what role to assume, with research supporting taking on more of an adult friend-like role and allowing the stepparent role to emerge over time (Sweeney, 2010; van Eeden-Moorefield & Pasley, 2012). Like other areas of stepfamily life, an important focus is to reexamine the expectations regarding roles and rules and adjust them slowly to fit the new family needs.

Much research suggests that the role of the stepparent is associated with a lack of normative expectations, and that stepfathers have an easier time than stepmothers. For example, stepfathers have greater flexibility in the roles they adopt with stepchildren, ranging from parent to friend to distant acquaintance (Ganong & Coleman, 2004). In the case study, it appears this would be consistent with Brian's stepfathering role. Such flexibility can create ambiguity between parents, resulting in coparenting conflict. This especially is seen among stepfamilies of shorter duration (Ganong & Coleman, 2004; Hetherington & Kelly, 2002). Alternatively, stepmothers often are gendered in that they are expected to take on traditional mothering behaviors early on in the stepfamily's development. This is linked to higher levels of depression, stress, and being poorly regarded by stepchildren (Shapiro & Stewart, 2011). Outcomes such as these may contribute to less closeness even as a stepchild moves into adulthood. It is possible that this partially provides insight into Carolyn's experiences.

Clearly, there is a steep learning curve for stepparents, and it is likely fraught with many opportunities for couple conflict (Favez et al., 2015; Pace et al., 2015). In general, when parent-stepparent conflict is high and stepchildren are involved, this does not bode well for the stepparent-stepchild relationship (Dunn, O'Connor, & Cheng, 2005) beyond issues of closeness. Accordingly, then, research would suggest the treating therapist assess the case study family for additional information about their conflict, as it likely is an important site for intervention. The ways in which the parent and stepparent work through issues in general, and concerns about parenting specifically, can help to establish a unified, cooperative coparenting relationship. This is considered one key to stepfamily success. In fact, recent research suggests that when parents (particularly mothers) feel secure in their parenting and have a working coparenting relationship with their ex-partners, they are more likely to expand the coparenting tasks to include the stepparent (Ganong et al., 2015). Research suggests the continuing tension between Carolyn and Anthony could be a barrier to Brian's involvement as a stepparent, and this would need to be managed better. Stepparent inclusion in coparenting fosters family cohesion (Favez et al., 2015) and marital quality (Pace et al., 2015). The relevance here is that building cooperative co-(step)parenting alliances within and across households is an important clinical goal.

We know that mothers often attempt to facilitate the development of the stepparent role with their new partner. However, frequently taking the side of their children when problems arise can serve as a barrier to creating a within-household family alliance. Research suggests that mothers may undermine the stepparent role in four ways: (1) they try to defend their children when they perceive the stepparent is attacking; (2) they attempt to control the level of closeness in the stepparent-stepchild relationship (gatekeeping); (3) they attempt to help resolve the problem by stepping in to mediate; and (4) they interrupt conflicts with explanations to help the stepparent gain more insight. As might be expected when mothers side with children and use these strategies, stepparents report feelings of frustration, alienation, and that their needs are least important in the family (Martin-Uzzi & Duval-Tsioles, 2013).

From the stepchild's point of view, it is likely he/she experiences the addition of a stepparent as a loss of time, affection, and attention from his/her parent (Cartwright & Seymour, 2002). This might be particularly relevant for Hope given the death of her mother and now reduced time with her father. Other research suggests living with a stepfather leads to greater declines in closeness between mother and adolescent compared with mothers of teens who remain single. This might explain some of the declines in closeness between Carolyn and her biological daughter, Maria. Although some stepchildren may hide their true emotions and display those that are more expected developmentally, it is not uncommon that stepchildren who were more congenial when the parent was dating the prospective stepparent are less so when the stepparent shares a household (Hetherington & Kelly, 2002). Stepchildren also affect how and what stepparents do by responding with a range of behaviors from openness and reciprocity to resistance, noncompliance, and hostility (Kinniburgh-White, Cartwright, & Seymour, 2010). As might be expected, the more negative the child's behavior, the more likely the stepparent is to reciprocate with negativity, although there is evidence that stepfathers are more likely to control their negative reactions to children compared with biological fathers (Bray & Kelly, 1998). Accordingly, feedback loops should be examined in clinical settings.

Specific to building alliances across households, parenting and stepparenting becomes more complicated when there are interested third parties beyond the single nonresident parent, as he or she also may be repartnered. When nonresident parents are repartnered, both must be included in parenting the shared child, and expectations must be negotiated across households with more players and the child's best interest in mind. It is likely that these nonresident stepparents have less chance to get to know their stepchild and form strong bonds, because of the limitations imposed by visitation and access agreements. Research shows that these nonresident parents and stepparents report tension in their couple relationship and their (step)parent-(step)child relationships (Henry & McCue, 2009). Specific to nonresident stepmothers, they report experiencing a lack of control where the stepchild is concerned, and this makes them feel powerless, angry, and resentful—all which collectively affects their couple relationship in negative ways (Henry & McCue, 2009). Both resident and nonresident stepmothers may be expected to assume more of a parental role and engage in discipline early, which can undermine their relationships with the stepchild. As stated earlier, it is likely that such expectations reflect overall gendered expectations for women's roles in families. Other research shows that nonresident stepcouples have more difficulty with triangulation (the child interferes in couple interaction, the parent interferes in stepparent-stepchild interaction, or the stepparent interferes in parent-child interaction), and such triangulations often are linked with exclusion of the stepparent from other interactions (Gosselin & David, 2007).

The literature is replete with recommendations for successful stepparenting. Primary among them is encouraging stepparents to adopt parenting behaviors gradually, particularly around matters requiring the use of discipline and limit-setting behaviors (e.g., Hetherington & Kelly, 2002; Pasley, Dollahite, & Ihinger-Tallman, 1993). Other scholars add that stepparents should provide support and warmth to stepchildren (Adamsons & Pasley, 2006; Mason et al., 2002)—a behavior also reflected in calls for "befriending" behaviors (Pasley, Dollahite, & Ihinger-Tallman, 1993) to facilitate a gradual evolution of the relationship over time. We believe that this gradual approach can enhance the coparenting relationship across households between former spouses and between stepparents and nonresident parents (Amato, King, & Thorsen, 2015; Ganong et al., 2015). This can reduce any potential conflict between the stepparent and nonresident parent, and the child is less likely to experience loyalty conflicts between stepparent and nonresident parent.

In addition to behaving in ways that may facilitate more positive relationships across households, there is some research showing that when coparental communication between the stepparent and nonresident parent is cooperative and nonantagonistic, stepparents report more relationship satisfaction with their partner and better mental health (Favez et al., 2015; Schrodt & Braithwaite, 2011). However, cooperative coparenting also was linked with partners reporting less, rather than more, relationship satisfaction and poorer mental health. Schrodt and Braithwaite (2011) also found antagonistic and supportive communication between the nonresident and resident parents influenced the nonresident parent's satisfaction with the stepparent and the stepparent's satisfaction with the nonresident parent. Reducing antagonistic and increasing supportive communication then is an intervention area. Taken together, creating a cooperative and inclusive alliance within and across households is likely to be a clinical issue that emerges and needs to be addressed. Within this, stepparents need to be supported.

Factors Affecting Stepparenting

A number of additional factors are shown to affect stepparenting. For example, stepfathers and stepsons have an easier time building a relationship than do stepfathers and stepdaughters (Schmeeckle, 2007); stepfathers express more warmth toward stepchildren who are highly active and sociable rather than shy (Ganiban, Ulbricht, Saudino, Reiss, & Neiderhiser, 2011); and living with one's stepchild also makes stepparenting less complicated (Schmeeckle, Giarrusso, Feng, & Bengtson, 2006). About half of all those who remarry give birth to a common child within the first two years, which can further reduce stepparent involvement with the stepchild (Stewart, 2005). This further can be problematic in that it serves as another transition that can negatively impact child adjustment.

Generally, evidence supports the recommendation that stepparents should not attempt to replace the nonresident parent nor should the nonresident parent's access to or involvement with the child be reduced or eliminated altogether, as ongoing contact with both parents is important to child well-being (Hetherington & Kelly, 2002). However, it is somewhat common that contact with a nonresident parent diminishes over time, especially fathers (e.g., Sweeney, 2010). Although contact with nonresident mothers also tends to decrease, they generally tend to be more involved, and such involvement can complicate the adjustment of a new stepfamily (Stewart, 2005). Decreases in involvement by nonresident parents also are associated with remarriage (Amato, Meyers, & Emery, 2009) or repartnering (Stewart, 2005) and having an older child (Amato et al., 2009). As the child moves into adulthood, there is some evidence that involvement may increase (Aquilino, 2006). Additionally, nonresident parent involvement also is compromised when the relationship between resident and nonresident parents is of poor quality (Jackson, Choi, & Franke, 2009), the nonresident parent fails to pay child support, or the child was born outside of marriage (Amato et al., 2009).

Children in Stepfamilies

Overwhelmingly, the effects of stepfamily life on children have been the primary focus of research, and numerous comprehensive reviews are available that summarize this work (e.g., Coleman & Ganong, 1990; Coleman et al., 2000; Sweeney, 2010; van Eeden-Moorefield & Pasley, 2012). Historically, research emphasizes between-group differences, comparing children in stepfamilies with children in single-parent households and children in two-biological-parent families (Coleman & Ganong, 1990; Coleman et al., 2000), so we know less about variations among stepfamilies—this is increasing (e.g., Amato et al., 2015; Ganong et al., 2015).

Although the effects of stepfamily life on children are important to understand, we take the position that children per se are not the key problem driving stepfamilies into therapy. Children's behavior may be offered as the presenting problem, somewhat similar to the case study in this chapter, but we suggest that the underlying issues around couple interaction and childrearing in stepfamilies are the likely sources of real concern. Thus, what is known about the effects of stepfamily life on children is less clinically relevant than is the research on couple relationships and childrearing in stepfamilies (Coleman et al., 2000; van Eeden-Moorefield & Pasley, 2012). With this assumption in mind, we briefly summarize the literature on child outcomes.

Children living in a stepfamily are at elevated risk for a number of academic, social, and psychological difficulties (e.g., academic achievement, externalizing and internalizing problem behaviors, substance use/abuse; Jeynes, 2006). Because the differences between groups are small and most stepchildren do well, these differences rarely rise to the level of clinical concern (van Eeden-Moorefield & Pasley, 2012). Moreover, most differences diminish over time, particularly when children are initiated into a stepfamily at a young age (e.g., Zill, Morrison, & Coiro, 1993). Academically, when children in stepfamilies perform more poorly (e.g., lower GPA/test scores, more school absences and suspensions), it often is associated with the experience of multiple family transitions (Halpern-Meekin & Tach, 2008; Jeynes, 2006), being an adolescent female (Ham, 2004), having a half or stepsibling (Halpern-Meekin & Tach, 2008), or being in a cohabiting stepfamily (Heard, 2007), especially that with stepfather (Artis, 2007; Heard, 2007).

Although many of these academic outcomes might be of concern, externalizing and internalizing behavior problems generally are of more concern, and more likely to lead a stepfamily into therapy, as was the case with Carolyn and Brian's stepfamily. Although early work tended to show that stepchildren experienced more internalizing problems (e.g., depression, anxiety; Coleman et al., 2000), more recent research suggests no direct effect of family structure (e.g., Willetts & Maroules, 2004). Like academic outcomes, the number of transitions experienced and other factors are more predictive of negative outcomes (e.g., Sweeney, 2007). Regarding the case study, this research suggests that the death of Hope and Melanie's mother, Hope's early adoption, and all the transitions related to becoming a stepfamily likely played a role in their internalizing symptoms. Still, other research shows that positive stepparenting (warmth, support, communication of acceptance and respect; e.g., Willetts & Maroules, 2004) and mattering to the stepparent (how important the child feels to the stepparent; Schenck et al., 2009) can buffer these effects. Clinically, these may be areas to strengthen.

Although symptoms of depression and anxiety can be problematic, it is likely that externalizing behavior problems in children more commonly serve as presenting issues in therapy. Examples of such behaviors include acts of aggression and hostility, delinquency (e.g., truancy, stealing), substance use, early dating (similar to Maria in the case study) and sexual debut, and other forms of acting out. Early research suggests that children in stepfamilies exhibit more externalizing behaviors than children in first families (Coleman et al., 2000). Some research supports these findings (e.g., Halpern-Meekin & Tach, 2008), whereas other research does not (Willetts & Maroules, 2004). Results from longitudinal studies confirm that externalizing behaviors are lower than noted previously in studies including only one time point (Collishaw, Goodman, Pickles, & Maughan, 2007). Further, some research shows that children in stepmother families and those that include half siblings and stepsiblings are most at risk for such problems (Harcourt, Adler-Baeder, Erath, & Pettit, 2015; Hoffmann, 2006). Gender differences are noted and suggest that aggressive behavior is 2.5 times higher among girls than boys in stepfamilies (Coleman et al., 2000). Other research shows that girls in stepfather families are more likely to discontinue their education (Song, Benin, & Glick, 2012), report early sexual debut (Merten & Henry, 2011), and cohabit or marry early compared with their same-sex peers in intact families (Zito, 2015). Moreover, adolescents in stepfamilies report lower-quality relationships with parents, including less communication and trust and more alienation (Ruschena, Prior, Sanson, & Smart, 2005). This is particularly concerning given the strong link between parent-child relationship quality and child adjustment (Amato et al., 2015).

Factors buffering these effects include closeness to (step)father (King, 2006) and mother (Merten & Henry, 2011), mattering to stepfather (Schenck et al., 2009), nonresident father involvement (Menning, 2006), parent involvement (Wojtkiewicz & Holtzman, 2011), and quality of parents' remarriage (Yu & Adler-Baeder, 2007). However, children's higher externalizing behaviors are linked with increased marital conflict about children and childrearing, and this relationship is stronger in complex stepfamilies than those in bio-families (Jenkins, Simpson, Dunn, Rasbash, & O'Connor, 2005). We anticipate that this relationship between children's externalizing behaviors and marital conflict is reciprocal in nature and can undermine the stability of the stepcouple relationship over time.

Sibling Interactions

Overall, there is little research on sibling relationships in stepfamilies (Sweeney, 2010). Typically, research on siblings addresses issues of contact, conflict, closeness, and communication, and much of it stems from studies of adult siblings. That which is available suggests that stepsibling relationships are characterized by more conflict and less closeness than are relationships with half and full siblings (Baham, Weimer, Braver, & Fabricius, 2008). However, Harcourt and associates (2015) found greater complications in stepfamilies when half siblings were present, although this was less common among Black compared to White stepfamilies. Much of the marital conflict in stepfamilies that include both stepchildren and biological children centers on how stepparents differentially treat children, and perceptions that stepparents are less responsive to stepchildren than biological children (e.g., Jenkins et al., 2005). Also, conflict about the differential treatment of siblings by stepparents is more pronounced in stepfather families, and stepmothers are less engaged with stepchildren. Examining the level of conflict among siblings in bio-families and stepfamilies, scholars found conflict was slightly higher among biological siblings (Deater-Deckard, Dunn, & Lussier, 2002). Regardless of type of sibling, higher sibling conflict and perceiving differential treatment by (step)parents is linked with more internalizing and externalizing problems in children in stepfamilies (Schenck et al., 2009). However, Yuan (2009) found that sibling structure (full, half, or step) was not related to mental health outcomes (depressive symptoms or positive well-being). However, spending time with siblings was linked with better mental health for half and stepsiblings but not for full siblings.

Interestingly, when asked to identify family members, children with stepsiblings are more likely to exclude them regardless of residency (Roe, Bridges, Dunn, & O'Connor, 2006); such exclusion is related to stepchildren feeling as if they do not belong in the family (Leake, 2007). Findings from a 20-year longitudinal study of children of divorce (Ahrons, 2007) found that being older when the stepfamily formed and infrequent contact with stepchildren was related to feeling excluded, although these feelings were tempered when a half sibling was present. Interestingly, some research shows that exclusion is related to higher levels of both internalizing and externalizing behaviors in children (Dunn, O'Connor, & Levy, 2002).

Conclusion

Stepfamilies are increasingly complex (Guzzo, 2016; Kreider & Lofquist, 2014), and such complexity is linked to heightened likelihoods for conflict (Favez et al., 2015), strained relationships (Slattery et al., 2011; van Eeden-Moorefield & Pasley, 2008), and more challenged (step)parenting (Ganong et al., 2015; Henry & McCue, 2009). Further, stepfamilies experience higher dissolution rates (Kreider, 2005), especially nonlegal stepfamilies (Cherlin, 2010), and slightly elevated risks for several negative outcomes (e.g., academic, depression) spanning each family member (e.g., van Eeden-Moorefield & Pasley, 2012). We know that viewing stepfamilies systemically with special attention given to assessing how various subsystems (e.g., stepparent-stepchild, child-nonresident parent, parent-stepparent-child) function can provide useful insight into the health of the entire stepfamily (Amato et al., 2015), as well as to determine key intervention sites. Additionally, research supports helping stepfamilies assess their beliefs about how a stepfamily should work (clarifying roles, rules, and boundaries) and navigating these new roles, rules, and boundaries that function to promote the stepfamily (Pasley, Dollahite, & Ihinger-Tallman, 1993; Sweeney, 2010). Important areas include promoting cooperative parenting alliances within and across households, with particular attention given to including the stepparent gradually over time (Favez et al., 2015; Henry & McCue, 2009). However, this does not mean the stepparent should be excluded in parenting decisions early on, but instead seen more as a consultant. Importantly, promoting open communication and teaching strong conflict resolution skills can help strengthen stepfamilies and lead to their success (Pace et al., 2015). Last, we acknowledge that stepfamily research continues to lack attention to broader issues of diversity. Accordingly, not all of this research will apply or work for all stepfamilies, and therapists play an important role in sharing the diversity they see and research needs they have to best work with increasingly complex stepfamilies.

References

Adamsons, K., & Pasley, K. (2006). Coparenting following divorce and relationship dissolution. In M. A. Fine & J. H. Harvey (Eds.), *Handbook of divorce and relationship dissolution* (pp. 241–262). Mahwah, NJ: Lawrence Erlbaum Associates, Inc.

Ahrons, C. R. (2007). Family ties after divorce: Long-term implications for children. *Family Process*, *46*, 53–65. doi: 10.1111/j.1545-5300.2006.00191.x

Amato, P. R. (2000). The consequences of divorce for adults and children. *Journal of Marriage and Family*, *62*, 1269–1287. doi: 2048/10.1111/j.1741-3737.2000.01269.x

Amato, P. R., King, V., & Thorsen, M. L. (2015). Parent—child relationships in stepfather families and adolescent adjustment: A latent class analysis. *Journal of Marriage and Family*, *77*, 1–16. doi: 10.1111/jomf.12267

Amato, P. R., Meyers, C. E., & Emery, R. E. (2009). Changes in nonresident father-child contact from 1976 to 2002. *Family Relations*, *58*, 41–53. doi: 2048/10.1111/j.1741-3729.2008.00533.x

Aquilino, W. S. (2006). The noncustodial father-child relationship from adolescence into young adulthood. *Journal of Marriage and Family*, *68*, 929–946. doi:10.1111/j.1741-3737.2006.00305.x

Artis, J. E. (2007). Maternal cohabitation and child well-being among kindergarten children. *Journal of Marriage and Family*, *69*, 222–236. doi: 2048/10.1111/j.1741-3737.2006.00355.x

Baham, M. E., Weimer, A. A., Braver, S. L., & Fabricius, W. V. (2008). Sibling relationships in blended families. In J. Pryor (Ed.), *The international handbook of stepfamilies: Policy and practice in legal, research, and clinical environments* (pp. 175–207). Hoboken, NJ: John Wiley & Sons.

Bray, J. H., & Kelly, J. (1998). *Stepfamilies: Love, marriage and parenting in the first decade*. New York: Broadway Books.

Cartwright, C. (2010). Preparing to repartner and live in a stepfamily: An exploratory investigation. *Journal of Family Studies*, *16*, 237–250. doi: 2048/10.5172/jfs.16.3.237

Cartwright, C., & Seymour, F. (2002). Young adults' perceptions of parents' responses in stepfamilies: What hurts? What helps? *Journal of Divorce & Remarriage*, *37*(3–4), 123–141.

Cherlin, A. J. (2010). Demographic trends in the United States: A review of research in the 2000s. *Journal of Marriage and Family*, *72*, 403–419. doi: 2048/10.1111/j.1741-3737.2010.00710.x

Coleman, M., & Ganong, L. H. (1990). The uses of juvenile fiction and self–help books with stepfamilies. *Journal of Counseling and Development, 68*, 327–331. doi: 2048/10.1002/j.1556-6676.1990.tb01384.x

Coleman, M., Ganong, L. H., & Fine, M. (2000). Reinvestigating remarriage: Another decade of progress. *Journal of Marriage and the Family, 62*, 1288–1307. doi: 2048/10.1111/j.1741-3737.2000.01288.x

Collishaw, S., Goodman, R., Pickles, A., & Maughan, B. (2007). Modeling the contribution of changes in family life to time trends in adolescent conduct problems. *Social Science & Medicine, 65*, 2576–2587.

Deater-Deckard, K., Dunn, J., & Lussier, G. (2002). Sibling relationships and socio emotional adjustment in different family contexts. *Social Development, 11*, 571–590.

DeLongis, A., Capreol, M., Holtzman, S., O'Brien, T., & Campbell, J. (2004). Social support and social strain among husbands and wives: A multilevel analysis. *Journal of Family Psychology, 18*, 470–479. doi: 2048/10.1037/0893-3200.18.3.470

Dunn, J., O'Connor, T. G., & Cheng, H. (2005). Children's responses to conflict between their different parents: Mothers, stepfathers, nonresident fathers, and nonresident stepmothers. *Journal of Clinical Child and Adolescent Psychology, 34*, 223–234. doi: 2048/10.1207/s15374424jccp3402_2

Dunn, J., O'Connor, T. G., & Levy, I. (2002). Out of the picture: A study of family drawings by children from step-, single-parent, and non-stepfamilies. *Journal of Clinical Child and Adolescent Psychology, 31*, 505–521. doi: 10.1207/S15374424JCCP3104_9

Ehrenberg, M. F., Robertson, M., & Pringle, J. (2012). Attachment style and marital commitment in the context of remarriage. *Journal of Divorce & Remarriage, 53*, 178–193.

Favez, N., Widmer, E. D., Doan, M. T., & Tissot, H. (2015). Coparenting in stepfamilies: Maternal promotion of family cohesiveness with partner and with father. *Journal of Child and Family Studies, 24*, 1–11. doi: 10.1007/s10826-015-0130-x

Ganiban, J.M., Ulbricht, J., Saudino, K.J., Reiss, D., & Neiderhiser, J.M. (2011). Understanding child-based effects on parenting: Temperament as a moderator of genetic and environmental contributions to parenting. *Developmental Psychology, 47*(3), 676–692. doi: 10.1037/a0021812

Ganong, L., & Coleman, M. (2004). *Stepfamily relationships: Development, dynamics, and intervention.* New York, NY: Springer.

Ganong, L., Coleman, M., Jamison, T., & Feistman, R. (2015). Divorced mothers' coparental boundary maintenance after parents repartner. *Journal of Family Psychology, 29*, 221. doi: 10.1037/fam0000064

Gosselin, J., & David, H. (2007). Risk and resilience factors linked with the psychosocial adjustment of adolescents, stepparents, and biological parents. *Journal of Divorce & Remarriage, 48*(1–2), 29–53.

Guzzo, K. B. (2016). *Stepfamilies in the U.S. family profiles*, FP-16–09. Bowling Green, OH: National Center for Family & Marriage Research.

Halford, K., Nicholson, J., & Sanders, M. (2007). Couple communication in stepfamilies. *Family Process, 46*, 471–483. doi: 10.1111/j.1545-5300.2007.00226.x

Halpern-Meekin, S., & Tach, L. (2008). Heterogeneity in two-parent families and adolescent well-being. *Journal of Marriage and Family, 70*, 435–451. doi: 2048/10.1111/j.1741-3737.2008.00492.x

Ham, B. D. (2004). The effects of divorce and remarriage on the academic achievement of high school seniors. *Journal of Divorce & Remarriage, 42*(1–2), 159–178. doi: 10.1300/J087v42n01_08

Harcourt, K. T., Adler-Baeder, F., Erath, S., & Pettit, G. S. (2015). Examining family structure and half-sibling influence on adolescent well-being. *Journal of Family Issues, 36*(2), 250–272. doi: 10.1177/0192513X13497350

Heard, H. E. (2007). Fathers, mothers, and family structure: Family trajectories, parent gender, and adolescent schooling. *Journal of Marriage and Family, 69*, 435–450. doi: 10.1111/j.1741-3737.2007.00375.x

Henry, P. J., & McCue, J. (2009). The experience of nonresidential stepmothers. *Journal of Divorce & Remarriage, 50*, 185–205. doi: 10.1080/10502550902717780

Hetherington, E. M., & Kelly, J. (2002). *For better or worse: Divorce reconsidered.* New York, NY: W. W. Norton & Company, Inc.

Hobart, C. W. (1991). Conflict in remarriages. *Journal of Divorce & Remarriage, 15*(3–4), 69–86. doi: 10.1300/J087v15n03_04

Hoffmann, J. P. (2006). Family structure, community context, and adolescent problem behaviors. *Journal of Youth Adolescence, 35*, 867–880. doi: 10.1007/s10964-006-9078-x

Jackson, A.P., Choi, J., & Franke, T.M. (2009). Poor single mothers with young children: Mastery, relations with nonresident fathers, and child outcomes. Social Work Research, 33, 95–106. doi: 10.1093/swr/33.2.95

Jenkins, J., Simpson, A., Dunn, J., Rasbash, J., & O'Connor, T. G. (2005). Mutual influence of marital conflict and children's behavior problems: Shared and nonshared family risks. *Child Development, 76*, 24–39. doi: 2048/10.1111/j.1467-8624.2005.00827.x

Jensen, T. M., Lombardi, B. M., & Larson, J. H. (2015). Adult attachment and stepparenting issues: Couple relationship quality as a mediating factor. *Journal of Divorce & Remarriage, 56*(1), 80–94. doi: 10.1080/10502556.2014.972201

Jeynes, W. H. (2006). The impact of parental remarriage on children: A meta-analysis. *Marriage & Family Review, 40*, 75–98. doi: 2048/10.1300/J002v40n04_05

King, V. (2006). The antecedents and consequences of adolescents' relationships with stepfathers and nonresident fathers. *Journal of Marriage and Family, 68*, 910–928. doi: 2048/10.1111/j.1741-3737.2006.00304.x

Kinniburgh-White, R., Cartwright, C., & Seymour, F. (2010). Young adults' narratives of relational development with stepfathers. *Journal of Social and Personal Relationships, 27*, 890–907. doi: 2048/10.1177/0265407510376252

Kreider, R. M. (2005). *Numbering, timing, and duration of marriages and divorces: 2001.* (Current Population Reports, P70–97). Washington, DC: U.S. Census Bureau.

Kreider, R. M. (2007). *Living arrangements of children: 2004.* (Current Population Reports, P70–114). Washington, DC: U.S. Census Bureau.

Kreider, R. M., & Elliott, D. B. (2009, May). The complex living arrangements of children and their unmarried parents. *Poster presented at the annual meeting of the Population Association of American*, Detroit, MI. Retrieved on November 30, 2009, from: http://www.census/gov/population/www.documentation/twps08.pdf

Kreider, R. M., & Lofquist, D. A. (2014). *Adopted children and stepchildren: 2010.* (Report No. P20–572). Washington, DC: U.S. Census Bureau. Retrieved from: http://www.census.gov/prod/2014pubs/p20–572.pdf

Leake, V. S. (2007). Personal, familial, and systematic factors associated with family belonging for stepfamily adolescents. *Journal of Divorce & Remarriage, 47*(1–2), 135–153.

Martin-Uzzi, M., & Duval-Tsioles, D. (2013). The experience of remarried couples in blended families. *Journal of Divorce & Remarriage, 54*(1), 43–57. doi: 10.1080/10502556.2012.743828

Mason, M. A., Harrison-Jay, S., Svare, G., & Wolfinger, N. (2002). Stepparents: De facto parents or legal strangers? *Journal of Family Issues*, *23*, 507–522. doi: 10.1177/0192513X02023004003

Menning, C. L. (2006). Nonresident fathers' involvement and adolescents' smoking. *Journal of Health and Social Behavior*, *47*, 32–46. doi: 2048/10.1177/002214650604700103

Merten, M. J., & Henry, C. S. (2011). Family structure, mother-daughter relationship quality, race and ethnicity, and adolescent girls' health risks. *Journal of Divorce & Remarriage*, *52*, 164–186. doi: 10.1080/10502556.2011.556966

Michaels, M. L. (2006). Factors that contribute to stepfamily success: A qualitative analysis. *Journal of Divorce & Remarriage*, *44*(3–4), 53–66. doi: 10.1300/J087v44n03_04

Pace, G. T., Shafer, K., Jensen, T. M., & Larson, J. H. (2015). Stepparenting issues and relationship quality: The role of clear communication. *Journal of Social Work*, *15*(1), 24–44. doi: 10.1177/1468017313504508

Pasley, K., Dollahite, D., & Ihinger-Tallman, M. (1993). Bridging the gap: Clinical applications of research findings on the spouse and stepparent roles in remarriage. *Family Relations*, *42*, 315–322. https://doi.org/10.2307/585561

Payne, K. K. (2015). *The remarriage rate: Geographic variation, 2013. Family profiles*, FP-15–08. Bowling Green, OH: National Center for Marriage & Family Research.

Roe, A., Bridges, L., Dunn, J., & O'Connor, T. G. (2006). Young children's representations of their families: A longitudinal follow-up study of family drawings by children living in different family settings. *International Journal of Behavioral Development*, *30*, 529–536. doi: 10.1177/0165025406072898

Schenck, C. E., Braver, S. L., Wolchik, S. A., Seanz, D., Cookston, J., & Fabricus, W. V. (2009). Relations between mattering to step- and non-resident fathers and adolescent mental health. *Fathering*, *7*, 70–90.

Schmeeckle, M. (2007). Gender dynamics in stepfamilies: Adult stepchildren's views. *Journal of Marriage and Family*, *69*, 174–189. doi: 2048/10.1111/j.1741-3737.2006.00352.x

Schmeeckle, M., Giarrusso, R., Feng, D., & Bengtson, V. L. (2006). What makes someone family? Adult children's perceptions of current and former stepparents. *Journal of Marriage and Family*, *68*, 595–610.

Schrodt, P. (2006). The Stepparent Relationship Index: Development, validation, and associations with stepchildren's perceptions of stepparent communication competence and closeness. *Personal Relationships*, *13*, 167–182. doi:10.1111/j.1475-6811.2006.00111.x

Schrodt, P., & Braithwaite, D. O. (2011). Coparental communication, relational satisfaction, and mental health in stepfamilies. *Personal Relationships*, *18*, 352–369.

Shafer, K., Jensen, T., Pace, G., & Larson, J. (2013). Former spouse ties and post-divorce relationship quality: Relationship effort as a mediator. *Journal of Social Service Research*, *39*, 629–645.

Shapiro, D.N., & Stewart, A.J. (2011). Parenting stress, perceived child regard, and depressive symptoms among stepmothers and biological mothers. *Family Relations*, *60*(5), 533–544. doi: 10.1011/j.1741-3729.2011.00665.x

Slattery, M., Bruce, V., Halford, K., & Nicholson, J. (2011). Predicting married and cohabiting couples' future from their descriptions of stepfamily life. *Journal of Family Psychology*, *25*, 590–569. doi: 10.1037/a0024538

Song, C., Benin, M., & Glick, J. (2012). Dropping out of high school: The effects of family structure and family transitions. *Journal of Divorce & Remarriage, 53*, 18–33. doi:/10.1080/10502556.2012.635964

Stewart, S. D. (2005). Boundary ambiguity in stepfamilies. *Journal of Family Issues, 26*, 1002–1029. doi: 10.1177/0192513X04273591

Sweeney, M. M. (2007). Stepfather families and the emotional well-being of adolescents. *Journal of Health and Social Behavior, 48*, 33–49. doi: 10.1177/002214650704800103

Sweeney, M. M. (2010). Remarriage and stepfamilies: Strategic sites for family scholarship in the 21st century. *Journal of Marriage and Family, 72*, 667–684. doi: 10.1111/j.1741-3737.2010.00724.x

van Eeden-Moorefield, B., & Pasley, K. (2008). A longitudinal examination of marital processes leading to instability in remarriages and stepfamilies. In J. Pryor (Ed.), *The international handbook of stepfamilies: Policy and practice in legal, research, and clinical environments* (pp. 231–249). Hoboken, NJ: John Wiley & Sons.

van Eeden-Moorefield, B., & Pasley, K. (2012). Remarriage and stepfamily life. In G. Peterson & K. Bush (Eds.), *Handbook of marriage and the family* (3rd ed., pp. 517–547). New York, NY: Springer Publishing Co.

Wilder, S. E. (2012). A comparative examination of reasons for and uses of uncertainty and topic avoidance in first and remarriage relationships. *Journal of Divorce & Remarriage, 53*, 292–310. https://doi.org/10.1080/10502556.2012.671660

Willetts, M. C., & Maroules, N. G. (2004). Does remarriage matter? The well-being of adolescents living with cohabiting versus remarried mothers. *Journal of Divorce & Remarriage, 41*(3–4), 115–133.

Wojtkiewicz, R. A., & Holtzman, M. (2011). Family structure and college graduation: Is the stepparent effect more negative than the single parent effect? *Sociological Spectrum, 31*(4), 498–521. doi: 10.1080/02732173.2011.574048

Xu, X., Hudspeth, C. D., & Bartokowski, J. P. (2006). The role of cohabitation in remarriage. *Journal of Marriage and Family, 68*, 261–274. doi: 10.1111/j.1741-3737.2006.00251.x

Yu, T., & Adler-Baeder, F. (2007). The intergenerational transmission of relationship quality: The effects of parental remarriage quality on young adults' relationships. *Journal of Divorce & Remarriage, 47*(3–4), 87–102. doi: 10.1300/J087v47n03_05

Yuan, A. S. V. (2009). Sibling relationships and adolescents' mental health. *Journal of Family Issues, 30*, 1221–1244.

Zill, N., Morrison, D. R., & Coiro, M. J. (1993). Long-term effects of parental divorce on parent-child relationships, adjustment, and achievement in young adulthood. *Journal of Family Psychology, 7*, 91–103. doi: 10.1037/0893-3200.7.1.91

Zito, R. C. (2015). Family structure history and teenage cohabitation: Instability, socioeconomic disadvantage, or transmission? *Journal of Family Issues, 36*, 299–325. doi: 10.1177/0192513X13490933

Clinical Theory and Intervention for Stepfamilies

Scott W. Browning

Stepfamilies: A Unique Family Form

Family therapy in the 1950s and 1960s began as a generalist movement by emphasizing systems theory to explain the dynamics of all types of families, and early family therapists avoided the creation of sub-groupings within the field. Accordingly, stepfamilies were seen as simply families that had a re-coupled member and were treated using a typical systems approach. In time it became clear that stepfamilies are different, in a number of ways, from first-union families, and that these differences influence the treatment process. Information about stepfamilies came from various fields (e.g., psychology, family science) and stepfamilies themselves, leading to a strong understanding of their uniqueness. Simultaneously, stepfamilies began to demand recognition that their needs were not being met in therapy.

Although ethnic and cultural backgrounds continue to be an important context for any family or stepfamily, stepfamilies can be regarded as a cultural marker. Once re-coupling occurs, the norms of a family shift, and a new structure begins to emerge. However, stepfamilies are a hidden culture. Pasley and van Eeden-Moorefield have compiled an extraordinary collection of studies that are directly relevant to the practitioner. In this clinical section, the stepfamily will be examined in light of the research, and a clinical approach will be outlined that addresses directly the adaptations to family therapy necessary to assist these complex families.

A Theoretical Foundation for Stepfamily Treatment

The origin of a theoretical understanding of the stepfamily is intimately tied to the research investigating the characteristics that make stepfamilies distinct from first-union families. Early on, many of the comparisons left stepfamilies appearing to be deficient, so efforts were made to reduce the stigma of comparison and concentrate on what makes stepfamilies stand out as a positive, but different, family form. The early research studies on stepfamilies took a deficit approach, one in which the stepfamily was compared, usually negatively, to the first-union family. Pasley and van Eeden-Moorefield specifically highlighted the normative adaptive perspective that envisions the stepfamily as an alternate, rather than lesser, family form.

Like all families, there is no template that fits every stepfamily; however, there are common factors that influence each stepfamily's experience. The evolution to a conceptualization of stepfamilies recognizes that these factors, when understood, can guide the therapist in supporting and assisting stepfamilies. Three primary factors (development, structure, and emotion) stand out in clinical theory about the nature of a stepfamily.

Stepfamily Development

Herein, development refers to a developmental sequence exclusive to stepfamilies. In first-union families, children commonly arrive after the couple has been together for some time, whereas in stepfamilies, children precede the couple relationship. As often is stated, a remarried or repartnered couple with children from prior marriages or partnerships is "honeymooning in front of an audience." Granted some conversations can and do occur away from others; yet many interactions between the members of a new stepfamily happen in "public spaces."

The relationship between a parent and child is different from the relationship between the stepparent and stepchild, and both must develop simultaneously. The stepparent/stepchild relationship can grow into a healthy and satisfying one, but it needs time to develop. In addition, the relationship between the remarried couple often is influenced strongly by how compatible the stepparent and stepchild are.

It is estimated that the time necessary for a stepfamily to develop a strong and supportive bond is approximately four to five years. This length of time is longer than many stepfamilies themselves believe should be necessary, which leads them to become discouraged. In addition to the larger issue of stepfamily development, a mismatch between the development of a stepfamily and the developmental stage of individuals within a stepfamily can prove to be troubling, referred to by Pasley as "competing developmental needs." There is a mismatch in the developmental stage of the stepfamily and the adolescent. Just as the adults are attempting to pull together to affirm the strength of the new family bonds, the adolescent is attempting to separate to gain a sense of independence. These two conflicting developmental forces lead to a friction commonly experienced by stepfamilies with adolescents.

Stepfamily Structure

A stepfamily is a system and, thus, can still be understood within the context of systems theory. However, the structure is different from that of first-union families. As such, the therapist must understand how a stepfamily structure affects the dynamics and interaction of its members. Constance Ahrons (1994; Ahrons & Wallisch, 1987) makes the interesting argument that following the break-up of a couple with children, the family no longer has a unified center; in other words, the family is "binuclear," meaning that each parent forms the center of a separate but interrelated family. A child now has two parents, living separately, each with their own extended family (aunts, grandparents, etc.), and it is the child that connects these two single-parent families. When one or both parents re-couple, the complexity of the interrelatedness increases as the child now has another "parental adult," as well as his or her extended family and potential stepsiblings.

To fully understand the effect of this added complexity, a great deal of research has examined the various dynamics that present in stepfamilies. Every structural combination of relationships must be taken into account when trying to understand a stepfamily that comes into treatment. In other words, the therapist must attempt to determine the nature of every relationship that exists in the stepfamily as part of assessing for treatment. For example, questions about structure include: Is the stepmother also a mother? Is the nonresident father involved in the child's life? How do the siblings get along in this stepfamily? Is the stepfather spending more time with his stepchildren than his own children from a previous relationship? Seeking answers to such questions allows the therapist to gain a clear picture of each unique case, since the potential variations in stepfamily structure are extensive.

There are two stepfamily structural variations that are common and designated by whether only one or both adult members of the stepcouple bring children to the new union. If only one person has a child from a previous relationship, this is referred to as a "simple stepfamily," whereas when both people bring children from previous relationships, and this new couple has a child who joins the stepfamily, this type of stepfamily is referred to as "complex." Although the language is useful for identification, it is unfortunate that it suggests that simple stepfamilies are more likely to coalesce with greater ease than complex stepfamilies. It is important to remember that these terms are labels, and do not convey any information other than the type of stepfamily they define.

Another feature to be taken into account when looking to understand the theoretical nature of a stepfamily is to understand the process by which this remarriage occurred. For example, if a stepfamily is formed after the death of one partner, which is much less common than one following divorce or dissolution, that stepfamily may be quite different from the stepfamily in which the nonresident parent is living. Also, the couple that re-couples and forms a stepfamily following an affair is certainly likely to have tensions originating from the children's anger at how the stepfamily was formed. Children tend to be reluctant to forgive the person who is perceived as the explicit reason for ending her or his parents' relationship.

Role of Emotion

The third factor that plays a dominant role in establishing a general understanding of stepfamilies is emotion. Establishing a stepfamily generates a range of emotions not fully expected by its members. Remarriage or re-coupling is not well simulated by dating. Based on limited research but ample clinical case studies, the dating process generally gives the participants somewhat of a false impression as to the relative ease of stepfamily formation. This occurs because during dating the parenting responsibilities are less powerful than they become after the stepfamily begins to live together.

Recognizing that the emotional climate of a stepfamily is often more charged than expected, the therapist's task is to search for the origin of strong feelings among the members within the unit. Is the child angry because she feels that the remarriage has caused her to lose her close relationship with her mother? Is the stepfather frustrated because he intended to be a coparent, only to find that his opinion is not highly regarded by his stepson? Does the mother in a stepfamily feel torn between the needs of her child and the demands of her new mate?

Once these and similar clinical questions appear, the therapist pushes for clarity (content) while simultaneously creating a deeper understanding for each person's hurt (process). The stepfamily particularly benefits from this back and forth use of process and content. The content helps establish the uniqueness of the stepfamily from the common template, the first-union family. The process parts of the intervention benefit from the fact that stepfamilies generally generate a great deal of emotion, so understanding the feelings from each stepfamily member creates some empathy, in most cases. The therapist is not trying to discuss empathy overtly, but by discussing and receiving confirmation of the accuracy of the therapist's hypothesis, an aura of empathy often just emerges. This combination of changed perspectives (from the linkage to research findings) to the recognition that every stepfamily member is wrestling with some hurt is a useful clinical approach.

Treatment: A Subsystem Approach

An understanding of stepfamily structure then serves as the basis for treatment by viewing this family as a collection of subsystems, some of which are bonded and others less so. The first task of the therapist is to determine which subsystem is most strongly bonded and to begin treatment with that group (Browning & Artelt, 2012). Unlike traditional family therapy, seeing the whole stepfamily together is not considered the optimal starting point for treatment, because the stepfamily needs to be assured that the therapist is actively aware of the volatility common to these families when in the early stages of development. Therefore, by starting from the most powerful subsystem, he or she is reassuring the stepfamily that agitating the family, in the name of change, will be done carefully and with respect for its fragile nature. Most commonly, the couple is seen first; their power is not necessarily based on the greatest love, since parental love is extremely potent, but this subsystem, in most cases, is running the stepfamily. This subsystem may need more than one session before moving on to the next most important subsystem, often a parent and her or his child(ren).

To approach therapy through work with subsystems, I recommend creating a *Consent to Treatment Form* that establishes the mental health professional as the person who is unwilling to hold "secrets" within the stepfamily. In many therapeutic settings, the default consent form is one that confirms the therapist will hold all secrets (except those the law mandates reporting) and does not share with other members. If the therapist is interested in working with various subsystems, with the explicit intention of strengthening one subsystem at a time to ultimately assist the whole stepfamily, he or she must be given the right to decide when information should be shared for the sake of the family as a whole. Any therapy model that highlights ethics and social justice (e.g., feminist or contextual therapy) will be fulfilling its mission by opening communication within the overall system. Each subsystem has to know the therapist is always attempting to do what is best for the overall stepfamily; therefore, toxic secrets are too potentially damaging to be permitted.

The mental health professional approaches each case by determining the manner in which the structure, development, and emotional volatility shape the stepfamily, and uses this to inform a diagnostic evaluation. With this information, a theory of stepfamily treatment can be superimposed on any recognized family therapy approach. Thus, the therapist and his or her therapeutic acumen and years of training in a family therapy model are still used. For example, if a particular therapist is well versed in conjoint family therapy (Virginia Satir), he or she will bring to the case a perspective that encourages the examination of the communication patterns, the family roles enacted, and ways to find the positive reframe to each situation.

What I call stepfamily therapy is not a comprehensive model that attempts to explain all factors that constitute a stepfamily. To do so inaccurately simplifies this complex family form. Rather, this "approach" provides an understanding of stepfamilies that can serve as the basis for assessing the status of a stepfamily, create a working hypothesis, and search for particular vulnerabilities. If the therapist can determine the presence of particular needs for the stepfamily in treatment, she or he is more likely to incorporate those needs into the treatment plan and comfort the members of the stepfamily with insights that demonstrate an understanding of the problems and challenges they are experiencing.

Common Vulnerabilities Experienced by Stepfamilies

Here, my goal is to introduce some vulnerabilities common in stepfamilies and to discuss some basic therapeutic approaches. Knowledge of these vulnerabilities can help the mental health professional become oriented to a stepfamily's problem quickly. Five areas of stepfamily vulnerability include rejection of the stepparent, intimate relationships under close scrutiny, parental guilt, loyalty binds, and increased volatility.

Rejection of the Stepparent

Although many stepparents are liked, and in time loved, many others experience rejection from a stepchild. Additionally, the rejection might be mutual; however, often it is not. Stepparents often sincerely desire a significant relationship with a stepchild only to find that their efforts at bonding are spurned. From the child's perspective, the stepparent is the symbol of anger and/or disappointment about the loss of the original family. Also, on occasion, the child is jealous of the attention the stepparent receives. When either of these dynamics is present, it is useful for the therapist to determine whether an intervention might motivate the stepchild to build a relationship with the stepparent. If a more functional relationship cannot be achieved, it may be necessary to lessen the stepparent's expectation, without encouraging him or her to react by angrily distancing from the stepchild.

The first step in this process is to determine whether the stepchild and stepparent want a relationship. Even when strong negative feelings exist, many people wish to reduce in-home tensions. Often a stepparent wants to start a relationship with the child, but he or she is convinced from off-the-cuff comments that the child does not desire this. However, if in the safety of the clinical office the child admits that some relationship is of interest, then the therapist can help to make that rapprochement possible.

Intimate Relationships Under Scrutiny

After remarrying/repartnering, the relationships within the family shift. The resulting change involves the fact that the parent now has a love interest, and a partner in parenting who is not biologically connected to the child. Because the bond between a parent and a child is often strained, especially for mothers and children following a divorce, the entrance of a stepparent can feel like an intrusion to the child who finds that sharing her or his parent with another adult is frustrating for two reasons. First, the child recognizes that her or his parent is now spending a great deal of time with the new spouse/partner; second, the child may find that having any time with her or his parent alone is difficult to achieve. In addition, there are situations whereby the child feels that time with a parent alone is rare, and the time spent with both a parent and stepparent is greatly influenced by the stepparent's opinions and beliefs. For example, conversations between a mother and her daughter may take on a different tone when the new stepfather is present; yet, he may be present a great deal because he both wishes to be involved, and his wife wants him involved. However, even the mother may begin to notice that her relationship with her daughter is shifting to accommodate to the standards or expectations put forth by the stepfather.

In observing this problem in a stepfamily, the mental health professional can intervene by recognizing that everyone is feeling frustrated by the tension surrounding these "family discussions." The intervention will flow from the therapist being clear that one-on-one conversations often are preferable to larger group discussions in the early formation of a stepfamily. This does not mean that the stepfather is relegated to a position of having no influence, but rather, his influence comes from discussions with his wife, or directly with his stepdaughter rather than as part of a triangle.

Guilt Experienced by a Parent

Guilt is a powerful and often insidious emotion. Whether the guilt is merited or not, the long-term effect of guilt is that an adult generally parents in a manner that is more permissive and unfocused. When a therapist recognizes that a parent is feeling guilty about some past behavior (e.g., the divorce, drug use, an affair), it is necessary to understand the effect this guilt has on the parenting of a child. In addition, the role of the stepparent also is influenced by the guilty parent, who may request that the stepparent fulfill a more primary disciplinarian parental role, a role that the guilty parent is unable or unwilling to fulfill.

If the parent is permitted to discuss why she or he feels guilty, the mental health professional can help him/her recognize that the outcome of this continued guilt is unhealthy for everyone involved. Assisting the parent to acknowledge mistakes from the past and to seek forgiveness is often a worthy therapeutic goal. However, teaching parents about the larger effect of this guilt-induced behavior often leads the guilt-ridden parents to address, and reduce, their guilt. In other words, a parent may have legitimate guilt, but most people who learn that their continued focus on personal guilt actually hurts loved ones frequently find that they can work towards moving past the guilt.

Existence of Loyalty Binds

Loyalty binds cause many problems in stepfamilies. Some loyalty binds may cause minor distress and are normal and expected whenever the complexity of a stepfamily increases. However, a line can be crossed in which loyalty stops an individual from being able to enjoy any relationship with someone else in the stepfamily. A loyalty bind may be present in any number of relationships within a stepfamily. The nonresident parent may challenge his or her child to be loyal and reject the stepparent. In addition, the resident parent may feel torn between showing loyalty to her or his child and showing loyalty toward the new spouse. Finally, it is not unusual to hear people (often men) report that they now feel close to their own child from a new relationship and less connected to their child from a past relationship. In a sense, remarriage/repartnering offers some men a second chance at being involved fathers.

Often the most useful intervention to address loyalty is to make sure that treatment includes the person for whom the loyalty is felt. For example, if a son speaks of his allegiance to his father and subsequent discomfort with his stepfather, his father should be invited into treatment. The therapist then asks the father directly about the need for absolute loyalty from his son. Psychologically healthy fathers will usually desire a clear sense of being beloved by their son but do not see a relationship between the son and the stepfather as disloyalty. The father may be able to acknowledge that he is grateful for the loyalty expressed, but he is not threatened by other important people in the son's life. On other occasions, loyalty is demanded, and the therapist's role is to help the stepfather, who feels unacknowledged, to understand the reason for the lesser relationship and learn not to set himself up for repeated hurts. For example, upon learning that his stepson is being pressured to reject him, a stepfather is better served by lowering his expectations about the potential for a bond between himself and his stepson until the boy begins to question his own father's motivation.

An Increase in Volatile Interactions

Stepfamilies often experience a pervasive increase in volatile interactions. The stepfamily is formed with people, some of whom express little warmth. Yet, this is a family with many of the interpersonal demands and powerful expectations one would experience in any family. This dynamic can be a recipe for volatile outbursts, even among those who pride themselves on not having hot tempers. The stepfamily situation itself generates a level of personal investment that is felt in few other circumstances. Dealing with "family issues" is the most emotionally fulfilling and taxing interaction most people encounter. A stepfamily is a family, and this reality ensures powerful feelings. As such, stepfamily life can lead to significant misinterpretations, emotional hurt, and dashed expectations.

The stakes are high in a stepfamily, because few want to see it dissolve, and yet they often feel relatively helpless as the emotional temperature of the home increases. Thus, it is incumbent on the therapist to function in such a way that the expressed emotion within the session is modulated. This can be done by working first with small groups (subsystems) within the stepfamily until eventually involving everyone. This therapeutic strategy is used to protect the members of the stepfamily from engaging in discussions that may open up too many wounds. In this way, the therapist must carefully monitor the emotion in the room and recognize any increase of negative emotion and work to diffuse it before it becomes overwhelming.

An awareness of potential vulnerabilities is not intended to provide such a clear roadmap that the mental health professional is jumping ahead and assuming to know what issues are important to the stepfamily in treatment. Rather, it provides an adequate general background so common vulnerabilities are understood quickly, and this offers the stepfamily support and relief.

Foundational Clinical Interventions for Stepfamilies

There are a myriad of interventions that are applied to stepfamilies. However, five overarching classes of interventions are predominately used in working with this population. These include psychoeducation; communication clarification; suspending unproductive, repetitive arguments; problem solving; and clarifying a stepfamily's own systemic pattern.

Psychoeducation

Intervening with education is particularly beneficial when it leads the clients to see themselves, in this case the members of a stepfamily, as behaving in a typical manner. The term often used to describe this process is "normalization." Evidence suggests that when clients begin to hear about situations that parallel their own, they feel calmer because they view their own stepfamily as less "dysfunctional." Most people enter a stepfamily expecting a particular timeline of adjustment. The actual adjustment period usually is longer than expected. The reality that adjustment requires more time than expected can be jarring and lead to a sense of panic that terrible mistakes have been made. Yet, providing education on typical stepfamily development often lessens the pressure felt by members, despite recognition that the situation is difficult. For example, a stepfamily that expects the stepparent to become the primary disciplinarian often finds that attempting to realize this expectation leads to increased conflict. The mother wishes to support her husband and new stepfather, and the stepfather believes that he is "doing the right thing" by helping his new wife who admits that she is "a little burned out after years of disciplining alone." The therapist intervenes by discussing the research supporting the idea that the stepparent is better off serving as a "monitor" for the first few years rather than as a full coparent. This intervention serves to create an understanding that is largely true—children in stepfamilies do not wish to see their parent as uninvolved, and they generally are not responsive to discipline from someone with whom they do not have a relationship. In essence, building a relationship must precede dispensing of discipline, but such knowledge is not always understood until someone helps to couch it in a clear statement.

Research on couple conflict is another example of useful information for psychoeducation. Specifically, although a high level of conflict/disagreement is common, research suggests that emotional exchanges in stepfamilies are more muted. In other words, bickering does not constitute an "emotional exchange." The honest emotional discussions that allow people to know each other do not occur as often in stepfamilies, so with fewer positive and negative exchanges occurring, members naturally withdraw. This finding can serve as the basis for helping stepfamily members actively engage in therapy, because a cardinal aspect of family therapy is an increased rate of emotional exchanges in a safe and supportive environment. Aided by the therapist, when the intensity of a stepfamily is regulated, an honest discussion between stepfamily members is a helpful intervention.

Another example of useful research findings for treatment is the evidence suggesting that men in stepfamilies are less involved with children in the home, regardless of whether the men were biological fathers or stepfathers. With this information, the therapist can be confident that intervening to increase men's connection with children and stepchildren will address a deficit.

A final example shows that a conflicted stepparent-stepchild relationship does negatively affect the marriage/partnership over time. Such information can be used to acknowledge predicable stress and begin the process of negotiating through this undeniable pressure. As an example, biological parents are in the unenviable position of being asked to take sides during conflict between the child and a stepparent. Inevitably, both spouse and child are correct some of the time, but the biological parent cannot support either party without being accused of betraying one or the other loved one.

There are many advantages to using psychoeducation, but there is a caveat that must be respected: Every stepfamily is different. Therefore, although it is critical to be aware of the common dynamics and research findings, the therapist should not be blinded to the uniqueness of the particular stepfamily in treatment. It is best to resist using active teaching until there is a solid understanding of the needs and difficulties of the specific case.

Communication Clarification

Clarifying the communication within a stepfamily is a necessary and effective intervention. Although communication is both central in many family therapies and connected with higher family functioning, stepfamilies have more opportunities for miscommunication because members do not share the same history. At times, miscommunication can be addressed in front of all parties; however, on other occasions, a subsystem approach allows the therapist to determine the intended meaning of a particular communication and help rectify a mistaken belief. For example, a stepmother might be overheard commenting on how she dislikes the kitchen in their home. Unbeknownst to the stepmother, this infuriates her stepchildren because their deceased mother organized the kitchen. Over time, any discussion about cooking, cleanup, or changing the kitchen is met with anger and silence from the children. During a subsystem therapy session with the children, the kitchen issue is brought up, and the strong personal feelings of hurt are clarified. The therapist could then foster a discussion so the stepmother has some idea of the importance of the kitchen to the stepchildren, and allow her to express her needs to feel like the house is hers as well, while respecting the unintended hurt that occurred.

Ending Repetitive Arguments

Stepcouples often have vastly different opinions about the nature of a child's intention when this child misbehaves, with stepparents often holding a less charitable view than do the parents. It is important that therapists convey this in terms of a history of the relationship and differences between a subjective and more objective view with a goal of moving couples from a circular, unresolvable argument to an acceptance of alternate viewpoints. It is critical in these moments that the therapist takes a constructivist view; neither position is the "right one." Individuals are often so convinced of the correctness of their position that they lose sight of the possibility of legitimate alternative explanations. Compromise and change is easier to achieve when appreciation of an alternate reality (the view held by the other) is recognized. For example, a mother and stepfather view the actions of the adolescent son from distinct vantage points. The mother remembers her son as an infant and his strengths are more evident, whereas the stepfather sees his stepson's current behavior and fears that he is heading in a wrong direction. The therapist's role is to generate empathy so both adults recognize the difficulty in trying to convince the other of their opinion and how working as a team becomes difficult with these attempts. Although they may not agree on their view of the child, they can work towards an acceptance that both have his best interests in mind.

This intervention appears to use empathy (asking each person to understand the view of the other); however, the end goal is to accept that some positions cannot be negotiated because different lived experiences produce dissimilar perspectives, rather than some middle ground or compromise. Interestingly, while the goal is not to get the couple to a middle ground, this intervention often has this result, as they become uninterested in staking out an extreme position about the child.

Problem Solving

Because adults often have different beliefs as to how best to solve a problem, doing so in stepfamilies is less straightforward. Stepcouples may agree on the problem to be solved (e.g., a child's poor grades), but the adults may have distinct ideas as to how to achieve this and unintentionally sabotage each other as a result. Certainly this phenomenon occurs in first-union families, but in stepfamilies the likelihood of seeing the child's actions from distinct positions is common. Not only does one adult have a longer shared history with the child, but the power structure between the two adults is also different from first unions. Therefore, therapists must be explicit in problem solving and provide ample time for the couple to explore why the solution chosen may not work in this situation. For example, a stepcouple may agree that both tutoring and consequences will be the response to a child's poor grades. The emphasis on each response needs to be worked out in great detail, because conversations whereby exact plans are discussed often are avoided in stepfamilies. Therefore, therapists must be persistent in establishing the family's rules on this issue, so concerns that are believed to have been resolved and later resurface as unresolved do not dishearten the couple.

Clarifying a Stepfamily's Own Systemic Functioning

Teaching stepfamilies about the way they function is a powerful intervention that can remove a great deal of blame. Awareness of how they function together eliminates perceptions of any one members' actions as resulting from being "unloving," "too strict," "permissive," or "gullible," rather than from a sequence of behaviors engaging all members. For example, a therapist can help two stepsisters begin to see that their tendency to fight is more likely in the presence of one's mother and stepmother. From this, a growing recognition occurs that the fighting is more about one stepsister's need to defend her mother as a good person, than any overwhelming dislike between the stepsisters. One very clear example comes from the case study. In the stepfamily, Carolyn is trying to reach out to Hope, and Hope, for legitimate psychological reasons, is not interested in this relationship, thus leaving Maria angry that her mother is being disrespected by her stepsister. So, the tension between Carolyn and her stepdaughter, Hope, is the result, in part, of Maria's deep anger at Hope. Seeing the systemic function of such arguing, the therapist can assist the mom to confirm with her daughter that she does not need her daughter to defend her. Carolyn and Hope need to establish their relationship, and Maria and Hope need to establish their own relationship. Triangles between people destroy relationships and can be damaging to a stepfamily (or family, for that matter). Without a rich systemic understanding, members of the stepfamily might believe that the stepsisters actively dislike each other, which is, in fact, untrue. This systemic understanding allows the clinician to intervene with relationships that might otherwise be considered unchangeable.

Applying Treatment Interventions to the Case Study

The brief case introduced at the start of the chapter is used here to demonstrate more specifically the steps to treatment and appropriate use of the five types of treatment interventions discussed. Doing stepfamily therapy, by definition, motivates the mental health professional to be visual, so working with a genogram is basic to working with these complicated families, as it serves as the map of the family functioning, much like GPS provides guidance in vehicles.

Initial Formulation and Therapeutic Direction

If a therapist is inclined toward stepfamily therapy, he or she benefits from determining the primary focus from the intake interview. Certainly, the issues of concern may shift, but the initial concerns must be addressed; however, a systems-oriented mental health provider will examine all issues to determine whether family intervention (or in this case, stepfamily intervention) is best to provide overall stability. Moving towards a stepfamily intervention is likely to help multiple family members and make individual work with any member more fruitful as well.

Challenges existed in this stepfamily and were the reason for seeking treatment. Carolyn reported feeling: (1) as though she and her daughter (Maria) were drifting apart; (2) that Brian seemed "down"; and (3) that she experienced hostile interactions with her younger stepdaughter, Hope. Brian was more vague about his concerns, but did comment that he was worried about how well his daughters were getting over the death of their mother.

In this case, the therapist sees the problems as: the couple needs to examine their relationship; interactional tensions will be addressed; the relationship between Carolyn and Maria will be discussed; Brian, Melanie, and Hope's grieving process requires attention; and Melanie's mild depression should be assessed. If the couple did not share any of these goals, then this aspect of treatment planning would be shifted accordingly. Other important issues are observable in the genogram, but the therapist must take care not to overwhelm the stepfamily with items that may not be part of treatment. Next, a consent form is provided that allows the therapist to "own the privilege" and determine what information needs to be shared across subsystems, when this information is toxic to the stepfamily in the form of a secret.

Session 1

This first meeting is with the spousal subsystem of Brian and Carolyn and focuses on gaining a clear description of "the problem." Defining the problem in relational terms is clearly one of the most useful common factors (Sprenkle, Davis, & Lebow, 2009). However, the tendency to blame one individual is logical to many stepfamily members, as the problems arise due to the new members in the home. Recall that the stepcouple is preceded historically by the parent-child relationship(s). This structure typically results in the adults having distinct perceptions of the child's behavior. Also, the adult roles in stepfamilies are less clearly defined, which creates expectations that are often not discussed. Such unrecognized expectations generate a sense of frustration, but the underlying reason remains unclear. Thus, the therapist needs to draw out concerns equally, being careful not to endorse one person's worldview too strongly over another.

There are numerous directions that can be followed early in treatment, and the genogram is a critical tool for getting clarity about who is involved and hypothesizing a logical sequence for the first few sessions. The agenda for this session is to understand the range of issues affecting them. Interestingly in stepfamilies, some issues will be predictable, while other concerns will be entirely unique to this stepfamily. Carolyn and Brian were interested in seeing their stepfamily succeed, and some positive things were already occurring. Clearly, the couple was in love, they expressed a desire to be close to each other's child(ren), and there was no profound mental health concern dominating the family's landscape.

Session 2

Included in this session were Carolyn and Maria, specifically to address the void that Carolyn felt was growing between them. In addition, Carolyn was worried about a new relationship that Maria now has with a young man, four years her senior. Both Maria and Carolyn affirmed a desire to regain some of the closer bond they had enjoyed prior to the remarriage. Maria expressed that she believed her mom had become "consumed" in trying to win over Hope and Melanie. Carolyn acknowledged that she has made a great effort to connect with them for the sake of the new marriage and because they had lost their mother. However, in hearing Maria's concern, Carolyn made a commitment to spend more time with Maria.

Session 3

This session focused on Brian and his two daughters, Melanie and Hope. Most striking was the range in temperament. Both Melanie and Brian were low key, with the possibility that Melanie fell within a diagnosable range of dysthymia. Hope, on the other hand, seemed to generate high energy and was prone toward combativeness. However, there was also clear familial love evident between all three. Hope's adoption (at 7 months from Korea), while not an overt presenting concern, is always some component of family identity.

Both girls acknowledged, upon the therapist's question, that they did try to protect their father since he "sort of fell apart" after Christine's death. Although Brian seems honestly surprised that they felt the need to protect him, he agreed that he had "turned a blind eye to some things cause I didn't feel up to heavy stuff." As this was explored it appeared evident that Brian's emotional style had also caused him to miss some problems between Hope and her stepsister, Maria, as well.

Session 4

This session was dedicated to the three young women, Melanie (20), Hope (17), and their stepsister, Maria (16). The tension between Maria and Hope was right on the surface. Melanie served as a buffer, but in her low-energy state, she just appeared to feel overwhelmed by their interactions. But, as the eldest, Melanie did have the ability to stop them from spiraling out of control; however, she generally just seemed exasperated. Hope and Maria challenged each other on various dimensions. Each thought the other was selfish, immature, over-using drugs or alcohol (one was drinking, one was taking pills). As the conversation progressed, part of the tension seemed to be due to Maria defending her mother from Hope's anger. Clearly, these two girls did not speak of any affection for one another, but there were some aspects that appeared to fit with typical sisterly fighting (some concern intertwined with annoyance).

Session 5

This session was a return to the couple. With the valuable information gained from the subsystem sessions, it was possible to clarify the specific issues needing to be addressed: the couple itself needed some attention, the incomplete mourning for Christine from Brian and her daughters, and the volatile relationships between Hope and both her stepsister and her stepmother. Returning to the couple after a series of subsystem sessions often results in significant clinical movement. Brian was more available to Carolyn, and he had made the link between the incomplete mourning for Christine and the stepfamily's slow formation. Carolyn had become more comfortable with her relationship with her daughter, Maria. The end of the session involved preparing the couple for a full stepfamily session. This preparation involved the therapist being clear about each person's opinion on a few topics that were to be covered in the next session.

Session 6

Carolyn met with Hope. One might inquire why Melanie (as the other stepsister) was not involved. The decision was made to offer Melanie an individual session to evaluate her depressive symptoms and determine if additional support (beyond the improved family functioning) was needed. So, Hope and Carolyn both described the tension in the home between them. Clinically, it was decided that if this relationship could be "softened," such a change would ripple positively throughout the entire stepfamily.

As might be expected, Carolyn tried to reach out to Hope, while Hope largely remained aloof. In such a situation, the therapist functions "as if" the agreement to meet together represents a tangible signal that some improved relationship is desired. It is important to remember that most people do not enjoy interfamilial tension. Identifying misperceptions can be an effective method to soften harsh interactions (Browning & Artelt, 2012).

Session 7

This session was an individual session for Melanie. When working from a subsystem perspective, any combination of people can be engaged, and this certainly includes individuals. Following a typical intake to assess depression, including two screening instruments, brought the working conclusion that Melanie needed some additional therapy, but a referral to a psychiatrist was not deemed necessary. On a systemic level, Melanie was able to provide critical information as to her dad's "shut down" after Christine's death, and the difficulty the two sisters had in simply returning to "life as usual." On a positive note, Melanie was glad to be engaged in the family, even though this involvement was frustrating.

Session 8

While this was not a final session, it represented the important transition from strictly subsystem to including the entire residential stepfamily. The clinical assumption is that the subsystems are sufficiently stable to withstand the pressures of everyone responding to each other's comments. The therapist should expect to be active in these sessions, as runaway emotions are put into check quickly. The purpose is to find a way to present the systemic pattern in such a way that people see their role, and a deeper understanding of the functionality of the stepfamily is apparent.

The case continued for three more sessions in which a number of improvements were solidified. Generally, if they are going to improve, stepfamilies, as with most family therapy, do so in 8–12 sessions. The mental health professional works to strengthen the family by strengthening various subsystems. If therapy is successful, as was the result in this case, most of the subsystems (the couple, the siblings, the step/parent-step/child, cross-generational subsystems, the coparenting biological parents) will be stronger and more satisfying. Of course, even successful treatment may end with one subsystem unimproved or even worse. Overall, there is greater love, respect, stability, and engagement following successful stepfamily treatment.

References

Ahrons, C. R. (1994). *The good divorce: Keeping your family together when your marriage comes apart*. New York, NY: HarperCollins Publishing.

Ahrons, C. R., & Wallisch, L. (1987). Parenting in the binuclear family: Relationships between biological and stepparents. In K. Pasley & M. Ihinger-Tallman (Eds.), *Remarriage and stepfamilies* (pp. 113–146). New York, NY: Guilford Press.

Browning, S., & Artelt, E. (2012). *Stepfamily therapy: A 10-step clinical approach*. Washington, DC: American Psychological Association.

Sprenkle, D. H., Davis, S. D., & Lebow, J. L. (2009). *Common factors in couple and family therapy: The overlooked foundation for effective practice*. New York, NY: Guilford Press.

4

FRAGILE FAMILIES

Case Study

C. Wayne Jones

When 17-year-old Marilyn was found by the police, after having been reported as missing by her mother, she was catatonic, naked, and wrapped in a cover from a gas grill. She was having both visual and auditory hallucinations. She was hospitalized for a week, where she was stabilized, then referred to a local intensive in-home family-based mental health program. Although she was no longer showing psychotic symptoms at discharge from the hospital, she remained shutdown emotionally, voicing considerable hopelessness about whether anyone could help her.

Marilyn struck the in-home family-based team as bright, intense, sensitive, and emotionally overwhelmed. She had been cutting, sporadically using drugs (mostly pot), and withdrawing through excessive sleeping. Although previously an A-B student, she was failing many of her classes at school. She talked a lot about being lonely both in her family and at school. Marilyn told the therapists that she had run away from her home because her 18-year-old brother, Allen, "puts me down and pushes me around." Although Marilyn is the identified patient in this case, the team noticed that both Marilyn's mother and her brother are equally distressed and symptomatic.

Marilyn's mother, Shelly, is divorced from the children's father. He lives across the country and is peripherally involved. Shelly is currently parenting alone and admits to being depressed, spending most days in her bedroom. She worries about Marilyn, but admits she is ready to throw in the towel on trying to parent her. She describes Marilyn as strong-willed and at times believes she may be "possessed." Disagreements between Shelly and Marilyn often escalate into dramatic shouting matches, pushing, and slamming of doors.

Caregivers in fragile families, like Marilyn's family, often present as alone, overwhelmed, and exhausted by their lives, with little energy left to parent. Caregivers are in conflict and not working together, whether they live in the same household or in different households. The more challenging the child's problems, the more likely therapists will be met with pressure from caregivers to send the child to an out-of-home placement. This was the case in Marilyn's family. There was little glue holding the family together—the bonds were fragile.

Family History

Shelly has a history of extreme trauma, yet she has never had any mental health treatment that has linked any of her symptoms of distress to it. Shelly is the youngest of five. Her next youngest sibling is 12 years older. Her father was a World War II veteran and is suspected to have had untreated war-related PTSD. He drank a lot, as did Shelly's mother. Her father would rage when angry and become violent. Although he physically abused all of his children (and also sexually abused some), her mother seemed to get the worst of it. The beatings were severe. Shelly's mother decided she could no longer be a parent (around age 30) and placed all four of her children in an orphanage, two years before Shelly was born. All of Shelly's siblings have struggled as adults with major mental health issues and substance abuse.

The story that Shelly has been told by her older siblings is that her mother did not want her when she was born and had said she would have aborted her, but discovered her pregnancy too late. Her mother died when Shelly was 2 years old from a brain aneurysm. She wonders if it was a result of the years of violence she had suffered at the hands of her father. From age 2 to 4 Shelly lived with several different people, finally being adopted by her older sister, Diane, at age 4. Tom, her stepfather, sexually abused Shelly between the ages of 11 and 16. Shelly told a school counselor and an investigation ensued, which eventually resulted in her adoptive parents separating and divorcing. However, her adoptive mother to this day still blames Shelly for causing it all by dressing too provocatively.

At age 20, Shelly met Larry at culinary school. When they graduated two years later, they moved in together and moved to the South, both finding jobs as chefs. Although they never formally married, they lived in one of 10 states in the United States that still recognize an informal handwritten signed note that states, "We intend to be a married couple." This is known as common law marriage. Shelly wanted this as "relationship insurance." Shelly describes their first six years together fondly; she felt "normal." They had fun together, went camping, traveled some, and had friends. All this began to change slightly after Allen was born, but changed substantially after Marilyn's birth. Larry says Shelly's personality changed once she became a parent, becoming more disorganized, not taking care of her daily hygiene, and behaving in a self-righteous manner. Shelly says Larry became more critical and distant. They started to fight frequently.

Larry describes his childhood and his family in mostly positive terms, with his mother being the one in charge of parenting since his father worked a lot. Although Larry's family does not seem to have the same level of abuse and trauma as Shelly's family, the family-based team felt that Larry was overly sanitizing his background to a great extent.

Shelly pushed for the family to move back to the Northeast to be closer to her extended family, hoping that they could support her as a young mother. Larry was reluctant but agreed to give it a try. Not only were Shelly's extended family not as supportive as she had hoped they would be, her young children ended up being sexually abused by her brother's son. They cut off all contact with this family after this incident.

Twelve years into the relationship, Larry found a job on the West Coast and moved out. Marilyn was 10 years old and Allen was 11. Shelly says she was devastated and notified the courts of their common law marriage, which meant Larry would have to go through a formal divorce process. Shelly refused to cooperate with the divorce process until granted full physical custody of the children. At about the same time, the sibling relationship deteriorated and they began fighting frequently. Marilyn says that Allen would beat her up and her mother would ignore it, implying she probably deserved it. Larry, her father, was physically and emotionally unavailable. Marilyn did not have close relationships with extended family because their family had cut off from them.

Since the divorce, Larry has fared much better in his life than Shelly with respect to income and friends. He has had several short-term girlfriends, marrying four years after he left Shelly to a woman who is 15 years younger. They now have a 3-year-old son. Shelly's life has gradually become narrower and emptier since Larry left the home. Shelly has had a few dates, but nothing very serious since the divorce.

Allen and Marilyn have pretty much raised themselves alone since their father left. Allen, however, acts like it does not bother him; instead, he stuffs it (he is significantly overweight). Since he does not complain to Shelly and listens well, this has earned him favored status. Marilyn, on the other hand, is painfully aware of her suffering and dramatically complains about it, further alienating Shelly and making her an easy target for scapegoating. Allen thinks he is helping his mother when he "disciplines" Marilyn when she is being difficult. He does not see it as aggressive. This parentified role that Allen plays in the home will need to be addressed firmly and quickly, given that this was the trigger for the most recent treatment episode.

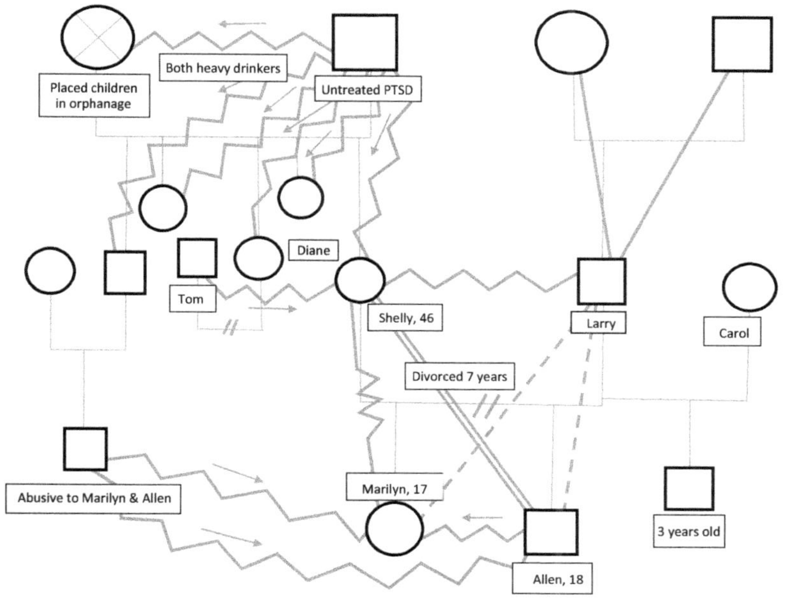

Figure 4.1 Family Vulnerabilities and the Pathway to Chronic SED

Research Perspectives on Fragile Families

Laura Tach

Fragile families like Marilyn's are defined by their economic and relationship insecurity, which leave them at a high risk of breaking up and living in poverty. Although poverty always has been a feature of the American economic landscape, socioeconomic inequality in family life has grown sharply over the past half century. Children born to the most educated parents have gained resources, whereas those born to the least educated have become more likely to experience unstable families and finances (McLanahan, 2004). In this chapter, I discuss research on how "fragile families" form, the experiences of insecurity that tend to befall them, and how these experiences shape family relationships and well-being. Although Marilyn's case may seem extreme with respect to the intensity and duration of trauma, her story illustrates common themes in the research literature. I conclude with a discussion of ways in which policymakers and practitioners can harness this research to support fragile families.

Childbearing in Fragile Families

There is a strong socioeconomic gradient in the timing and relationship contexts of childbearing. Today, women and men with low levels of education are substantially more likely to begin their childbearing early and outside of marriage than their college-educated counterparts. According to nationally representative data from the National Survey of Family Growth (NSFG), becoming a parent during young adulthood (before age 25) is the norm for men with a high school degree or less (52.6%), and is nearly ubiquitous for less-educated women (81.5%). Alternatively, parenthood during young adulthood is rare for college-educated women (25.1%), and almost nonexistent for college-educated men (6.1%; Edin & Tach, 2012). Early childbearing is often nonmarital childbearing: a majority of young-adult mothers (65%) and fathers (60%) were unmarried at the time of their child's birth, and the share of births outside of marriage among teen parents is over 80% (Edin & Tach, 2012; Hamilton, Martin, & Ventura, 2009).

Parents who have children at young ages and outside of marriage tend to exhibit a number of economic, psychological, and relational risk factors. Many have insecure attachments to work, low and unstable earnings, and histories of welfare receipt (Sum, Khatiwada, McLaughlin, & Palma, 2011). Much of what we know about the personal and family characteristics of unmarried parents comes from the Fragile Families and Child Wellbeing Study, a longitudinal survey of children born to unmarried parents in large U.S. cities. In this survey, about one-quarter of young-adult fathers who had children outside of marriage were not employed when their child was born, and their average annual earnings were $16,000. Young-adult mothers did not fare much better: over half did not have their high school diplomas, and 40% were receiving public assistance at the time of the child's birth (Edin & Tach, 2012). Many parents also have health issues that make it hard to sustain work and family obligations. In fact, 17% of new unmarried mothers and 12% of unmarried fathers reported depressive symptoms in the year after their child was born, rates twice as high as their married counterparts (McLanahan, 2009). Unmarried fathers were also twice as likely as married fathers to have problems with drug use, three times as likely to be violent, and nearly seven times as likely to have been incarcerated in the past (McLanahan, 2009). It is within these circumstances that couples conceive and give birth, forming what researchers call fragile families.

The romantic relationships that produce fragile families tend to be haphazard and casual. Unmarried parents' qualitative accounts of their relationships reveal that the median length of relationship prior to conception is only six to seven months, and fully half described their relationships prior to conception as casual (Edin, England, Fitzgibbons Shafer, & Reed, 2007; Tach & Edin, 2011). According to NSFG data, most unmarried parents (74%) report that their child's birth was unplanned (Finer & Henshaw, 2006). Pregnancy intentions are difficult to measure, however, and qualitative research suggests that most pregnancies to unmarried parents are neither fully planned nor fully avoided. Many reported an ambivalent desire to have children and inconsistent contraceptive use (Augustine, Nelson, & Edin, 2009; Edin & Kefalas, 2005; Waller, 2002).

Despite rapid progression to childbearing, most who form fragile families are optimistic about their prospects as parents and partners. Most fathers readily acknowledge paternity rather than contest it (Edin, Tach, & Mincy, 2009; Waller, 2002), and many eagerly embrace the role of father (Augustine et al., 2009; Edin & Nelson, 2013). In the Fragile Families survey, three-fourths of unmarried fathers offered financial support to the mother during her pregnancy, and seven in 10 visited the mother and child in the hospital (Edin & Tach, 2012). Nationally, fully half of children born outside of marriage are born to parents who are cohabiting, and another third are born to parents who are romantically involved but not living together—just 20% occur to parents who are not romantically involved with one another (Tach & Edin, 2011). Thus, while being married is not the norm for disadvantaged parents, being in a romantic relationship is. Further, at the time of their child's birth couples reported that they were optimistic about their future together, including the possibility of marrying (Center for Research on Child Wellbeing, 2003). This has led researchers to dub the time of the child's birth as *the magic moment* for fragile families—a moment full of optimism and commitment, and one with potential for intervention and outreach.

Dynamics of Insecurity Factors Among Fragile Families

Economic Insecurity

Children thrive in stable, secure environments. A host of research across economics, sociology, and psychology has documented the ways in which relationship instability and economic insecurity create chaos in the home and undermine children's cognitive and socioemotional development, with lasting effects that persist into adulthood (for reviews, see Evans, 2004; Shonkoff, 2010). The interdisciplinary body of research that has emerged to identify how poverty produces adverse outcomes clearly shows that poverty is a multilevel phenomenon that shapes a child's *macroenvironment* via access to broader structures of opportunity such as quality schools, services, housing, and neighborhoods, as well as the child's *microenvironment* within the home, including the quality and stability of relationships with parents, parenting style, and learning materials (Bronfenbrenner, 2009). Accordingly, newer poverty research often focuses on identifying the precise causal effects of particular modifiable factors, understanding how these effects vary based on the developmental timing and duration of a child's exposure to poverty, and uncovering the biosocial mechanisms that link environmental exposures to adverse outcomes for children. These innovations will help identify particular sources of risk and resilience, as well as promising levers for interventions.

A major concern in poverty research is whether the effects of poverty are causal: Is low income itself responsible for adverse child outcomes, or is this association produced by other parental characteristics that result in both low incomes and poor child outcomes? The answer to this question is important from a policy and intervention standpoint because it tells us which environmental or personal conditions to target. Among the most careful analyses of the causal effect of poverty on children's outcomes is the New Hope Study, a policy experiment fielded in the mid-1990s in Milwaukee, Wisconsin, that raised parents' income by offering cash and in-kind assistance in exchange for employment. Led by the economist Greg Duncan, a team of researchers fielded a randomized experimental evaluation of the New Hope program and found that children of participants in the experimental group performed better in school and had fewer behavioral problems compared to controls (Duncan, Huston, & Weisner, 2007). Other quasi-experimental evaluations of cash transfers to poor parents have identified similar positive effects on children's health and educational achievement (Dahl & Lochner, 2012; Hoynes, Miller, & Simon, 2015). These studies reveal that not only does poverty have a causal effect on children, it is also a factor that can be modified to improve parental and child well-being.

Careful analyses of the dynamics and developmental timing of poverty revealed the experience of poverty is particularly detrimental during early childhood and when spells of poverty are of long duration (Brooks-Gunn & Duncan, 1997). Researchers also examined the adverse effects of economic insecurity—unexpected and/or involuntary fluctuations in income—on parenting and child outcomes (see Western, Bloome, Sosnaud, & Tach, 2012, for a review). Unstable incomes produced by job, housing, and family instability increase parental stress and hinder parents' ability to plan for and invest in the future, which undermines their investments in their children. This body of work points to the dynamics of poverty that matter most: early developmental periods, long durations, and unpredictable fluctuations are particularly pernicious forms of poverty, and thus may be particularly effective moments for intervention.

Researchers also made strides in identifying biosocial pathways by which extreme stress and material deprivation affect brain functioning in children. Prenatal and early-life experiences of stress are thought to reduce a child's stress reactivity, due in part to epigenetic modification of gene expression and the alteration of developing neural circuits that control responses to stress (see Phillips & Shonkoff, 2000, for a review). Although short-term reactivity to stress is advantageous, prolonged exposure can wear on one's organs, leading to poor physical and mental health—what researchers have dubbed *toxic stress* (Shonkoff et al., 2012). Because these early-childhood exposures can have lasting repercussions, researchers and practitioners' interventions targeting toxic stressors associated with poverty could be effective in reducing socioeconomic inequalities as well as inequalities in mental and physical health during adulthood. Taken together, these emerging areas of research reinforce that the deleterious effects of poverty have lasting biosocial consequences, especially when experienced during early childhood, but that these effects can be mitigated via social policies.

Family Insecurity

Unstable family relationships are an additional source of risk for children born to low-income, unmarried parents. Although most parents who form fragile families are optimistic about their relationships, these relationships are typically quite unstable. For example, almost 40% of urban unmarried parents ended their relationships within a year of the child's birth and fully two-thirds had ended by the child's fifth birthday (Tach & Edin, 2011). There are stark socioeconomic gradients and racial inequalities in the experience of family instability. Cohabiting and marital unions are less stable for low-income and Black couples than they are for affluent and White couples (Graefe & Lichter, 1999; Manning, Smock, & Majumdar, 2004). Risky behaviors like drug use, alcohol, smoking, and domestic violence are among the most common reasons couples cite for ending relationships (Reed, 2007; Waller & Swisher, 2006; Wilson & Brooks-Gunn, 2001). As a result, a majority of children in these families see their parents' unions end by their fifth birthday.

Not all nonmarital unions end in dissolution. A handful remain stably cohabiting, and almost a third transition to marriage (Tach & Edin, 2011). In-depth qualitative research reveals that standards low-income unmarried parents have for marriage closely resemble those of their middle-class counterparts, even though their chances for meeting them are far lower. For the typical low-income unmarried father or mother, a prerequisite for marriage is a set of financial assets that demonstrate that the couple has "arrived" economically. Most say that before they can marry, they need a mortgage on a modest home, a car note, furniture, some money in the bank, and enough left over for a wedding. Without these marks of financial achievement—often called the *marriage bar* by researchers—it would not be right to get married (Edin & Kefalas, 2005; Gibson-Davis, Edin, & McLanahan, 2005).

Clashing with the reality of poor economic prospects, these standards lead to an indeterminate delay in marriage for many couples (Gibson-Davis et al., 2005). Marriage is more likely if a couple is able to improve their economic prospects, while becoming poorer decreases the likelihood of marriage (Osborne, 2005). Men's economic standing is particularly important, and those with less education, low earnings, and weaker attachment to the labor force are especially unlikely to marry (Goldstein & Kenney, 2001; Manning & Smock, 1995). On an aggregate level, the concentration of economic disadvantage within particular communities, above and beyond one's personal characteristics, reduces the availability of suitable marriage partners and may influence marriage rates among disadvantaged populations (McLanahan & Watson, 2009; Wilson & Neckerman, 1986).

Incarceration is another form of family insecurity that is deeply implicated in the romantic relationships of fragile families, particularly for African-Americans (Western & Wildeman, 2009). Incarceration undermines relationships via men's absence from the family and the community, the logistical problems of visitation, and the shame men feel as a result of their incarceration (Edin, Nelson, & Paranal, 2004; Roy & Dyson, 2007; Waller, 2002). Men's absence during incarceration, for example, imposes both economic pressures and opportunities for women to move on to new partners. Even when this does not occur, the physical separation and lack of ability to monitor one another's behavior fuels suspicion and mistrust (Edin & Kefalas, 2005). Partner relationships are marked by confusion and conflict during the period of incarceration, and deteriorating commitments between partners persist after men are released (Roy, 2005).

Among couples that end their relationships, transitions to new romantic relationships occur quickly. Almost two-thirds of mothers who end their marriages, and over three-fourths of mothers who end their cohabiting relationships, had a new romantic partner by the time their child was 5 years old (Tach & Edin, 2011). Many even had two or more different partnerships during that time period, what researchers call *churning* (Giordano, Manning, Longmore, & Flanigan, 2012). And new relationships can produce additional children, resulting in a proliferation of step- and half siblings. Among recent cohorts, about one-third of children spent time in a stepfamily (Bumpass, Raley, & Sweet, 1995), and 20% of women and 16% of men had children with more than one partner by midlife (Dorius, 2012; Guzzo, 2014; Guzzo & Furstenberg, 2007). Complexity is even more widespread among economically disadvantaged and racial minority families, where the prevalence of multiple-partner fertility approaches 50% (Dorius, 2012; Guzzo, 2014; Guzzo & Furstenberg, 2007). This combination of relationship instability and childbearing with multiple partners results in exceedingly complex family structures, with children experiencing two, three, or even more different father figures and a host of different resident and nonresident half siblings.

Parenting and Attachment Insecurity

Unstable family structures have the potential to undermine child well-being, but they do not always do so. Although there is a great deal of political and empirical debate around the effects of family structure, studies using a range of methodological techniques (e.g., growth curve models, sibling fixed effects, propensity score matching) to identify causal effects tend to find significant negative effects, on average, of family instability for children's cognitive and behavioral outcomes (see McLanahan, Tach, & Schneider, 2013, for a review). Amato and Anthony (2014) examined heterogeneity in the effects of divorce and found that a nontrivial share of children experienced no observable negative effects of divorce on the cognitive and socioemotional outcomes measured. Similarly, Musick and Meier (2010) found that the effects of divorce were weak or nonexistent when parents had low-quality relationships prior to dissolution, suggesting that not all divorces necessarily undermine children's well-being.

Research has attempted to elucidate the mechanisms by which unstable family structures affect parental and child well-being. A key theme in this regard is the idea of attachment insecurity: The fragile nature of attachments among parents, partners, and children leave them vulnerable to emotional and relationship problems. From qualitative work and a growing body of research using the Fragile Families and Child Wellbeing survey, we know that parents' often-scarce resources of time and money must be spread across several households in complex families systems, and this presents a challenge to maintaining meaningful involvement with all of the households to which they may be obligated (Tach, Edin, Harvey, & Bryant, 2014). Furstenberg and his colleagues suggested that parents' priorities might shift as they move from one family to the next, taking on commitments and obligations with a new romantic partner (Furstenberg & Cherlin, 1991; Furstenberg & Harris, 1992). Fathers visit their nonresident children less frequently (Carlson & Furstenberg, 2007; Tach, Mincy, & Edin, 2010) and provide less economic support to them via formal and informal arrangements (Manning & Smock, 2000) when they have children with new partners. Parents with children in different households are also less intensively involved with their current residential children (Carlson, McLanahan, & Brooks-Gunn, 2008), creating strain on current family relationships (Carlson & Furstenberg, 2007; Edin et al., 2009; Hill, 2007). Prior partners, who often continue to engage with the mother via child visitation, are a significant source of tension in new couple relationships as the prior partner's visits can fuel jealousy (Hill, 2007). Harknett and Knab (2007) also found that parents' kin networks provide less social support to them when they have children by other partners.

Maintaining high-quality relationships between the mother and father is crucial for the intensity and quality of fathers' involvement with their children, both in the context of romantic relationships and after those relationships have ended (Furstenberg & Cherlin, 1991). In other words, good partners are likely to make good parents (Carlson, McLanahan, & Brooks-Gunn, 2006). Cooperative coparenting—the ability of mothers and fathers to actively engage with one another in order to share childrearing responsibilities (Furstenberg & Cherlin, 1991)—is relatively uncommon, but it predicts more frequent and higher-quality father-child contact (Sobolewski & King, 2005). Custodial mothers play an important role as "gatekeepers," either facilitating or hindering a nonresident father's involvement (Buchanan, Maccoby, & Dornbusch, 1996), and mothers are more likely to grant access when the two have a strong relationship (Waller & Swisher, 2006). Thus, interventions to support effective coparenting, especially when parents are no longer in romantic relationships, may help promote continued, high-quality relationships between fathers and their nonresident children.

The formation of stable, secure attachment relationships with caregivers during childhood is important for the development of healthy relationships throughout the life course (Hazan & Shaver, 1987). The less committed, volatile relationships among members of unstable families make it more challenging for children to develop secure attachment relationships with their caregivers, and may have lasting effects on their ability to form secure relationships when they become adults (Stanley, Rhoades, & Whitton, 2010). In this way, children who grow up in fragile families are more likely to form fragile families themselves when they become adults (Musick & Mare, 2006), contributing to the reproduction of family inequality over time.

Conclusions

Increasingly, researchers have attempted to consider the host of insecurities and risk factors that affect the family environment under the term *chaos*: the disruption of daily activities and the feelings that such experiences engender (Fiese & Winter, 2010). Family chaos is more common among economically disadvantaged families, and is particularly sensitive to residential mobility, nonstandard work schedules, and unreliable childcare settings (Corapci, 2010; Repetti & Wang, 2010). Researchers have found that chaos leads to lower levels of investment in family relationships and parenting, with families spending less time together to establish and maintain family rituals and routines that are linked to positive relationships (Fiese & Winter, 2010). Parents in chaotic settings are less responsive, more authoritarian, and invest less money and time in their children (Evans, 2004). The new frontiers of research in this area offer some nuance to these findings—there is considerable heterogeneity in children's reactions to stress, which are shaped in part by biological risk factors, but stressful life events are particularly detrimental when they happen during early childhood and over sustained periods of time.

U.S. social policy and service delivery are not well equipped to address the needs of fragile families living in chaos, however. Most social policies either fail to recognize fragile families in the determination of benefits or penalize parents for not sharing biology or residence with their children. For example, SNAP (food stamps) allows only one household to receive benefits for a child. Similarly, the Earned Income Tax Credit (EITC) offers a substantial refundable tax credit for custodial parents and little for noncustodial parents. The all-or-nothing structure of both policies ignores the fact that many children in fragile families spend time in multiple households and with multiple parental figures. The current system, thus, has the potential to undermine the material resources available to children in fragile families, to increase within-family inequality by rendering children in the same family system eligible for different benefits, and to stigmatize them in the determination and recertification of eligibility.

In a similar vein, fragile families struggle to receive coordinated, high-quality physical and mental health services. They are less likely to be insured or to have a regular source of care, are more likely to forego treatment because of cost, and are less likely to receive timely preventive services (NCHS, 2012). Their lives present a number of logistical barriers to receiving stable care, including a lack of access to transportation and difficulties making and keeping appointments because of unpredictable family and employment circumstances (Diamant et al., 2004). Although there is little national research documenting disparities in the quality of services, qualitative case studies suggest that poor individuals can receive lower-quality care from practitioners due to a lack of provider understanding of what it is like to live in poverty. Further, this can manifest itself via a failure to collect adequate data about patients' social circumstances, the development of care plans patients are unable to follow, and a lack of awareness of social and community resources that could benefit patients (Bernheim, Ross, Krumholz, & Bradley, 2008; Willems, De Maesschalck, Deveugele, Derese, & De Maeseneer, 2005). In this way, contemporary social policies and services typically have failed to recognize the fluidity of resources, relationships, and living arrangements within fragile family systems.

The research evidence on the costs of family instability is painfully evident in Marilyn's case. Her mother, Shelly, experienced a series of troubled relationships with parents, relatives, and the foster care system as a child. As an adult, she struggled to form secure and stable relationships with her community, family, and treatment team. Shelly is now recreating the insecurity of her childhood with her own children, Allen and Marilyn, who each present the socioemotional consequences of their insecure family attachments in distinct ways. At the same time, Marilyn's case reveals areas where research evidence is lacking. There is little nationally representative data on rates of mental health issues and trauma among fragile families, the role of undertreated mental health problems in family formation, functioning, and dissolution, or the accessibility of quality mental and physical health services. These are ripe areas for future research that would advance our scientific understanding of the social determinants of health, improve service delivery among practitioners, and enhance the early detection and treatment of health problems among children like Marilyn.

References

Amato, P. R., & Anthony, C. J. (2014). Estimating the effects of parental divorce and death with fixed effects models. *Journal of Marriage and Family*, *76*, 370–386. doi: 10.1111/jomf.12100

Augustine, J., Nelson, T., & Edin, K. (2009). Why do poor men have children? Fertility intentions among low-income unmarried U.S. fathers. *Annals of the American Academy of Political and Social Sciences*, *624*, 99–117. doi: 10.1177/0002716209334694

Bernheim, S. M., Ross, J. S., Krumholz, H. M., & Bradley, E. H. (2008). Influence of patients' socioeconomic status on clinical management decisions: A qualitative study. *The Annals of Family Medicine*, *6*(1), 53–59. doi: 10.1370/afm.749

Bronfenbrenner, U. (2009). *The ecology of human development: Experiments by nature and design*. Cambridge, MA: Harvard University Press.

Brooks-Gunn, J., & Duncan, G. J. (1997). The effects of poverty on children. *The Future of Children*, *7*(2), 55–71. doi: 10.2307/1602387

Buchanan, C. M., Maccoby, E. E., & Dornbusch, S. M. (1996). *Adolescents after divorce*. Cambridge, MA: Harvard University Press.

Bumpass, L. L., Raley, R. K., & Sweet, J. A. (1995). The changing character of stepfamilies: Implications of cohabitation and nonmarital childbearing. *Demography*, *32*, 425–436. doi: 10.2307/2061689

Carlson, M. J., & Furstenberg, F. F. (2007). *The consequences of multi-partnered fertility for parental resources and relationships*. (Center for Research on Child Wellbeing Working Paper # 06-28-FF). Princeton, NJ: Princeton University Press.

Carlson, M. J., McLanahan, S. S., & Brooks-Gunn, J. (2006). *Do good partners make good parents? Relationship quality and parenting in two-parent families*. (Center for Research on Child Wellbeing Working Paper). Princeton, NJ: Princeton University Press. Retrieved from: http://crcw.princeton.edu/workingpapers/WP06-28-FF.pdf

Carlson, M. J., McLanahan, S. S., & Brooks-Gunn, J. (2008). Coparenting and nonresident fathers' involvement with young children after a nonmarital birth. *Demography, 45*, 461–488. doi: 10.1353/dem.0.0007

Center for Research on Child Wellbeing. (2003). *Introduction to the fragile families one-year public use data*. Princeton, NJ: Bendheim Thoman Center for Child Wellbeing. Retrieved from: http://www.fragilefamilies.princeton.edu/documentation/core/4waves_ff_public.pdf

Corapci, F. (2010). Child care chaos and child development. In G. Evans & T. D. Wachs (Eds.), *Chaos and its influence on children's development: An ecological perspective* (pp. 67–82). Washington, DC: American Psychological Association.

Dahl, G. B., & Lochner, L. (2012). The impact of family income on child achievement: Evidence from the earned income tax credit. *The American Economic Review, 102*, 1927–1956. doi: 10.1257/aer.102.5.1927

Diamant, A. L., Hays, R. D., Morales, L. S., Ford, W., Calmes, D., Asch, S., & Sumner, G. (2004). Delays and unmet need for health care among adult primary care patients in a restructured urban public health system. *American Journal of Public Health, 94*(5), 783–789. doi: 10.2105/AJPH.94.5.783

Dorius, C. (2012). *New approaches to measuring multipartnered fertility over the life course*. (PSC Research Report No. 12-769). Ann Arbor: University of Michigan. Retrieved from: http://www.psc.isr.umich.edu/pubs/pdf/rr12-769.pdf

Duncan, G. J., Huston, A. C., & Weisner, T. S. (2007). *Higher ground: New hope for the working poor and their children*. New York: Russell Sage Foundation.

Edin, K., England, P., Fitzgibbons Shafer, E., & Reed, J. (2007). Forming fragile families: Was the baby planned, unplanned, or in between? In P. England & K. Edin (Eds.), *Unmarried couples with children* (pp. 25–54). New York: Russell Sage Foundation.

Edin, K., & Kefalas, M. (2005). *Promises I can keep: Why poor women put motherhood before marriage*. Berkeley, CA: University of California Press.

Edin, K., & Nelson, T. J. (2013). *Doing the best I can: Fatherhood in the inner city*. Berkeley, CA: University of California Press.

Edin, K., & Tach, L. (2012). Becoming a parent: The social contexts of fertility during young adulthood. In A. Booth, S. Landale, N. S. Manning, & S. M. McHale (Eds.), *Early adulthood in a family context* (pp. 185–207). New York, NY: Springer Publishing Co.

Edin, K., Tach, L., & Mincy, R. (2009). Claiming fatherhood: Race and the dynamics of paternal involvement among unmarried men. *The Annals of the American Academy of Political and Social Science, 621*, 149–177. doi: 10.1177/0002716208325548

Evans, G. W. (2004). The environment of childhood poverty. *American Psychologist, 59*, 77–92. doi: 10.1037/0003-066X.59.2.77

Fiese, B. H., & Winter, M. A. (2010). Family stories and rituals. In J. Bray & M. Stanton (Eds.), *Handbook of family psychology* (pp. 625–636). Oxford, UK: Blackwell.

Finer, L. B., & Henshaw, S. K. (2006). Disparities in rates of unintended pregnancy in the United States, 1994 and 2001. *Perspectives on Sexual and Reproductive Health, 38*, 90–96. doi: 10.1363/3809006

Furstenberg, F. F., & Cherlin, A. J. (1991). *Divided families: What happens to children when parents part*. Cambridge, MA: Harvard University Press.

Furstenberg, F. F., & Harris, K. M. (1992). The disappearing American father? Divorce and the waning significance of biological parenthood. In S. South & S. Tolnay (Eds.), *The changing American family: Sociological and demographic perspectives* (pp. 197–223). Boulder, CO: Westview.

Gibson-Davis, C. M., Edin, K., & McLanahan, S. (2005). High hopes but even higher expectations: The retreat from marriage among low-income couples. *Journal of Marriage and Family*, *67*, 1301–1312. doi: 10.1111/j.1741-3737.2005.00218.x

Giordano, P. C., Manning, W. D., Longmore, M. A., & Flanigan, C. M. (2012). Developmental shifts in the character of romantic and sexual relationships from adolescence to young adulthood. In A. Booth, S. Landale, N. S. Manning, & S. M. McHale (Eds.), *Early adulthood in a family context* (pp. 133–164). New York, NY: Springer Publishing Co.

Goldstein, J. R., & Kenney, C. T. (2001). Marriage delayed or marriage foregone? New cohort forecasts of first marriage for US women. *American Sociological Review*, *66*, 506–519. doi: 10.2307/3088920

Graefe, D. R., & Lichter, D. T. (1999). Life course transitions of American children: Parental cohabitation, marriage, and single motherhood. *Demography*, *36*, 205–218. doi: 10.2307/2648109

Guzzo, K. B. (2014). New partners, more kids: Multiple-partner fertility in the United States. *The Annals of the American Academy of Political and Social Science*, *654*, 66–86. doi: 10.1177/0002716214525571

Guzzo, K. B., & Furstenberg, F. F. (2007). Multipartnered fertility among young women with a nonmarital first birth: Prevalence and risk factors. *Perspectives on Sexual and Reproductive Health*, *39*, 29–38. doi: 10.1363/3902907

Hamilton, B. E., Martin, J. A., & Ventura, S. J. (2009). Births: Preliminary data for 2007. *National Vital Statistics Reports*, *57*(12), 1–23. Retrieved from: http://www.cdc.gov/nchs/data/nvsr/nvsr57/nvsr57_12.pdf

Harknett, K., & Knab, J. (2007). More kin, less support: Multipartnered fertility and perceived support among mothers. *Journal of Marriage and Family*, *69*, 237–253. doi: 10.1111/j.1741-3737.2006.00356.x

Hazan, C., & Shaver, P. (1987). Romantic love conceptualized as an attachment process. *Journal of Personality and Social Psychology*, *52*(3), 511–524. doi: 10.1037/0022-3514.52.3.511

Hill, H. D. (2007). Steppin' out: Infidelity and sexual jealousy among unmarried parents. In P. England & K. Edin (Eds.), *Unmarried couples with children* (pp. 104–132). New York: Russell Sage Foundation.

Hoynes, H., Miller, D., & Simon, D. (2015). Income, the earned income tax credit, and infant health. *American Economic Journal: Economic Policy*, *7*, 172–211. doi: 10.1257/pol.20120179

Manning, W. D., & Smock, P. J. (1995). Why marry? Race and the transition to marriage among cohabitors. *Demography*, *32*, 509–520.

Manning, W. D., & Smock, P. J. (2000). "Swapping" families: Serial parenting and economic support for children. *Journal of Marriage and the Family*, *62*, 111–122.

Manning, W. D., Smock, P. J., & Majumdar, D. (2004). The relative stability of cohabiting and marital unions for children. *Population Research and Policy Review*, *6*, 135–159.

McLanahan, S. (2004). Diverging destinies: How children are faring under the second demographic transition. *Demography*, *41*, 607–627. doi: 10.1353/dem.2004.0033

McLanahan, S. (2009). Fragile families and the reproduction of poverty. *The Annals of the American Academy of Political and Social Science*, *621*(1), 111–131. doi: 10.1177/0002716208324862

McLanahan, S., Tach, L., & Schneider, D. (2013). The causal effects of father absence. *Annual Review of Sociology*, *39*, 399–427. doi: 10.1146/annurev-soc-071312-145704

McLanahan, S., & Watson, T. (2009). *Marriage meets the Joneses: Relative income, identity, and marital status.* (National Bureau of Economic Research Working Paper No. 14773). Cambridge, MA. Retrieved from: http://www.nber.org/papers/w14773

Musick, K., & Mare, R. D. (2006). Recent trends in the inheritance of poverty and family structure. *Social Science Research, 35*(2), 471–499. doi: 10.1016/j.ssresearch.2004.11.006

Musick, K., & Meier, A. (2010). Are both parents always better than one? Parental conflict and young adult well-being. *Social Science Research, 39*, 814–830. doi: 10.1016/j.ssresearch.2010.03.002

National Center for Health Statistics. (2012). Summary health statistics for US adults: National health interview survey, 2010. *Vital and Health Statistics, 252*, 1–207. Retrieved from: http://www.cdc.gov/nchs/data/series/sr_10/sr10_252.pdf

Osborne, C. (2005). Marriage following the birth of a child for cohabiting and visiting parents. *Journal of Marriage and Family, 67*, 14–26. doi: 10.1111/j.0022-2445.2005.00002.x

Phillips, D. A., & Shonkoff, J. P. (Eds.). (2000). *From neurons to neighborhoods: The science of early childhood development.* Washington, DC: National Academies Press.

Reed, J. (2007). Anatomy of a breakup: How and why do unmarried couples with children break up? In P. England & K. Edin (Eds.), *Unmarried couples with children* (pp. 133–156). New York: Russell Sage Foundation.

Repetti, R. L., & Wang, S. (2010). Work-family spillover. In H. T. Reis & S. K. Sprecher (Eds.), *Encyclopedia of human relationships* (pp. 1694–1697). Thousand Oaks, CA: Sage Publications.

Roy, K. M. (2005). Transitions on the margins of work and family for low-income African American fathers. *Journal of Family and Economic Issues, 26*, 77–100. doi: 10.1007/s10834-004-1413-3

Roy, K. M., & Dyson, O. L. (2007). Gatekeeping in context: Babymama drama and the involvement of incarcerated fathers. *Fathering, 3*, 289–310. doi: 10.3149/fth.0303.289

Shonkoff, J. P. (2010). Building a new biodevelopmental framework to guide the future of early childhood policy. *Child Development, 81*(1), 257–367. doi: 10.1111/j.1467-8624.2009.01399.x

Shonkoff, J. P., Garner, A. S., Siegel, B. S., Dobbins, M. I., Earls, M. F., McGuinn, L., & Wood, D. L. (2012). The lifelong effects of early childhood adversity and toxic stress. *Pediatrics, 129*, e232–e246. doi: 10.1542/peds.2011-2663

Sobolewski, J. M., & King, V. (2005). The importance of the coparental relationship for nonresident fathers' ties to children. *Journal of Marriage and Family, 67*, 1196–1212. doi: 10.1111/j.1741-3737.2005.00210.x

Stanley, S. M., Rhoades, G. K., & Whitton, S. W. (2010). Commitment: Functions, formation, and the securing of romantic attachment. *Journal of Family Theory & Review, 2*(4), 243–257. doi: 10.1111/j.1756-2589.2010.00060.x

Sum, A., Khatiwada, I., McLaughlin, J., & Palma, S. (2011). No country for young men: Deteriorating labor market prospects for low-skilled men in the United States. *The Annals of the American Academy of Political and Social Science, 635*(1), 24–55. doi: 10.1177/0002716210393694

Tach, L., & Edin, K. (2011). The relationship contexts of young disadvantaged men. *Annals of the American Academy of Political and Social Sciences, 635*, 56–75. doi: 10.1177/0002716210393680

Tach, L., Edin, K., Harvey, H., & Bryant, B. (2014). The family-go-round: Family complexity and father involvement from a father's perspective. *Annals of the American Academy of Political and Social Sciences, 654*, 169–184. doi: 10.1177/0002716214528655

Tach, L., Mincy, R., & Edin, K. (2010). Parenting as a package deal: Relationships, fertility, and nonresident father involvement among unmarried parents. *Demography, 47*, 181–204. doi: 10.1353/dem.0.0096

Waller, M. R. (2002). *My baby's father: Unwed parents and paternal responsibilities.* Ithaca, NY: Cornell University Press.

Waller, M. R., & Swisher, R. (2006). Fathers' risk factors in fragile families: Implications for "healthy" relationships and father involvement. *Social Problems, 53*(3), 392–420. doi: 10.1525/sp.2006.53.3.392

Western, B., Bloome, D., Sosnaud, B., & Tach, L. (2012). Economic insecurity and social stratification. *Annual Review of Sociology, 38*, 341–359. doi: 10.1146/annurev-soc-071811-145434

Western, B., & Wildeman, C. (2009). The Black family and mass incarceration. *Annals of the American Academy of Social and Political Science, 621*, 221–242. doi: 10.1177/0002716208324850

Willems, S., De Maesschalck, S., Deveugele, M., Derese, A., & De Maeseneer, J. (2005). Socio-economic status of the patient and doctor—patient communication: Does it make a difference? *Patient Education and Counseling, 56*(2), 139–146. doi: 10.1016/j.pec.2004.02.011

Wilson, M., & Brooks-Gunn, J. (2001). Health status and behaviors of unwed fathers. *Children and Youth Services Review, 23*, 377–401. doi: 10.1016/S0190-7409(01)00138-4

Wilson, W., & Neckerman, K. (1986). Poverty and family structure: The widening gap between evidence and public policy issues. In S. Danziger & D. Weinberg (Eds.), *Fighting poverty: What works and what doesn't* (pp. 232–259). Cambridge, MA: Harvard University Press.

An Eco-Systemic Approach to Strengthening Fragile Families

C. Wayne Jones

In the previous section, Tach focused on the unique risks and challenges faced by fragile families, a family structure associated with frequent chaos and, more often than not, poverty. This chapter focuses on the emotional and relational lives of fragile families, with special attention given to the role of emotion dysregulation and attachment insecurity in undermining family stability and the mental health of family members. Although fragile families may care about one another, minor conflicts easily escalate into major conflicts, abrupt family breakups, violence, and trauma. It is not surprising that the vast majority of children and adolescents showing severe emotional disturbance (SED) treated in community-based behavioral health programs live in fragile, multi-stressed families.

SED is characterized by extra sensitivity to stress, under-regulation of emotions, and a tendency toward severe and extreme reactions when upset (Jones, 2010). Without effective treatment, these children accumulate repeated failures in their lives and become the creators of the next generation of fragile families. For example, children with SED have the highest dropout rate of all recognized disabilities under the Individuals with Disabilities Education Act (IDEA; Lehr, Johnson, Bremer, Cosio, & Thompson, 2004). Of those who graduate, only 30% do so with a standard diploma (Reimer & Smink, 2005). Twenty percent are arrested once before leaving high school, and 50% are arrested within five years post high school (Davis & Vander Stoep, 1997).

Children and adolescents with SED often enter the behavioral health system at an early age, usually for disruptive behavioral problems. Most often, they receive treatments that focus strictly on symptoms, including psychopharmacology, behavioral management, and the teaching of coping or social skills. For those children who live in emotionally reactive fragile families, these interventions are rarely effective. These children cannot integrate new coping skills and sustain changes when their families are unstable and relationships insecure.

When children have multiple treatments and they do not feel their lives are any better as a result, they may give up on the possibility of change, concluding they are defective, and then become less open to further intervention. This is the mindset that Marilyn had when she came into treatment. The treatment team understood why Marilyn held this perspective. For several years in elementary school, she had *wrap-around* services. This mostly involved a one-on-one person who helped her manage transitions and regulate her behavior in the classroom. Marilyn recalls that she did better in school with the extra structure and support, but that it did not help her feel better about herself because it did not change anything at home, where she felt unwanted. She also complained that every time she started liking the workers, they would leave and be replaced with someone else. Before the service ended, she had four different workers. She also had a brief episode of outpatient therapy with someone she says mostly focused on helping her to identify and express her feelings. Marilyn told the team, "She was kind but she never really understood that if I express my feelings at home, my mother will just go crazy on me."

Marilyn had her first inpatient hospitalization at age 11 following suicidal ideation, not long after her father moved away. This began a six-year negative cycle involving the behavioral health system, Marilyn, and her family. Marilyn would be prescribed medicine and outpatient therapy, would stabilize for a month or two, and then all treatment would stop, leading to another hospitalization. There were six in all. The hospital functioned to regulate Marilyn when Shelly could not. Although some providers viewed Shelly's failure to follow through with treatment recommendations for her daughter as neglectful and resistant, Shelly's response also could be viewed as a consequence of treatment that did not fully involve her as a partner. Providers gave her information about Marilyn's treatment but did not elicit her agenda or her perspective, nor did they assess the family context. Marilyn's father was not included at all. This acontextual, child-centric approach often is standard treatment of children with SED living in fragile families.

In this chapter, I describe eco-systemic structural family therapy (ESFT), an evidence-informed approach developed specifically to treat children and adolescents with SED within the context of their fragile, multi-stressed families. I explain the treatment model and demonstrate its application using excerpts from the case study, identifying: (1) core vulnerabilities and negative patterns in fragile, multi-stressed families most associated with SED, (2) how these core vulnerabilities shape the development of a therapeutic alliance and the focus of treatment, and (3) the principles and methods of change. Finally, a detailed description is provided as to how ESFT was used with Marilyn and her family to help them make changes in each of the four core vulnerabilities targeted by ESFT. (Although this case study is based on an actual case, any information that might lead to identification of members of this family has been altered.)

A Brief History of ESFT

ESFT is an adaptation of structural family therapy (SFT), developed by Salvador Minuchin (1974) and colleagues at the Philadelphia Child Guidance Clinic in the 1970s. It is grounded in systems theory, which assumes that what caregivers and their children feel, think, and do are a function of recursive relationship patterns in the family. These relationship patterns are, in turn, a function of the family's interactions with their extended family and the community in which they live. Most importantly in ESFT, like SFT, treatment is strengths-based and collaborative, driven by a deep belief that most families, regardless of their circumstances or current problems, are capable of change with the right support. Therapists in this model are action-oriented and experiential, focused on identifying and then shifting negative relationship patterns in the family system to more functional ones.

Early formulations of ESFT were developed by Lindblad-Goldberg at the Philadelphia Child Guidance Center in response to an initiative by the Children's Bureau at Pennsylvania's Office of Mental Health and Substance Abuse in the late 1980s to create an intensive, in-home, community-based family treatment program that would prevent children and adolescents with SED from cycling in and out of inpatient hospitals and residential treatment centers (Lindblad-Goldberg, Dore, & Stern, 1998). The SFT model was expanded so it could be team-delivered and more easily implemented in the home and community. Additionally, ESFT incorporates services such as parent education, service coordination, crisis intervention, family support, and case management.

ESFT became more integrative beginning in the late 1990s. Although still systemic at its core, the current clinical model incorporates more recent theory and research about the role of attachment, development, and trauma in shaping children and their caregivers' interactions with one another and the larger community, as well as their response to treatment (Jones, 2010; Jones & Lindblad-Goldberg, 2002). ESFT can best be described as an eco-systemic, trauma-informed, attachment-focused, developmentally based family treatment program. The concepts and practices of ESFT were further specified and operationalized in a treatment manual published by Jones in 2010. The manual, together with a standardized clinical management system and measures of treatment adherence, has allowed the model to be more consistently implemented by community behavioral health providers, measure treatment outcomes, and study its effectiveness.

Core Vulnerabilities of Fragile Families With an SED Child

In ESFT, treatment is constructed around the observation that what causes and maintains SED symptoms is a family environment that is *hyper-arousing and under-supporting* (Jones, 2010). Although this can be found in any family across the socioeconomic, cultural spectrum, this is a particularly common situation in fragile families. At critical moments when a child needs comfort, calm, and connection most urgently, caregivers become activated and dysregulated by the child's emotionality, and then respond with name-calling, yelling, withdrawal, threats of abandonment, and criticism. Family members are out of sync with one another's emotional needs at the most critical moments in their relationships with one another. The effect on everyone in an *SED system* is frustration and isolation, so communication becomes derailed easily, preventing resolution of routine conflicts.

In Marilyn's family, the core negative interactional cycle usually began with Marilyn distressed about peer conflicts at school, interactions with her brother, or anxieties about her studies. Marilyn struggled with regulating her attention and staying organized, which created considerable stress for her at school. Shelly would not notice her daughter's distress, often expressed as irritability, because she spent most of her time in her bedroom watching TV or reading her Bible. Marilyn would try to handle her distress alone, playing her music loudly and smoking pot, but when this did not work, would angrily barge into her mother's bedroom to criticize her for not cooking meals. Shelly, who belongs to a small evangelical church, would tell Marilyn that she was selfish and that her behavior was caused by the devil, and then she would begin praying and talking in tongues. This would send Marilyn into a rage, quickly sending her mother back into her bedroom and creating further distance and aloneness for both of them. These episodes would also activate Allen, her elder brother, who would take his mother's side and try to "punish" Marilyn for making their mother upset.

Although there is tremendous diversity among fragile families who have a child with SED, there are four general patterns they share that leave them vulnerable when they are in conflict or stressed (see Figure 4.2). First, caregivers are extra-sensitive to stress and have tremendous difficulty regulating their emotions when in conflict with their children and vice versa. This usually results in an insecure or ruptured caregiver-child bond since secure attachments are built on calm, soothing responses that bring relief from stress and anxiety. The family is then off balance when conflict occurs and they are unable to regulate or de-escalate the hyper-aroused family members. This is in part because the executive components of parenting are often weak and inconsistent. Caregivers tend to be overly harsh or not pay sufficient attention, and many times swing between these extremes depending on the mood or context of the caregivers on that particular day. Finally, the caregivers' relationships with one another and with those in their extended social network are organized in a way that undermines support for a non-reactive, positive approach to parenting. Caregivers need consistent emotional support and soothing themselves in order to give it to their children.

Implications for Creating a Therapeutic Alliance

The first task of any intensive, in-home family-based treatment is to establish a balanced therapeutic alliance with all family members. In Marilyn's family, the therapists believed the most important person to connect with was Shelly. They recognized Shelly was extremely suspicious of outsiders, so being invited into

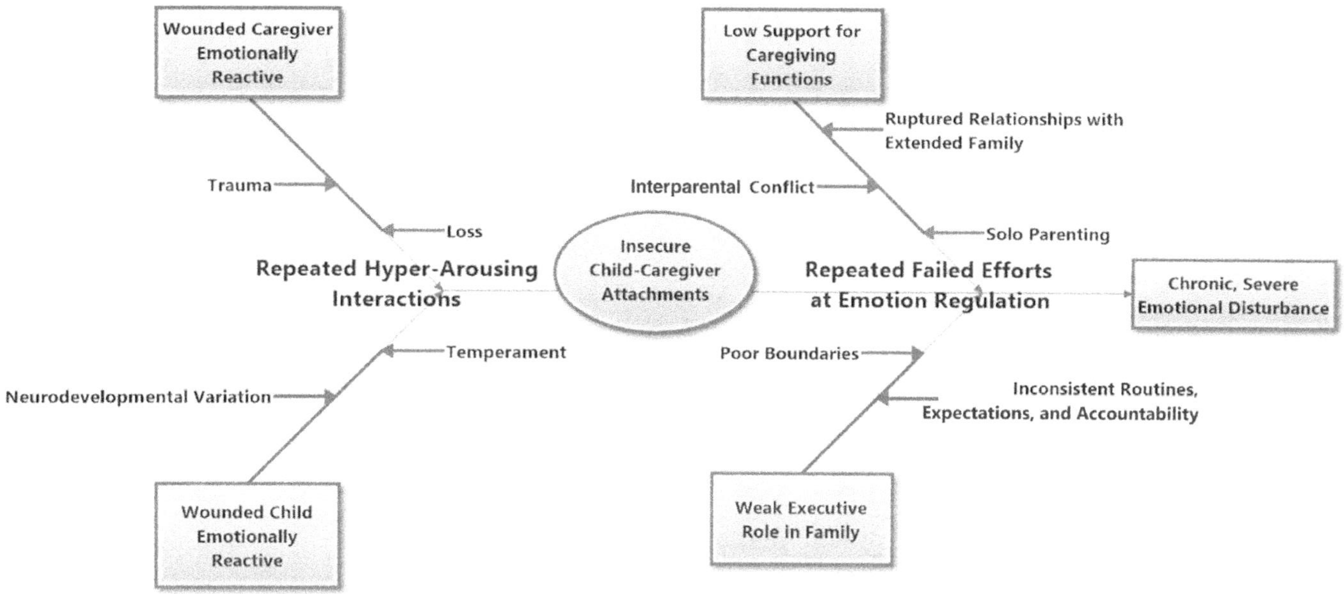

Figure 4.2 Family Vulnerabilities and the Pathway to Chronic SED

Source: Permission to republish granted by The Center for Family Based Training (Jones 2010)

the home on a regular basis was going to be a struggle. Marilyn was equally challenging because she had given up all hope. For the first month of treatment, Marilyn withdrew to her room or left the house when they showed up. Since Allen believed all the problems in the family were Marilyn's fault, he also initially refused to participate.

The treatment team anticipated some initial defensiveness and guardedness, and they normalized it. They viewed it as an adaptation to what the family had experienced thus far in their relationships with other agencies, family of origin, and with one another. Shelly's experience with the service system to some extent mirrored her experience in her family of origin. That is, she felt a sense of failure and disempowerment. Shelly told the team that she had encountered a few service providers who treated her as a "bad" or "harmful" parent, uninterested in the welfare of her daughter.

The team had a negative internal reaction when Shelly stated angrily that she wanted Marilyn out of the home and was not interested in being personally involved in the treatment, but they did not judge her or react in the same way others had when they heard her talk in such a rejecting, hostile manner about her daughter. They reminded themselves that caregivers' initial presentations do not always accurately represent the full extent of who they have been in the past or who they are capable of being with more support. The team knew that no one looks their best when they are in crisis and are overwhelmed. This is when families are most likely to present with significant despair, chaos, and hostility. The team made it clear, however, that they would not recommend out-of-home placement and reminded Shelly how Marilyn's previous hospitalizations made it more difficult for Shelly to parent her.

No matter how strong the desire to be a good parent, untreated trauma, loss, and isolation can transform ordinary family conflicts into desperate fights for emotional survival, hijacking caregivers' executive potential to the point that their children, and sometimes even their partners, are perceived as the enemy. They are doing well just to survive, given their own high levels of internal distress. At times it can seem that childhood can be toxic to caregivers who are "wounded" by histories of complex traumatic stress and loss. This is certainly Shelly's history. She grew up with caregivers compromised by alcoholism, drug abuse, and mental illness. Like many of the caregivers in fragile families, she also experienced harsh or abusive parenting, deprivation and neglect, sexual exploitation, and loss of an important caregiver at an early age.

In ESFT, the treatment flows through the caregivers. At first glance, this seems like an impossibility to therapists new to the model when they meet caregivers with major mental health issues like Shelly who are parenting alone and seemingly in no condition to take on such an active role. The treatment team addressed this dilemma by giving Shelly three important messages, all of which are essential in creating the therapeutic alliance and fully engaging caregivers in family treatment. First, they genuinely empathized with Shelly and acknowledged how overwhelmed she was. "This is an incredibly difficult situation and would be hard for anyone." The second message to Shelly was that Marilyn would recover more quickly if she knew her family was working just as hard as she was. "Marilyn needs to know that you are there and will be a major player on her recovery team. . . . It would mean even more to her knowing how depressed you are." This message serves as an important value statement about the importance of families sticking by one another and begins a psychoeducational process about how change happens. "Marilyn can't fully recover from her illness without you." The third message that makes it easier to digest the previous one is that she will not be alone. "We are here for you, Shelly, we will work alongside you as a team every step of the way, doing whatever it takes to help you with your daughter."

Marilyn's trust of the therapists grew as she noticed how effectively and persistently they were working with her mother. Allen was very anxious about the therapists placing so much pressure on his mother, because he anticipated she may deteriorate and things would be even worse for him in the home. He managed this anxiety by remaining in earshot of the team's sessions with Shelly, slowly relaxing as he saw that the therapists were sensitive to his mother's emotional fragility. The team developed an alliance with Allen by taking care not to leave him out, checking in with him briefly after sessions with his mother and Marilyn, asking for his observations and acknowledging the role he has played in the family. He grew to respect their leadership abilities and agreed to fully participate in the treatment about two months into it.

An important principle here is, when caregivers are compromised and not fully participating in the parental role, the therapists' alliance with children is contingent on how effective they have been in creating an emotionally safe relationship with the caregivers. When therapists are successful in creating a collaborative partnership with the caregivers on behalf of the child, a relationship in which caregivers are credited for the strengths and assets they bring to the team, the alliance with both the caregivers and the children is established. To feel respected and to be listened to as collaborative partners is a new experience for many caregivers in fragile families with a history of having multiple community services. And, it is often a unique experience for children in these families to witness therapists treating their parents respectfully while holding them accountable. This is an essential part of setting the stage of effective treatment for any family, but for these families it carries considerable weight.

The ESFT Treatment Model

The overarching goal of ESFT treatment is to create a context within the family system that fosters greater relationship stability and greater emotion regulation, a context that is more growth-promoting and functional for its members. In short, a less fragile family. When therapists are successful, the children referred for treatment show significantly reduced symptoms of distress, they are no longer a safety concern, and they are better able to handle the typical demands of participating in home, school, and the community. Most importantly, caregivers come to believe they can manage and parent their children in their home. They are no longer talking about out-of-home placement. If caregivers do not have confidence in their ability to parent a child, the caregiver-child bond remains fragile and insecure, and the cycle of reactivity and rejection continues when caregivers become stressed by the child's behavior.

To create this outcome, ESFT therapists directly target the four core patterns that leave families vulnerable to dysregulation and chaos (see Figure 4.3). These are the cornerstones of ESFT treatment: (1) strengthen the co-caregiver alliance, (2) strengthen the caregivers' emotional availability to the child,

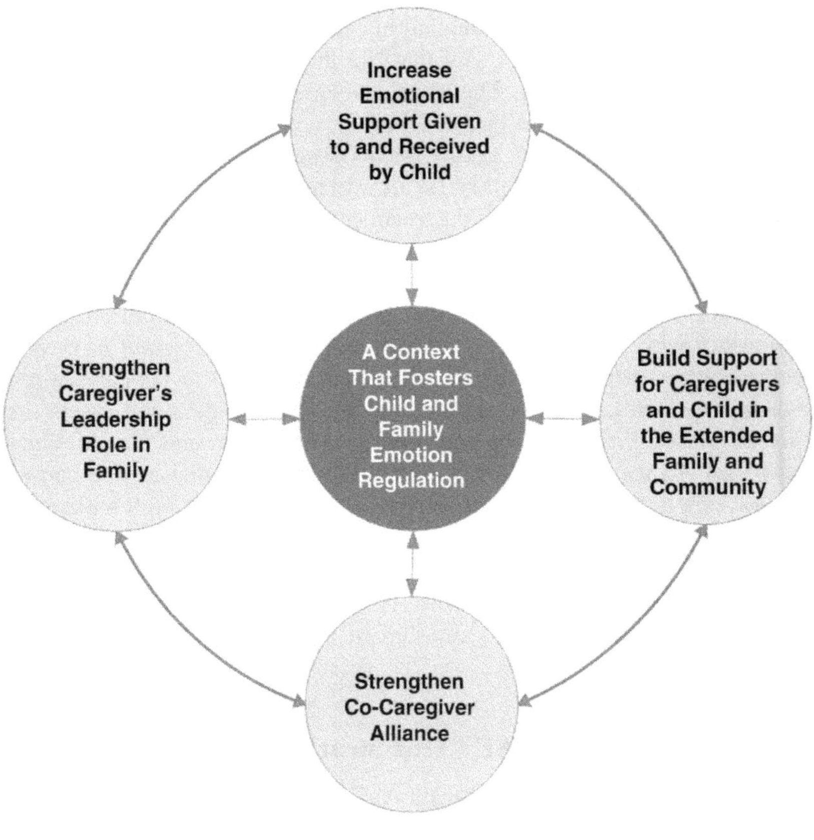

Figure 4.3 The Four Cornerstones (Drivers) of ESFT Treatment

Source: Permission to reprint granted by The Center for Family Based Training (Jones, 2010)

(3) strengthen the caregivers' leadership role in the family, and (4) build support for the caregivers and the child in the extended family and community.

Core Mechanisms of Change in ESFT

In ESFT, there are six conditions (i.e., *mechanisms of change*) that, when present, are assumed to account for positive and meaningful change in fragile families with a child who has SED. Although the particular way in which these mechanisms are operationalized is specific to ESFT, they reflect common factors found in all current evidence-based family intervention models (Sprenkle & Blow, 2004). In the next section, the particular ways in which these conditions are created in ongoing treatment with Marilyn and her family are described. A therapist is fully implementing the ESFT model when they are working to establish the following six treatment conditions (known as the core mechanisms of change):

- *All family members who can influence the functioning of the child and the caregivers and their relationship with one another are included in treatment.*
- *A strong therapeutic alliance is established between therapists and all family members.*
- *Family members experience themselves as being part of a respectful, collaborative, and accountable relationship with therapists.*
- *Family members experience themselves as safe, calm, regulated, and emotionally connected with one another in the presence of the therapists.*
- *Negative, judgmental behavioral views of the child and one another are moving in the direction of a more compassionate, relational one.*
- *Family members experience themselves as successfully practicing new, more functional patterns with one another.*

Setting the Stage for Change

Beginning with the first session, ESFT therapists work intensively to cultivate a treatment context where all of the above mentioned conditions are present. Therapists typically meet with families a minimum of three times per week (once with the identified patient alone, once with the caregivers, and once with the entire family), particularly during the first 90 days of involvement. They ensure there is full consent from caregivers to work on an agreed upon treatment plan. All initial operations of setting the stage are given equal weight. Together, these conditions create a treatment structure that stabilizes families and creates opportunities for meaningful engagement. To keep the treatment moving at a faster pace, ESFT therapists employ *strengths-based straight talk* with families. In order for family members to hear therapists above the background noise of the chaos of their daily lives, therapists must be clear, focused, and persistent. The sixth operation, practicing more functional patterns, becomes the main focus of treatment once the stage has been successfully set. Below, the process for creating the stage for treatment with Marilyn and her family is described.

One of the more critical early tasks of ESFT treatment, but often the most challenging, is engaging peripheral or uninvolved caregivers. Rather than passively accepting whoever shows up, the ESFT therapist works with the involved caregiver to elicit permission to contact the other caregiver. Marilyn and Allen's father, Larry, has lived on the other side of the country for the last seven years of her life. Shelly was cut off from Larry after the divorce and does not speak with him about the children. Marilyn and Allen have sporadic phone calls with him. Not unexpectedly, Shelly firmly rejected the idea when the treatment team initially brought it up. She harbored significant resentments toward him for "abandoning" her and the kids. Marilyn also initially refused the therapists' request to contact her father for similar reasons. Allen was okay with it, having maintained more contact with Larry than Marilyn after he left the home.

The team more strongly pushed the idea of contacting Larry during the next session when they were completing an eco-map of family members' connections with people outside the household and the kids included their father. The treatment team told Shelly that "sometimes even a small connection with a father can be helpful to recovery, . . . your daughter is in real crisis here . . . why should you bear all the responsibility for her future mental health alone." Shelly remained reluctant because she feared the team would become influenced by negative things Larry might say about her. The team addressed this by reassuring Shelly, "No matter what Larry might tell us about you, we know you are the one that stayed with your children and faced the challenges of raising them alone." Marilyn softened in her opposition to involving her father a few weeks after her mother gave permission.

ESFT therapists are trained to be persistent in their efforts to repair cutoffs and reestablish some type of relationship with others who could possibly strengthen the caregiving system. In this case, the team knew that Shelly could not help Marilyn alone and their efforts would be limited without Larry's involvement. Larry eagerly accepted the call from the therapists, but it seemed that his initial agenda was to justify why he "had to leave" Shelly and the kids. Of course, Larry told the team many negative things about Shelly, many of which turned out to be true, but were not relevant to the task of helping his daughter in the present. He was reluctant initially to become involved in an ongoing way with treatment. The team's clarity with Larry about the importance of his role engaged him, giving him a purpose. By engaging Larry in treatment, even if long distance, the team had begun to develop an executive team, and had seeded the idea of at least some minimal coparenting.

The team's success in engaging Larry had the effect of deepening their alliance with both Shelly and Marilyn, because it was the first time anyone they had worked with showed this level of potency. Another important set of early actions by the team that deepened their alliance with the family had to do with creating emotional safety, providing an experience for mother and daughter that it was possible to talk to one another in sessions without emotions escalating into a yelling match. They interrupted and shifted the direction of the conversation when Marilyn began cursing at her mother in sessions, which she had a strong penchant for doing. The team also interrupted and shifted the conversation when Shelly began to talk about Marilyn's behavior as being caused by demon possession. Early on they did not challenge this belief because it was deeply held. However, they established strong boundaries around bringing it up when they were doing family sessions, pointing out that it makes her daughter stop listening to her and only increases her cursing. The treatment team brought in something new to the family—consistent structure, along with a calm and nonjudgmental presence.

The next critical set of tasks in setting the stage for treatment involves softening the caregivers' negative, behavioral views of the child, and moving all family members towards a more compassionate, relational frame of the problems they want to resolve. This requires developing some awareness on the part of family members that they are a system. When families are in crisis or living in survival mode, they usually do not pause to reflect on how they mutually affect one another. Their perspective is narrowly focused on sorting people into allies or adversaries. Many of the techniques used in ESFT are designed to help family members become more aware of themselves as a system of mutual influence.

Two informal process-oriented methods used for this purpose involve therapists (1) calling attention to and highlighting an interaction occurring in the room that seems to be part of a recurring pattern and then (2) punctuating the link between this interaction and either the problem or its solution. Therapists do not have to interpret or explain what is happening. Instead, therapists help ensure that family members attune to what they see in the room at the present moment, and then reflect upon it. The meaning that any particular interaction may have is co-constructed through conversations between family members and the therapists. This is how the treatment team began to shift Shelly's negative view of her daughter, not so much by directly challenging the view she held, but by drawing her attention to the link between her behavior and that of her daughter, and vice versa.

Two structured methods for developing a more relational and contextual perspective are genograms and relational timelines. Although these methods sometimes are used as assessments, in ESFT they are used more as interventions with the goal of increasing awareness of the big picture of their family relationships. During the Genogram interview, as Shelly's history of sexual, emotional, and physical abuse was shared, the treatment team noticed Marilyn's sadness for her mother and they pointed it out to Shelly, with the goal of punctuating how much her daughter cares about her, and that when she lets herself be vulnerable, it pulls her daughter towards her. Shelly initially rejected the team's comments until Marilyn validated their observation. The final step in setting the stage for change is gaining the consent of everyone to a relational plan of action. This involves highlighting the team's observation of the family structure and the core negative interactional cycle, having family members reflect on and discuss the team's observations, and then refining this hypothesis until it resonates with everyone and becomes a shared narrative about the process.

After highlighting many times the way Marilyn would escalate and de-escalate based on whether she was emotionally available to her or not, Shelly began to soften her perspective. After much discussion, the team and the family eventually settled on the following working systemic hypothesis: "The more that Shelly is distant and unavailable to her daughter, and the more she tells her she is possessed, the more Marilyn is alone and defenseless, vulnerable to negative influences inside her head and outside the home." Another component of this problem definition involved Allen. "And Shelly, when Allen sees that you are unavailable to Marilyn, he believes he needs to parent her . . . leaving him with the awful decision of whether to attend school or stay home and take care of you and Marilyn." This resonated with Shelly and it created a clear role for her in the change process. This frame also validated Marilyn and Allen's experience and validated their desire to have their mother step more fully into a parenting role.

Applying ESFT: Working the Four Cornerstones

Once everyone has signed onto a clear, systemic, psychologically informed definition of the problem, ESFT therapists collaboratively develop a plan with the family that is organized around the four cornerstones of treatment. Therapists then devote their focus to supporting family members in taking the action steps to which they have committed. It is at this point that the sixth core mechanism of change is most prominent.

In ESFT, all four cornerstones are worked on simultaneously, meeting with the family as a whole, as well as with different subsystems, depending on the action step being addressed. In this case, the team occasionally met with each family member alone, initially to join and learn more about them, then to prepare them for focused conversations in sessions involving mother-daughter, mother-son, coparent, and the family as a whole. Regardless of the specific content the family may bring up in sessions, therapists attend to opportunities within each of the four treatment domains for family members to use their strengths and resources to take the actions they have agreed to in the plan.

Strengthening the Caregivers' Emotional Support of the Child

The focus of the work in this arena is the caregiver-child relationship, helping it to become a resource for the child, particularly in the child's efforts to self-calm and regulate behavior. Here, therapists focus on both the caregivers' emotional availability to the child and the child's receptivity to the caregivers when they are trying to support them. Outcomes include: (1) caregivers are showing more curiosity, empathy, and acceptance of the child, (2) caregivers are more often seeing their children's misbehavior as a sign of potential distress, not an effort to defy or irritate them, and (3) children are learning to be less provocative when initially met with a disappointing parental response. To achieve these outcomes, therapists help both caregivers and their children learn to pause when they are agitated and then to regulate themselves before responding. The best evidence that children are beginning to see their parents as a real source of emotional support is when they begin going to them for comforting and problem solving. This new relationship pattern greatly reduces the child's risk for a wide range of negative outcomes because caregivers are working to soothe and de-escalate their children.

In the treatment of Marilyn's family, the initial step was to cultivate a less hostile, rejecting relationship between mother and daughter. The therapists saw this as a longer-term goal, not possible at this juncture. Just getting this mother and daughter into the same room together and keeping them there for more than 10 minutes took the entire first 30 days of treatment. The therapists were patient because they understood that Marilyn was as much of a trigger for Shelly's overwhelming anxiety and sense of danger as Shelly was for Marilyn. The team acted as an accepting, calm emotional anchor for Shelly and Marilyn, setting their first action step small—just being in the same room together with the team while talking about non-emotionally charged topics for 20 minutes.

Once Shelly and Marilyn achieved this goal, the team and family set another action step—successfully talking about one sensitive, emotionally upsetting topic without either of them storming out of the room or yelling. In ESFT, all conversations in treatment sessions are seen as opportunities to help families expand their tolerable range of emotional intensity, to communicate past the point at which they usually stop talking, and to resist customary negative coping patterns such as avoidance and attack. When therapists set up and facilitate these conversations between family members with this intent, they are using a technique known as *enactments*. The majority of conjoint family sessions in ESFT involve repeated enactments. It is this vehicle that creates the condition for family members to practice new, more functional patterns of relating.

An example of how this works can be seen in the following excerpt from one such conversation between Marilyn and Shelly, which was triggered by Marilyn bringing up how she does not feel her mother knows much about her. Shelly reacted to the introduction of this topic by distancing from Marilyn and making an attempt to shut down the conversation. The therapists intervened quickly to remind the family of the negative interactional cycle that they have both agreed they want to change, while refocusing them on the topic at hand. You will note the therapists do no coaching or teaching in this exchange, but instead facilitate and remind them of previous successes. The goal is to successfully complete an emotionally charged conversation because it is this repeated experience that is assumed to build competency and more stable relationships.

SHELLY (softly, looking away from her daughter): *I've lived on this earth a lot longer than you and I have experienced a lot of things . . .* (Marilyn interrupts)

MARILYN (sharply, but with incredulous laughter): *And I've experienced a lot of things too, woman. You have no fucking idea!*

Shelly begins to shut down, looking like she was about to retreat to her bedroom.

THERAPIST (calmly, but firmly): *This is what we talked about last time, Shelly, when the exact same thing happened. And I know how much you hate the cursing. But remember how you discovered that you can easily trigger Marilyn when it sounds like you are dismissing or judging her. Is it possible that is what is happening right now?*

MARILYN (more calmly): *I don't like it when you make assumptions about me, Mom. You make assumptions about me and then you close your ears and don't listen to anything I might try to tell you. It gets me fuming.*

Shelly begins shaking her head and then puts her head in her hands looking down, which escalates Marilyn again, who begins cursing and getting loud, criticizing her mother's religious beliefs. The therapist interrupts Marilyn by beginning to talk directly to Shelly.

THERAPIST (calmly, with curiosity): *What's happening for you, Shelly, when she's screaming? I'm betting it's pretty hard to listen, even if it is because she's hurt.*

Shelly feels the therapist's support but comes back vigorously defending her religious beliefs, further escalating Marilyn, and requiring the therapist to interpret and remind Shelly of her successes in other sessions avoiding the current negative cycle.

THERAPIST (softly with persistence, while Shelly continues to pontificate about religion): *Shelly . . . Shelly . . . Shelly . . . (Shelly pauses and looks at the therapist.) What do you think Marilyn wants from you at this moment? You did an excellent job last week when the exact same thing happened. A subject came up, one you didn't want to talk about, and you started to shut down, Marilyn was insistent on pursuing the issue. But then you were able to shift and become softer with her and you had a very productive conversation, a different experience for both of you. Try to give her what she needs at this moment so you guys can go there again. I know you know what that is . . . she just wants you to listen to what she thinks, you don't have to agree with it.*

SHELLY (looking directly at Marilyn, voice a little stronger, more present): *OK, we can talk about your beliefs, if that's what you think is important. I want to know, just don't curse.*

Although the therapists needed to interrupt and redirect many times when Marilyn and Shelly would become reactive, they maintained their role as *keepers of the conversation*, remaining neutral with respect to content. Marilyn tearfully explained to her mother the pain caused by her accusations that she is demon possessed and her threats to take her to an exorcist. Shelly opened herself up enough to hear Marilyn describing how hard she tries to be a good daughter and believes in God just as much as her mother, but needs her help. The conversation became pivotal in softening the mother-daughter relationship. In the eight months this family was in treatment, over 25 similarly intense conversations about many different emotionally laden topics were facilitated by the therapists, including Marilyn's relationship with her father and her brother, her drug use, a molestation that had occurred as a preschooler, and the impact of Shelly's mental health on her.

Equally important were the sessions with Shelly and Allen. Although he was not the target of as much hostility and rejection, he received little emotional support from his mother. Given his protective role with Shelly, Allen needed much more support and reassurance from the therapists than Marilyn to talk about his distress and needs with Shelly. As long as Shelly maintained her belief that Allen was the "good child," she was unlikely to become more curious about his suffering, which was significant.

Marilyn's mother, Shelly, has PTSD but has never sought counseling of any kind. It is this history that normally accounts for caregivers in fragile families to present with depression, emotional reactivity, and many times, lack of empathy for their children. It did not occur to Shelly that the way she felt might be a treatable mental illness because she had felt this way her entire life—it was normal. Further into treatment, once Marilyn and the family had stabilized, the team provided Shelly with psychoeducation about the link between her experiences, trauma, and her current reactions to Marilyn and Allen. By the end of family treatment, they were able to evoke more concern for her own emotional health and get her linked to an outpatient therapist. This is an important part of intervening in this treatment domain when it operates as a barrier to a caregiver providing emotional support to his or her children.

Strengthen the Co-Caregiver Alliance

The focus of the work in this arena is to create support for stable caregiving within the family and reduce the leaking of parental conflict and negativity across generational lines. ESFT therapists have four general goals when addressing this treatment domain, which include: (1) ensure all family members involved in caregiving are engaged in the treatment, (2) ensure each caregiver is interacting with the children so they have real data to draw upon when discussing them, (3) encourage the sharing of all information with one another that is relevant to daily parenting, and (4) work to help caregivers set boundaries, containing their conflicts to the caregiving subsystem and not involving the children in them.

In Marilyn's family, the first goal was accomplished early in the treatment. The team next addressed the distance between Larry and his children. The emotional distance between Shelly and Larry was similar to that between Larry and each of his children. The treatment team encouraged Larry to check in more frequently with his children, and they encouraged his children to reach out more to him. When one caregiver has little involvement with the children, this places even more stress on the caregiver who is left to raise the children, which can be overwhelming. As Larry and the children had more contact, Shelly relaxed a little and felt less alone. Shelly became more willing to meet with Larry (via phone) and the treatment team.

The next step in strengthening the co-caregiving relationship was to have conjoint sessions with Shelly and Larry, where the treatment team directly addressed the negative patterns they fall into when interacting about the children. When they were living together, Shelly was highly reactive, negatively interpreting all of Larry's comments about their messy house and the amount of time she spent in bed. She would then shut down and stop speaking to him for weeks at a time. Even though it has been seven years since they have lived together, they were each still easily triggered into the old pattern. The treatment team urged Shelly to work through her frustration with Larry when he said something offensive and to refrain from shutting down. They worked with Larry to help him have more empathy for Shelly and to be less critical. Before treatment ended and after, Shelly was reaching out to Larry more frequently for support with Marilyn and had begun to share more information with him.

Strengthen the Caregivers' Leadership Role in the Family

The focus of treatment in this domain is to build more consistent, predictable structure in the home for everyone, particularly the children. Therapists know they have been successful in strengthening the caregivers' leadership or executive role in the home when caregivers have established a few reasonable daily routines and household rules, monitor follow-through with them, and provide reasonable consequences when necessary. The caregivers' consistency in maintaining such a structure is the key outcome because this equates with stability. To accomplish this, therapists need to help caregivers shift their mindsets from reactive, mood-based parenting to one that is more intentional and grounded in what their children need. Basic parenting education is another important component of intervention in this treatment domain.

The treatment team saw, as a strength, that Shelly was able to establish routines for herself, although they all revolved around church and religious practices. There was no structure for managing the household or the children. When the treatment team initially came to the home, they were overwhelmed by the amount of trash, dirty dishes, clutter, and so forth around the house. There were no regular mealtimes or bedtimes. The house itself was in such disrepair that the team had safety concerns. Given the chaos in the home and real safety issues, the treatment team decided that helping Shelly to make a commitment to reclaiming the house for her family was a priority. This meant making some repairs and evicting two boarders renting the living room space. Although it took a while for Shelly to build the courage, she eventually evicted the renters, which became an important victory for her and her children. The treatment team helped Shelly build on this success and referred to it often as they discussed small ways she could bring more leadership to the home. The other major leadership role she followed through on was monitoring Marilyn's medication. This was an essential component of Marilyn's recovery because Marilyn often forgot and this would have a direct effect on her daily functioning.

The treatment team had frank talks with Shelly about how much Marilyn required structure to function. This was a challenge to Shelly's belief that Marilyn should be self-sufficient. The team used Marilyn's timeline, from age 8 to 17, to show how Marilyn's functioning in school and at home was directly related to the availability of another adult in overseeing her day-to-day activities. For example, she did best in the classroom when she had wrap-around services and she did better in the home when her father was still present or when Shelly was functioning better as a parent. They also pointed out how Marilyn has deteriorated when Shelly was depressed and not functioning in a caregiving role.

The team made a clear link between consistent structure, ongoing parental attention and nurturing, and Marilyn's ability to make a full recovery from mental illness. Although Shelly was making significant changes, the team also was aware there was a possibility her own recovery from severe mental illness may not proceed quickly enough for her to parent at the level Marilyn would require at this moment in time. Marilyn remained vulnerable, having had a significant psychotic break only six months earlier. As part of preparing for discharge and thinking about aftercare, the team brought this dilemma up with Shelly.

The therapists' objective was to empower Shelly to make a responsible decision about whether Marilyn should live in a therapeutic foster home. They reviewed how she would know when this became necessary and encouraged it to be a collaborative decision made with Marilyn. The team made it clear that not having a fully functioning parent in the home was not an option for Marilyn. Previously, Shelly had blocked all such discussions. This time, she was able to separate her guilt and fear about losing control from listening to Marilyn's needs. This was pivotal for Marilyn, who now knew that she could request to leave her mother's home if necessary without feeling tremendous fear that her mother would never speak to her again.

Build Support for the Caregivers and the Child in the Extended Family and Community

The fourth cornerstone of ESFT treatment is often the most challenging because the family may be cut off or alienated from many relationships with extended family, and they may distrust their neighbors and organized community organizations. Yet, this component of the treatment is critical for sustaining changes the family has made during a course of treatment. The goals are specific when working in this arena. One, the caregivers are working toward establishing at least one adult relationship outside the nuclear family who supports their efforts to be a better parent. Two, the child is developing a relationship with another adult outside the nuclear family, whether in the extended family, school, or community, who the child trusts to provide guidance and support when his or her parents are not available. Belonging to a group of prosocial peers is a protective factor for adolescents in fragile families.

One of the major community-based interventions in the treatment of Marilyn's family involved Shelly's pastor and members of her church. Midway into their eight months with the family, the team asked Shelly for permission to speak with her pastor and invite him to a session. He came along with a deacon. The team told them that they respected how Shelly's faith was an important asset for the family. At the same time, they spoke frankly about how fragile Marilyn's mental health is and how much she needs her mother to believe in her ability to recover. They told the pastor and the deacon that talk of demon possession pushes her more into mental illness and hopelessness. The pastor and deacon were receptive to the team and seemed appreciative to have a coherent explanation about what was going on with Marilyn in the context of her family. They did not know Marilyn and had only heard frightening stories from Shelly. The pastor and deacon made an agreement with Shelly that they would support her relationship with her daughter by reminding her to have faith, and invited her to call them for support when she feels like giving up and thinking about demons.

Clinical Outcomes

Fragile families can become less fragile and more functional with targeted eco-systemic interventions. At the end of eight months of intensive, in-home family-based treatment using ESFT, Marilyn's mental health was more stable, there were no safety concerns, and she had returned to school. This was a good child-focused outcome given the state she was in when treatment began. ESFT therapists would not be satisfied with this outcome alone, however, if they could not also say with confidence that the family was more stable and functional as a result of the treatment. ESFT therapists ask themselves, can the changes we see in this child be supported and sustained by her environment? One of the main points of this chapter was to demonstrate that children with emotional problems who live in fragile families are unlikely to remain success stories when their families do not become more stable and supportive. When families are not involved in treatment and do not change, children with SED often become trapped in a cycle of failure and under-functioning, regardless of momentary successes in the various treatments they are likely to receive over their life course.

Here, Marilyn stands a reasonably good chance of remaining stable and returning to a more positive developmental pathway because there were significant changes in the way her family organizes their relationships. For example, Larry, her father, continued to stay involved by phone with Marilyn and Allen. This new relationship pattern continued without the therapists because they each got something important out of their interactions with one another, and Shelly supported it. Although Marilyn never felt she could turn to her mother for deep emotional support, they developed a more positive relationship. Shelly's hostility subsided. She stopped saying her daughter was possessed, because she no longer thought this. As Shelly developed more understanding of how her history of trauma and PTSD had compromised her ability to be the person she wanted, she became more empathic and open to getting to know her daughter.

About three months after the treatment ended, Marilyn felt her mental health slipping again as she confronted old challenges of dealing with unkind peers and trying to catch up on academic work she fell behind on while out of school. This time Shelly noticed Marilyn's distress, but acknowledged she was not yet able to provide what she needed to get through it. Together, Shelly, in collaboration with Larry and Marilyn, decided that short-term placement in a therapeutic foster home would be beneficial, which they were able to arrange. Marilyn remained in communication with her parents throughout her six months there.

Marilyn still suffers from bipolar illness, and must remain vigilant about managing it, but she no longer feels unstable and does not see herself as hopelessly and chronically mentally ill like before. Marilyn has had no further inpatient hospitalizations as of the last follow-up one-year post-treatment. A successful treatment does not necessarily mean everything is working well. Post-treatment, Marilyn still faces many day-to-day stressors and there remains much pain about her family life, but she is slowly reentering the world of peers and work. Unlike many of her peers with similar conditions living in fragile families, Marilyn has not become one of the statistics of failure among children with SED mentioned earlier in the chapter, nor has Allen.

References

Davis, M., & Vander Stoep, A. (1997). The transition to adulthood for youth who have serious emotional disturbance: Developmental transition and young adult outcomes. *The Journal of Mental Health Administration, 24*(2), 400–427.

Jones, C. W. (2010). *Setting the stage for change: In-home, family based treatment.* Bala Cynwyd, PA: Center for Family Based Training.

Jones, C. W., & Lindblad-Goldberg, M. (2002). Eco-systemic structural family therapy. In F. Kaslow (Series Ed.) & R. Massey & S. Massey (Vol. Eds.), *Comprehensive handbook of psychotherapy: Vol. 3: Interpersonal, humanistic, and existential models* (pp. 3–33). New York: John Wiley & Sons.

Lehr, C. A., Johnson, D. R., Bremer, C. D., Cosio, A., & Thompson, M. (2004, May). *Essential tools: Increasing rates of school completion: Moving from policy and research to practice: A manual for policymakers, administrators, and educators.* Retrieved from: http://www.ncset.org/publications/essentialtools/dropout/default.asp

Lindblad-Goldberg, M., Dore, M., & Stern, L. (1998). *Creating competence from chaos: A comprehensive guide to home-based services.* New York, NY: W. W. Norton & Company, Inc.

Minuchin, S. (1974). *Families and family therapy.* Cambridge, MA: Harvard University Press.

Reimer, M., & Smink, J. (2005). *Information about the school dropout issue: Selected facts and statistics.* Clemson, SC: National Dropout Prevention Center.

Sprenkle, D. H., & Blow, A. J. (2004). Common factors and our sacred models. *Journal of Marital and Family Therapy, 30*(2), 113–129. doi: 10.1011/j.1752-0606.2004.tb01228.x

5

ADDICTION AND FAMILIES

Case Study

Sara Smock Jordan

Henry grew up in Alabama, the youngest of five children. From an early age he watched his father get drunk and beat up on his mother. As he grew older, Henry began to try to protect his mother from the violence. At the age of 12, Henry started to drink his father's moonshine as a way to cope with the hurt and abuse he experienced. Despite his aversion to the effects of booze, Henry developed a love/hate relationship with alcohol. He would try to drink only enough to "dull the pain" but occasionally would get drunk and pass out. Over the years Henry's tolerance grew and he would "unintentionally" drink too much. This pattern escalated until he met his true love, Veronica. Henry said it was "love at first sight." Henry made a promise to himself that he would never be like his father and immediately cut down on his drinking. After only a few months of dating, Veronica became pregnant with their first son, Mykuhl. Even though Henry was able to "control drink," he was now more determined to overcome his battle with alcohol and began to totally abstain from alcohol while Veronica was pregnant. He was successful for weeks at a time but would end up binge drinking. Henry tried AA a few times but over the years found that its approach of abstinence was too rigid. After many years of trying to abstain from alcohol, Henry would tell people, "Not drinking simply doesn't work for me." Nevertheless, Henry's drinking continued to escalate. Veronica continued to stay in their tumultuous relationship, and when Mykuhl was 3 years old, Veronica unexpectedly got pregnant with their daughter Tiffany. Veronica was devastated when she found out that she was pregnant again. She was unhappy and wanted out of the relationship. Soon after Tiffany was born, Veronica finally left Henry and moved in with her sister, Loretta, to raise her children in a sober household. Henry has had little contact with Veronica and the kids over the last three years.

Recently Henry had a health scare and realized that at the age of 47 he was willing to do "whatever it takes" to reestablish a relationship with his children, now 6 (Mykuhl) and 3 (Tiffany) years of age. In an effort to prove to his children that he is serious about controlling his drinking this time, Henry has cut his drinking down to four beers a day. He finds that if he can "take the edge off" of his stress and anxiety with a few beers he is a "much better person to be around." Henry is pleased with his efforts to "control drink," because he has gone four months without getting drunk. This is the longest period of time he has gone without passing out from drinking. He is finally ready to make contact with his children and hopes that they learn to accept him for who he is. His siblings all currently drink heavily, so Henry does not feel like they can be supportive in his journey to control his drinking. Henry has a few friends in his neighborhood, but they don't really see a problem with drinking and smoking pot around their children, so he cannot rely on them for support. He has thought about trying AA again but fears their "abstinence only" message will only set him up for a binge drinking cycle. After struggling to keep a job over the years, Henry has finally been able to hold down his position at a local tortilla factory. While he doesn't have any close friends at work, there are a few people with whom he enjoys taking smoke breaks during the day.

Veronica has been in a bad place for several months now. She recently moved in with her boyfriend, Hank, who also struggles with binge drinking behaviors. Over the past few months, Veronica has engaged in heavy drinking with Hank around the children. Last week Veronica found out that she is pregnant with Hank's baby. She is very concerned because she is having trouble "putting the bottle down," so to speak. Her sister Loretta used to be supportive but has not talked to Veronica since she moved in with Hank. Veronica's other family members are in and out of jail for drug possession. Veronica has not worked in years because she cannot find affordable child care for Tiffany. She relies on food stamps and government aid to feed her children and pay her bills.

A few days ago Henry started calling Veronica to try and see Mykuhl and Tiffany. Veronica has dreaded receiving phone calls from Henry because she is under too much stress right now to communicate with him. Veronica wants Tiffany and Mykuhl to know their father but does not know what to do. Veronica has a neighbor who told her about a local community agency that offers free family therapy. In her desperation to "get her life back together," Veronica sets up an appointment to meet with a therapist.

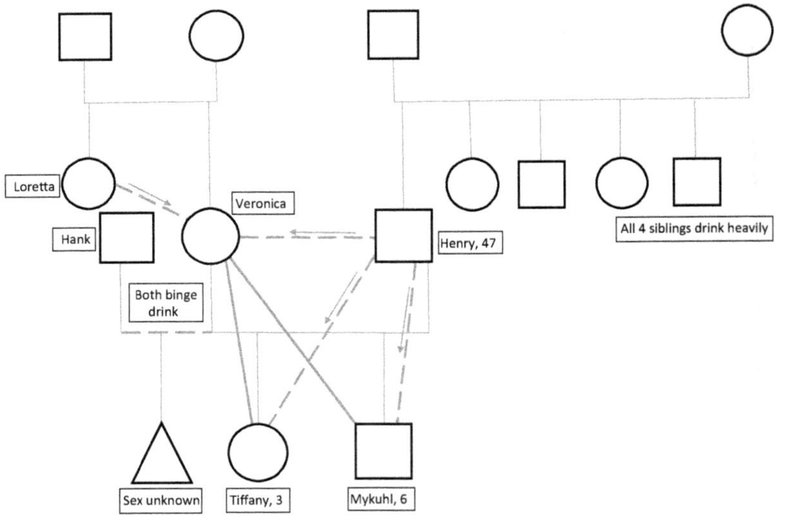

Figure 5.1 Addiction and Families Genogram: Veronica and Henry

A Research Perspective on Substance Abuse in Families

Karen Milligan, Tamara Meixner, and Amelia Usher

Substance use, including consumption of alcohol and illicit substances, is common and a highly visible part of North American popular culture. National survey data suggests 87% of adults have consumed alcohol within their lifetime, 55% of them within the past month (SAMHSA, 2013). Similarly, over half of adults report illicit substance use in their lifetime, with cannabis use being most common, followed by nonmedical use of psychotherapeutics and opiates (SAMHSA, 2013). For some, use evolves into problematic patterns characterized by a cluster of behavioral and physical symptoms relating to withdrawal, tolerance, and cravings. These symptoms significantly impact on daily functioning in multiple domains including home, school, and/or work (APA, 2013). Problematic patterns of use are most common for alcohol, with current prevalence rates for alcohol use disorders (AUD) being 13.9% for the past 12 months and 29.1% for the past year, equivalent to 32,648,000 and 68.5 million individuals, respectively (Grant et al., 2015). Although less common, substance use disorders (SUD) specific to illicit substances impact 8.2% of the population, or approximately 21.6 million people aged 12 and over (SAMHSA, 2013; Stinson et al., 2005). The cost of alcohol and illicit drug abuse to society exceeds $400 billion when health care, work productivity, and crime are considered (National Institute on Drug Abuse, 2016).

Although these statistics pertain to individuals, the prevalence of those affected by substance abuse (hereafter used to refer to both alcohol and illicit substances) increases significantly when one considers its impact on the entire family system. Family members carry considerable burden in supporting individuals with substance abuse issues and often provide unacknowledged health and social support. However, there is considerable variability. Research suggests that substance abuse has important consequences for the couple relationship and partner well-being, parenting, child outcomes, and the lifestyle and ability of families to secure essential social determinants of health (e.g., housing, food, employment, social support; Galea & Vlahov, 2002). Further, there is substantial evidence that supports an intergenerational transmission perspective of substance use (e.g., Mares, Aschoff-Lichtwarck, & Engels, 2013).

This chapter focuses on the family unit as a context for understanding the development, maintenance, and intergenerational transmission of substance abuse, with the goal of informing treatment for these families. Although the primary focus of the chapter is on the family system, putative factors involved in the development and maintenance of substance use are numerous and varied, with the most meaningful conceptualizations of the disorder's progression arising from an integration of interrelated individual (e.g., emotional, biological), interpersonal (e.g., family), and contextual (e.g., poverty) factors. As seen in the case study, Henry was exposed to multiple factors that increased his substance abuse risk. These factors included genetic risk given his father's alcohol abuse and early emotional risk given his experience of abuse by his father and witnessing the abuse of his mother. Henry began to use alcohol as a means of coping with strong negative emotions, as had been modeled by his father. The alcohol working to "take the edge off" negatively reinforced Henry's substance abuse. This means of coping was associated with interpersonal risks such as relationship challenges and contextual risks (e.g., poverty, unemployment) that could be considered secondary to substance abuse. Further, Veronica also drank alcohol as a means of coping with stress, with biological risks now heightened due to her pregnancy and the potential impact for her child.

This type of family picture is not uncommon due to the myriad factors that interact to place individuals at risk for substance abuse and that serve to maintain these behaviors over the long term. This chapter addresses some of the broad factors that place individuals at risk from an individual and a contextual level in order to provide a comprehensive picture of the dynamic and complex array of variables at play in families affected by substance abuse. The dominant theories of substance use are then discussed and applied to explore family risk in the context of substance abuse. We revisit Henry and Veronica throughout the chapter to better understand how these factors may have influenced their trajectory.

Understanding Substance Abuse From an Individual Perspective

As we can see from Henry and Veronica, issues such as gender, concurrent mental health, and motivational factors related to emotion regulation have influenced their substance abuse, with sequela influencing the functioning of the entire family. These select individual factors are discussed below, with the understanding that a comprehensive formulation might also include additional factors not discussed in this chapter, including genetics and other biological factors such as neurotransmitters and reward systems and psychological factors, including cognitions such as expectancy effects.

Gender: A Narrowing Divide

Historically, scholars and clinicians considered the occurrence of alcohol and substance abuse to be primarily among men, and investigated, understood, and treated almost exclusively as such (Finkelstein, 1994; Greenfield, 2002). According to Kandall (2010), however, the history of women and substance use/abuse in America dates back 150 years. Although denial of this rendered the epidemiological landscape challenging to decipher, several key themes have endured: neglect for the range and degree of drug use among females; a general lack of treatment services, in particular those that acknowledge women's unique needs; and pervasive societal attitudes of "ostracism, vilification, and prosecution" related to women's unique role of bearing and rearing children (Finkelstein, 1994; Kandall, 2010, p. 125). This latter point has been a central impetus for much societal reproach (e.g., they are solely to blame for their situation, and are negligent and/or incapable of successful mothering; Finkelstein, 1994; Reid, Greaves, & Poole, 2008). These beliefs, in concert with growing understanding and evidence of the short- and long-term impacts of prenatal exposure to alcohol and drugs, child neglect attributable to maternal substance use, and associated monetary costs have contributed to the conceptualization of female substance use and abuse as a "moral failing," which in turn has fostered concealment of substance use issues (Kandall, 2010). As a result, the development of effective substance use treatments for women has been slow relative to men.

Though progress has been realized over the past few decades, women continue to face barriers that are undoubtedly rooted in the historical context of their substance use. When asked about this, women describe feeling resistant to subjecting themselves to the community- and at times provider-based stigma and scrutiny that accompanies being a woman seeking help for addiction (Howell & Chasnoff, 1999). Further, they express two main pregnancy- or child-oriented concerns: (1) fear of being reported to child protection services and/or losing custody of their child and (2) frustration at the lack of resources specifically geared toward pregnancy and parenting, including direct and ancillary services such as child care or transportation (Howell & Chasnoff, 1999; Poole & Greaves, 2009). Existing barriers and slowed program development continue to hinder our ability to sufficiently address existing needs.

While rates of substance use and abuse in North America remain elevated among men relative to women (SAMHSA, 2013), evidence has accumulated over the past three decades to suggest that this gender gap is converging (e.g., Holdcraft & Iacono, 2002; Keyes, Grant, & Hasin, 2008). Studies comparing general and problematic alcohol and substance use among male and female populations report prevalence patterns in which decreased gender-related disparities are observed among younger age cohorts compared to their older counterparts (e.g., Poole & Dell, 2005; SAMHSA, 2013). This diminishing inequity appears to be most prevalent among individuals aged 12–17, where gender-specific differences increasingly are negligible (e.g., SAMHSA, 2013). One might question whether these patterns of convergence are attributable to a true narrowing of disparity in use between the sexes or if this can be better explained by an increased recognition of use among girls and women. While it is difficult to discern the origin with exactness, results from the 2013 National Survey on Drug Use and Health (SAMHSA, 2013) suggest that trends may differ according to age, gender, and drug type. For example, while rates of illicit drug use in 2012 among persons aged 12 to 17 years was comparable among males (9.6%) relative to females (9.5%), females showed a decrease in use in 2013 (8.0%) relative to males (9.6%), who remained stable. With respect to alcohol use, however, rates among males and females were comparable (11.2% and 11.9%) in 2013. Relative to those aged 12 or 18 years and older, where males show higher rates of substance dependence or abuse than females (10.8% versus 5.8% and 11.4% versus 5.8%), rates are nearly equivalent in the 12 to 17 age group (5.3% versus 5.2%). Among youths aged 12–17, females exceed males in the nonmedical use of all psychotherapeutic medication, including stimulants, tranquilizers, sedatives, and pain relievers, and in their likelihood to exhibit dependence (Cotto et al., 2010). Interestingly, however, rates of use may not necessarily map onto prevalence of abuse and/or dependence. For instance, Cotto et al. (2010) reported that although males aged 18 to 25 reported greater overall use of psychotherapeutic drugs, females were more likely to exhibit dependence. Results such as these point to the importance of understanding how additional factors contribute to the development of abuse.

Gender-focused epidemiological research also suggests that males and females are differentially motivated to use and abuse substances (e.g., Teter, McCabe, LaGrange, Cranford, & Boyd, 2006), exhibit distinct patterns of use and abuse (e.g., Cotto et al., 2010), and experience physical (Brady & Randall, 1999; Cormier, Dell, & Poole, 2004; Greenfield, 2002), mental (Rush et al., 2008; Zilberman, Tavares, Blume, & el-Guebaly, 2003), and interpersonal (Brady & Randall, 1999; Kauffman, Silver, & Poulin, 1997) consequences that differ both qualitatively and quantitatively. Biologically, women exhibit a more rapid progression to alcohol and opioid dependence and greater vulnerability to health consequences, including circulatory disorders, cirrhosis of the liver, hypertension, and premature death than their male counterparts (e.g., Brady & Randall, 1999; Cormier et al., 2004; Greenfield, 2002). Additionally, about 66% of women experience concurrent mental health disorders that further complicate abuse and treatment. One important aspect of mental health is the experience of trauma. Although both men and women with substance abuse report higher rates of trauma than those without, the majority of women in treatment for substance abuse report a history of interpersonal trauma, including sexual, physical, or emotional abuse, with rates estimated at approximately 85% (Cormier et al., 2004). Referring back to the case study, both Henry and Veronica presented with a trauma history. For Henry, this began in early life with abuse by his father as well as witnessing violence against his mother. For Veronica, her experience of abuse was within the context of intimate relationships, with a continued cycle of involvement in abusive relationships. Henry and Veronica used substances to cope with the pain and the emotional distress of the abuse they experienced. A trauma history, when coupled with symptoms of post-traumatic stress disorder and complex trauma, can complicate substance abuse treatment (Cottler, Nishith, & Compton, 2001) and lead to poorer treatment outcomes (Zweben, Clark, & Smith, 1994). This is due, in part, to magnified social, physical, and mental health challenges within the context of the comorbid condition (Brady, Dansky, Sonne, & Saladin, 1998) discussed further in the next section.

Concurrent Mental Health Disorders

Considerable evidence has amassed over the past 20 years documenting the co-occurrence of substance abuse and mental health disorders. Among alcohol-dependent men and women, research suggests comorbidity rates of 78% and 86%, respectively (Brady & Sinha, 2005). Rates of concurrent disorders appear to be elevated among individuals using illicit drugs as compared to alcohol, with rates doubling for those using both alcohol and illicit substances (Kandel, Huang, & Davies, 2001). Although this research is correlational, the relationship between substance use and mental health issues appears to be bidirectional. On the one hand, mental health disorders pose risk for subsequent substance use, abuse, and dependence. In their prospective examination of the relation between specific mental health disorders and risk for substance use, abuse, and dependence 10 years later in a nationally representative sample of over 5000 individuals, Swendsen et al. (2010) found that disruptive behavior disorders and previous substance abuse were most commonly associated with increased risk from use to abuse and abuse to dependence. Anxiety and mood disorders (particularly bipolar disorder) increased risk for movement from substance abuse to dependence. This suggests that mental health disorders both increase the risk for a substance use disorder and are associated with increased severity of disorder. Chronic alcohol and drug use is associated with brain-based changes that may increase emotional distress and produce secondary symptoms of mental health disorders, which in turn may also serve to perpetuate or worsen disordered patterns of substance use (Brady & Sinha, 2005). The pattern of concurrent anxiety with substance abuse is apparent for Henry and appears to be a factor related to his use of alcohol to assist in the regulation of anxiety and stress.

Substance Use and Emotion Regulation

Substance use often is associated with regulation of distress and negative emotion (Brady & Sinha, 2005). Emotion regulation is “the extrinsic and intrinsic processes responsible for monitoring, evaluating, and modifying emotional reactions, especially their intensive and temporal features, to accomplish one's goals" (Thompson, 1994, pp. 27–28). Henry used alcohol as an external means of regulating his emotional reaction and decreasing the intensity of negative emotion (i.e., "dulling the pain") to the abuse in childhood. This pattern of regulating or coping with negative emotion was maintained well into adulthood as he faced new challenges with his relationship with his family and a health scare. The experience of alcohol being able to regulate emotions supports the development of positive beliefs or expectations about drinking on emotional outcomes, which in turn increases motivation for use and predicts disordered patterns of alcohol use (Sher, Grekin, & Williams, 2005).

With respect to the emotional impact of substance use, those who expect drinking will be associated with enhanced positive affect may be more likely to engage in this behavior than those who do not foresee positive gains (e.g., Earlywine, 1994). Similarly, one who views alcohol consumption as a coping strategy for negative affect might also have a stronger affinity for use (e.g., Sher et al., 2005). In the case, Henry was motivated to use because he believed that alcohol had the power to "take the edge off." When these negative emotions were reduced after he consumed alcohol, his drinking behavior was negatively reinforced.

Alcohol consumption as a means of regulating negative emotion is fueled by increased frequency and intensity of stress, including the presence of behavioral (e.g., sleep changes), cognitive (e.g., attention, memory), and physical (e.g., alcohol craving, appetite) symptoms, as well as decreased functioning of the neurochemical response systems responsible for adapting to stress. This includes changes in brain reward and motivation pathways that increase cravings for alcohol in the context of stress, as well as changes in the hypothalamic pituitary adrenal axis (involved in the body's adaptation to stress) and autonomous components of stress regulation. This pattern is particularly prevalent in the early abstinence period, which may result in increased risk of relapse (Sinha, 2012). This certainly was the case for Henry, who found that he relapsed repeatedly after being involved in Alcoholics Anonymous, which uses an abstinence approach to treatment.

Understanding Substance Abuse From a Social Contextual Perspective

Social epidemiology, in particular, is concerned with documenting how the distribution of substance-related behaviors within the population is shaped by social factors (Galea, Nandi, & Vlahov, 2004). In the case of Henry and Veronica, challenges with poverty, unemployment, and family and friends using substances all influenced their substance abuse. These factors are consistent with some of the social epidemiological factors shown to be important. Galea et al. (2004), in their review of studies examining social factors and drug use, found that characteristics of one's social network, particularly drug use in the social network, play an important role in the initiation of both alcohol and illicit substance use. Two prospective cohort studies carried out in Germany (von Sydow, Lieb, Pfister, Hofler, & Wittchen, 2002) and the United States (Miller & Miller, 1997) found that peer drug use was associated with cannabis use. Both studies concluded that measures of familial disadvantage (e.g., low socioeconomic status) were associated with use. Neighborhood disadvantage and availability of drugs more generally have been associated with the initiation of drug use, and this is particularly true with respect to illicit drugs (Kadushin, Reber, Saxe, & Livert, 1998).

An interesting recent contextual factor is the legalization of recreational marijuana in four states and medical marijuana in 23 states. A recent review by Guttmannova et al. (2016) suggests that legalization (which increases availability and access) is associated with increased medical and recreational use. Interestingly, it was further suggested that increased access might result in substance substitution. For example, in a sample of 238 students in Washington, Mason, Hanson, Fleming, Ringle, and Haggerty (2015) compared rates of use between a cohort of grade 9 students when use was legal and grade 9 students when use was not legal. They found that legalization resulted in students being more likely to use marijuana than alcohol. These results highlight the impact that policies and laws can have on patterns of use and rates of substance abuse. This brief overview suggests these factors exert influence at all points from use to abuse to recovery and need to be considered in the conceptualization of families affected by substance abuse.

Theories of Families of Substance Abuse

From a family perspective, there is no single theory used in the extant literature that can adequately explain or account for how substance abuse progressively impacts families. However, three prominent theories provide some level of explanatory guidance: the family disease model, family systems theory, and stress and coping models (see Table 5.1 for summary). These theoretical perspectives provide explanatory insight into the progression and impact of substance use on the family and are distinguished from therapy models discussed later in this chapter.

Table 5.1 Comparison of Theoretical Models of Families of Substance Abuse

Assumptions	*Family Disease*	*Family Systems*	*Stress and Coping*
Source of family dysfunction	Disease of addiction	Family imbalance	Stress
Impact on family members	Codependence Defense mechanisms (e.g., denial, minimization)	Disrupted family roles Distorted boundaries Low family cohesion Poor parenting practices	Maladaptive coping strategies Poor physical and mental health

The family disease model views substance abuse as a disease. This disease is thought to affect all members of the family (O'Farrell & Fals-Stewart, 1999), with members displaying defense mechanisms (e.g., denial, minimization; Werner, Joffe, & Graham, 1999) and codependence (e.g., excessive caretaking and rescuing behaviors) that can contribute to the perpetuation of substance abuse. The family systems approach also views substance use as affecting all members of the family, but conceptualizes substance use differently. Rather than seeing substance abuse as a disorder, it is seen as one of a number of personal dysfunctions that can cause imbalance within the family system (Bowen, 1974). This theory proposes that family members function as an integrated system that is continuously adjusting to and compensating for changes within the family, and assumes a "reciprocal relationship between the family's functioning and the substance abuse" (Smock, Froerer, & Blakeslee, 2011, p. 184). From a family systems perspective, family members seek to adapt addiction-related interactions, such that homeostasis is maintained. For example, substance use may exert a stabilizing function within a family through serving to divert attention away from underlying conflicts. This could, for instance, take the form of an adolescent with substance abuse issues, who, within the context of marital problems, protects the alliance between mother and father by displacing conflict and pain onto him or herself (Klagsbrun & Davis, 1977). Disrupted family roles, distorted boundaries, role reversal, low levels of family cohesion, and poor parenting practices are key aspects of this model (O'Farrell & Fals-Stewart, 1999).

Finally, stress and coping models also assume an impact of substance abuse on all family members but place the emphasis on the experience of stress by individual family members and their ability to cope rather than on substance abuse or homeostasis. Within this model, stress is thought to promote the intensification of substance abuse, resulting in negative physical and mental health outcomes for the individual and family (Orford, Copello, Velleman, & Templeton, 2010a). Social support is considered a key factor in supporting family members given its ability to enhance adaptation and positive coping with stress. A 2010 review of qualitative research conducted with family members affected by substance abuse concluded that positive social support was highly valued as a coping mechanism for regulating emotions, yet is often absent from families' lives due to reluctance to disclose to those outside the immediate family (Orford, Velleman, Copello, Templeton, & Ibanga, 2010b). Stigma and shame associated with substance abuse contributes to the experience of stress in this model.

Characteristics of Families of Substance Abuse

Although there is considerable variability among families of substance abuse, there are some common characteristics and patterns, including increased risk for unstable or chaotic home environments and problems within the different family relationships, including the couple relationship (Gruber & Taylor, 2006) and the parent-child relationship (Mayes & Truman, 2002). Similar to the mental health challenges described above, these relationships are complex and often bidirectional in nature, with characteristics often serving as both a precipitate and a consequence of substance abuse.

Unstable or Chaotic Environment

Families of substance abuse often are characterized by disrupted family roles, poor communication, and lack of predictability, which have the ability to impact the relationship between the couple, as well as the parent and child (Gruber & Taylor, 2006). The home environment often is marked with instability or chaos due to frequent cycles of relapse or general neglect due to parental substance use (Barnard & McKeganey, 2004). Disrupted family routines and rituals also are common, contributing to an overall lack of structure (Velleman & Templeton, 2007). For example, family celebrations may be associated with increased stress and lead to increases in substance use. Consistency and predictability within the context of everyday routines such as meal planning and the availability of supervision for children may be disrupted. Evidence suggests that when substance use becomes entrenched within family routines and rituals, it becomes increasingly difficult for the family to challenge those behaviors (Gruber & Taylor, 2006). This may, in turn, increase the risk to children, as they have been found to be at even greater risk themselves of developing a substance use disorder when they simultaneously experience such disruptions and lack of structure within the family environment. This type of disruption of family routines and rituals was present for Henry and Veronica. Henry experienced challenges in staying sober, which led to a roller coaster of use. This was associated with unpredictable behavior and adherence to his responsibilities at home and at work. Henry and Veronica's children did not have consistent contact with their father due to his substance use as well as Veronica's challenges in communicating with him and regulating the associated stress.

Difficulties Within Families

Characteristics of the Couple Relationship

A complex relationship exists between substance use and the couple dyad, with substance use being both a precipitant and a consequence of marital discord (Gruber & Taylor, 2006). These relationships tend to be characterized by high levels of relationship dissatisfaction (Marshall, 2003), instability, high prevalence and frequency of physical and verbal aggression (Fals-Stewart, Birchler, & O'Farrell, 1999; Newcomb, 1994), significant sexual problems (O'Farrell, Choquette, Cutter, & Birchler, 1997), and often significantly heightened levels of psychological distress in both partners and other family members (Kelley & Fals-Stewart, 2002). Further, marital and family problems (e.g., poor communication, financial stressors) can promote or serve as precursors to excessive use as a means of coping with relationship distress (e.g., Maisto, O'Farrell, McKay, Connors, & Pelcovitz, 1988). Interestingly, there is some evidence to suggest that it is not simply the presence of alcohol use, but rather the discrepancy of use between partners that results in relationship dissatisfaction. For example, Mudar, Leonard, and Soltysinski (2001) found that newlywed couples with concordant heavy drinking had marital satisfaction scores that were comparable to couples with concordant nonheavy drinking, and both groups had higher marital satisfaction than couples with discordant drinking patterns. Further, the discrepancy between husband and wife heavy drinking predicted lower levels of marital satisfaction over time (e.g., Homish & Leonard, 2007). Research also has suggested a mediating role of mood and anxiety disorders in the link between substance use and marital dissatisfaction (Whisman, 1999).

Substance abuse also has been documented as a risk factor for domestic violence (Gruber & Taylor, 2006). Marital conflict is common in substance-abusing families and can manifest itself as verbal or physical aggression (Lam & O'Farrell, 2011). Research reviews suggest that alcohol consumption by either partner is common in a large proportion of domestic assault cases (Klostermann & Fals-Stewart, 2006). For example, in cases of male-to-female domestic violence, physical aggression was substantially higher on days where male partners consumed alcohol relative to days in which they did not. Among men in alcoholism treatment programs, the odds of any male-to-female physical aggression occurring on a given day were 11 times higher on days where drinking occurred. The odds of severe male-to-female physical aggression were 11 times higher on drinking days relative to nondrinking days, and days of heavy drinking by male partners made it 18 and 19 times more likely that any and severe male-to-female violence would occur, respectively (Fals-Steward, 2003). Quigley and Leonard (2000) also found that early-marriage drinking patterns of the husband were predictive of violence over the following two years when the wife's alcohol use was also taken into account; highest levels of violence were observed in couples where the husband was a heavy drinker and the wife was not.

Characteristics of the Parent-Child Relationship

In the United States, most individuals seeking treatment are parents (over 80% of women and 68% of men). Similarly, approximately 10.5% of all children in the United States live with either one or two parents who abuse alcohol. Despite good intentions, parenting challenges and skills deficits are common among parents who abuse substances and typically reflect the interaction of child, maternal, and environmental factors (Mayes & Truman, 2002). The relation between substance use and parenting behavior is complex and transactional, with both direct and indirect pathways that increase risk for poor parenting and child maltreatment (Guterman & Lee, 2005).

In the context of parenting, physical/emotional (e.g., cravings, withdrawal symptoms) aspects of substance use, resurfacing of unresolved past traumas, or limited exposure to effective parenting role models (Niccols et al., 2012) may impede a parent's ability to understand and sensitively respond to the needs and cues of the child, potentially precluding the development of a secure attachment. When parents are unable to assist their infants to self-regulate in the face of internal and external stimulation, infants experience chronic stress that hinders maturation of the regulatory system (Motz, Leslie, Pepler, Moore, & Freeman, 2006), thereby reducing their ability to moderate reactions to stress later in life (Bradley, 2000). The majority of children born to women who use substances develop disorganized attachments (Espinosa, Beckwith, Howard, Tyler, & Swanson, 2001) that can, in turn, set the stage for unfavorable child outcomes (e.g., difficulties managing affective responses, poor self-esteem; Main & Hesse, 1990).

Research supports the notion that parents who abuse substances also engage in more negative parenting, such as poor monitoring and inconsistent discipline, and less positive parenting, such as praise, emotional responsiveness, warmth, and guidance (Barnard & McKeganey, 2004; Stanger, Dumenci, Kamon, & Burstein, 2004). Additionally, substance use can interfere with emotion regulation, higher-order cognitive abilities that support problem solving (i.e., executive functions), and sensitivity to environmental cues, all of which are necessary for responsive and stable parenting (Mayes & Truman, 2002). Further, parental substance abuse has been correlated with child maltreatment (Dunn et al., 2002), with children being nearly three times more likely to be abused and more than four times more likely to be neglected than children of parents who do not engage in substance use (Walsh, MacMillan, & Jamieson, 2003).

Parental stress, low frustration tolerance, and poor emotion regulation have been cited as possible mediators (Gruber & Taylor, 2006; Lander, Howsare, & Byrne, 2013). The stress underlying the experiences of these families and the ability to regulate emotion and frustration may mediate the relation between substance use and increased risk of child abuse (Gruber & Taylor, 2006; Lander et al., 2013). As noted above, drugs and alcohol can disrupt the ability to regulate emotions and modulate arousal (Fox, Hong, & Sinha, 2008). Thus, substance-abusing parents may have difficulty responding to their child's cues, contributing to a stressful environment, in turn perpetuating the use of substances as a form of coping (Mayes & Truman, 2002). Qualitative research conducted with family members living in the context of substance abuse has uncovered some common themes that characterize the stressful nature of this relationship. These include aggressive or disagreeable relationships, increased financial conflict, the experience of uncertainty, worry about the addicted family member, and disrupted family life (Orford et al., 2010b). The common co-occurrence of substance abuse with other mental health problems is also important to consider, as it may exacerbate the relationship between substance abuse and negative parenting practices (Lam & O'Farrell, 2011; Mayes & Truman, 2002). In their examination of parenting in fathers with substance abuse issues, Stover, Urdahl, & Eason (2012) found that depression status significantly mediated the relationship between severity of parental drug use and engagement in hostile-aggressive parenting.

Pregnancy and Substance Use

The role of substance use during pregnancy is of paramount importance. Among women with substance use issues, the majority are of child-bearing age (Tjepkema, 2004), and the profound and far-reaching implications of substance use during pregnancy for mother and baby are extensively documented. In fact, data indicate that 14%–20% of mothers report drinking alcohol during pregnancy (McCourt, Paquette, Pelletier, & Reyes, 2005). The use of alcohol and other substances during pregnancy confers biological risk to the developing fetus for a range of unfavorable outcomes. Prenatal alcohol exposure is associated with a range of negative child development outcomes, including Fetal Alcohol Spectrum Disorder (FASD). FASD is associated with intellectual impairment, developmental delay, behavioral disorders, learning disabilities, and attention deficit disorder and hyperactivity (Motz et al., 2006). The negative impact of substance use during pregnancy extends to other substances as well, including tobacco, crack/cocaine, methamphetamines, marijuana, and opiates. Cigarette smoke, for example, has been associated with behavioral, attentional, and temperamental difficulties (e.g., conduct disorder, aggression, hyperactivity; Brook, Brook, & Whiteman, 2000; Wakschlag, Leventhal, Pine, & Carter, 2006). Infants who have been exposed prenatally to crack/cocaine demonstrate increased behavioral reactivity in response to stress (Mayes, Grillon, Granger, & Schottenfeld, 1998) and display symptoms such as irritability, hyperactivity, and abnormal feeding and sleeping patterns (PRIMA Project, 2004). Prenatal marijuana exposure is associated with child hyperactivity, inattention, and impulsivity at age 10 years old.

Challenges associated with prenatal exposure are important to incorporate into an understanding of family functioning, regardless of whether a woman is pregnant. There is a complex transactional relationship at play that extends beyond pregnancy to later childhood. Further, parenting in the context of behavioral and neurodevelopmental challenges may fuel feelings of parental ineffectiveness, guilt, shame, and grief, which may perpetuate the use of substances for managing painful thoughts and feelings (Luthar, Cushing, Merikangas, & Rounsaville, 1998). Veronica's pregnancy is therefore an important factor that increases risk for both Veronica and her baby, both due to primary and secondary substances impact on the development of the fetus, including stress, poverty, nutrition, and access to prenatal care. An integrated treatment program that provides comprehensive services for pregnant and parenting women with substance use disorders may be particularly appropriate for Veronica. These programs address the individual, contextual, and family needs of women, including child care and food security, and have been shown to improve birth outcomes compared to no treatment and to a traditional treatment program (Milligan, Niccols, Sword, Thabane, Henderson, & Smith, 2011).

Children Living in the Context of Substance Abuse

Children are particularly vulnerable when exposed to parental substance abuse. Decades of research demonstrate that children of parents with substance abuse issues are at increased risk for negative psychosocial and developmental outcomes, and a substantial proportion will go on to develop a substance use disorder themselves (Johnson & Leff, 1999; Straussner, 2011). Genetic heritability of alcoholism is estimated to range from 50%–60% (Gruber & Taylor, 2006), although it remains difficult to tease out the unique effects of genetic and environmental influences. Twin studies of inherited alcoholism confirm a modest causal effect of direct exposure to parental substance abuse. Biederman, Faraone, Monuteaux, and Feighner (2000), for instance, demonstrated that exposure to parental substance abuse predicted adolescent substance use over and above genetic risk factors and socioeconomic status, suggesting that family environment plays a critical role in understanding substance abuse transmission. It is likely that characteristics associated with the substance-abusing family environment, such as inconsistent caretaking, transient living conditions, and attitudes towards drugs and alcohol, have compounding effects on preexisting genetic risk factors (Gruber & Taylor, 2006).

The negative consequences for children living in households marked by parental substance abuse are well documented. Such children are at increased risk for a range of psychological, behavioral, cognitive, and social problems (Francis, 2010; Johnson & Leff, 1999). A review of research on children raised by parents with substance abuse issues suggests increased prevalence of psychiatric diagnoses of any kind, with major depression and anxiety being the most prevalent (Barnard & McKeganey, 2004; Diaz et al., 2008). Increased risks of behavioral and social challenges also are common, and include conduct disorders and ADHD (Barnard & McKeganey, 2004). Socially, children are more likely to experience loneliness and low self-esteem.

Conclusion

The challenges faced by Henry and Veronica are numerous and act in concert to create a pattern of risk that maintains substance use. This pattern is not uncommon, and this chapter focused on aspects of the individual, context, and family associated with increased risk. Understanding the interplay of risk factors will aid in the development of comprehensive treatment plans that address the myriad patterns of risk. The body of research reviewed suggests that substance use can have a significant impact on the functioning of the couple. This certainly was the case for Henry's parents, for Henry and Veronica, and for Veronica and her new partner, where substance abuse led to physical abuse, and, in turn, maintained substance use and contributed to the intergenerational transmission. These findings appear to support a stress and coping model of family substance use. Enduring patterns of marital conflict and distress resulting from discordant alcohol use or domestic violence may perpetuate the use of substances as a coping mechanism. Further, underlying mental health disorders and emotion regulation difficulties in combination with substance use may exacerbate this issue. Problems often continue or intensify over a long period of time, thus creating an enduring stressful environment within the couple (Orford et al., 2010a). In addition, poor communication and inadequate boundaries within the couple can be conceptualized within a family systems perspective, and may function as a pathway towards dysfunction, leading to either enmeshed or disengaged relationships (Ripple & Luthar, 1996). Finally, theoretical understanding from a family disease perspective suggests that behaviors such as minimization, denial, or codependence between partners serve to perpetuate and enable continued substance use within the couple (O'Farrell & Fals-Stewart, 1999), as avoidance of conflict with the substance using partner may serve to reinforce such behavior (Gruber & Taylor, 2006).

Parenting challenges and the far-reaching negative consequences of substance use on children can be understood from multiple theoretical perspectives. From a family disease perspective, evidence of loneliness and low self-esteem support the notion that family substance use is inherently socially isolating and shame inducing for children. Reluctance to disclose substance use within the family may foster a culture of secrecy, and fear leads to significant social isolation for many of these children (Peleg-Oren & Teichman, 2006). Family systems perspectives account for findings relating to poor parenting practices, poor boundaries, and unstable family environments that characterize substance-involved families. The theory suggests that parental substance use is directly implicated in development of poor parenting skills and poor family cohesion, in turn leading to childhood psychosocial problems, delinquency, and eventually substance use (Lochman & van den Steenhoven, 2002; Thompson, Pomeroy, & Gober, 2005). Finally, there is evidence of significant distress in relation to substance use within the family. Emotion regulation deficits may be the direct result of substance use or an underlying by-product of living in a stressful environment (Fox et al., 2008; Orford et al., 2010a). Regardless of the directionality of this relationship, a stress and coping theoretical model of family substance use predicts that parents may be less responsive to children's emotional needs and cues, thereby perpetuating perceived stress in parenting, domestic distress, and the continued use of substances as coping mechanism (Mayes & Truman, 2002).

Although not the focus of this chapter, there are also many protective factors that can be capitalized on in treatment to improve family outcomes. Some factors present for Henry and Veronica include relationships with others or social support on treatment retention (Dobkin, Civita, & Paraherakis, 2002), as was seen in Veronica having an initial positive impact on Henry's use, and increased motivation to seek treatment when pregnant or parenting to improve outcomes for their children, as was seen with both Henry and Veronica. Research has consistently shown that pregnancy and parenting opens a "window of opportunity" during which motivation to seek and persist with treatment may be enhanced (Sword et al., 2009). It is possible that this window has opened for Henry and Veronica.

References

American Psychiatric Association. (2013). *Diagnostic and statistical manual of mental disorders* (5th ed.). Arlington, VA: American Psychiatric Publishing.

Barnard, M., & McKeganey, N. (2004). The impact of parental problem drug use on children: What is the problem and what can be done to help? *Addiction*, *99*, 552–559.

Biederman, J., Faraone, S. V., Monuteaux, M. C., & Feighner, J. A. (2000). Patterns of alcohol use and drug use in adolescents can be predicted by parental substance use disorders. *Pediatrics*, *106*(4), 792–797.

Bowen, M. (1974). Alcoholism as viewed through family systems theory and family psychotherapy. *Annals of the New York Academy of Sciences*, *233*(1), 115–122.

Bradley, S. J. (2000). *Affect regulation and the development of psychopathology*. New York, NY: Guildford Press.

Brady, K. T., Dansky, B. S., Sonne, S. C., & Saladin, M. E. (1998). Posttraumatic stress disorder and cocaine dependence: Order of onset. *The American Journal on Addictions*, *7*(2), 128–135.

Brady, K. T., & Randall, C. L. (1999). Gender differences in substance use disorders. *Addictive Disorders*, *22*, 241–252.

Brady, K. T., & Sinha, R. (2005). Co-occurring mental and substance use disorders: The neurobiological effects of chronic stress. *The American Journal of Psychiatry*, *162*(8), 1483–1493.

Brook, J., Brook, D., & Whiteman, M. (2000). The influence of maternal smoking during pregnancy on the toddler's negativity. *Archives of Pediatric and Adolescent Medicine*, *154*, 381–385.

Cormier, R. A., Dell, C. A., & Poole, N. (2004). Women and substance abuse problems. *BMC Women's Health*, *4*(Suppl 1), S8.

Cottler, L. B., Nishith, P., & Compton, W. (2001). Gender differences in risk factors for trauma exposure and post-traumatic stress disorder among inner city drug abusers in and out of treatment. *Comprehensive Psychiatry*, *42*, 111–117.

Cotto, J. H., Davis, E., Dowling, G. J., Elcano, J. C., Staton, A. B., & Weiss, S. R. B. (2010). Gender effects on drug use, abuse, and dependence: A special analysis of results from the national survey on drug use and health. *Gender Medicine*, *7*, 402–413.

Diaz, R., Gual, A., Garcia, M., Arnau, J., Pascual, F., Cañuelo, B., Rubio, G., Dios, Y., Fernández-Eire, Y. C., Valdés, R., & Garbayo, I. (2008). Children of alcoholics in

Spain: From risk to pathology: Results from the ALFIL program. *Social Psychiatry and Psychiatric Epidemiology*, *43*, 1–10.

Dobkin, P. L., Civita, M. D., Paraherakis, A., & Gill, K. (2002). The role of functional social support in treatment retention and outcomes among outpatient adult substance abusers. *Addiction*, *97*, 347–356. https://doi.org/10.1046/j.1360-0443.2002.00083.x

Dunn, M. G., Tarter, R. E., Mezzich, A. C., Vanyukov, M., Kirisci, L., & Kirillova, G. (2002). Origins and consequences of child neglect in substance abuse families. *Clinical Psychology Review*, *22*, 1063–1090.

Earlywine, M. (1994). Personality risk for alcoholism and alcohol expectancies. *Addictive Behaviours*, *19*, 577–582.

Espinosa, M., Beckwith, L., Howard, J., Tyler, R., & Swanson, K. (2001). Maternal psychopathology and attachment in toddlers of heavy cocaine-using mothers. *Infant Mental Health Journal*, *22*, 316–333.

Fals-Steward, W. (2003). The occurrence of partner physical aggression on days of alcohol consumption: A longitudinal diary study. *Journal of Consulting and Clinical Psychology*, *71*, 41–52.

Fals-Stewart, W., Birchler, G. R., & O'Farrell, T. J. (1999). Drug-abusing patients and their partners: Dyadic adjustment, relationship stability and substance use. *Journal of Abnormal Psychology*, *108*, 11–23.

Finkelstein, N. (1994). Treatment issues for alcohol- and drug-dependent pregnant and parenting women. *Health and Social Work*, *19*, 7–15.

Fox, H. C., Hong, K. A., & Sinha, R. (2008). Difficulties in emotion regulation and impulse control in recently abstinent alcoholics compared with social drinkers. *Addictive Behaviours*, *33*(2), 388–394.

Francis, S. A. (2010). Using a framework to explore associations between parental substance use and the health outcomes of their adolescent children. *Journal of Child and Adolescent Substance Abuse*, *20*(1), 1–14.

Galea, S., Nandi, A., & Vlahov, D. (2004). The social epidemiology of substance use. *Epidemiological Reviews*, *26*, 36–52.

Galea, S., & Vlahov, D. (2002). Social determinants of the health of drug users: Socioeconomic status, homelessness, and incarceration. *Public Helath Reports*, *1*, 35–45.

Grant, B. F., Goldstein, R. B., Saha, T. D., Chou, P., Jung, J., Zhang, H., . . . Hasin, D. S. (2015). Epidemiology of *DSM-5* alcohol use disorder results from the national epidemiologic survey on alcohol and related conditions III. *Journal of the American Medical Association*, *72*, 757–766.

Greenfield, S. F. (2002). Women and alcohol use disorders. *Harvard Review of Psychiatry*, *10*, 76–85.

Gruber, K. J., & Taylor, M. F. (2006). A family perspective for substance abuse: Implications from the literature. *Journal of Social Work Practice in the Addictions*, *6*, 1–29.

Guterman, N. B., & Lee, Y. (2005). The role of fathers in risk for physical child abuse and neglect: Possible pathways and unanswered questions. *Child Maltreatment*, *10*, 136–149.

Guttmannova, K., Lee, C. M., Kilmer, J. R., Fleming, C. B., Rhew, I. C., Kosterman, R., & Larimer, M. E. (2016). Impacts of changing marijuana policies on alcohol use in the United States. *Alcoholism: Clinical and Experimental Research*, *40*, 33–46.

Holdcraft, L. C., & Iacono, W. G. (2002). Cohort effects on gender differences in alcohol dependence. *Addiction, 97*, 1025–1036.

Homish, G. G., & Leonard, K. E. (2007). The drinking patnership and martical satisfaction: The longitudinal influence of discrepant drinking. *Journal of Consulting and Clinical Psychology, 75*, 43–51.

Howell, E. M., & Chasnoff, I. J. (1999). Perinatal substnace abuse treatment: Findings from focus groups with clients and providers. *Journal of Substance Abuse Treatment, 17*, 139–148.

Johnson, S. S., & Leff, M. (1999). Children of substance abusers: Overview of research findings. *Pediatrics, 103*, 1085–1099.

Kadushin, C., Reber, E., Saxe, L., & Livert, D. (1998). The substance use system: Social and neighborhood environments associated with substance use and misuse. *Substance Use and Misuse, 33*, 1681–1710.

Kandall, S. R. (2010). Women and drug addiction: A historical perspective. *Journal of Addictive Diseases, 29*, 117–126.

Kandel, D.B., Huang, F.Y., & Davies, M. (2001). Comorbidity between patterns of substance use dependence and psychiatric syndromes. *Drug and Alcohol Dependence, 64*(2), 233–241. doi: 10.1016/S0376-8716(01)00126-0

Kauffman, S. E., Silver, P., & Poulin, J. (1997). Gender differences in attitudes toward alcohol, tobacco, and other drugs. *Social Work, 42*, 231–241.

Kelley, M. L., & Fals-Stewart, W. (2002). Couples- versus individual-based therapy for alcoholism and drug abuse: Effects on children's psychosocial functioning. *Journal of Consulting and Clinical Psychology, 70*, 417–427.

Keyes, K. M., Grant, B. F., & Hasin, D. S. (2008). Evidence for a closing gender gap in alcohol use, abuse, and dependence in the United States population. *Drug and Alcohol Dependence, 93*, 21–29.

Klagsbrun, M., & Davis, D. I. (1977). Substance abuse and family interaction. *Family Process, 16*, 149–164.

Klostermann. K., & Fals-Stewart, W. (2006). Intimate partner violence and alcohol abuse: Exploring the role of drinking in partner violence and its implication for intervention. *Journal of Violence and Aggression, 11*(6), 587–597.

Lam, W. K., & O'Farrell, T. J. (2011). Dynamics of substance-abusing families and implications for treatment. In S. L. A. Straussner & C. H. Fewell (Eds.), *Children of substance abusing parents: Dynamics and treatment* (pp. 49–75). New York, NY: Springer Publishing Co.

Lander, L., Howsare, J., & Byrne, M. (2013). The impact of substance use disorders on families and children: From theory to practice. *Social Work and Public Health, 28*, 194–205.

Lochman, J. E., & van den Steenhoven, A. (2002). Family-based approaches to substance abuse prevention. *Journal of Primary Prevention, 23*, 49–114.

Luthar, S. S., Cushing, G., Merikangas, K. R., & Rounsaville, B. J. (1998). Multiple jeopardy: Risk and protective factors among addicted mothers' offspring. *Development and Psychopathology, 10*, 117–136.

Main, M., & Hesse, E. (1990). Parents' unresolved traumatic experiences are related to infant disorganized attachment status: Is frightened or frightening parental behaviour the linking mechanism? In M. T. Greenberg, D. Cicchetti, & E. M. Cummings (Eds.), *Attachment in the preschool years: Theory, research and intervention* (pp. 161–182). Chicago, IL: University of Chicago Press.

Maisto, S. A., O'Farrell, T. J., McKay, J., Connors, G. J., & Pelcovitz, M. A. (1988). Alcoholics' attributions of factors affecting their relapse to drinking and reasons for terminating relapse events. *Addictive Behaviors*, *13*, 79–82.

Mares, S. H. W., Aschoff-Lichtwarck, A., & Engels, R. C. M. E. (2013). Intergenerational transmission of drinking motives and how they relate to young adults' alcohol use. *Alcohol and Alcoholism*, *48*, 445–451.

Marshall, M. P. (2003). For better or for worse? The effects of alcohol use on marital functioning. *Clinical Psychology Review*, *23*, 959–997.

Mason, W. A., Hanson, K., Fleming, C. B., Ringle, J. L., & Haggerty, K. P. (2015). Washington state recreational marijuana legalization: Parent and adolescent perceptions, knowledge, and discussions in a sample of low-income families. *Substance Use & Misuse*, *50*(5), 541–545.

Mayes, L. C., Grillon, C., Granger, R. H., & Schottenfeld, R. (1998). Regulation of arousal and attention in preschool children exposed to cocaine prenatally. In J. A. Harvey & B. E. Kosofsky (Eds.), *Cocaine: Effects on the developing brain: Vol. 846: Annals of the New York Academy of Sciences* (pp. 126–143). New York, NY: New York Academy of Sciences.

Mayes, L. C., & Truman, S. D. (2002). Substance abuse and parenting. In M. H. Bornstein (Ed.), *Handbook of parenting: Vol. 4: Social conditions and applied parenting* (pp. 329–360). Mahwah, NJ: Lawrence Erlbaum Associates, Inc.

McCourt, C., Paquette, D., Pelletier, L., & Reyes, R. (2005). *Report on maternal and child health in Canada: Making every mother and child count.* Ottawa: Public Health Agency of Canada.

Miller, D. S., & Miller, T. Q. (1997). A test of socioeconomic status as a predictor of initial marijuana use. *Addictive Behavior*, *22*, 479–489.

Milligan, K., Niccols, A., Sword, W., Thabane, L., Henderson, J., & Smith, A. (2011). Birth outcomes for infants born to women participating in integrated treatment programs: A meta-analysis. *Addiction Research and Theory*, *19*, 542–555. https://doi.org/10.3109/16066359.2010.545153

Motz, M., Leslie, M., Pepler, D. J., Moore, T. E., & Freeman, P. A. (2006). Breaking the cycle: Measures of progress. *Journal of Fetal Alcohol Syndrome International*, *4*. Retrieved from: http://www.motherisk.org/JFAS_documents/BTC_JFAS_Report FINAL.pdf

Mudar, P., Leonard, K. E., & Soltysinski, K. (2001). Discrepant substance use and marital functioning in newlywed couples. *Journal of Counselling and Clinical Psychology*, *69*, 130–134.

National Institute on Drug Abuse. *Trends & statistics*. Retrieved on August 5, 2016 from: https://www.drugabuse.gov/related-topics/trends-statistics

Newcomb, M. D. (1994). Drug use and intimate relationships among women and men: Separating specific from general effects in prospective data using structural equation models. *Journal of Consulting and Clinical Psychology*, *62*, 463–476.

Niccols, A., Milligan, K., Sword, W., Thabane, L., Henderson, J., & Smith, A. (2012). Integrated programs for mothers with substance abuse issues: A systematic review of studies reporting on parenting outcomes. *Harm Reduction Journal*, *9*, 14.

O'Farrell, T. J., Choquette, K. A., Cutter, H. S., & Birchler, G. R. (1997). Sexual satisfaction and dysfunction in marriages of male alcoholics: Comparison with non-alcoholic maritally conflicted and noncomplicated couples. *Journal of Studies on Alcohol*, *58*, 91–99.

O'Farrell, T. J., & Fals-Stewart, W. (1999). Treatment models and methods: Family models. In B. S. McCrady & E. E. Epstein (Eds.), *Addiction: A comprehensive guidebook* (pp. 287–305). New York: Oxford University Press.

Orford, J., Copello, A., Velleman, R., & Templeton, L. (2010a). Family members affected by a close relative's addiction: The stress-strain-coping-support model. *Drugs: Education, Prevention and Policy, 17*, 36–43.

Orford, J., Velleman, R., Copello, A., Templeton, L., & Ibanga, A. (2010b). The experiences of affected family members: A summary of two decades of qualitative research. *Drugs: Education, Prevention and Policy, 17*, 44–62.

Peleg-Oren, N., & Teichman, M. (2006). Young children of parents with Substance Use Disorders (SUD): A review of the literature and implications for social work practice. *Journal of Social Work Practice in Addictions, 6*, 49–61.

Poole, N., & Dell, C. A. (2005). *Girls, women and substance use*. (Report No. 1-896323-67-7). Retrieved from the Canadian Centre on Substance Abuse (CCSA) website: http://www.ccsa.ca/Resource%20Library/ccsa-011142–2005.pdf

Poole, N., & Greaves, L. (2009). Mother and child reunion: Achieving balance in policies affecting substance-using mothers and their children. *Women's Health and Urban Life, 8*, 54–66.

PRIMA Project. (2004). *Pregnancy related issues in the management of addictions: A reference for obstetrical care providers*. Retrieved from: http://www.addiction pregnancy.ca

Quigley, B. M., & Leonard, K. E. (2000). Alcohol and the continuation of early marital aggression. *Alcoholism: Clinical and Experimental Research, 24*, 1003–1010.

Reid, C., Greaves, L., & Poole, N. (2008). Good, bad, thwarted or addicted? Discourses of substance-using mothers. *Critical Social Policy, 28*, 211–234.

Ripple, C. H., & Luthar, S. S. (1996). Familial factors in illicit drug abuse: An interdisciplinary perspective. *The American Journal of Drug and Alcohol Abuse, 22*(2), 147–172.

Rush, B., Urbanoski, K., Bassani, D., Castel, S., Wild, T. C., Strike, K., & Somers, J. (2008). Prevalence of co-occurring substance use and other mental disorders in the Canadian population. *Canadian Journal of Psychiatry, 53*, 800–809.

Sher, K. J., Grekin, E. R., & Williams, N. A. (2005). The development of alcohol use disorders. *Annual Review of Clinical Psychology, 1*, 493–523.

Sinha, R. (2012). How does stress lead to risk of alcohol relapse? *Alcohol Research: Current Reviews, 34*(4), 423–440.

Smock, S. A., Froerer, A. S., & Blakeslee, S. E. (2011). Systemic interventions in substance abuse treatment: Past, present, and future. *Journal of Family Psychotherapy, 22*(3), 177–192.

Stanger, C., Dumenci, L., Kamon, J., & Burstein, M. (2004). Parenting and children's externalizing problems in substance-abusing families. *Journal of Clinical Child and Adolescent Psychology, 33*, 590–600.

Stinson, F. S., Grant, B. F., Dawson, D. A., Ruan, W. J., Huang, B., & Saha, T. (2005). Comorbidity between DSM-IV alcohol and specific drug use disorders in the United States: Results from the national epidemiological survey on alcohol and related conditions. *Drug and Alcohol Dependence, 80*(1), 105–116.

Stover, C. S., Urdahl, A., & Eason, C. (2012). Depression as a mediator of the association between substance abuse and negative parenting of fathers. *American Journal of Drug and Alcohol Abuse, 38*, 344–349.

Straussner, S. L. A. (2011). Children of substance abusing parents: An overview. In S. L. A. Straussner & C. H. Fewell (Eds.), *Children of substance abusing parents: Dynamics and treatment* (pp. 1–28). New York, NY: Springer Publishing Co.

Substance Abuse and Mental Health Services Administration (SAMHSA). (2013). *Results from the 2012 national survey on drug use and health: Summary of national findings*. (NSDUH Series H-46, HHA Publication No. (SMA) 13-4795). Rockville, MD: SAMHSA, US Department of Health and Human Services.

Swendsen, J., Conway, K. P., Degenhardt, L., Glantz, M., Jin, R., Merikangas, K. R., . . . Kessler, R. C. (2010). Mental disorders as risk factors for substance use, abuse and dependence: Results from the 10-year follow-up of the national comorbidity survey. *Addiction, 105*, 1117–1128.

Sword, W., Jack, S., Niccols, A., Milligan, K., Henderson, J., & Thabane, L. (2009). Integrated programs for women with substance use issues and their children: A qualitative meta-synthesis of process and outcomes. *Harm Reduction Journal, 6*, 32.

Teter, C. J., McCabe, S. E., LaGrange, K., Cranford, J. A., & Boyd, C. J. (2006). Illicit use of specific prescription stimulants among college students: Prevalence, motives, and routes of administration. *Pharmacotherapy, 26*, 1501–1510.

Thompson, R. A. (1994). Emotion regulation: A theme in search of definition. *Monographs of the Society for Research in Child Development, 59*, 25–52.

Thompson, S. J., Pomeroy, E. C., & Gober, K. (2005). Family-based treatment models targeting substance use and high-risk behaviors among adolescents: A review. *The Journal of Evidence-Based Social Work, 2*, 207–233.

Tjepkema, M. (2004). Alcohol and illicit drug dependence. *Health Reports, 15*, 9–19.

Velleman, R. D. B., & Templeton, L. J. (2007). Substance misuse by children and young people: The role of the family and implications for intervention and prevention. *Pediatrics and Child Health, 17*, 25–30.

von Sydow, K., Lieb, R., Pfister, H., Hofler, M., & Wittchen, H. W. (2002). What predicts incident use of cannabis and progression to abuse and dependence? A 4-year prospective examination of risk factors in a community sample of adolescents and young adults. *Drug and Alcohol Dependence, 1*, 49–64.

Wakschlag, L. S., Leventhal, B. L., Pine, D. S., Pickett, K. E., & Carter, A. S. (2006). Elucidating early mechanisms of developmental psychopathology: The case of prenatal smoking and disruptive behaviour. *Child Development, 77*, 893–906.

Walsh, C. A., MacMillan, H., & Jamieson, E. (2003). The relationship between parental substance abuse and child maltreatment: Findings from the Ontario Health Supplement. *Child Abuse and Neglect, 27*, 1409–1425.

Werner, M. J., Joffe, A., & Graham, A. V. (1999). Screening, early identification, and office-based intervention with children and youth living in substance abusing families. *Pediatrics, 103*, 1099–1112.

Whisman, M. A. (1999). Marital dissatisfaction and psychiatric disorders: Results from the national comorbidity survey. *Journal of Abnormal Psychology, 108*, 701–706.

Zilberman, M. L., Tavares, H., Blume, S. B., & el-Guebaly, N. (2003). Substance use disorders: Sex differences and psychiatric comorbidities. *Canadian Journal of Psychiatry, 48*, 5–13.

Zweben, J. E., Clark, H. W., & Smith, D. E. (1994). Traumatic experiences and substance use: Mapping the territory. *Journal of Psychoactive Drugs, 26*(4), 327–344.

Using Solution-Focused Brief Therapy With Substance-Abusing Families

Sara Smock Jordan

Focusing on the family as a context for the development, maintenance, and intergenerational transmission of substance abuse is essential to treatment. The systemic treatment of substance abuse is explained best by defining first the levels of family participation in treatment, and second the interventions used in the process. Doherty and Baird (1986) originally proposed five levels of involvement, later accepted by SAMHSA (2015b) as levels of systemic substance abuse treatment. Level one does not include family involvement of any type. At the second level, psychoeducation is provided to the addict's family. The third level includes some interaction between the clinician and the family, but it is not until the fourth level that an assessment with the family occurs. The final level is the only one where family members are directly involved in therapy. Increasingly, substance abuse treatment centers are adding family therapy to services provided, given the evidence of its effectiveness (Stanton & Todd, 1982).

Despite the level of family involvement, prevention remains the overarching goal of substance abuse family therapy. Research shows that the single greatest predictor of substance abuse is whether one's parents abused drugs and/or alcohol (Johnson & Leff, 1999). Because families are systems that transmit patterns of behavior, as well as genetic predispositions to substance abuse, treating individuals from a systemic perspective aids in preventing misuse and dependence of other family members and future generations. By drawing on a family's strengths and lessening the impact of addiction on other family members, family therapy can have a much wider effect than individual intervention.

Issues to Consider in Systemic Substance Abuse Treatment

When working with individuals and families struggling with substance abuse, many factors can complicate treatment. Besides the specific training that family therapists need to work with families, the likelihood that several family members are struggling with chemical dependency, and lack of treatment facilities that provide counseling for the entire family, several additional issues should be considered.

Legal Issues

Court-mandated substance abuse treatment is common for individuals who have violated the law. In cases involving minors, family therapy may be required. In legal cases involving adults, family therapy may not be mandated but recommended. When working with a family where one member is mandated to attend substance abuse treatment, it is important to inform them about your role. For example, when working with legal mandates, the therapist may be asked to report on the progress, or lack thereof. It is important for clients to understand that the therapist has a dual role, to report and to treat.

Financial Issues

The cost of substance abuse treatment can be a major barrier. For those who have insurance coverage, one member of the family must be diagnosed with a substance use disorder in order for treatment to be covered. However, insurance companies do not reimburse for couple or family therapy, so providers must incorporate the relational component into their services for the individual. In addition, most insurance companies have a lifetime limit for inpatient and/or outpatient services. Given the high relapse rate in the United States, many insured substance abusers run out of episodes of care at some point in their life.

Many individuals and families struggling with substance abuse/dependency do not have insurance coverage for treatment. This may be directly related to their extensive use of alcohol and/or drugs (i.e., not being able to hold down a job, growing up in a lower socioeconomic status home due to addiction in the family) or may be present for other reasons. For some, wealthier family members may pay for their treatment, which can cause strain within the family system. For others, a lack of family financial resources could result in any of the following: receiving educational classes instead of therapy, being placed on a wait list for managed care, incarceration, and/or no intervention, which may lead to social, emotional, occupational, psychological, and/or physical decline.

Unique Needs of Women

As mentioned earlier in the chapter, a gender divide exists in substance use. Women use for different reasons (e.g., Teter et al., 2006), experience difference consequences of use (e.g., Brady & Randall, 1999), and have unique patterns of misuse (e.g., Cotto et al., 2010). Additionally, women have unique needs in substance abuse treatment (SAMHSA, 2015a). First, women experience different physiological responses to substances compared to men. It takes a smaller amount of a substance for women to be intoxicated or high, and health declines occur much faster for women compared to men. Heavy drinking and drug use can also lead to reproductive difficulties, concerns about pregnancy and prenatal health, as well as an increased risk of cancer and STIs. In terms of mental health, women who abuse substances have a greater likelihood of having co-occurring conditions such as depression, PTSD, anxiety, and eating disorders. These co-occurring disorders also factor in the likelihood of substance-abusing women being physically and sexually traumatized by violence. In some cases, the abuse (in childhood) precipitates the misuse of substances as a means of coping.

Socially, women are more likely than men to be influenced by relationships when it comes to substance abuse, treatment, and relapse. Pregnancy and child care are additional factors that influence a woman's ability to enter and complete treatment. In the late 1980s NIDA funded a project called Perinatal 20, which established a treatment facility (called PAR Village) allowing women to bring their children with them to residential treatment. When compared to a traditional woman's residential program, the residents in the PAR Village had a significantly higher retention rate, which has been shown to be the best predictor of behavioral and psychological outcomes (De Leon, 1989). Another prominent social factor is that women tend to be more stigmatized for abusing substances than men. This stigmatization can play a role in women seeking treatment.

Domestic Violence

As previously mentioned in the research section of this chapter, one of the main areas of concern in doing couples or family therapy with one or more substance abuse member is the risk of domestic or intimate partner violence. SAMHSA reports that a dominant theme for women who abuse substances is being in unhealthy relationships, resulting in a higher risk of experiencing violence. Thus, the safety of all family members receiving treatment needs to be considered. It is important to assess whether couple or family therapy is appropriate. McCollum and Trepper (2001) state two important points to consider when making a treatment plan for violent families. First, if the victim feels safe around the family member who has been violent, then joint treatment can be considered. In addition, the following conditions must be met: violence is not currently present in the relationship, a nonviolence agreement is signed by the perpetrator, a safety plan is in place for any potential violence, and the perpetrator takes full responsibility for the violent behavior. If the above conditions are met, the therapist can proceed with couples or family substance abuse treatment as long as an ongoing assessment of safety is maintained by the therapist.

Models and Interventions

Several philosophies and approaches to family therapy with substance abusers exist. The root or cause of abusing substances usually has a systemic origin in traditional family therapy interventions. Some perspectives view the system as the root of the problem (i.e., the family disease model), whereas others view the substance as the systemic obstacle. The following are some traditional approaches to treating families with at least one substance abuse member.

Traditional Approaches

One of the most well-known traditional family treatments comes from the medical model. This approach believes there is a genetic component to abusing alcohol and drugs. It sees chemical addiction as a disease that can be passed intergenerationally. Specific approaches include multifamily groups, network therapy, AA, and the family disease model (SAMHSA, 2015b; Smock et al., 2011). Pharmacological advances may help to treat biological predispositions in families suffering from chemical addictions.

Another traditional approach to treating families is the sociocultural model. This approach takes into account all environmental and social factors present that may be contributing to abusing alcohol and or drugs. Altering the sociocultural aspects of a family seems necessary to create positive change, but the practicality of making these alterations is difficult. Examples of sociocultural interventions include multisystemic therapy (MST), sociological stress models, and the family systems model (SAMHSA, 2015b; Smock et al., 2011).

Evidence-Based Approaches

Over the past few years, the use of evidence-based practice in substance abuse treatment has become standard. The Substance Abuse and Mental Health Services Administration (SAMHSA) has developed the National Registry of Evidence-based Programs and Practices (NREPP) to review and list programs with evidence-based criteria. While neither NREPP nor SAMHSA endorse the programs listed on their website, reviews provide information to providers about empirically supported approaches. Solution-focused group therapy (SFGT) is one of many evidence-based practice programs with clinical outcome data (Smock et al., 2008), and it is detailed in the next section.

SFBT: An Overview

History of SFBT

A team of therapists led by Steve de Shazer and Insoo Kim Berg developed solution-focused brief therapy (SFBT). By paying close attention to what the therapist did in session that was helpful to clients, SFBT emerged as an approach influenced by family therapy and social constructionism. The developers used a paradigm shift away from a problem-solving approach to focusing on what the client wants in her or his preferred future. Solution building became a process of describing the client's problem, developing well-formed goals, looking for exceptions to the problems, gaining client feedback, and evaluating the client's progress (De Jong & Berg, 2013).

Techniques

Although SFBT is not a technique-driven model, key interventions do exist. The following are hallmark SFBT techniques, questions, or interventions: goal-formulating questions, the miracle question, exception questions, coping questions, relational questions, scaling questions, taking a break, giving compliments, and giving homework. A detailed description of these techniques, applied to the case study, will be given later in the chapter along with an outline of when to use them.

SFBT and Substance Abuse

SFBT has been applied most often to the treatment of substance abuse, with nearly a dozen SFBT books on the topic, and several reasons exist that underscore its use. First, SFBT is a brief approach that has been shown to be just as effective as longer models. Writing on SFBT also talks about its usefulness with clients who are seen as resistant or in denial. SFBT works well with chronically relapsing clients due to its view that clients are experts of their own lives. Finally, SFBT can be used individually, with families, and in a group format.

Doing SFBT Family Therapy: Session Outlines

Pichot and Smock (2009) provide a session outline for conducting SFBT individual and group sessions. The following is a first family therapy session outline incorporating De Jong and Berg's (2013) suggestions as well as Pichot and Smock's (2009):

1. The therapist asks each family member to tell a little bit about him or herself (e.g., what the individual is good at, how the individual spends his or her days).
2. The therapist asks each family member what he or she would like to get out of therapy (his or her goals).
3. Since each family member may have a different goal, the therapist develops a common goal based on the theme of each member's individual preferred future.
4. The therapist shares the family theme (goal) with everyone to verify that it fits for all members. If it does not, ask how the goal can be modified. (Note: This could take more than one session.)
5. Once a family goal is established, the therapist asks the miracle question to gather more information about the details of their preferred future.

6. The therapist asks about if and when there are times when pieces of the miracle are already occurring (highlighting exceptions). If family members have trouble giving exceptions, the therapist can move to #7 and ask coping and/or confidence scaling questions.
7. The therapist asks each member one or more scaling questions about their current level of progress towards the family goal. If members of the family did not identify exceptions (from #6), the therapist can ask scaling questions about how they are coping with the issue that brought them to therapy and/or how confident they are that things will improve in their family.
8. The therapist can ask different family members where they would rate each other's progress towards the family goal (especially if a family member is not expressing his or her own progress towards the family goal).
9. The therapist can ask each family member what difference that individual's progress would make to others. For example, the therapist can ask the daughter, "So what difference would it make to your father if you _____ [details about making progress towards the family goal]?"
10. The therapist then can ask each family member where he or she would like to be (from #7) on a scale from 1 to 10 (or 0 to 10) by the next session.
11. Next, the therapist can either leave the room or stay and take a few moments to gather his or her thoughts about possible compliments that can be given to the family.
12. Compliments are given to the family by the therapist. Solution-focused compliments are based on: (1) what the clients like about themselves; (2) what they are proud of; and/or (3) things they are doing well.
13. Finally, the therapist gives the family homework to complete based on what the members have mentioned as being useful/helpful in reaching their mutual goal.

It is mentioned above in the fourth step that finding a mutual family goal may take more than one session. In this case, the second session should begin with asking, "What's been better?" (see below for details) and then continue with exploring a mutual family goal. Once a joint family goal is established, the follow-up SFBT family session outline, adapted from De Jong and Berg, should be used for all additional sessions:

1. Begin the session by asking a variation of the question, "So what's been better since the last time we met?" Allow all family members to answer this question.
2. Listen to what the family has to report.
    a. If anyone in the family reports improvement, the therapist should follow by asking, "So how did you do that?" and then, "What difference did you notice?"

b. If no one in the family reports improvement, the therapist can ask the following:

   i. "Has anything been even slightly better?" or "How have you kept things from getting worse?"

c. If the family reports that things have gotten worse, the therapist can:

   i. Ask the family how they were able to all come to therapy today.
   ii. "How did you keep things from getting MUCH worse?"

3. Next, if the family reports improvement, the therapist then asks, "So what else is better?" The therapist should re-ask the questions in Step 2a until the family can't come up with anything else that's better. If the family doesn't report improvement (or says things are worse), skip to Step 5.
4. If the family reports improvement, the therapist should ask, "So what will it take to keep this going?"
5. The therapist asks each family member to scale his or her progress towards the family goal by asking, "On a scale of 1 to 10 (or 0 to 10), where 10 is your goal and 1 (or 0) is furthest from that, where are you this week?"
6. The therapist then asks each family member what the family will look like when any of them move up one point on the scale: "When you or another family member moves up on the scale of [define goal], what will things look like?"
7. The therapist then either takes a break or remains and gathers his or her thoughts about potential compliments for the family. (Note: Steps 7 through 9 are the same as in the initial therapy session.)
8. Solution-focused compliments are given to the family by the therapist.
9. Homework is given to the family based on what the members have mentioned will be useful/helpful in reaching their mutual goal.

Creating Safety

For family therapy to be helpful, all family members should have the freedom and ability to vocalize their concerns. Ensuring the safety of all individuals in family therapy is important. There are only a few situations when family therapy might not be safe. As mentioned above, the presence of domestic violence may be a reason to not use family therapy. Child abuse and/or neglect is another serious safety issue that can contraindicate family therapy. Depending on the severity of the abuse and whether or not it is still occurring, individual therapy may be preferred. Violence and/or abuse need to be assessed by the therapist to determine whether or not family therapy is recommended.

Incorporating Research for Psychoeducation

Psychoeducation is a common practice in substance abuse treatment. Disease and medical model-based approaches value psychoeducation because educating individuals and families about addiction is key to treating the ailment. Some treatment centers and facilities only use psychoeducation to involve family members, whereas others use multifamily groups that include psychoeducation (SAMHSA, 2015b). Psychoeducation within multifamily groups is shown to motivate family involvement in treatment (Wermuth & Scheid, 1986). In solution-focused brief therapy, psychoeducation is done with teachable moments (Berg & Reuss, 1998). Questions such as "So what effect does alcohol have on your body?" are a way to ask clients about what they know already. Depending on their answer, the therapist can provide appropriate information, or psychoeducation, in an informative yet respectful manner.

Cultural Issues Regarding Families and Addiction

When considering cultural issues within families facing addiction it is important to remember that culture is multifaceted. Credentialing disciplines in substance abuse treatment offer culturally competent guidelines to help minority clients.

Racial and Ethnic Minority Groups

As mentioned earlier in the chapter, racial and ethnic inequalities influence substance use, abstinence, and relapse rates. Unfortunately, these disparities create treatment barriers for ethnic and racial minorities needing services, including recognition of the severity of problem drinking, the cost of treatment, cultural messages about seeking professional help, negative beliefs about treatment, and lack of providers for poor individuals (Kline, 1996). These barriers, and others, should be addressed in treatment settings by providing culturally responsive services.

Religion and Spirituality

Beliefs and values surrounding substance use, abuse, and treatment vary among religious groups. Is substance use acceptable but substance abuse not tolerable? Is drinking and/or substance use part of religious ceremonies or rituals? Many factors must be considered when assessing a client's religious and/or spiritual beliefs and practices. The distinction between religion and spirituality is an important one in treatment. Although a religious perspective to treatment usually is not part of most treatment centers, spirituality is a major component in a lot of programs. Alcoholics Anonymous (AA), as well as other 12-step groups, views spirituality as an important piece in recovery. Because treatment for substance use disorders is more likely to incorporate spiritual principles than help for other mental illnesses, cultural sensitivity for minority religious and spiritual clients is important. Non-Christian clients often worry about the role spirituality plays in some treatment facilities. Thus, providers must assess the client's religious and/or spiritual needs just as they would assess other cultural needs.

Applying SFBT Family Therapy to the Case Example

The next section of this chapter provides a step-by-step illustration, including dialogue, of applying SFBT family therapy to Veronica and Henry's case. Both Henry and Veronica attended the first session. Due to the children's ages, both Veronica and Henry thought it would be best to exclude them from the initial session. Since creating safety is an important piece to doing substance abuse family therapy, when concerns arise it is important to make sure they are addressed. One way for assessing safety in SFBT is to ask during the intake procedures, "Who would be most helpful, if anyone, in attending therapy with you?" In SFBT, clients are asked to include supportive individuals in their life in session if it is helpful to them. In times when safety is an issue, clients should have the opportunity to talk with the therapist individually about who would be helpful to attend therapy with them. SFBT is not technique driven nor should it be used formulaically. However, to illustrate the major pieces of SFBT, this section applies dialogue to the guidelines for a first SFBT session (De Jong & Berg, 2013; Pichot & Smock, 2009).

Session 1

This first meeting begins with the therapist getting to know Veronica and Henry and establishing their goals. Since SFBT uses specific language to co-construct one's preferred future, giving example dialogue is helpful in learning how to use the model. The following are example dialogue segments that illustrate the first session outline.

(Step 1) THERAPIST: *So, tell me a bit about yourself. . . . How you spend your days?*

VERONICA: *Well, right now I'm just trying to keep my kids fed and safe.*

HENRY: *Yeah, with that no-good boyfriend you're living with, I'm sure that's a full-time job.*

THERAPIST: *Trying to keep your kids fed and safe is very important. Tell me about your kids.*

As you can see, right from the beginning Veronica and Henry are taking jabs at each other. This type of interaction is not uncommon. The SFBT therapist is careful to not get pulled into the problem talk. Alternatively, the SFBT therapist does not ignore problem talk. The therapist here acknowledges the problem(s) that Henry and Veronica bring to session without asking detailed questions about those problems. Instead of asking about Henry and Veronica's problem specially, the therapists says:

(Step 2) THERAPIST: *So, how can I be helpful to the two of you?*

HENRY: *If you could help us figure out how to get along enough for Veronica to let me see the kids.*

THERAPIST: *So what do you think it would take for you and Veronica to get along enough for this to happen?*

HENRY: *Well, I guess her trusting me with them. It's not like my home environment is any worse than where they are currently living.*

THERAPIST: *So more trust.*

The therapist continues to ask Henry and Veronica questions that help narrow down their goals. In SFBT, it is believed that the solution is not always connected to the problem. Thus, the therapist asks Henry and Veronica how he/she can be helpful or some variation in order to understand what they want in their preferred future. The real goal for Henry is not to stop using alcohol, but to reestablish the estranged relationship with his kids. However, in order for Henry to reestablish his relationship with his kids he needs to abstain from drinking. This is important due to safety reasons concerning the children and Veronica. Setting client-centered, realistic goals for Henry and Veronica is one of the most important aspects of this first session.

(Steps 3 and 4) THERAPIST: *So Veronica, you want to be more stable for your kids, and Henry, you want Veronica to trust you with the kids. It sounds like a common goal for both of you is to be your best for your kids.*

HENRY: *Yeah, I want to be my best for the kids . . . so I can see them and be part of their lives.*

VERONICA: *I want the best for my kids too, no matter what happens between me and Henry. I know he wants to be in my life, but I'm not sure that I want that yet.*

THERAPIST: *When the two of you are being the best you can be for your kids, what will that look like?*

The therapist has proposed a theme to Veronica and Henry's goals, which they accepted.

Developing a common goal in substance abuse treatment is an important developmental milestone. Henry and Veronica agree that their common goal is for both of them to be the best for their kids.

In Step 5, the therapist asks Henry and Veronica the miracle question, a hallmark question asked in SFBT.

(Step 5) THERAPIST: *Do you mind if I ask you a strange question?*

VERONICA: *Sure.*

HENRY: *OK.*

THERAPIST: *Great. Suppose you leave here today, you go home and go about your regular day. You do what you normally do in the evening and eventually . . . maybe that's watching TV or putting the kids to bed . . . and eventually you go to bed and go to sleep. And while you are sleeping something shifts, a miracle occurs . . . the problems that brought you here today are gone just like that (snaps fingers). But this miracle happens while you are asleep, so you don't know it has happened. When you wake up the next day, what would be the first thing that you would notice that was different?*

Veronica's answer to this question is that she would be living independently and active in her children's lives. Henry's miracle is that his children would remember him.

In steps 6 and 7 the therapist used a scaling technique to determine where Henry and Veronica were on their goal progression. In Step 6, the therapist asks Henry and Veronica: *Tell me about times in both of your lives when you wake up sober or wake up looking forward to playing with your kids.* The therapist continues to measure the progress of Henry and Veronica's goals throughout the course of their therapy to mark milestones in their treatment progress.

In Step 8, the therapist really tied in the relational component of SFBT by asking the relational question: *So what would you notice Veronica doing if she were closer to being the best for your kids?* Henry responded by saying that he would notice Veronica talking more about the kids around him. The therapist then asked Veronica what she would notice about Henry. She said that Henry would start saving the money he spent on alcohol for the kids.

Step 9 involved asking difference questions about how each other's progress will impact the other people in their family.

(Step 9) THERAPIST: *So Veronica, what difference would it make to Henry if you were able to be your best for the kids?*

VERONICA: *I think it would make all of the difference to him because it would mean that he would be in their lives.*

HENRY: *I agree.*

By asking Veronica and Henry difference questions, they begin to realize what impact their behavioral changes have on each other. This is another way to track milestones in treatment. Next the therapist asks Veronica and Henry where they would like to be when they meet next time.

(Step 10) THERAPIST: *So Henry and Veronica, where would you like to be on the scale towards your goal by the next time we meet?*

HENRY: *Well, I would like to be at an 8.5. Veronica has already started to trust me a bit by following through with the appointment. I would like to be an 8.5 next time.*

THERAPIST: *What would that look like?*

HENRY: *It would mean that we would start to talk about when I might be able to see the kids. Perhaps we could set up a time during next session to have lunch with Veronica and the kids.*

THERAPIST: *And Veronica, where would you like to be on your scale next time?*

VERONICA: *I want to be at a 6 . . . break up with Hank. I think Henry's confidence in me and my sister's support is what I need to do it. I really think I can do that pretty soon.*

This is one way that SFBT gives some direction to Henry and Veronica about what to work on outside of therapy.

In steps 11 and 12, the therapist takes some time to give Henry and Veronica one or more compliments. The key in SFBT compliments is that they come directly from the client. The phrasing of the compliments use the clients' words and reflect what the clients have already said that they are proud of or like about themselves. For example:

(Steps 11 and 12) THERAPIST: *I would like to take a few minutes to gather some thoughts I have for the two of you.* (Therapist puts together on paper a few compliments to share.) *Veronica, I want to say that I'm very impressed that you want to be stable enough for your kids. I also think that you are very wise to make sure that their environment is safe. And Henry, I think that it says a lot that you have been able to control your drinking for some time now. You also have been able to hold down your job as well. You both seem motivated to be the best you can for your kids, which says a lot about you as parents.*

The last step in any SFBT session is focused on giving clients homework based on what the clients have reported as being useful in reaching their goal.

(Step 13) THERAPIST: *So between now and the next time we meet, which we will talk about in a few moments, I would like the two of you to keep doing those things that will move you up on your scale. As you work on your goal, I want you to notice what is useful and what is not useful. Do more of the things that are useful and less of those that aren't.*

Veronica is asked to think about what it would take to reach her next step of breaking up with Hank. Henry is asked to think about how he can have some conversations with Veronica about when he might be able to see the kids. A lot has been accomplished within this first session. Henry and Veronica have set detailed goals, have a plan for their next steps towards these goals, and have homework to work on between sessions.

Session 2

In session 2, the therapist begins by saying the following to Henry and Veronica.

(Steps 1–4 alternative) THERAPIST: *So, what's been better since the last time we met?*

VERONICA: *Nothing that I can think of.*

HENRY: *Yeah, things have been pretty bad.*

THERAPIST: *I'm sorry to hear that. So how have you kept things from getting worse?*

HENRY: *Well, I haven't gotten drunk.*

THERAPIST: *That's good. How were you able to do that?*

HENRY: *I've just stayed focused on work.*

THERAPIST: *And you, Veronica, what have you done to make it through the week without things getting worse?*

VERONICA: *I'm not sure. I'm kinda surprised that things didn't get worse.*

THERAPIST: *What would the kids say that you did to keep things from getting worse?*

VERONICA: *Hmmm. I guess they would say that I spent some time with them this week.*

In session 2, Veronica and Henry reported that the week was pretty bad, but Henry was able to not get drunk and Veronica spent more time with the kids. After gathering this information the therapist checks in with them about their miracle and both of them report that they had moments where their miracle seemed a bit closer despite the challenges of the week. The therapist further explores in detail what they did to keep things from getting worse during the week.

Session 3

During session 3 Henry and Veronica reported that things had gotten better. Veronica had broken up with Hank, and Henry did not drink at all during the week. Henry and Veronica hung out together for the first time with the kids, and they reported an enjoyable time together. When the therapist asked Henry the same scaling question from the first session, he reported being an 8.5 (increased from a 7 during session 1) because he has been able to control his drinking, see his kids, and noticed that Veronica is starting to trust him more. Veronica was at a 9 on the same scale because she broke up with Hank and had started to trust Henry more. This was an important milestone in treatment because they had or were doing what they stated in session 1.

Session 4

At the beginning of session 4, Veronica reported some doubts about having Henry around the children. She stated that Henry was doing everything he needs to do but she was just getting scared he might slip back into his old behavior. The therapist asked her several questions about how she has coped with fear in the past and what has worked. Henry was supportive of Veronica in session, and the therapist could tell that their bond was continuing to grow.

Session 5

The therapist checked in with Veronica and Henry, and they both reported feeling confident about reaching their current goals. When the therapist asked, *When would the two of you know that you no longer needed to come to therapy anymore?* they both stated that they thought that this might be their last session. They had grown as a couple and even talked about moving back in together. The therapist asked them questions about how they were going to maintain their goals after therapy. Veronica and Henry reported that they had a plan to keep things moving in the right direction. The therapist offered to meet with them in the future if they ever needed to talk.

In SFBT, treatment ends once all family goals are accomplished. Sometimes this takes a few sessions, and other times treatment occurs for several months. The therapist is available if new things come up that would be helpful to bring to therapy. Solution-focused brief family therapy is helpful because it works in a brief amount of time; can be used when working with "resistant" and/or chronically relapsing clients; can be used individually, with families, or in groups; and is recognized as an evidence-based approach for substance abusers.

References

Berg, I. K., & Reuss, N. H. (1998). *Solutions step by step: A substance abuse treatment manual*. New York, NY: W. W. Norton & Company, Inc.

Brady, K. T., & Randall, C. L. (1999). Gender differences in substance use disorders. *Psychiatric Clinics of North America, 22*(2), 241–252. doi: 10.1016/S0193-953X(05)70074-5

Cotto, J. H., Davis, E., Dowling, G. J., Elcano, J. C., Stanton, A. B., & Weiss, S. R. (2010). Gender effects on drug use, abuse, and dependence: A special analysis from the national survey on drug use and health. *Gender Medicine, 7*(5), 402–413. doi: 10.1016/j.frnm.2010.09.004

De Jong, P., & Berg, I. K. (2013). *Interviewing for solutions* (4th ed.). Belmont, CA: Brooks/Cole.

De Leon, G., & Rosenthal, M. S. (1989). Treatment in residential therapeutic communities. In H. Kleber (Ed.), *Treatment of psychiatric disorders: A task force report of the American Psychiatric Association* (Vol. 2, pp. 1379–1396). Washington, DC: American Psychiatric Association.

Doherty, W. J., & Baird, M. A. (1986). Developmental levels in family-centered medical care. *Family Medicine, 18*(3), 153–156.

Johnson, J. L., & Leff, M. (1999). Children of substance abusers: Overview of research findings. *Pediatrics, 103*, 1085–1099.

Kline, A. (1996). Pathways into drug user treatment: The influence of gender and racial/ethnic identity. *Substance Use and Misuse, 31*(3), 323–342.

McCollum, E. E., & Trepper, T. S. (2001). *Family solutions for drug and alcohol abuse: Clinical and counseling approaches*. New York: Routledge/Taylor & Francis.

Pichot, T., & Smock, S. A. (2009). *Solution-focused substance abuse treatment*. New York: Haworth.

SAMHSA. (2015a). *Substance abuse treatment: Addressing the specific needs of women.* (TIP 5). Rockville, MD: U.S. Department of Health and Human Services.

SAMHSA. (2015b). *Substance abuse treatment and family therapy.* (TIP 39). Rockville, MD: U.S. Department of Health and Human Services.

Smock, S. A., Froerer, A. S., & Blakeslee, S. E. (2011). The history of systemic substance abuse treatment. *Journal of Family Psychotherapy, 22*, 177–192. doi: 10.1080/08975353.2011.602613

Smock, S. A., Trepper, T. S., Wetchler, J., McCollum, E., Ray, R., & Pierce, K. (2008). Solution-focused group therapy for level 1 substance abusers. *Journal of Marital and Family Therapy, 34*, 107–120. doi: 10.1111/j.1752-0606.2008.00056.x

Stanton, M. D., & Todd, T. C. (1982). *The family therapy of drug abuse and addiction.* New York, NY: Guilford Press.

Teter, C. J., McCabe, S. E., LaGrange, K., Cranford, J. A., & Boyd, C. J. (2006). Illicit use of specific prescription stimulants among college students: Prevalence, motives, and routes of administration. *Pharmacotherapy, 26*, 1501–1510. doi: 10.1592/phco.26.10.1501

Wermuth, L., & Scheidt, S. (1986). Enlisting family support in drug treatment. *Family Process, 25*, 25–33.

6

FAMILIES THAT EXPERIENCE HOMICIDE

Case Study

Mary Beth Hays and Scott W. Browning

Janis (age 30) called requesting therapy for her son, Ethan (age 8). She reported that her husband, Michael (age 35), was killed by a gunshot and that she wanted her son to talk to someone. Janis stated that Michael was a chef who, on his way home from work six weeks ago, was robbed and murdered. Michael's killer was found. He was a neighborhood juvenile who had become addicted to drugs and was seeking means to meet his addiction. He reportedly never intended to kill anyone.

Janis and her deceased husband have two children, Ethan and Sarai (age 3). Ethan presented as a healthy boy who had successfully completed first grade and was initially performing above grade level at the start of second grade. However, it appeared that Ethan was suffering from his father's traumatic loss in many ways. He was struggling with both reading and math and had begun to withdraw from his mother and friends. Ethan was also experiencing frustration, sleep disturbances, crying spells, and a loss of appetite. Ethan had also begun to act in a parentified manner with his younger sister, Sarai.

During the initial assessment process when Janis was asked what she absolutely loved about Ethan, she described his smile and his laughter. She stated that she missed seeing his smile and certainly missed hearing his laughter. Janis went on to describe that Ethan and Sarai had very warm and loving attachments with their father and miss him daily. When asked about how Ethan learned of his father's death, Janis began to cry. She stated that she was initially unable to tell him that his father had been murdered and originally told him that Michael was taken to the hospital because he was sick. At that point it became clear that Janis could use her own grief support, specifically around parenting. It was during this same session that I learned Janis had not yet told Sarai of her father's death. When I previously asked who attended Michael's funeral, Janis had remarked that everyone had been there. It was at this point that I took the therapeutic stance that Sarai deserved to know the truth, after all it was *her* story too.

When disclosing her family history, Janis shared that her father died when she was 7 years old. It was stated that he was in a fatal car accident and died from a severe head injury. Janis reports that she was initially never told of her father's death. She recalled being told that he was working far away and, over time, began to believe that her father had abandoned the family. In regard to current family composition, the remaining three grandparents of Ethan and Sarai are alive. Janis's mother lives close and is involved with the children. Michael's parents live further away and have been reluctant to engage the children following Michael's murder. Janis has a younger brother, Jason, who is available to spend some time with Ethan and Sarai, although he is busy and living the casual life of a young adult.

Janis reports that she is open to the treatment recommendations of the therapist and is willing to have the children seen, engage in family therapy, seek some support for herself, and even invite in extended family if that would be perceived as useful. Janis works a full-time job, but is willing to leave on occasion for herself or her children. In addition, Theresa (Janis's mother) can bring the children to sessions if needed.

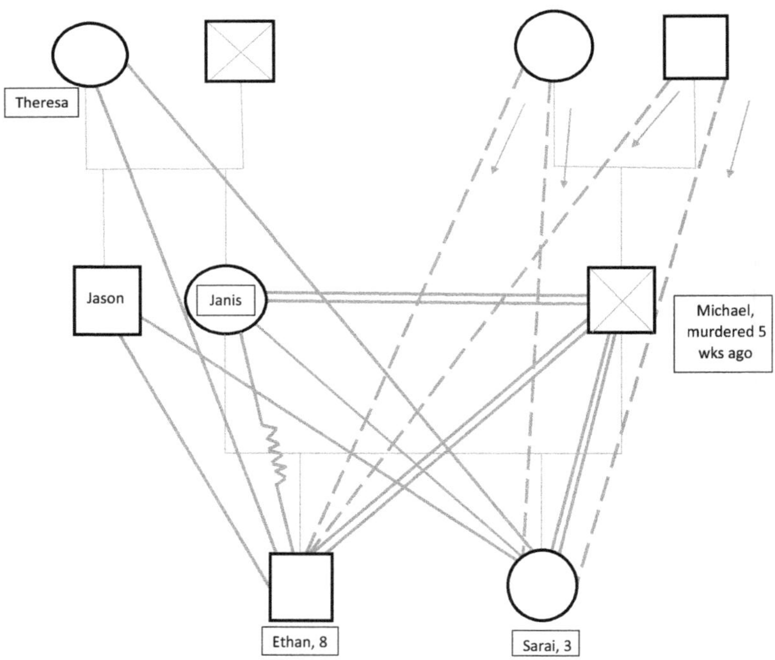

Figure 6.1 Families of Homicide Genogram: Janis and Her Children

Research on Understanding the Surviving Families of Homicide

Ashley Wellman

When we think about murder, it is usually the subject of a crime drama or a news story that discusses details about the offender and the victim. It is something that we imagine could never happen to us or to someone we love. There are statistics that detail who commits these crimes and numbers to demonstrate the annual number of victims. However, too frequently we overlook the fact that behind the statistics is an often forgotten group: the surviving family members of homicide victims. These are the people who are left to cope with the aftermath of homicide on a daily basis. This chapter presents the current state of research about homicide and homicide survivors in the United States, along with various manifestations and types of grief. An overview of the impact of homicide on family and nonfamilial relationships and roles also is discussed. Finally, methods of coping and the unique experience of cold case homicide survivors are presented.

Defining Homicide and Homicide Survivors

A homicide is defined by the FBI's Uniform Crime Reporting Program as "the willful (non-negligent) killing of one human being by another" (USDOJ FBI, 2015, p. 1). In 2014, 14,249 homicides were reported and resulted in a law enforcement clearance rate of 64.5% for the year. This means that law enforcement was able to resolve nearly two-thirds of 2014 homicide cases. Officers may officially close the case, thus officially noting the case as "cleared," through the identification and arrest of a suspect or by other exceptional means such as the death of the main suspect prior to charges being filed.

Murphy (1996) suggested there are at least four surviving individuals closely connected or related to each homicide victim. Using Murphy's formula and the 2014 UCR data, these rates indicate that there would be approximately 56,996 individuals that became surviving individuals in 2014. We can estimate that with a clearance rate of 64.5% approximately 36,800 survivors had a resolution in their case and another 20,200 survivors were left without answers due to the unsolved nature of their case. Individuals without a resolution in their case are at risk of becoming known as cold case homicide survivors. Although no universal definition exists for a cold case homicide, Walton (2006) notes that a cold case homicide occurs when the original detective has been reassigned or no longer works the case, there are no promising leads or information in the case, and the case is at least one year old without activity. Survivors who are left to cope with a cold case homicide may experience prolonged grief and unique challenges compared to traditional homicide survivors (Wellman, 2014b).

Based on a conservative estimate, nearly 38,000 people a year will become survivors of homicide. Bard and Sangrey (1979) were the first scholars to suggest survivors of a homicide victim may also suffer from victimization. While they are not the direct victims of murder, the surviving family members are left behind to handle the financial and emotional damages of the crime. The surviving family members will be the direct contacts for medical personnel, law enforcement agents, and media professionals. If an offender is apprehended, the family will be directly exposed to the criminal justice process and forced to relive the events of their loved one's murder. These difficult responsibilities, relationships, and unexpected challenges that occur when someone is murdered often result in the family members developing mental, physical, spiritual, and financial struggles. Although coworkers and friends certainly are impacted by the sudden, violent nature of homicidal deaths of someone they know, this chapter examines the impact murder has on the immediate surviving family members. Utilizing Amick-McMullan, Kilpatrick, and Resnick's (1991) conceptualization, immediate family members include parents, children, spouses, siblings, grandparents, and grandchildren of homicide victims.

Manifestations of Grief

Survivors of homicide face many emotional and physical challenges as part of the grieving process. Response to such traumatic stress often is complicated and variable across survivors (Malone, 2007), thus requiring health care providers to understand a wide scope of conditions and indications of grief. Survivors may expect the emotional distress to subside after a year following the homicide, and when it does not, they may feel even greater distress (Kristensen, Weisæth, & Heir, 2012). It is important for both the survivors and treatment providers to recognize the normalcy of these complications as the symptoms and conditions manifest themselves.

The sudden, violent nature of death caused by homicide leads to great emotional turmoil for surviving family members. For some, they witnessed the death, thus having to cope with the event experience and the homicide simultaneously. Survivors who witnessed the death may have faced threats to their own life and may struggle with replaying images of the homicide (Hussain, Weisaeth, & Heir, 2010). For others, great physical damage to the victim's body prevent them from viewing the body at time of burial, thus inhibiting the survivor's ability to formally say goodbye. Despite the concern that viewing the body of someone who has died a tragic death may lead to emotional complications, research shows that this is rarely the case. Few survivors of sudden, violent deaths regret viewing their loved one's body, while those who did not view the body reported increased remorse in their decision (Chapple & Ziebland, 2010; Winje & Ulvik, 1995). In fact, those reporting increased anxiety after viewing the body felt less long-term distress than those who did not view the body at all (Hodgkinson, Joseph, Yule, & Williams, 1993). Some families do not regain possession of a body. Thus, despite the suspicion of murder, the finality of the death cannot be fully realized. For example, in the case of a missing person, additional anxiety and denial of death are exaggerated. These families struggle with the lack of a body, a formal burial. or a gravesite to visit. Delay in death confirmation is noted as one of the greatest stressors for surviving family members (Raphael, 1986).

Nearly a quarter of homicide survivors develop post-traumatic stress disorder (PTSD; Amick-McMullan et al., 1991), with women displaying signs of PTSD more than men (Murphy, Clark Johnson, Wu, Fan, & Lohan, 2003). PTSD is related to reliving moments and details of the death, even if the survivor did not witness the homicide; thus, further complicating the recovery process (Rynearson, 2001). Depression and anxiety, accompanied by preoccupation with the deceased loved one, loss of interest, and numbness are common (Mezey, Evans, & Hobdell, 2002). Sleep disturbances are frequently experienced by survivors due to intrusive thoughts that can become obsessions, causing survivors to fixate on the exact manner of death and potential ways it could have been prevented (Hardison, Neimeyer, & Lichstein, 2005). Missing information and unanswered questions about the homicide can prevent survivors from being able to process, make meaning of it, and fully grieve (Merlevede et al., 2004). Even if formal, factual information is provided, survivors who continue to focus on information seeking, such as understanding the victim's last thoughts, level of suffering, and so forth, are likely to experience long-term maladjustment (Winje, 1998).

Emotional distress may lead to risky and dangerous behaviors by the survivors. Survivors may turn to alcohol, prescription pills, or illegal drugs as a method of coping. Thoughts of guilt, self-blame, and a lack of control may result in increased rates of suicidal thoughts and self-harming behaviors such as cutting. There often are heightened feelings of anger, rage, and a desire for revenge that can overwhelm survivors. Mezey et al. (2002) studied survivors of homicide and found that nearly two-thirds of survivors noted that they were "more angry" post-homicide. Specifically, half of the respondents noted that they were more verbally aggressive with people, and 7% noted they were more physically aggressive. The anger was most often conceptualized in feelings of revenge against the perpetrator, anger against one's self for "allowing" the crime to happen, and towards others who may have been able to prevent the death.

Survivors of homicide often experience a physical toll as well (Armour, 2002; Hardison et al., 2005; Kenney, 2003; Miller, 2009a). Changes in appetite, weight, and sleep patterns are present. Trauma can lead to gastrointestinal problems, cardiovascular disorders, and immune system suppression. Several studies have found that family members of slain victims are at an increased risk of death due to post-homicide health complications (Armour, 2003; Prigerson et al., 1997; Sprang & McNeil, 1995). Specifically, men may have an elevated risk for heart issues and premature death due to commonly repressed emotions, whereas women are most likely to suffer with emotional and psychological disorders such as anxiety and depression.

Experiences and Types of Grief

Much research exists on the "traditional" manner in which people grieve. However, scholars agree that survivors of a traumatic event or violent death do not follow the traditional bereavement grief model (Armour, 2002; Feldman Hertz, Prothrow-Stith, & Chery, 2005; Malone, 2007; Rando, 1993; Rynearson, 1984, 1988). Janoff-Bulman (1985) identifies three basic assumptions that are challenged when a traumatic incident occurs. Most operate with a feeling of invulnerability, rarely focusing on one's own mortality. Yet, when one survives a traumatic event such as the homicide of a loved one, personal feelings of safety and invulnerability are shattered (Asaro, 1992; Burgess, 1975; Janoff-Bulman, 1985). Additionally, survivors are forced to reconsider the concept that the world is a just and meaningful place. The questions of how this happened to the victim, the unfair nature of death, and individual purpose are all ideas present in the aftermath of trauma. Survivors often perceive an inability to control events in their own lives. Finally, it is common to question one's own purpose and struggle to view one's self in a positive light. It becomes increasingly difficult for the survivor to see himself or herself as good and cautious. To heal it becomes critical for survivors to maintain or reshape an optimistic view of the world and of themselves (Klass, 1993).

Bereavement specialists encourage survivors to release the emotional and psychological bonds once shared with the deceased family member and to form a new life that is independent of that individual (Rando, 1993). For homicide survivors, this idea seems unrealistic and unachievable. Due to sudden loss, homicide survivors struggle to move on, and emotionally detaching seems unbearable. Many survivors associate emotional detachment with disregarding the homicide (Armour, 2002; Miller, 1999). While traditional grief models describe how individuals can reach a final stage of acceptance (Kübler-Ross, 1969; Kübler-Ross & Kessler, 2005), these survivors are unlikely to ever reach that final stage (Armour, 2002; Rando, 1993).

The sudden, violent, and unexplainable nature of homicide does not allow survivors to emotionally prepare for the victim's death. In addition to the unique emotional challenges, the external obligations for survivors that accompany homicide elongate and may prohibit grief progress. For example, interactions with the police and media following the murder cause survivors to relive the death. As time passes, survivors may interact with the criminal justice system. Even if an offender is convicted, appeals will continue to inundate survivors. If not solved, many survivors will continue to seek answers, hunt for justice, and focus on the homicide in an effort to find a resolution that may never occur (Wellman, 2011). Each of these factors contributes to the inability for many survivors to grieve the death in a traditional manner. Accordingly, scholars posed models of traumatic grief, complicated grief, and disenfranchised grief that allow for the complexity, suddenness, and unnatural manner that come with homicide.

Traumatic Grief

Traumatic grief can be understood as the emotional and physical responses to bereavement in which survivors struggle to understand the world around them (Spungen, 1998). Traumatic grief commonly occurs when the death is sudden, involves a child, or is viewed as preventable (Rando, 1993). Those who have a fractured relationship prior to the death or feel alone in their grief are more likely to experience a traumatic bereavement period. Individuals who display traumatic grief experience separation anxiety, overwhelming preoccupation with the deceased, hypervigilance, and/or a feeling that their life is useless—lasting for at least two months. Additionally, many struggle to acknowledge the death and have excessive feelings of anger and frustration around the unfair nature of the death, and experience prolonged impaired social and occupational functioning (Steele, 2013).

Complicated Grief

Approximately 10% of survivors present with complicated grief, marked by elongated and unresolved expressions of grief (Middleton, Raphael, Burnett, & Martinek, 1998). Horowitz et al. (1997) established seven criteria (present for at least one year) demonstrating complicated grief: disturbing memories or thoughts related to the death, severe emotional reactions related to the death, feelings of isolation, deep desire for the deceased loved one to be present, clear avoidance of any reminders of the deceased, unusual sleep disturbances, and a significant loss of interest. The American Psychiatric Association (2000) notes that a patient experiencing complicated grief often also presents with substance abuse, post-traumatic stress disorder (PTSD), major depressive disorder, and/or an anxiety disorder. Applebaum and Burns (1991) found that parents of homicide are more likely to develop PTSD, most indicative of complicated grief, than siblings of homicide and parents of children killed in an accident, due to their ability to make meaning of the event.

Disenfranchised Grief

When a homicide victim was involved in a criminal lifestyle, such as drugs, prostitution, or violence, survivors may experience disenfranchised grief (Doka, 2002; Jones & Beck, 2007). Disenfranchised grief occurs when the surviving family feels that other people do not value the victim or the magnitude of the death. The family may feel the media or police did not recognize the murder (Wellman, 2011, 2013). Survivors may also believe that their surrounding community views the death as less important, thus further isolating grieving individuals. Such grief may be intensified when survivors are part of a minority family (Doka, 2002). The dismissive reaction to the homicide may lead people to feel discriminated against and misunderstood. When this occurs, survivors are left to not only battle the murder of their loved one but also to cope with the secondary harm caused by individuals and institutions. Perceived inappropriate, insensitive, and inadequate reactions by others can cause further damage to the survivor, known as secondary victimization (Neimeyer & Jordan, 2002; Rando, 1993; Rynearson, 1994).

Impact on Family Relationships and Roles

Beginning to rebuild life without the murdered family member can be overwhelming and can complicate the survivors' grieving process and their relationships with the other survivors within their family. Depending on the victim's family role, several challenges are likely to arise. If the slain individual was the primary income earner, the family must seek ways to compensate for lost income (Asaro, 2001). If the murder victim was the childcare provider, it becomes critical for survivors to locate resources and proper child care (Asaro & Clements, 2005). Families recognize gaps that exist when a member is killed, leaving roles such as emotional supporter or disciplinarian absent in the family's fiber. Roles, responsibilities, and personal inventory of purpose are likely to shift post-homicide.

Impact on Parents

Parents who experience the murder of their child are in a challenging position to mourn the death of one child and often simultaneously care for and maintain the role of parent for surviving children (Asaro & Clements, 2005; Rando, 1993). For those parents who only had one child, they are left to question their purpose and role in life. Parents naturally do not plan to outlive their children, thus making the death of a child most difficult to understand and process (Asaro, 1992; Grebstein, 1986).

Many times parents will struggle with self-blame, guilt, and anger after the death of a child (Armour, 2002). The parental role is defined by the ability to care for and protect one's child, and when a murder occurs, the parent is likely to struggle with the concept of self-worth and ability (Miller, 1999). Parents who survive the homicide of a child are more likely to blame themselves for the death and question their value as a parent, compared to parents of accident-related deaths (Matthews & Marwit, 2004). Due to the malicious nature of murder, parents may focus on self-blame in an effort to rationalize the event and to reconstruct feelings of safety and well-being (Rando, 1993).

The parent of a murdered child may develop feelings of hypervigilance, becoming overprotective of surviving children (Armour, 2002). Additionally, the parent may become fixated on the deceased child, leading to hallucinations of the child's presences or a fierce attachment to the deceased's belongings (Klass, 1993). Some parents many continue to set the child's place at the table or preserve the child's room, in an effort to maintain a sense of normalcy and closeness (Wellman, 2011).

The death can have dramatic effects on the marital relationship of the surviving parents as well. When comparing surviving parents of homicide to bereaved parents of an accident or suicide death, the homicide parents report the lowest level of marital satisfaction (Murphy et al., 2003) For some couples, they will seek to blame one another for "allowing" the death to happen, thus creating a wedge between spouses. In these instances, divorce may become an option. For other couples, the death of a child further strengthens their relationship, turning to one another for hope and solace.

Impact on Spouses

The death of a spouse is an incredibly multifaceted issue. The relationship prior to the death will greatly impact the way in which a surviving partner grieves (Jacobs, Wellman, Fuller, Anderson, & Jurado 2016). If there was frustration and dissatisfaction prior to the murder, there could be intense feelings of guilt. For those partners who had strong marital relationships, they will grieve an even greater loss of a friend, companion, and sexual partner. If the couple had children, the surviving spouse is left to assume all of the parental roles and responsibilities, which can seem daunting (Parents of Murdered and Missing Children, 2015). Survivors may struggle to balance the stresses with coexisting pressures like returning to work (Miller, 2009a; Spungen, 1998).

When a former spouse is murdered, surviving ex-spouses often experience disenfranchised grief (Doka, 2002; Jones & Beck, 2007). Those around them often assume that the death is not as important since the couple is divorced (Doka, 2002). However, many divorced couples maintain family relationships with children and in-laws, continue to share financial responsibilities, and may even retain strong feelings for their ex-spouse. These continuing interactions and feelings contribute to the grief that divorced individuals experience following the death of a former spouse (Scott, 2000).

Impact on Children

The relationship between the victim and the child may impact the child's reaction. A child whose parent is murdered may feel the intense pressure to grow up quickly (Asaro & Clements, 2005) and seek ways to fulfill the responsibilities and roles of the deceased parent. A young boy whose father is killed may be told or perceive his new role to be that of the man of the house, or a young girl may seek to fulfill matriarchal duties after the death of her mother. For the surviving children, the death of a sibling poses unique challenges. In light of their parent's grief, children may feel as though their pain is ignored or minimized by family, friends, and service providers (Asaro & Clements, 2005). The surviving child may also feel forgotten, overshadowed, or less important than the memory of the deceased sibling. Survivor guilt for siblings is common, leaving the child to wish they had died instead of the victim (Clements & Burgess, 2002). There is likely to be an element of fear from a surviving sibling, questioning their own personal safety (Asaro & Clements, 2005).

Yalom (1980) noted that adults commonly overlook and underestimate the anxiety and understanding children have surrounding death. It is critical for both parents and clinicians to acknowledge children's ability to process trauma, recognize how their age and maturity may impact their interpretation and meaning making of the message presented to them, and how they may have questions and reactions that must be addressed (Poltorak & Glazer, 2006; Ronen, 2002). In one study, 132 bereaved children and their caregivers were asked to disclose how they were coping with traumatic death (Brown et al., 2008). Children who questioned their own mortality, who witnessed a caregiver's extreme reaction at the time of death, who lived in an environment with pervasive sadness and distress, and who were less removed from the time of death were most likely to suffer from childhood traumatic grief.

According to Miller (2009a), age dictates much of the child's reaction to the homicide of a loved one. Caregiver responses and treatment plans must be age-appropriate. Children under the age of 3 are not likely to understand the concept of death, but will react to the turmoil and grief, will have difficulty articulating the related frustration, and may lash out. Normalcy and stability are important with these children. Children aged 4–7 may not fully grasp the full scope of death, but do recognize the abrupt absence and loss of their family member. Therefore, these children must have the reality of the homicide explained to them in age-appropriate terms, accompanied by statements of comfort and safety. Older children, aged 8–12, are likely to find a distraction and preoccupation with their involvement in school, extracurricular activities, and friends. Adults should be aware that these children may appear to be less impacted by the crime, but are still likely to struggle with the reality of the deceased family member, have questions, and need specialized attention. Those aged 13–18 may have the most difficult time processing death, fully aware of the universality of death, and may become obsessed with their death. Their natural growth and independence may be halted or stunted due to the trauma.

Research indicates that school performance and developmental behavior may regress following the homicide (Brown et al., 2008; Eth & Pynoos, 1994; Kristensen et al., 2012; Miller, 2009a, 2009b; Vigil & Clements, 2003). The trauma of a homicide poses a great disruption to a child's routine and often is associated with significant risks and symptoms of PTSD. Physically, young children may revert to infantile behaviors such as bedwetting or trouble with potty training, inability to sleep through the night, throwing tantrums and crying to express frustration (Eth & Pynoos, 1994).

Children will struggle with cognitive manifestations of grief. School-aged children are likely to experience a decline in school performance (Eth & Pynoos, 1994). The inability to concentrate, being easily distracted, displaying signs of anxiety and depression, and the lack of inhibition often contribute to difficulties in the school environment. As the child ages, he or she may act out with behaviors such as truancy, substance abuse, sexual promiscuity, and delinquency. In interviews with teenage survivors who witnessed their parents' murders, many appeared to be guarded, uncooperative, and plagued by guilt associated with thoughts of how their own behavior may have contributed to the death of their loved one (Eth & Pynoos, 1994). Additionally, the child's conceptualization of the consequences of his or her behavior, moral reasoning, and understanding of mortality can be greatly impacted (Vigil & Clements, 2003). Psychosomatic manifestations of grief were commonly noted among children. These included stomach pains, headaches, and other physical ailments. Often the presentation of symptoms mirrored the injuries their deceased loved one experienced (Eth & Pynoos, 1994).

Impact on the Larger Family System

There are two components of grief when a family experiences a homicide: the individual processing of the event and the need to cope as a family unit (Armour, 2002). Although both pose unique challenges, families face several difficulties when trying to incorporate and understand coping strategies used by individual family members. One challenge is that each individual within the group will grieve and progress at a different rate. When individual members feel that others have grieved too quickly, it may be perceived that they do not care, the deceased was not as important, or that their own grief pattern is abnormal. Likewise, many family members may grow frustrated with members of the family who experience an elongated grief period, are unable to contribute to the family restructuring, and/or have not resumed a healthy personal routine. Therapists and counselors must remind family members that there is no proper timeline for healing and that family support and recognition of different grief stages among members is important (Jacobs et al., 2016).

Additionally, the different manner in which family members express emotions may increase the struggles a family faces. Post-homicide, individuals in certain roles or genders may feel the need to be strong, grieve privately, and conceal their pain to protect the other family members. Particularly heterosexual men and heads of household often attempt to shield and conceal their emotional distress to appear as the family's source of stability and strength (Jacobs et al., 2016; Miller, 2009b). However, this lack of emotional presentation can be perceived as insensitive and cold. All members should be encouraged to communicate their feelings and express their pain without the belief that their emotional expression will complicate other members' grief.

Finally, family members must respect each member's ability and willingness to contribute to the family unit's healing process. For some survivors, there is a deep need to be present and acknowledged in the healing plan. Yet, other survivors need the group to recognize their need and desire for private, separate grieving. Grieving individually and grieving together must be carefully balanced to meet the needs of the various family members. Families may need help recognizing and articulating the proper balance (Armour, 2002).

In the event that the perpetrator and the victim were related, there is the additional strain on the family, as various members take different sides, further deteriorating the remaining family structure (Asaro, 2001). Future family events, formal court proceedings, and even custody of children may become a source of frustration and a reminder of the murder. Survivors without a resolution in their case may question or suspect that a family member is responsible for the death, leading to increased pain and frustration. According to Jacobs et al. (2016), cold case homicide survivors struggle within the family unit similarly to those survivors with answers. By analyzing the experiences of four families comprised of 12 cold case survivors, the authors found that families with unsolved cases most commonly reported difficulty managing time with other related survivors, becoming overprotective, influence of pre-homicide familial relationships on coping, pressure to remain strong, and complications surrounding family traditions.

For family therapists, understanding the diverse family dynamics becomes critical in offering the proper treatment to homicide survivors. Vesper and Cohen (1999) detailed five common family reactions that often present themselves after a traumatic event. The first family reaction is that of *the Contemptuous Family*, which are often categorized by their secrecy and deception, presence of anger, blaming, and denying the evident problems. Therapists most successfully connect with these families by developing a commonality and foundation on noncontroversial issues, such as the family's daily routine, and then moving forward to tackle larger issues. The second family type is *the Brittle Family*, who often worry that the other surviving family members are too fragile to rely on for emotional support and thus turn to external support systems, at the expense of the other family members' healing. These families can be encouraged to trust and strengthen the inner family relationships to progress as a unit. Third, *the Hierarchical Family* operates with an inflexible definition of family roles and turn to the senior members of the family for guidance. The stability can be a positive aspect of this family type, but there should be an encouragement for members of this type of family to expand the definitions of individual roles and responsibilities. *The Enduring Family* is the fourth reactionary type, relying on faith to provide order and support in times of turmoil. Finally, *the Functional Family* operates in a manner where each member works together to support and care for one another, helping to strengthen the family's commitment and bond despite tragedy.

Impact of Nonfamilial Relationships

Friends, Acquaintances, and Coworkers

Many survivors seek support and meaning in relationships outside of the family. For these survivors, the reaction they received from their friends and coworkers can be powerful in the healing process. When individuals demonstrated behaviors such as listening to the survivor, attempting to help problem solve or serve as a companion, they were often perceived as supportive (Asaro, 1992, 2001; Bard, 1982). Those who were deemed by survivors as unexpectedly kind and helpful, despite the casual nature of their connection, were incredibly important to the grieving process (Bard, 1982). External actors, such as friends and coworkers, often do not understand the difficulties of coping with homicide, and therefore might offer hurtful responses (Doka, 2002; Neimeyer & Jordan, 2002; Rando, 1993; Rynearson, 1994). People who appear to be impatient with the survivors' elongated grief are likely to arouse feelings of isolation and loneliness in moments when the survivor is seeking social support the most (Symonds, 1980).

Typically, fellow homicide survivors are some of the strongest tools for survivors in understanding their own grief and navigating through the recovery process post-homicide. Due to the unique, unexpected, and violent manner of death, families of homicide victims believe that no one can truly relate to their experience, unless they too have had a murder in their family (Rock, 1998). Within the homicide survivor social network, there is likely to be comparison amongst cases. Wellman (2013) found that cold case homicide survivors often think of homicide as different and more complex than any other type of death. Yet, within the same sample, some cold case homicide survivors viewed their lack of answers as worse than a homicide survivor who has a resolution, whereas others reported that the absence of a resolution had spared their family the immense pain associated with a trial and subsequent legal proceedings. Fellow survivors may become angry when their own family member's homicide is overshadowed, feeling as if others viewed them as unentitled to the continuing grief (Asaro, 1992, 2001).

Personnel From Related Systems

Following a homicide, surviving family members are thrust into unexpected and often undesired relationships with professionals, such as media personnel, law enforcement officers, victim advocates, and courtroom actors (Malone, 2007; Wellman, 2011). Each has the ability to significantly influence survivors, and persons interacting with a survivor of homicide must be careful not to cause secondary victimization. Survivors report both positive and negative interactions with the professionals who handle their case. What is critical is that each person interacting with a survivor of homicide must be careful not to commit (un)intentional secondary victimization.

Traditional homicide literature establishes that media personnel often distort the meaning of the tragedy for the surviving families (Miller, 2009a). The media often brings unwanted attention to the family and the victim, claiming that the public has a right to know the details of the case (Armour, 2002). Wellman (2013) found that among cold case homicide survivors, families often were revictimized and hurt by the perceived inadequate case coverage, inaccurate information, and the negative portrayal of the victim. Regardless of their experiences with the media, most survivors agreed that they needed and wanted coverage of their loved one's case, thus committing them to continuing the often troublesome relationship.

Many families will turn to the police and to the criminal justice system for answers and for assistance with the bereavement process. Research notes that these interactions also often result in revictimization (Bucholz, 2002; Karmen, 2007). In a study of unsolved homicide survivors, common themes emerged including the lack of communication with law enforcement, a perceived change in law enforcement behavior based on the victim's status, prosecutors' unwillingness to prosecute, and police inactivity (Stretesky, Shelley, Hogan, & Unnithan, 2010). Survivors often note feeling angry and dissatisfied by the treatment they received throughout the criminal justice process, often reporting that they felt minimized and as if they were denied justice (Baliko & Tuck, 2008; Bucholz, 2002). To reduce the potential trauma and secondary victimization often common from interactions with practitioners and the justice system, it may help families to appoint a non-family member to serve as the family contact for the media, friends, and law enforcement agencies while the family seeks privacy (Malone, 2007; Wellman, 2013). Cold case survivors will experience an even greater challenge of continuing these forced professional relationships for years in an effort to keep their case in the minds of those who may be able to help solve their loved ones' murder (Wellman, 2011).

Coping After Homicide

Survivors of homicide use a variety of methods and mechanisms, both formal and informal, to heal. Some use professional counseling as an individual and/or with their families. Many seek mental health care, both in the form of therapy and medication. One study found that slightly more than half of survivors sampled were prescribed psychotropic medication post-homicide (Mezey et al., 2002). Community homicide bereavement groups and grief support organizations may also offer solace. To process and cope with the trauma of homicide, many survivors turn to their faith (Asaro, 1992; Wellman, 2014a). Several studies have presented mixed results on the impact of religion on survivors' grief, ranging from detrimental to therapeutic (Czillinger, 1986; Hathaway & Pargament, 1991; Kashka & Beard, 1999; Thompson & Vardaman, 1997). A study focusing on cold case survivors and religion found that despite initial anger with God, survivors do not blame God for the murder (Wellman, 2014a). Instead these survivors turn to religion for peace and purpose in the midst of not having any other answers in their case.

Regardless of the formal care that survivors seek, it is common for the bereaved to also engage in informal methods of coping (Wellman, 2011). Artistic expressions of grief, such as songwriting, drawing, and poetry, can be therapeutic and allow survivors an opportunity to visually express their pain. Serving others who are in need may be a healthy outlet as well. Survivors note that being able to reach out to another family who has suffered a homicide and help is a step in their own healing process (Wellman, 2014b). Survivors may feel empowered or motivated to combat injustices in the community around them as a way to cope with their own feelings of being wronged. A crusade for justice in their own case, in other homicide cases, or for inequality may be a healthy mechanism for healing, as long as it does not become an all-consuming mission for the survivor (Miller, 2009b).

As survivors progress through the coping process, they must eventually face the reality that life must go on without the presence of their loved one. Survivors of homicide can struggle with the concept of "moving forward" after their family member's murder, in fear that moving on will signify that they are letting go or have forgotten about their loved one. However, resuming normal routines and learning to memorialize their loved one may be the most effective way to progress through the grief (Miller, 2009b; Sprang & McNeil, 1995; Spungen, 1998). Miller (2009b) proposed that families honor the deceased by pinpointing an item or photograph that may provide comfort. Together, the families may seek to process through photo albums to reposition positive memories and images in the forefront of their thoughts instead of the gruesome intrusions of the murder. Creating a scrapbook together may also help the family bond and advance in a positive direction of healing. Establishing a memorial event, ritual, or project together may also be a helpful exercise for the family unit. However, it is again important to remember that all family members may not be able to or may not desire to participate in the memorialization process. Each member should be encouraged to continue with their personal grieving and join the family when emotionally ready to do so, if at all (Barnes, 1998; Miller, 1999).

Unique Challenges for Cold Case Homicide Survivors

Those survivors who do not have a resolution in their case avoid the difficult experiences of court but are left to address several unique challenges (Wellman, 2011). Without a perpetrator, the anger and blame often is displaced among cold case homicide survivors (Wellman, 2011). Anger commonly is placed with first responders and the medical team who treated the victim, "failed" to save him or her, or did not gather the proper evidence to aid the investigation. Blame most commonly will be placed with the police for failing to interview the proper witnesses or investigate the case fully in the first place. The survivors view the police as the ones most responsible for catching their perpetrator. Thus, when the offender remains at large it reflects poorly on the officers' ability to close the case (Stretesky et al., 2010; Wellman, 2011).

Fear is another common emotion that is present in an unsolved murder. Without an apprehension, there is always the risk of the perpetrator killing someone else or returning to kill another member of the family. Even more frightening is the realization that without identification cold case survivors are left questioning who the killer could be. Family members, friends, associates, and strangers all become potential suspects, creating an additional challenge to the grieving process. The potential to be living, or associating, with the killer can cause the cold case homicide survivors to internalize their grief and isolate themselves from their social groups.

Case Study Reflection

In the case study, the mother, Janis, is working hard to grieve her husband's death while trying to parent her two young children. Despite resuming work, Janis has several challenges for both her own healing and for the grief journey of her children. Janis is approaching her children as too fragile to handle the reality of their father's death, thus mirroring the Brittle Family detailed by Vesper and Cohen (1999).

Janis is unaware of how to talk to her children about their father's death, so in an effort to protect them, she originally misled her son to think his father was sick and has yet to disclose the death to her daughter, who was present at the funeral. It is easy to understand why Janis has defaulted to this protection mechanism of avoiding the topic of death with her children, because as a child, she too was misled about her own father's sudden traumatic death. However, Ethan may now struggle with the reality of his father's death, may fear others becoming "sick" as his father's "sickness" meant he died, and may not trust his mother or may display anger towards her for hiding the truth of his father's murder. Her daughter, while young, is also at risk of complications if Janis does not tell her about her father's death.

It becomes critical to develop age-appropriate explanations of the murder of their father and to establish an open communication policy within the family.

Utilizing Miller's (2009a) age breakdown, it is possible that Sarai, aged 3, may not fully understand the concept of death but is likely observing the turmoil and distress in the home. By age 4, Miller notes children do understand the absence of a loved one and need their safety reassured. Ethan is in the age bracket that may present as being preoccupied and detached from grief, but may struggle with the loss of the family member and need to have his questions addressed. His presentation of difficulties in the classroom and lack of joy are consistent with the literature (Eth & Pynoos, 1994). The children are also likely reacting to the presentation of emotions by their caregivers (mother, grandparents, and uncle) and to the perceived chaos and distress in the home caused by the reassignment of roles and lack of comfort from their father (Brown et al., 2008). Ethan is becoming overprotective and a fatherly figure to his sister, establishing that he feels the pressure to assume the void that his father left (Asaro & Clements, 2005).

References

American Psychiatric Association. (2000). *Diagnostic and statistical manual of mental disorders* (4th ed., text rev.). Washington, DC: American Psychiatric Association.

Amick-McMullan, A., Kilpatrick, D. G., & Resnick, H. S. (1991). Homicide as a risk factor for PTSD among surviving family members. *Behavior Modification, 15*, 545–559. doi: 10.1177/01454455910154005

Applebaum, D. R., & Burns, G. L. (1991). Unexpected childhood death: Posttraumatic stress disorder in surviving siblings and parents. *Journal of Clinical Child Psychology, 20*, 114–120. doi: 10.1207/s15374424jccp2002_1

Armour, M. P. (2002). Journey of family members of homicide victims: A qualitative study of their posthomicide experience. *American Journal of Orthopsychiatry, 72*, 372–382. doi: 10.1037/0002-9432.72.3.372

Armour, M. P. (2003). Meaning making in the aftermath of homicide. *Death Studies, 27*, 519–540. doi: 10.1080/07481180302884

Asaro, M. R. (1992). *Families of homicide victims: Reactions and coping experiences* (Unpublished master's thesis). Ann Arbor, MI: University Microfilm.

Asaro, M. R. (2001). Working with adult homicide survivors, Part 1: Impact and sequelae of murder. *Perspectives in Psychiatric Care, 37*(3), 95–101. doi: 10.1111/j.1744-6163.2001.tb00633.x

Asaro, M. R., & Clements, P. T. (2005). Homicide bereavement: A family affair. *Journal of Forensic Nursing, 1*(3), 101–106. doi: 10.1111/j.1939-3938.2005.tb00025.x

Baliko, B., & Tuck, I. (2008). Perceptions of survivors of loss by homicide: Opportunities for nursing practice. *Journal of Psychosocial Nursing and Mental Health Services, 46*(5), 26–34. doi: 10.3928/02793695-20080501-02

Bard, M. (1982). *A retrospective study of homicide survivor adaptation*. (Final Report, Grant No. R01 MH31685). Rockville, MD: National Institute of Mental Health.

Bard, M., & Sangrey, D. (1979). *Things fall apart: Victims in crisis*. New York, NY: Basic Books.

Barnes, M. F. (1998). Understanding the secondary traumatic stress of parents. In C. R. Figley (Ed.), *Burnout in families: The systematic cost of caring* (pp. 75–89). Boca Raton, FL: CRC Press.

Brown, E. J., Amaya-Jackson, L., Cohen, J., Handel, S., Bocanegra, H. T. D., Zatta, E., . . . Mannarino, A. (2008). Childhood traumatic grief: A multi-site empirical examination of the construct and its correlates. *Death Studies*, *32*, 899–923.

Bucholz, J. A. (2002). *Homicide survivors: Misunderstood grievers*. Amityville, NY: Baywood.

Burgess, A. W. (1975). Family reaction to homicide. *American Journal of Orthopsychiatry*, *45*, 391–398. doi: 10.1111/j.1939-0025.1975.tb02550.x

Chapple, A., & Ziebland, S. (2010). Viewing the body after bereavement due to a traumatic death: Qualitative study in the UK. *British Medical Journal*, *340*, c2032. doi: 10.1136/bmj.c2032

Clements, P. T., & Burgess, A. W. (2002). Children's responses to family member homicide. *Family and Community Health*, *25*, 32–42.

Czillinger, K. J. (1986). Advice to clergy on counseling bereaved parents. In T. A. Rando (Ed.), *Parental loss of a child* (pp. 465–471). Champaign, IL: Research Press.

Doka, K. J. (Ed.). (2002). *Disenfranchised grief: New directions, challenges, and strategies for practice*. Champaign, IL: Research Press.

Eth, S., & Pynoos, R. S. (1994). Children who witness the homicide of a parent. *Psychiatry*, *57*(4), 287–306. doi: 10.1521/00332747.1994.11024694

Feldman Hertz, M., Prothrow-Stith, D., & Chery, C. (2005). Homicide survivors: Research and practice implications. *American Journal of Preventive Medicine*, *29*, 288–295. doi: 10.1016/j.amepre.2005.08.027

Grebstein, L. C. (1986). Family therapy after a child's death. In T. A. Rando (Ed.), *Parental loss of a child* (pp. 429–449). Champaign, IL: Research Press.

Hardison, H. G., Neimeyer, R. A., & Lichstein, K. L. (2005). Insomnia and complicated grief symptoms in bereaved college students. *Behavioral Sleep Medicine*, *3*, 99–111. doi: 10.1207/s15402010bsm0302_4

Hathaway, W. L., & Pargament, K. I. (1991). The religious dimensions of coping: Implications for prevention and promotion. *Prevention in Human Services*, *9*, 65–92. doi: 10.1300/J293v09n02_04

Hodgkinson, P. E., Joseph, S., Yule, W., & Williams, R. (1993). Viewing human remains following disaster: Helpful or harmful? *Medicine, Science and Law*, *33*, 197–202.

Horowitz, M. J., Siegel, B., Holen, A., Bonanno, G. A., Milbrath, C., & Stinson, C. H. (1997). Diagnostic criteria for complicated grief disorder. *American Journal of Psychiatry*, *154*, 904–910.

Hussain, A., Weisaeth, L., & Heir, T. (2010). Psychiatric disorders and functional impairment among disaster victims after exposure to a natural disaster: A population-based study. *Journal of Affective Disorders*, *128*, 135–141. doi: 10.1016/j.jad.2010.06.018

Jacobs, K. A., Wellman, A. R., Fuller, A. M., Anderson, C. P., & Jurado, S. M. (2016). Exploring the familial impact of cold case homicides. *Journal of Family Studies*, *22*, 1–16. doi: 10.1080/13229400.2015.1065195

Janoff-Bulman, R. (1985). The aftermath of victimization: Rebuilding shattered assumptions. In C. R. Figley (Ed.), *Trauma and its wake: The study and treatment of post-traumatic stress disorder* (pp. 15–31). New York, NY: Brunner/Mazel, Inc.

Jones, S. J., & Beck, E. (2007). Disenfranchised grief and nonfinite loss as experienced by the families of death row inmates. *OMEGA-Journal of Death and Dying*, *54*, 281–299.

Karmen, A. (2007). *Crime victims: An introduction to victimology*. Belmont, CA: Wadsworth.

Kashka, M. S., & Beard, M. T. (1999). The grief of parents of murdered children: A suggested model for intervention. *Holistic Nursing, 14*, 22–36.
Kenney, J. S. (2003). Gender roles and grief cycles: Observations on models of grief and coping in homicide cases. *International Review of Victimology, 10*, 19–47. doi: 10.1177/026975800301000102
Klass, D. (1993). The inner representation of the dead child and the world views of bereaved parents. *OMEGA-Journal of Death and Dying, 26*, 255–272. doi: 10.2190/GEYM-BQWN-9N98-23Y5
Kristensen, P., Weisæth, L., & Heir, T. (2012). Bereavement and mental health after sudden and violent losses: A review. *Psychiatry, 75*, 76–97. doi: 10.1521/psyc.2012.75.1.76
Kübler-Ross, E. (1969). *On death and dying*. New York, NY: Macmillan.
Kübler-Ross, E., & Kessler, D. (2005). *On grief and grieving: Finding the meaning of grief through the five stages of loss*. New York, NY: Scribner.
Malone, L. (2007). In the aftermath: Listening to people bereaved by homicide. *Probation Journal, 54*, 383–393. doi: 10.1177/0264550507083537
Matthews, L. T., & Marwit, S. J. (2004). Examining the assumptive world views of parents bereaved by accident, murder, and illness. *OMEGA-Journal of Death and Dying, 48*, 115–136. doi: 10.2190/KCB0-NNVB-UGY6-NPYR
Merlevede, E., Spooren, D., Henderick, H., Portzky, G., Buylaert, W., Jannes, C., . . . Michem, N. (2004). Perceptions, needs and mourning reactions of bereaved relatives confronted with a sudden unexpected death. *Resuscitation, 61*, 341–348. doi: 10.1016/j.resuscitation.2004.01.024
Mezey, G., Evans, C., & Hobdell, K. (2002). Families of homicide victims: Psychiatric responses and help-seeking. *Psychology and Psychotherapy: Theory, Research and Practice, 75*, 65–75. doi: 10.1348/147608302169553
Middleton, W., Raphael, B., Burnett, P., & Martinek, N. (1998). A longitudinal study comparing bereavement phenomena in recently bereaved spouses, adult children and parents. *Australian and New Zealand Journal of Psychiatry, 32*, 235–241. doi: 10.3109/00048679809062734
Miller, L. (1999). Treating posttraumatic stress disorder in children and families: Basic principles and clinical application. *American Journal of Family Therapy, 27*, 21–34. doi: 10.1080/019261899262078
Miller, L. (2009a). Family survivors of homicide: I. Symptoms, syndromes, and reaction patterns. *The American Journal of Family Therapy, 37*, 67–79. doi: 10.1080/01926180801960625
Miller, L. (2009b). Family survivors of homicide: II. Practical therapeutic strategies. *The American Journal of Family Therapy, 37*, 85–98. doi: 10.1080/01926180801960633
Murphy, S. A. (1996). Parent bereavement stress and preventive intervention following the violent deaths of adolescent or young adult children. *Death Studies, 20*, 441–452. doi: 10.1080/07481189608252753
Murphy, S. A., Johnson, L. C., Wu, L., Fan, J. J., & Lohan, J. (2003). Bereaved parents' outcomes 4 to 60 months after their children's deaths by accident, suicide, or homicide: A comparative study demonstrating differences. *Death Studies, 27*, 39–61. doi: 10.1080/07481180302871
Neimeyer, R. A., & Jordan, J. R. (2002). Disenfranchisement as empathic failure: Grief therapy and the co-construction of meaning. In K. Doka (Ed.), *Disenfranchised grief* (pp. 95–117). Champaign, IL: Research Press.

Parents of Murdered and Missing Children. (2015). *Survivors of homicide*. Retrieved from: http://www.pomc.com/survivors.html

Poltorak, D. Y., & Glazer, J. P. (2006). The development of children's understanding of death: Cognitive and psychodynamic considerations. *Child and Adolescent Clinics of North America, 15*, 567–573.

Prigerson, H. G., Bierhals, A. J., Kasl, S. V., Reynolds, C., Shear, M. K., Day, N., Beery, L. C., Newsom, J. T., & Jacobs, S. (1997). Traumatic grief as a risk factor for mental and physical morbidity. *American Journal of Psychiatry, 154*, 616–623. doi: 10.1176/ajp.154.5.616

Rando, T. A. (1993). *Treatment of complicated mourning*. Champaign, IL: Research Press.

Raphael, B. (1986). *When disaster strikes: How individuals and communities cope with catastrophe*. New York, NY: Basic Books.

Rock, P. (1998). Murderers, victims and "survivors": The social construction of deviance. *The British Journal of Criminology, 38*, 185–200.

Ronen, T. (2002). Difficulties in assessing traumatic reactions in children. *Journal of Loss & Trauma, 7*, 87–106. doi: 10.1080/153250202753472264

Rynearson, E. K. (1984). Bereavement after homicide: A descriptive study. *American Journal of Psychiatry, 141*, 1452–1454. doi: 10.1176/ajp.141.11.1452

Rynearson, E. K. (1988). The homicide of a child. In F. M. Ochberg (Ed.), *Post-traumatic therapy and victims of violence* (pp. 213–224). New York, NY: Brunner/Mazel, Inc.

Rynearson, E. K. (2001). *Retelling violent death*. Philadelphia: Brunner-Routledge.

Rynearson, T. (1994). Psychotherapy of bereavement after homicide. *The Journal of Psychotherapy Practice and Research, 3*, 341–347.

Scott, S. (2000). Grief reactions to the death of a divorced spouse revisited. *OMEGA-Journal of Death and Dying, 41*, 207–219. doi: 10.2190/KKML-1RGK-105U-L9PE

Sprang, G., & McNeil, J. S. (1995). *The many faces of bereavement: The nature and treatment of natural, traumatic, and stigmatized grief.* New York, NY: Brunner/Mazel.

Spungen, D. (1998). *Homicide: The hidden victims: A resource for professionals* (Vol. 20). Thousand Oaks, CA: Sage.

Steele, W. (2013). Grief and trauma: The confusion, the difference. *TLC Starr*. Retrieved from: https://www.starr.org/sites/default/files/articles/confusiondifference.pdf

Stretesky, P. B., Shelley, T. O. C., Hogan, M. J., & Unnithan, N. P. (2010). Sense-making and secondary victimization among unsolved homicide co-victims. *Journal of Criminal Justice, 38*(5), 880–888. doi: 10.1016/j.jcrimjus.2010.06.003

Symonds, M. (1980). The "second injury" to victims. *Evaluation and Change, 7*, 36–38.

Thompson, M. P., & Vardaman, P. J. (1997). The role of religion in coping with the loss of a family member to homicide. *Journal for the Scientific Study of Religion, 36*, 44–51. doi: 10.2307/1387881

United States Department of Justice, Federal Bureau of Investigation. (2015). *Crime in the United States, 2014*. Retrieved on February 21, 2016 from: https://www.fbi.gov/about-us/cjis/ucr/crime-in-the-u.s/2014/crime-in-the-u.s.-2014/offenses-known-to-law-enforcement/murder/murder/murder.pdf

Vesper, J. H., & Cohen, L. J. (1999). Litigating posttraumatic stress disorder: Effects on the family. *The Journal of Psychiatry & Law, 27*, 313–337. doi: 10.1177/009318539902700204

Vigil, G. J., & Clements, P. T. (2003). Child and adolescent homicide survivors: Complicated grief and altered worldviews. *Journal of Psychosocial Nursing and Mental Health Services*, *41*, 30–39. doi: 10.3928/0279-3695-20030101-11

Walton, R. H. (Ed.). (2006). *Cold case homicides: Practical investigative techniques*. Boca Raton, FL: CRC Press.

Wellman, A. R. P. (2011). Breaking the ice: Understanding the experiences of cold case homicide survivors (Unpublished doctoral dissertation). Gainesville, FL: University of Florida.

Wellman, A. R. P. (2013). Real to reel: The impact of media crime coverage on cold case homicide survivors. *Annual Meeting of American Society of Criminology*. Atlanta Marriott Marquis. Atlanta, GA. November 21, 2013.

Wellman, A. R. P. (2014a). Faith without answers: The use of religion among cold case homicide survivors. *OMEGA-Journal of Death and Dying*, *69*, 19–39. doi: 10.2190/OM.69.1.b

Wellman, A. R. P. (2014b). Grief in comparison: Use of social comparison among cold case homicide survivors. *Journal of Loss and Trauma*, *19*, 462–473. doi: 10.1080/15325024.2013.801306

Winje, D. (1998). Cognitive coping: The psychological significance of knowing what happened in the traumatic event. *Journal of Traumatic Stress*, *11*, 627–643. doi: 10.1023/A:1024433114095

Winje, D., & Ulvik, A. (1995). Confrontations with reality: Crisis intervention services for traumatized families after a school bus accident in Norway. *Journal of Traumatic Stress*, *8*, 429–444. doi: 10.1002/jts.2490080306

Yalom, I. D. (1980). *Existential psychotherapy*. New York, NY: Basic Books.

Clinical Work With Families of Homicide

Mary Beth Hays and Scott W. Browning

The psychological treatment of families of homicide (FoH) demands therapists are competent in addressing systems and highly attuned to trauma. One significant difference from traditional family therapy is that the clinician needs to understand the legal system in order to support and recognize the burden on the family. Additionally, a therapist must be more aware of her or his own reaction than typical. Stabilizing the family involves providing absolute safety and support, while building a clear understanding of the effect of the trauma on all family members. How is this family being forced to adapt? How are the various effects of the murder being understood and discussed by family members? It is in addressing these issues that the skilled therapist excels.

The Families

Families of homicide (FoH) exist with a significant systemic void. In each family (of any composition) the abrupt loss of a family member pushes the system toward instability. Although we do not wish to suggest that all families move into a state of severe dysfunction, many do suffer greatly. Alternatively, some families marshal resources and find a way to adapt quickly. Also, if most members of the family are psychologically healthy, their personal stability spreads throughout the family. Instability, in this context, refers to the extraordinary shift in both communication patterns and family structure. A family is more than the sum of its parts (Watzlawick, Bavelas, & Jackson, 1967). Therefore, the loss of an individual creates a redefined system. While most of the members still exist and "life goes on," it goes on in a new manner. The role of each person is altered by the loss of a family member. Commonly, the remaining parent and eldest child experience needs that demand focused attention since their status within the home has gone through the greatest change.

The new system is structurally different and has altered communication. The structural aspects can be addressed, to an extent, by filling the void. While a family never is the same as prior to the loss, the void in the system can be made less gaping by increasing the family's engagement with others. Two common interventions are getting the family involved in group activities and increasing contact with extended family and good friends. However, it is in addressing communication that this approach is most distinct.

Once the murder has occurred, the deceased has altered four channels of communication. The murdered individual is no longer a: (1) speaker, (2) listener, (3) topic of a changing conversation, or (4) an influence on how others are perceived. Thus, almost all communication within a family is somewhat altered following the murder. In the midst of this turbulence, the clinical professional needs to assist these families either through individual, group, or family treatment. In other words, communication must be increased among those left in the family due to the void left by having one member be murdered.

Treatment Considerations and Approaches

This section is dedicated to family-based treatment, even when the initial client of record is an individual. Our treatment is grounded in a systemically informed (Guttman, 1991) contextual therapy model (Boszormenyi-Nagy & Krasner, 1986) that makes important use of Mindfulness-Based Play-Family Therapy, MBPFT (Higgins-Klein, 2013) strategies as well. Importantly, the works of Badenoch (2008), Bloom (2013), Gil and Terr (2010), and Mahler, Pine, and Bergman (2008) provide critical contributions to the philosophical underpinnings and trauma-informed techniques of this approach. Accordingly, readers may seek additional information in those works.

Specific to our approach, there are five pillars we highlight. The initial overarching feature of a family in which a member has been murdered is a sense of stigma (Spungen, 1998). The idea of murder is so uncomfortable that it stretches our empathic capacity. Accordingly, the therapist's *nonjudgmental acceptance* is a critical first pillar. A clinician must be able to understand the profound grief as well as assist all members to survive this trauma. A second pillar involves *offering direction*. Due to feeling aimless, members of the family seek advice. They are not asking for, nor expecting, a standard guidebook to follow, but they do expect a clinician to serve as a coach in figuring out how life continues (both practically and emotionally) after such a loss.

The third pillar includes the legion of *evidence-based treatment (EBT)* interventions that can assist family members with specific, diagnosable problems (e.g., depression, panic, parent-child conflict). These interventions do not represent the totality of treatment, but they can assist some members of the family to better cope, thus strengthening the overall family. The fourth pillar is the understanding of *common factors* (Frank, 1995; Norcross, 1999; Rosenzweig, 1936). Common factors are those universal therapeutic positions that fall outside the category of "techniques," but clearly are part of effective therapy no matter which model of treatment is being utilized. For example, empathy, goal clarity, and the therapeutic alliance are consistently part of effective treatment.

Finally, the fifth pillar consists of those *interventions aimed at this specific population* (families of homicide), which is the focus here. This section provides foundational concepts for treating FoH, in addition to a description of the approach. The specific treatment offered to the case study family is presented as well. Generally, the therapist balances the primary needs of the family, while focusing on grief, trauma, legal difficulties, and family stability and role confusion. This particular approach evolved due to an agency that has as its sole mission, the care of those family members remaining after a murder. The Anti-Violence Partnership, the clinical arm of Families of Homicide Victims, was incorporated in Philadelphia, Pennsylvania, in 1982.

Creating Safety

Although cliché, there is great wisdom in the adage that, as clinicians, we must look at ourselves and do our own therapeutic work before asking anyone else to do the same. This practice does not suggest that histories, experiences, and cultures must be matched between the therapist and the client. Instead, what it offers is some clarity as to a therapist's unconscious agendas that might compromise the ability to be fully and authentically present. In other words, it is crucial for the therapist to be self-aware in order to simultaneously be aware of others. One might challenge that if we are completely attending to our clients, then how could "we" get in the way. Utilizing contextual therapy the therapist lends her or himself in a balanced and calm manner when working with trauma. Bloom describes the value of this deftness:

> *People can have an enormous positive influence on a highly aroused individual. If they can maintain clarity and calmness, this too can be contagious, thus reducing the other person's level of arousal both emotionally and physiologically. We actually have an enormous, underestimated, and often neglected role to play in other people's emotional lives.*
>
> (Bloom, 2013, p. 43)

The therapist who consciously or unconsciously is focused on her or his agenda will inevitably be less present to a client. This sort of a distraction creates an imbalance, which can create a disturbance in the trust and safety of the therapeutic process. There is a presence of humility when a clinician recognizes her or his own biases or agenda, even when one wishes to deny such an agenda exists—this in turn exhibits clinical competence (Bloom, 2013). The authenticity of the therapist directly increases trust, which in turn builds safety in the therapeutic space. Safety can also be determined by who is invited, discussed, and/or present in the room. The therapeutic pacing must match the client's vulnerability. In other words, clinical work involves a clear assessment of each person's vulnerability when the whole family has been traumatized. Determining the level of vulnerability means that the clinician gauges the client's mood, defensiveness, and affect. Helping a family become more stable is an essential goal and is dependent on creating a sense of clinical safety, especially in a family that has experienced homicide and is, by definition, less secure.

Predictable Milestones

For the members of an FoH, there are various milestones that collide. As with any traumatic loss, shock, denial, numbness, sadness, and anger may occur. A general distrust and hypervigilance to outsiders is a common reaction to the family system's experience of a homicide. Therapists may need to address traumatic responses and grief in a manner that acknowledges how each is influenced by the other. Emotional issues, psychological concerns, and legal challenges all confront the family simultaneously. However, the members of an FoH also are suddenly distrustful, hypervigilant, and anxious.

With the traumatic loss of a family member, particularly when it is a parent, a child's developmental process is likely to be affected. Regulation theory (Schore & Schore, 2008) suggests that this level of trauma has specific effects on brain functioning. Simultaneously, psychological development and brain functioning are altered, and those providing clinical care should understand this process. This knowledge base is necessary to both fully empathize with family members and provide some education as to the physiological basis of their changed behaviors.

Clinically, therapists must be well versed in typical development. As this pertains to working with co-victims, it is important to understand where possible emotional, psychological, and physical disruptions can occur. For those clinicians regularly utilizing the DSM-5, it is important to not overly diagnose the natural consequences of trauma, as it can increase the chance of misdiagnosing. Traumatic grief in children can look like ADHD, anxiety, depression, OCD, ODD, PTSD, and more. Children and adults alike develop coping skills that best serve the individual in that moment. It is the responsibility of the therapist to understand typical development and to be mindful of the possible interruptions and how they might present. Bessel van der Kolk (2014) speaks to the effects of the mind-body connection offering an understanding of how trauma gets stored in the body and presents within the *self*. Treating practitioners should be informed of the mind-body relationship to traumatic events and the host of possibilities in which the experiences are held and manifested. Reaching into the histories of possible psychological and physiological expressions of trauma and their cognitive impact is critical in attempting to understand and treat the root of trauma.

Understanding the nuances of a particular criminal justice system is extremely beneficial to the family as they negotiate this system. The sheer range of personnel and procedures involved in the investigation, possible arrest, and trial are relevant. FoH must interact with police, detectives, attorneys, and advocates. They also are exposed to the defendant's family members and supporters, and possible media attention. If an arrest is made, then the process expands again to include court proceedings, trials, verdicts, sentencing, pleas, parole, and so forth. The length of time required for this process is something of which clinicians should be aware, given each significantly can impact the emotional milestones.

As if the layers of confusion and complexity confronting the FoH are not enough, the clinician must be prepared to address the possible stigma of homicide co-victims. Co-victims also can experience a real or imagined threat from the community, financial losses, and sometimes, relocation by choice. If the victim was a significant earner in the family, the loss of income can impact lifestyle, residence, work life, schools, transportation, health, and insurance. When defendants and victims are related, there is the opportunity for family and community divides. Race and class are typically woven into many aspects of the co-victim's experience (i.e., "innocent" vs. "guilty/deserving" victims). Having a family member murdered shifts almost every relationship across one's entire life.

Inclusion of Education in Treatment

It is clinically responsible to provide psychoeducation pertaining to homicide, traumatic grief, typical development, and information about the potential judicial system experience. Informing clients about the realities of living with traumatic grief after homicide can be both daunting yet validating. Clients often want to know if what they are experiencing is typical and when it will stop. Clinicians can never assure someone of the exact process, although traumatic grief due to a violent death does have some predictable stages. In the first half of this chapter by Wellman, the wide range of responses to homicide within the family are described. When individual worldviews are impacted by murder, it can be a tremendous battle to reenter the family system or even society. The immediate reconfiguration, for most families, leaves individuals often feeling powerless and victimized as well. Parenting demands can seem impossible for some, while others may become overly vigilant and feel the need to restrict their children dramatically. Often there is such a surreal quality to the death that daily functioning is challenged by reality. For spouses, they are suddenly alone. If the couple had children, the status of single parenthood is immediate.

Although clinical safety has been discussed, these families often are conscious of actual physical safety as well. For some, an actual threat of being killed by association is possible, especially when defendants are not apprehended in a timely fashion. In the case of a witness, it is all too real that their lives also might be at risk for homicide as a way to prevent potential testimony. It is most necessary to begin these dialogues before getting into the deeper clinical work in case witness protection or relocation services are warranted.

As stated earlier, it can be helpful to educate clients on what might be occurring with their brain as a reaction to trauma. Clinically, one should not overtax individuals with an inordinate amount of information, but instead integrate basic science regarding the mind with practical life experiences. For example, trauma is considered to be stored primarily in the right hemisphere, thus a treatment that activates that part of the brain is effective. Play therapy is dependent on actions that help strengthen pathways in the brain that generate trauma recall. The strengthening of this pathway reacquaints the individual to the traumatic imagery, and serves as a safe approach to exposure treatment—a treatment effective for panic, trauma, and anxiety.

Conveying an understandable rationale about intrusive imagery (and how these images can be triggers) provides trauma survivors with some sense of predictability. When working with homicide co-victims, the notion of reigning in powerlessness is challenging at best, especially when they are enduring the judicial process and simultaneously trying to grieve. It is helpful to understand that many coping mechanisms are related to and/or influenced by their family of origin and presiding cultural identity. In other words, styles of grief may be inherited; thus, a particularly stoic individual may have learned that talking about loss is useless. Behaviors and mechanisms of coping may differ as much as the individuals themselves.

An example of the importance of education for parents and teachers on behalf of children is that it can provide the appropriate context for reducing judgment and increasing acceptance. For example, the caregivers may begin to understand that when the bell rings in the presence of a child who has experienced a trauma, the student may become triggered by the startling auditory stimulation. The trauma connection then unfolds—the ringing of the bell increases the child's startle response, which then makes it hard for the child to remain emotionally regulated. If within a school community there is a shared understanding that a child's brain becomes activated and overly hypervigilant as a means of trauma-related self-protection (and not with the expressed intent to disrupt the classroom), the educational community can then provide the student with an opportunity to experience a supportive (not punitive) environment. When children and adults are understood and accepted, it is far easier to clarify intentions; thus, relationships can be healed. Explaining to both caretakers as well as educators that trauma is stored in a part of the mind where there is no language can help to support the child who is forced into overly cognitive dialogues about the trauma symptoms in regard to the homicide (e.g., regression, sleep disturbances). This potentially can inform necessary accommodations. A common trend is that as children begin to integrate the trauma and loss, their academic performance will rise again.

Traumatic grief is often exhibited in regressive behaviors. Explaining to parents, family members, and outside caretakers about the possible disruption that a 3-year-old co-victim may experience is hugely relevant to the anticipation and expectation of normal developmental milestones. Communicating that children between the ages of 18 months and 3 years of age are working on mastering their sense of emotions is critical to the potential disruption of the developmental phase. If this development is impacted by a sudden violent loss, then one would expect to see poor emotional regulation.

The Genogram

One useful treatment tool is the genogram. Not only does a clear genogram offer clarity for the clinician in understanding the numerous systemic factors, but it is also an educational tool. While showing a family the genogram, it is informative to explain the need to remain connected to extended family, especially on the victim's side. The family's norms and values become clear when learning about their intergenerational history. This process often generates a space for increased self-reflection as families are reminded of the context in which they were raised and how inherited relational traits inform them on many levels, even in the way that they grieve and manage the loss of control. The expanding genogram creates a platform of nonjudgment held by the therapist. In a sense, a genogram provides an opportunity for one to see that all people are affected by the loss. While typical curiosity often encourages the therapist to look for one person suffering the most (or most responsible for certain problems in the family), the underpinnings of contextual family therapy push the therapist to be "partial" to all those in the family system.

A Direct and Non-Partial Clinical Stance

The clients can experience this nonjudgment and partiality in many ways. Often the connections of relational inheritance are not even seen until the genogram process occurs. The therapist then will be informed by the family trauma. It is more likely that the therapist is able to revisit the genogram as a part of the therapeutic process, updating and learning more as clients are able to remember and/or trust more to share. As the therapist has a greater understanding of the intergenerational concepts that have been passed on consciously and unconsciously, it informs the direction of the work. Admittedly, clients often are blind to realities of their family history that could be described by the therapist as clearly identifiable. The therapist must balance when to invite the client to look further while maintaining safety with patience (and, more often, silence), which is a skill that must be practiced and looked to as a constant goal. Genuine therapeutic shifts are quite transformative when the therapist only guides individuals and allows for clients to come to their own awareness.

When working with homicide co-victims, it is important to gain an increased understanding of the family dynamics present prior to the homicide, including both previous losses and traumas, as families are not defined entirely by one event. Health, addictions, divorce, parenting styles, adoption, domestic violence, abuse, positive attachment, siblings to great-grandparent relational dynamics, marriage, sexual orientation, and more all influence the individual and the family system. All that has happened in one's life prior to the homicide (as well as after the sudden loss) informs the process, notwithstanding previous traumas, varied losses, and all else that occurs in a person's life that is a part of his or her personal narrative. Social teachings, either verbal or nonverbal, inform how one grieves, how one perceives something traumatic, as well as how one sees oneself within one's own narrative. For example, when the community norm is saturated with violence, it can be difficult to notably identify, acknowledge, and respond to such grave injustices. Hence, if violence is so much a part of the individual's fabric, the threads are often indistinguishable to the self. Therefore, it is the role of the therapist to begin to unravel and identify the multiple emotional and psychological injuries sustained throughout one's life, much like magnifying the threads of a beautifully woven piece of material.

Through family histories, individuals are given directives on the social/cultural/familial practices and acceptance of how one should or should not grieve, how one should manage stress reactions, and/or the consequences of either position. For instance, if silence is the family/cultural practice, then how does verbalizing about the traumatic grief impact this individual's loyalty to the family system? The concept of exploring the costs, consequences, or possible freedom should always be explored. If outward expression of traumatic grief is expected, then how might an individual who is silently distraught (nondemonstrative) become interpreted within the family system? These positions or social practices of how one should grieve and manage violent tragedy are passed through generations.

When approaching treatment in which there was previous family violence, it is important to not overly direct the agenda, as many traumatic memories may surface well beyond the homicide itself. Having the necessary training and supervision with domestic violence is an ethical imperative in order to obtain a full understanding about family violence without judgment or pretense. In the event where the victim was an abuser/offender, it can naturally further complicate the trauma and loss. The therapist must always be prepared for anyone's "truth" to invite the complexity of responses, from rage to relief, that the client's loved one has been murdered.

Clinical Approach for the Case Study

After Janis called requesting therapy, the therapist acknowledged the family's loss. In keeping with MBPFT, the therapist listened to the mother's request to treat Ethan and then began to explain the theory of working with the child of most concern (CMC) within the framework of the family. Hence, the therapist welcomed the opportunity to work with Ethan, but also suggested therapeutic interest in the mother's well-being while not excluding Sarai. This family approach is much more respectful to the systemic pulse of the traumatic loss than focusing solely on the CMC as the potential symptom bearer for the family. At the point of referral, the therapist invited the mother to come to the initial session alone in order to gain more information about both Ethan and the family. This style of pacing allowed for the parent to assess and connect with the therapist, so that when the child meets the therapist at the next session he or she can experience how the parent validates the therapy at the clinician's request. While initially meeting with just the adult(s) the therapist also will have a chance to hear any information with great sensitivity and attunement without the age-appropriate censoring that occurs when children are present. Taking particular notice of how families are impacted by a homicide clearly highlights the need for individual space, often due to graphic specifics of the violent death. The descriptions of homicide events can easily create secondary traumatization to other family members, depending on the proximity to the event. Hence, the clinician should be diligent in differentiating those who have been exposed to the crime as direct witnesses and those who have learned of the homicide otherwise, while incorporating developmental age and relationship as a treatment cursor. Ensuring that individuals have their own trauma narrative is critical and is not to be influenced by the descriptors of direct witnesses as much as possible. This same opportunity for traumatization often happens during both preliminary hearings and homicide trials, where graphic details are essential.

Upon meeting at the intake session, the therapist acknowledged the loss of Janis's husband and the loss of the children's father. The therapist went on to provide an overview of a possible agenda to explore over the next several sessions, with a focus on learning how the death impacted individuals and the family to date, as well as obtaining a developmental history on Ethan. Co-victims of homicide often feel compelled to share the details of days prior and the events leading up to the loved one's death. In the event where family members potentially witness the homicide or violent assaults, this also can include the specifics of the crime. This pointed information provides the therapist with an opportunity to gather trauma and loss details as the assessment begins. When working with homicide co-victims, or those "victimized" by violent loss, it is tremendously relevant to ask about who is in the family system as a way to acknowledge those directly impacted by the loss. Introducing and naming the concept of co-victimization is one of the initial tenets of defining the difference of a sudden violent death of a loved one versus traditional grief. Understanding and employing the term "co-victim" has the potential to highlight the relationship between the client and the loved one. From a victim advocacy perspective, we acknowledge the stigma sometimes attached to the use of the word "victim", and, instead, suggest use of "survivor" as the preferred term. Therefore, in the case of a co-victim who might take offense to being qualified in any way as a victim, the therapist can also describe the client as a survivor after the murder of his or her loved one. This level of conversation begins to set the stage for the therapist's openness to learning about the individual's/family's self-assessment regarding the impact of the sudden loss and death itself. This exploration invites the client to examine both the homicide and the specter of living with the fear of unexpected violence. This process generates an initial clinical sketch that often leads into a fuller genogram. This can provide a map into such family issues as support, attachment, or disconnectedness, all of which assist the therapist in understanding the family of origin, as well as the extended family.

Janis explained that each child had warm and loving connections with their father and they miss him daily. When asked about how Ethan learned of his father's death, Janis began to cry. She was initially unable to tell Ethan that his father had been murdered and instead told him that Michael was taken to the hospital because he was sick. At this point, Janis could not continue and it became clear that her needs were at the forefront in the moment. The therapist attended to Janis's pain of having to inform her son of his father's tragic death. One critical theme in this family's treatment was the emergence of Janis's struggle to be honest with Ethan, worrying that to do so would shatter his innocence. Janis felt conflicted because she disliked being dishonest, but she truly believed she was protecting her children. Janis avoided telling Ethan the facts, which frustrated him terribly and began to decrease his trust in his mother. Over time, this process of Ethan's demanding the truth and Janis's resistance to being honest was uncovered as a well-established family dynamic prior to the homicide. It was revealed that Janis learned this in her family of origin and was unaware of the cost of passing this tradition along. She described incidents of Ethan's behaviors as vacillating between blatant disobedience and catatonic passivity.

Ethan was described as a healthy boy who successfully completed first grade and was performing above grade level at the start of second grade. However, it appeared that Ethan was suffering from his father's traumatic loss in many ways. He started struggling with both reading and math and began to withdraw from his mother and friends. Ethan also was becoming easily frustrated, experiencing sleep disturbances, crying spells, and a loss of appetite. Ethan began to act in a parentified manner with his younger sister, Sarai. During the initial assessment process, when the mother was asked what she absolutely loved about Ethan, she described his smile and his laughter. She stated that she missed seeing his smile and certainly missed hearing his laughter. When asked who attended Michael's funeral, Janis remarked "everyone." It was during this assessment that Janis acknowledged that she had not yet told Sarai of her father's death. The therapeutic stance taken was that Sarai deserved to know the truth since this was *her* story too. The clinician must be partial to the anguish, from Janis's perspective, of explaining to her young daughter that her father was no longer to return because he had died, while also being partial to the necessity of Sarai knowing the truth. Offering Janis samples of language regarding how to share the sudden death of her father with Sarai would become part of the clinical agenda.

When gaining a family history through the genogram process it was learned that Janis's father had died when she was 7 years old. He was in a fatal car accident and died from a severe head injury. Janis reports that she was initially not informed of her father's death. She recalled being told that he was working far away, and over time she began to believe that her father had abandoned the family. Through this clinical lens the family relational dynamics were magnified. In this situation, the therapist's understanding of the generational resemblances was more complete than was Janis's. The only similarity Janis recognized between herself and her children was that they had all suffered childhood losses. She struggled to see that in both cases, the withholding of critical information (even with the best intentions) only added to confusion and mistrust. It would seem easily justifiable why any mother would never want to tell her children that their father had been murdered. But when a mother is already unconsciously informed about traumatic grief in her family of origin and has her own trauma narrative, it then becomes the task of the therapist to gently begin to highlight the generational parenting likenesses that were intended to be beneficial, originating from an innocent place of parental protection and trauma, yet consequentially destructive.

Although understandable given her history, Janis's reluctance to speak "the unspeakable" has potential long-term effects on a child's trust and security. Hence, Janis's history of traumatic grief directly affected her ability to deal with both her own historical grief and the current grief around her husband. For example, the fact that neither Sarai nor Ethan was initially told of their father's death highlights the depths of relational disruption. Janis's reluctance to share information with her children directly damaged Ethan, resulting in a boy who just months prior had been developmentally on track and was now regressed and full of fear. Therapy is uniquely able to highlight how a significant loss can compromise any child's developmental progress. As the treatment progressed, Ethan benefited from his individual play therapy and Sarai often joined family sessions. As opportunities presented, clinical openings occurred in which the therapist was able to draw the connection between the absence of Janis's directness and truthfulness in correlation with Ethan's negative behaviors as a form of distress and dissatisfaction of not knowing.

As is common in most homicide cases, there is a judicial process that parallels the loss—all attempts at justice, and/or the lack thereof, are experienced by all family members. In this family, Michael's killer was found. The murderer was a neighborhood juvenile who had become addicted to drugs and was seeking means to meet his addiction, reportedly never intending to kill Michael. The fact that the family actually knew this young defendant aroused Janis's early experiences of feeling betrayed as a layer of traumatic grief. The sense of betrayal needed to be addressed clinically. Narratives generated included her sense of pain, anger, powerlessness, efforts, vulnerabilities, systems, and trust.

These issues became central to the ongoing treatment. Treatment lasted for two years, and the goals achieved included both Ethan and Sarai being told of and about their father's death (concretely and age appropriately), as well as Janis engaging in her own individual therapy. Sarai began her own non-directive play therapy and continued with the family therapy, and Ethan's PTSD symptoms were significantly reduced. The central focus of treatment shifted to providing Janis with a tremendous amount of support including around parenting issues, addressing her own family history, and identifying her current needs as a single parent. Providing the safe space for the family to learn how to communicate honestly well beyond the "truths" of the homicide was critical to the management of their traumatic grief and daily functioning in both present and future. The mother/son relationship became far more transparent. Ethan responded to the treatment process quite favorably. He engaged in play therapy with great depth as he began to find expressive language for his need for honesty while grieving the traumatic loss of his father. This in turn allowed for fewer behavioral disruptions in all settings. He began to demonstrate the ability to identify his emotional state and needs, which was imperative for developing his sense of regulation and control. Janis's receptivity to having dialogues with her children that were not stifled by fear also fostered Ethan's capacity to speak and feel heard. Academically, Ethan finished treatment ahead of his educational milestones and was able to regain his momentum of learning with great stride. Sarai successfully engaged in her own play therapy communicating themes of loss, anger, and aggression. Developmentally, Sarai has remained on track with the support of MBPFT, her childcare team, and Janis's ability to be present and witness her pain and sorrow.

So much of this family's success was anchored in Janis's deep desire to help her son. Oftentimes the children of most concern lead their families into great healing opportunities (Higgins-Klein, 2013). Janis had the ability to reach out and accept resources that were beyond her initial scope of treatment needs, including modalities such as play therapy, family therapy, and her own individual therapy. She was able to process the concepts of intergenerational loyalties and practices that afforded her insight into her own trauma and pain. This constructive examination adjoined with clinical guidance afforded Janis the ability to care for herself and parent her children productively through an inordinate amount of trauma and loss. The clinical foundation regarding families and homicide moves into the greater awareness and practice of familial injustice, justice, and repair as it pertains to trauma, death, and grief.

The Clinical/Clinician's Process

The clinician must be open to the client's pain. This strength is often nonverbal but can be demonstrated by the therapist's comfort with witnessing profound psychological and emotional pain and trauma. The concept of this language of attunement is explicit in the discipline of interpersonal neurobiology (Badenoch, 2008). Not hurrying through the silence of tears, anger, and reminiscent thoughts is a tenet of building the relationship. This bold embrace of someone's pain, shock, and often confusion after a homicide affords the client a felt sense of experience and acceptance. Having knowledge of the impact of violence as it infects nations, communities, neighborhoods, schools, and households is imperative to the clinician's efforts of being present for all who have been afflicted by its contagion. The impression of traumatic grief is a prominent factor; yet, the clinician needs to balance this work with traditional family therapy concerns. FoH present the unusual challenge of supporting the surviving family members' past, present, and future functioning while simultaneously keeping the loss of the murdered family member in the balance of treatment. The clinician relies on an array of trauma-informed modalities depending on the needs of each member of the system as a comprehensive treatment approach.

References

Badenoch, B. (2008). *Being a brain-wise therapist: A practical guide to interpersonal neurobiology*. New York, NY: W. W. Norton & Company, Inc.

Bloom, S. (2013). *Creating sanctuary: Toward the evolution of sane societies* (Revised ed.). New York, NY: Taylor & Francis.

Boszormenyi-Nagy, I., & Krasner, B. R. (1986). *Between give and take: A clinical guide to contextual therapy*. New York, NY: Brunner/Mazel, Inc.

Frank, J. D. (1995). Psychotherapy as rhetoric: Some implications. *Clinical Psychology: Science and Practice*, *2*, 90–93. doi: 10.1111/j.1468-2850.1995.tb00030.x

Gil, E., & Terr, L. (2010). *Working with children to heal interpersonal trauma: The power of play*. New York, NY: Guilford Press.

Guttman, H. A. (1991). Systems theory, cybernetics, and epistemology. In A. S. Gurman & D. P. Kniskern (Eds.), *Handbook of family therapy* (pp. 41–62). New York, NY: Brunner/Mazel, Inc.

Higgins-Klein, D. (2013). *Mindfulness-based play-family therapy: Theory and practice*. New York, NY: W. W. Norton & Company, Inc.

Mahler, M. S., Pine, F., & Bergman, A. (2008). *The psychological birth of the human infant: Symbiosis and individuation*. New York, NY: Basic Books.

Norcross, J. (1999). Foreword. In M. A. Hubble, B. L. Duncan, & S. D. Miller (Eds.), *The heart and soul of change: What works in therapy* (pp. xvii–xix). Washington, DC: American Psychological Association.

Rosenzweig, S. (1936). Some implicit common factors in diverse methods of psychotherapy. *American Journal of Orthopsychiatry*, *6*, 412–415. doi: 10.1111/j.1939-0025.1936.tb05248.x

Schore, J. R., & Schore, A. N. (2008). Modern attachment theory: The central role of affect regulation in development and treatment. *Clinical Social Work Journal*, *36*(1), 9–20.

Spungen, D. (1998). *Homicide: The hidden victims: A guide for professionals*. Thousand Oaks, CA: Sage Publications.

Stretesky, P. B., Shelley, T.O.C., Hogan, M. J., & Unnithan, N. P. (2010). Sense-making and secondary victimization among unsolved homicide co-victims. *Journal of Criminal Justice*, 38, 880–888. https://doi.org/10.1016/j.jcrimjus.2010.06.003

Van der Kolk, B. (2014). *The body keeps the score: Brain, mind, and body in the healing of trauma*. New York: The Penguin Group.

Watzlawick, P., Bavelas, J. B., & Jackson, D. D. (1967). *Pragmatics of human communication: A study of interactional patterns, pathologies, and paradoxes*. New York, NY: W. W. Norton & Company, Inc.

7

FAMILIES OF INCARCERATION AND REENTRY

Case Study

John R. Hart, Kevin M. Roy, and Lorig Charkoudian

Tamika is a 35-year-old African-American. She and her 32-year-old boyfriend, Mychal, have been dating off and on for 10 years. Mychal is Puerto Rican and African-American, but self-identifies as African-American. Both consider themselves Christians but do not attend church regularly. Both Tamika and Mychal are from the South. They have three children together, a 14-year-old son (Chris) from Tamika's previous relationship, and a 10-year-old daughter (Jessica) and 7-year-old son (Luke). Mychal had a daughter with his previous fiancée, but the baby died shortly after the birth (Mychal was locked up for two years during the pregnancy and death). Mychal was in prison for the last four years, and since his release last month the family has experienced several difficulties.

Mychal's father, Jeff, was a known criminal and hustler, and his mother, Sandra, was a strong-minded Christian woman. They married young and got divorced shortly after his older brother's (Andre) birth. Sandra always dedicated her life to her boys and has been a great source of support financially, spiritually, emotionally, and relationally. Mychal expressed that it was hard watching his brother follow their father's criminal behaviors because it always broke his mother's heart. Tamika's mother, Lucille, and her maternal grandmother, Charlotte, raised her. Tamika's father, Riley, was killed in a car accident when Tamika was 2. Even though she does not remember much about her father, she loved hearing her mom talk about their marriage (e.g., Lucille would often tell Tamika, "He knew what it meant to show me love"). Tamika describes her upbringing and current relationships with her mother, grandmother, and older sister, Melinda, as loving and nurturing although they live three hours apart. Tamika even reported that all three made frequent trips to provide support to her and the kids while Mychal was locked up. Tamika admits that her sister Melinda is the only one supportive of her relationship with Mychal.

Tamika and Mychal both report that their relationship as a couple and as parents has been strained since Mychal has been released from prison. As a couple, Tamika shares that this last prison term has "hardened" Mychal; he struggles to meet her needs as a girlfriend and she feels that Mychal is trying to control her. Mychal expresses that Tamika has been "threatening to report me to my parole officer if she does not get her way." Mychal feels that he may be distant from Tamika because she did not visit him often while locked up and did not write regularly. Tamika claims that she could not take off work to travel 100 miles to the prison as often as he may have wanted, and it was emotionally hard on her. Tamika feels that she has a more nurturing approach with their children whereas Mychal has a tough approach with a lot of yelling at the kids.

Tamika shares that Chris was a fairly well-adjusted kid growing up. Chris's biological father has never been involved with Chris other than paying partial child support. Chris attached to Mychal when Tamika started dating him. Chris became angry when Mychal was incarcerated, though, as evidenced by his snapping at Tamika and his younger siblings often. Tamika mentions that Chris has been hanging around with known gang members and has been fighting a lot in school. Since his release, Mychal has not been as involved with Chris. Mychal does admit that he is worried about Chris's future and how he may get locked up one day. Tamika shares that Chris's relationship with his Aunt Melinda has been a major source of support, and Chris tends to listen to his aunt.

Parenting has been hard for Mychal. Mychal expresses that his own children do not respond to him because Tamika did not bring them to see him while he was locked up and so "this [parenting] is on her." Tamika reports that her two younger children have been struggling with engaging their father since he has been home. Tamika also reports that Jessica and Luke fight all the time, and is worried it is because they see her and Mychal fighting all the time. Mychal anxiously shares that while he is blessed that Tamika had so much support with the kids from his mom and her family, he feels "left out" of parenting duties and responsibilities now. Mychal states, "My kids are confused—they do not know who to listen to, when to listen to someone, because there are too many chefs in the kitchen." Tamika even adds that it did not help the kids' ability to connect with Mychal when he returned home from prison as her mother and grandmother would often "slam him" at every opportunity his name came up.

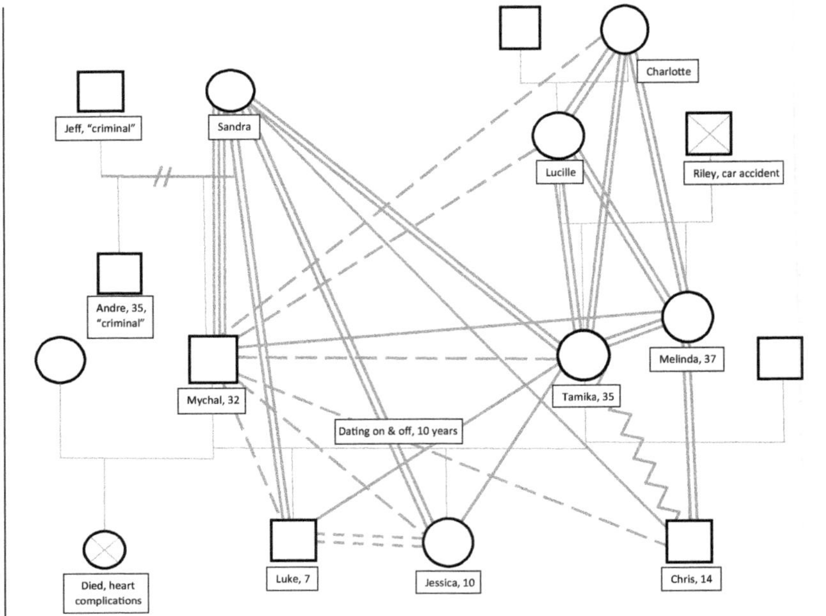

Figure 7.1 Families of Incarceration and Reentry Genogram: Tamika and Mychal

Research on Families of Incarceration and Reentry

Joyce A. Arditti and Mathis V. Kennington

Tamika and Mychal's story has become an all too common experience of American lives punctuated by criminal justice involvement. Approximately 1.6 million people are in federal or state prison, 735,601 offenders are confined to local jails (Glaze & Herberman, 2013; Minton, 2012), four million people are on probation, and nearly 65 million individuals have a criminal record (Rodriguez & Emsellen, 2011). Importantly, 52% of state and 63% of federal inmates are parents to an estimated 1.7 million minor children, accounting for 2.3% of the U.S. child population (Glaze & Maruschak, 2010). Up to 2.7 million children, or 3.6% of all children under 18, have an incarcerated parent, inclusive of jail populations (Western & Pettit, 2010b), and this number rises to 3.2 million children when paroled and recently released parents are considered, the largest proportions of whom are Black and have incarcerated fathers (Glaze & Maruschak, 2008).

As a group, families that interface with the criminal justice system tend to face multiple risks, and children may be particularly vulnerable. A growing body of evidence suggests that even after controlling for other risk markers such as parental substance abuse, parental mental health, compromised parenting, and poverty, parental incarceration continues to predict externalizing (Wildeman, 2010), internalizing problems such as depression (Dallaire, Zeman, & Thrash, 2015), child trauma symptomology (Arditti & Savla, 2013), antisocial behavior (Will, Whalen, & Loper, 2014), and overall poor health (Lee, Fang, & Luo, 2013). Wakefield and Wildeman's (2014) stringent analyses of several secondary data sets provide some of the most compelling evidence that parental incarceration (particularly paternal incarceration) uniquely contributes to substantial increases in children's externalizing, internalizing, physically aggressive, and total behavioral problems.

In this chapter, we take a *family perspective* on Mychal's criminal justice involvement, which highlights not only how his incarceration might have impacted his relationships with his children and intimate partner, but also considers the experience from the vantage point of his family members. Criminal justice policy generally has not been formulated with family well-being in mind, and yet, we can see that incarceration and related interventions have far-reaching effects on the family. A family perspective acknowledges the "important role of family" with respect to a broad range of policy issues (Bogenschneider, 2002, p. 25). Such a view supports an examination of how Mychal's family-of-origin risks may have contributed to his own incarceration, Mychal's experience as a father himself, and how his incarceration has impacted Tamika's ability to carry out her parenting responsibilities, as well as the effects of his involvement in the criminal justice system on his children.

The effects of incarceration on families have been defined as the *collateral costs* of imprisonment (Hagan & Dinovitzer, 1999). These collateral costs include unemployment, loss of income, homelessness, and the need for public assistance (Arditti, Lambert-Shute, & Joest, 2003; Sugie, 2012; Wakefield & Wildeman, 2014). Collateral costs represent a *ripple effect* that involves repercussions to children and the diminished economic and social capital of their families and communities. Social scientists struggle to answer why the repercussions of parental incarceration generally are negative. One reason it is difficult to disentangle the effects of incarceration on children is because children with incarcerated parents *already* are likely to display behavior problems and other developmental and academic shortfalls due to their disadvantaged social and community environments (Wakefield & Wildeman, 2014). Therefore, in order to understand family changes that may connect to parental incarceration, we must first contextualize what it means to be incarcerated in the United States.

The Context of Parental Incarceration

The rapid and remarkable growth in the number of incarcerated persons has been referred to as *mass imprisonment*. Mass imprisonment signifies a rate of incarceration well above the historical and comparative norm for the United States, and far exceeds what one might expect due to population growth (King, Mauer, & Young, 2005). Tough criminal policies like mandatory minimum sentencing and the war on drugs created a drastic demand for resources that state and federal budgets cannot sustain. Although there has been a modest downward trend in prison population growth in some states, largely accounted for by the release of offenders in California's overcrowded facilities, the decline may be attributed to the taxing economy of incarceration on government budgets, as opposed to reform-based policy directives (Glaze & Herberman, 2013).

Some argue penal involvement tends to "crystallize" social inequality, as prisoners are often the least advantaged members of society and drawn from its "bottom rung" (Western & Pettit, 2010a). Indeed, mass imprisonment disproportionately impacts people of color: more than 60% of prisoners are minorities (The Sentencing Project, n.d.), with Blacks, on average, eight times more likely to be in prison than Whites (Pettit & Western, 2004). Such a disparity may reflect growing physical, socioeconomic, and emotional health divides between African-Americans, Hispanics, and Whites (Lopez & Light, 2009).

Youth of color also are disproportionately affected by mass imprisonment. One in four Black children born in 1990 had a father in prison, compared to less than 4% of White children (Sykes & Pettit, 2014; Wildeman, 2010). Tamika and Mychal's family is representative of the larger population of families impacted by incarceration.

Parental Incarceration and the Reproduction of Disadvantage

Like Mychal, most prisoners come from intense histories of disadvantage characterized by multiple risks. These risks include family histories of victimization, low education, neighborhood disadvantage, mental health difficulties, substance misuse and addiction, and intergenerational criminality (Arditti, 2012; Phillips, Erkanli, Keeler, Costello, & Angold, 2006). On a macro level, accumulated risk seems to be related to increased rates of both first-time and repeat incarceration rates (Morenoff & Harding, 2011). The fact that Mychal's father was involved in the criminal justice system is not surprising, as there is a positive connection between parental incarceration, children's delinquency, and their subsequent involvement in the criminal justice system (Johnson, 2009).

It remains to be seen whether Chris will end up in the juvenile system, and it will depend on several factors. His family's level of economic disadvantage, his social and educational exclusion as a result of Mychal's imprisonment, and poor neighborhood conditions may increase Chris's risk. Mounting evidence also describes a disturbing pattern of racial and ethnic differences pertaining to the effects of parental incarceration whereby the intergenerational transmission of criminal justice involvement and behavioral disadvantage appears to be more profound for Black children (Haskins, 2014; Sykes & Pettit, 2014). Chris's minority status likely equates with greater risk exposure, which in conjunction with his risky behavior (fighting in school; hanging out with gangs) subsequently contributes to the likelihood he will end up following in Mychal's footsteps. Intergenerational incarceration is increased for youth whose background consists of exposure to their parents' negative life events like substance abuse, criminal justice activities, or stigma (Ng, Sarri, & Stoffregen, 2013).

There is compelling evidence that children who have or have had an incarcerated parent are particularly vulnerable to disadvantage (Phillips et al., 2006). Children with incarcerated parents are significantly more likely to experience homelessness and food insecurity (Wakefield & Wildeman, 2014). This is particularly likely for minority children with incarcerated fathers (Johnson, 2009). For example, the risk of Black youth experiencing housing instability is 144% larger if they have an incarcerated father compared to children who do not (Cox & Wallace, 2013). Additionally, children of color may be selectively strained by paternal imprisonment for lower rates of educational achievement (Foster & Hagan, 2009; Haskins, 2014). Lack of educational achievement in young men of color is especially correlated with increased risk of imprisonment, among other poor outcomes, and as a result produces a cyclical pattern of risk that is difficult to change without resources and meaningful intervention (Arum & LaFree, 2008; Foster & Hagan, 2009).

Indeed, parental incarceration appears to intensify any preexisting disadvantage among families due in part to declining social capital (Wakefield & Wildeman, 2014). As a result of incarceration, families may withdraw from previously supportive informal social networks. Prior incarceration suppresses fathers' financial contributions to their children in part because it connects with the dissolution of the parental relationship (Geller, Garfinkel, & Western, 2011). Formerly incarcerated persons' status as "ex-felons" diminishes their ability to earn a standard living wage, accumulate assets, or participate in civic behaviors like voting (Geller et al., 2011; Maroto, 2015). Families of prisoners often are left with the burden of providing housing and economic resources for ex-prisoners who cannot find work or cannot meet hefty post-release demands like probation or parole fees (Phillips & Spencer, 2013). Thus, disadvantages are accumulated systemically, accrued both by prisoners as well as by families.

It is no surprise then that parental incarceration is associated with economic and health declines in families (Arditti et al., 2003; Wakefield & Wildeman, 2014). For example, a recent study of 712 incarcerated individuals and their family members found that two out of three families struggled to meet their basic needs while also continuing to support their incarcerated family member financially (deVuono-powell, Schweidler, Walters, & Zohrabi, 2015). Health and educational risks are then reproduced in subsequent generations that ultimately hamper offspring's ability to form healthy families, sustain health and well-being, and generate income in adulthood (Maroto, 2015). In sum, incarceration is both an outcome of and contributor to cumulative disadvantage and compounds the risk of imprisonment within and across intergenerational cohorts. Whole kin networks are impacted by imprisonment as risk accumulates between and across generations, leaving families strained to provide resources for the children that remain. This loss of resources may be associated with an increase in delinquent behaviors like truancy and gang membership, thus compounding risk further.

Proximal Processes Associated With Parental Incarceration

Understanding the context of incarceration points to its scope and intensity among disadvantaged communities of color. However, that is only part of the picture. Incarceration of a family member, and in particular a parent, dramatically can alter proximal family processes. Within ecological theory, proximal processes are defined as dynamic and enduring interactions that "drive" development (Bronfenbrenner, 1999). These interdependent processes occur at the individual, family, and broader social level. Examining processes helps us explain why parental incarceration negatively affects children and what we can do about it. Key processes on Mychal's and Tamika's family well-being include the psychological impact of incarceration on Mychal, the effects of the contact that Mychal had with Tamika and the children during his confinement, the day-to-day quality of parenting that the children received from Tamika and other key persons, and the coparenting relationship between Mychal and Tamika.

"Prisonization" and Offender Adjustment

We begin our examination of how parental incarceration influences processes at the intraindividual level by focusing on the psychological effects of incarceration on parents in prison. In the case study, Tamika reports that prison has "hardened" Mychal. What does she mean by that? It may be that Tamika is sensing Mychal is different now compared to before he went into prison. Mychal is likely "prisonized"—a term used to refer to institutionalization that occurs in corrections settings and is shorthand for the negative psychological effects of imprisonment on offenders (Clemmer, 1940). Prisonization refers to how prisoners import criminogenic characteristics such as accumulated risks, are assimilated into prison society, and are deprived by prison culture. Originally thought to emerge and exist solely within prisons and jails, where prisonized social hierarchies thrived (Clemmer, 1940; Sykes 1958), scholars now suggest it extends beyond prison walls and after release (Comfort, 2007).

Prisonization, then, involves the incorporation of the norms of prison life into one's way of "thinking, feeling, and acting" (Haney, 2002, p. 80) that are vastly inconsistent with life as a free person and the enactment of family roles. For example, adaptation to penal life requires that inmates abandon self-sufficiency and are absolutely dependent on the institutional structure. It is no surprise then that parenting identities that emerge and gain prominence during incarceration can become "prisonized," characterized by a loss of agency, helplessness, and a great deal of distress (Arditti, Smock, & Parkman, 2005; Dyer, Wardle, & Day, 2004). Incarceration constitutes a profound identity interruption, and parents may perceive themselves as losing their place with respect to their children (Enos, 1997). Offender parents miss important family life benchmarks (in our case study, Mychal missed the birth and death of his infant daughter), which can contribute to feelings of distress, frustration, and a sense of being forgotten.

Ultimately, the prolonged adaptation to prison life, and its corresponding deprivations and frustrations (commonly referred to as the *pains of imprisonment* per Sykes, 1958), result in a diminished capacity for incarcerated parents to fulfill family roles during confinement as well as after. Not only was the imprisoned parent unavailable to contribute to the family during incarceration, but the psychological effects reverberate after the prison sentence is served. These pains extract a high toll on the family in that parents who return from incarceration may struggle to exercise the initiative necessary to effectively parent, or as a result of suffering the "negative effects of a distrusting and hypervigilant adaptation to prison life," find it difficult to engage in trusting and authentic relationships with their children and intimate partners (Haney, 2002, p. 15). In this manner, cycles of pain may be reproduced as Mychal reenacts the sense of helplessness, lack of control, and mistrust he experienced in prison by feeling helpless and unworthy at home. He may respond to these feelings by trying to assert his authority in unhealthy ways (Hairston & Oliver, 2006) or withdrawing further (Haney, 2002). In sum, fathers like Mychal may experience paternal identity ambiguity during reentry as a result of prisonization.

Visitation and Contact Processes During Confinement

Contact during confinement influences how families and offenders adjust to incarceration as well as the nature of family relationships after release. Unfortunately, the empirical literature provides an incomplete picture of visitation and contact processes due, in part, to the difficulties inherent in collecting data from families impacted by incarceration. The picture that does emerge suggests that in-person visitation may be a developmental paradox that serves as a source of both positive emotional connection and as a traumatic reminder of painful separation (Arditti, 2012).

Although there is considerable variation with regard to the nature and extent of children's contact with their incarcerated parent, like Mychal, the majority of incarcerated parents report at least some contact during their confinement. The most comprehensive information about contact between incarcerated parents and their children comes from a 2007 special report by the Bureau of Justice, which surveys state and federal prisoners. This report revealed that 70% of state and 84% of federal inmates had mail contact with their children, more than half (53% of state and 85% of federal) had spoken by telephone with their children, and 42% of state prisoner parents and 55% of federal prisoner parents report having an in-person visit. Mothers were more likely than fathers to have received in-person visits, and also to have some form of weekly contact with their children. This may be due to the fact that female inmates were also more likely to have resided with their children prior to their incarceration (Glaze & Maruschak, 2008) and are confined in facilities with more liberal visitation policies (Hoffmann, Dickinson, & Dunn, 2007).

Ecologically speaking, in-person visits are the most proximal form of contact. Much of the variation with regard to in-person visiting has to do with the type of facility where the parent is confined (e.g., jail or prison), how far the inmate is from family members, and the institutional policies regulating contact (Cochran & Mears, 2013; Shlafer, Loper, & Schillmoeller, 2015). For example, jails are operated locally and offenders tend to be in much closer proximity to their families. However, jails also by and large have "no contact" visitation policies, which involve only seeing the incarcerated person behind a glass partition or barrier for a short period of time (typically 20–30 minutes;

Boudin, Stutz, & Littman, 2013; Shlafer et al., 2015). These visits can be particularly difficult for young children who may not understand why they cannot touch their parent (Poehlmann, Dallaire, Loper, & Shear, 2010). Alternatively, prisons tend to house more serious offenders for longer periods of time. It is not uncommon, though, for incarcerated persons in state and federal prisons to be held far from home, with the average distance approximately 100 miles (Glaze & Maruschak, 2008). The fact that Mychal was so far from home during his confinement likely discouraged visits from Tamika and the children. Going on visits entails major resource expenditures of time, money, and energy with little return (Christian, 2005), and is likely to wane or stop during the course of a lengthy sentence (Glaze & Maruschak, 2008). Therefore, it makes sense that families who live closer to the corrections facility along with families who report fewer visitation difficulties have more frequent visits with the incarcerated family member (Beckmeyer & Arditti, 2014). Mychal's difficulties at home may reflect devitalized ties that resulted in part from a lack of contact with family during his confinement.

On balance, visits from family during confinement seem to benefit incarcerated parents. Several studies have demonstrated that in-person visits may strengthen family bonds, lessen parental distress (with some exceptions—see Arditti, 2012, for a review), improve the behavior of incarcerated persons in prison and after release (Cochran & Mears, 2013), and promote paternal involvement (LaVigne, Naser, Brooks, & Castro, 2005). Supportive relationships with family are seen as critical to reentry success (Shanahan & Agudelo, 2012), although the empirical literature is not entirely consistent on this point. It does appear that family conflict in particular is linked to negative reentry outcomes such as drug use and recidivism (Mowen & Visher, 2015); therefore, Mychal's sense of disconnection with Tamika and the children as well as the frequent conflict at home between Mychal and Tamika run counter to Mychal's successful reintegration.

While family contact via visitation can be a source of continuity and support for incarcerated parents and their families, less clear are the effects of in-person visits on children. Some studies show positive benefits for youth, particularly those who reported regular visits with incarcerated mothers (Shlafer & Poehlmann, 2010; Trice & Brewster, 2004). Visits can be hard for families and children, and it is no surprise that Tamika chose not to bring the children to see Mychal frequently. Visitation conditions often involve tedious and lengthy waits, rude treatment by correctional officers, and visiting in crowded, noisy, and uninviting facilities lacking in privacy (Arditti, 2003; Comfort, 2008). These barriers serve to discourage visitation (Hoffmann, Byrd, & Kightlinger, 2010).

Like Tamika, caregivers and children may experience emotional difficulties after visitation (Arditti, 2003; Dallaire, Zeman, & Thrash, 2014). Visitation experiences may evoke painful emotions among family members and potentially involve reliving traumatic separation from the parent (Arditti & Savla,

2013). Additionally, traditional visits put a great deal of stress on caregivers to monitor their children and ensure they behave (Cecil, McHale, Strozier, & Pietsch, 2008), as visits can be terminated or denied by the correctional facility if parents cannot control their children (Boudin et al., 2013). The reaction of the incarcerated also can influence the nature and frequency of visits, as some incarcerated parents may discourage visitation because they feel they are too difficult or emotionally painful (Nesmith & Ruhland, 2008). In sum, family contact, and in particular in-person visits, during incarceration is a complicated enterprise. There are many barriers that keep families at bay, and the incarcerated themselves may actively disengage from the family during confinement. On the other hand, given the challenges associated with traditional forms of visitation, it is really quite remarkable how many families do make the effort to sustain ties with the offender parent. Moreover, when visits are enhanced or "family friendly," children and their families seem to benefit (Kalkan & Smith, 2014; Poehlmann et al., 2010). Enhanced visits typically feature more relaxed or child-sensitive security procedures, longer visiting periods, structured and unstructured activities such as arts and crafts, games, and so forth, and visiting environments more conducive to typical family interactions (Boudin et al., 2013; Shlafer et al., 2015).

Caregiver Quality and Stability

As the story of Mychal and Tamika illustrates, incarceration often is associated with the creation of an involuntary single-parent household. Growth in single-parent households has been matched by the mass incarceration of men across the country and disproportionately impacts families of color (Western, Lopoo, & McLanahan, 2004). The single parent may experience psychological distress, relationship instability, and role strain (Arditti et al., 2003). Incarceration, then, not only alters the parental role of the offender parent, but can connect with changes in the quality and stability of the care children receive from other family members. The ability of caregivers to provide competent and responsive care to their children will vary to the extent that they have the resources necessary to cope with any challenges and complexities that are a function of a family member's incarceration, along with the routine demands of parenting. Unfortunately, children with a history of parental incarceration are likely to experience *caregiver risk*, such as caregiver mental health problems, caregiver stress, caregiver substance abuse, and caregiver health problems (Arditti et al., 2003; Phillips et al., 2006), along with poor parenting practices and family victimization (Aaron & Dallaire, 2010; Phillips et al., 2006).

Yet, how a parent's incarceration impacts the family can vary widely, and there are instances when incarceration might actually *improve* children's caregiving scenarios by removing an abusive or neglectful parent from the home or protecting them from harmful behaviors (Hanlon, O'Grady, Bennett-Sears, & Callaman, 2005). Moreover, several studies examining the effects of maternal incarceration on children have revealed null effects with regard to child outcomes or caregiver scenarios, probably because children were already in stable and alternative care prior to their mothers' confinement (Hanlon et al., 2005). For example, Turanovic, Rodriguez, and Pratt (2012) conducted a qualitative study of maternal incarceration in which caregivers of women's children expressed either positive changes or no changes to their lives as a result of the incarceration. Findings from the interview data revealed that many caregivers in the study assumed parenting roles in children's lives long before the incarceration and had "distanced themselves from their children's mothers" or "otherwise experienced . . . relief in their absence" (Turanovic et al., 2012, p. 945).

Findings pertaining to maternal incarceration point to the diverse experiences of families who interface with the criminal justice system. The preponderance of evidence seems to suggest that parental incarceration is in fact more often related to a lack of quality parenting by nonincarcerated parents and caregivers (Kjellstrand & Eddy, 2011; Phillips et al., 2006). The mechanisms underlying this shift are not entirely clear, but likely have to do with how paternal incarceration is associated with family instability (Lopoo & Western, 2005) and female caregiver's repartnering and multi-partner fertility (Carlson & Furstenberg, 2006; Sykes & Pettit, 2014; Turney & Wildeman, 2014). To the extent that repartnering and childrearing across households or among larger numbers of children diminishes resources or introduces instability to the family, children's well-being may be compromised (Carlson & Furstenberg, 2006).

The fact that Tamika has a great deal of family support bodes well for her and her children. Close kin networks in which children are a shared responsibility, often characteristic of African-American families, enhance the likelihood of producing positive developmental trajectories for children with incarcerated parents (Miller, 2007). Tamika's nurturing upbringing as well her current, supportive intergenerational family relationships are important protective factors that contribute to effective caregiving on her part as well as her children's ability to overcome adversity (Nesmith & Ruhland, 2008). Social support is also a protective factor that moderates incarceration-related stigma (Hagen & Myers, 2003). By extension, it would make sense that the presence of Tamika's kin in her and her children's lives helped her enormously during Mychal's incarceration, and will serve as a stable influence now that he is back.

Coparenting

As we see in Mychal and Tamika's story, their inability to come together with regard to parenting and dealing with their children is putting a great deal of strain on the family. A cooperative and functioning coparenting alliance is a "potent family force" that helps improve parental adjustment, parental involvement, and emotional/behavioral outcomes in children (Cecil et al., 2008, p. 514). Coparenting theory emphasizes the importance of parents' mutual investment in their children's lives, valuing the partner parent's judgments and involvement with regard to children, and positive communication between parents about child-related issues (Loper, Phillips, Nichols, & Dallaire, 2014). Parental incarceration poses particular challenges for the development and/or maintenance of a strong coparenting relationship due in part to the logistics of co-caregiving within correctional systems that place real restrictions on contact and communication (Poehlmann et al., 2010). For example, phone use is limited and may be at exorbitant prices, costing far more than placing and receiving calls outside of prison walls (FCC, 2014). Phone constraints and the typically long distances between the correctional facility and home serve to discourage family contact and the formation of positive coparenting alliances (Loper & Clarke, 2013).

While theoretically significant, unfortunately there is scant literature that directly examines coparenting relationships between offender parents and their children's caregivers.

We can draw some conclusions based on the research available, as well as by extrapolating from other literatures (such as studies on divorced families and the culture of grandmothering). Existing research predominantly focuses on co-caregiving between incarcerated mothers and their children's caregivers—usually a grandmother (Hanlon, Carswell, & Rose, 2007). For example, findings from a study by Baker, McHale, Strozier, and Cecil (2010) that examined the co-caregiving relationships between 40 incarcerated mothers and their children's caregiver were consistent with the coparenting literature in that coparenting quality was related to fewer behavior problems in children. Yet, the literature on incarcerated mothers suggests a history of troubled family relationships that may be difficult to mend (O'Brien, 2001). Vulnerability in co-caregiving relationships may stem from caregivers' shame and disappointment in the incarcerated mother (Hungerford, 1996) as well as differing perspectives between caregiver and mother (Loper et al., 2014). Despite these potential difficulties, caregivers who are relatives are believed to do more to keep the incarcerated parent's psychological presence alive for the children and facilitate contact during confinement than would an estranged spouse (Cecil et al., 2008). Positive coparenting appears to be particularly likely in instances when incarcerated mothers report warm and accepting relationships with maternal grandmothers and trust the care they are providing for children (Loper & Clarke, 2013).

Unfortunately, we know little about the dynamics of coparenting between incarcerated men and their children's caregivers, and even less about how these relationships may evolve after release. When fathers are incarcerated, children are likely to be cared for by their biological mothers (rather than paternal kin), and may be spread across multiple households (Hairston, 2009; Nurse, 2002). Consequently, fathers' coparenting alliances are likely more fragile than incarcerated mothers' coparenting relationships due in part to the female partner's *gatekeeping* function relative to children. Maternal gatekeeping broadly refers to mothers' general reluctance to relinquish family responsibility, and a belief that their own parenting identity and roles are more important than that of fathers (Allen & Hawkins, 1999). Low levels of trust, high levels of dissatisfaction with the children's father, and high levels of hostility toward the father are associated with more pronounced gatekeeping and lower levels of father involvement (McBride et al., 2005).

We can see how conditions associated with paternal incarceration create a scenario that is ripe for maternal gatekeeping. Intimate partners who also have the responsibility for children's care usually unilaterally control the incarcerated parent's access to his children (Arditti et al., 2005; Edin, Nelson, & Paranal, 2004). Therefore, the quality of the father's relationships with his children, and by extension, child outcomes that are a function of paternal incarceration, will largely depend on his relationships to the child's mother (Tach, Mincy, & Edin, 2010). These bonds between incarcerated fathers and their children's mothers tend to deteriorate as a result of imprisonment, with low levels of trust, estrangement, and disappointment characterizing such relationships. Roy and Dyson (2005) describe these relationships as the "babymama drama" and explain: "Babymama drama was a process of negotiation of men's roles as fathers. It reflected a risky balance of conflict and support between incarcerated fathers and their former or current partners" (p. 296). Mychal's resentment of Tamika for not bringing the children to see him during confinement, along with her distrust of his parenting, reflects the "babymama drama" continuing beyond prison walls.

Implications for Reentry

Formerly incarcerated persons may return to their families and communities "prisonized," with mobility, financial, and time challenges that are difficult to navigate, placing great strain on families upon whose shoulders the burden of rehabilitation rests. Approximately 700,000 prisoners are released from prison or jail every year (Durose, Cooper, & Snyder, 2014), the great majority of whom are men of color. Many of these same men will return to prison, typically within three years of release (Langan & Levin, 2002). Research has documented the multiple challenges associated with reentry, like housing and employment, along with complying with the requirements of probation or parole (Travis, 2005). Former prisoners' histories of disadvantage and the stigma attached to incarceration further contribute to the difficulties they may have in making it on the "outside" (Foster & Hagan, 2007). Families foster successful reintegration and crime desistance among ex-offenders even though they are also dealing with the typical strains of family life.

Large, close family networks contribute to men's ability to avoid criminal behavior, as does parenthood (Bahr, Armstrong, Gibbs, Harris, & Fisher, 2005). For example, married men who resided with wives and children after release seem better able to reintegrate than those ex-offenders who did not (Visher & Travis, 2003). But family life is complicated for ex-offenders. Comfort (2007) reported that families who visit incarcerated family members experience prisons as a "domestic satellite," in which family members enact domestic behaviors like discipline and parenting, and even wedding ceremonies. Mychal and Tamika's relationship suggests a similar, albeit reversed, situation in which home life after prison became a kind of "prison satellite." Tamika, for example, threatens to report Mychal to his probation officer to compel his compliance with household activities. Indeed, ex-prisoners experience freedom ambiguously fraught with uncertainty about the ability to sustain life outside of prison walls (Kennington, 2013).

Invisible Punishments

Ex-offenders are subject to invisible punishments, which are policies and practices purposely designed to isolate former prisoners from employment, civic activities, and important resources following release (Travis, 2002). African-American families uniquely are impacted by invisible punishments as a result of their disparate incarceration rates (Mauer & Chesney-Lind, 2002). Invisible punishments involve denying ex-offenders access to (1) cultural capital like educational loans, (2) social redistribution such as federally funded health and welfare benefits, and (3) political participation like the right to vote. Invisible punishments are a means to perpetuate and intensify social inequities beyond prison by not only marginalizing the ex-offender, but causing difficulties for those parents and families most in need. In this manner, family well-being is systematically undermined, and fairness and equality is thwarted. Prison rehabilitation programs often are designed around prosocial behaviors between prisoners and their families. Upon release, many rehabilitative programs promote ongoing support and contact between family members and former prisoners to contribute to reduced rates of recidivism. However, because invisible punishments are designed to restrict social and physical mobility of former offenders, the burden of care is placed on family members already disenfranchised by limited resources.

Invisible punishments exist in the former prisoners' immediate experience, such as former prisoners who cannot find gainful employment due to a criminal record that should not legally prohibit work, but still does (Pager & Western, 2009). Intangible punishments like social stigma, the loss of social and civil privileges, and criminal records that make it difficult to acquire a living wage represent invisible punishments.

Conclusions and Recommendations

In this chapter, we presented a family perspective of how parental incarceration and subsequent reentry impacts families across and between generations. Our coverage of proximal processes suggests key intervention points involve strengthening the identities and competencies of incarcerated parents, enhancing in-person visitation and promoting cooperative coparenting when possible during confinement and beyond, and the provision of support and resources for children's nonincarcerated caregivers. Unfortunately, research on justice-involved individuals and families suggests that incarceration is associated with cumulative disadvantage and the accumulation of risks that diminish healthy outcomes like educational achievement, positive relationships, and upward social mobility. These disadvantages may leave Mychal and Tamika without the ability to adequately thrive in life after prison. Chris, Jessica, and Luke, by virtue of their exposure to Mychal's incarceration and all the challenges that accompany it, are at risk to follow the same path. For this reason, the conversation about reentry is imperative.

However, no discussion of the risks associated with criminal justice involvement is complete without considering protective factors and resilience processes that serve to counterbalance risks. There is evidence that many children experiencing parental incarceration do well at home and school. For example, Nesmith and Ruhland (2008) found evidence of family strengths (e.g., strong, supportive social networks) among children aged 8–17 whose parents were incarcerated. Stable caregiving and close relationships with kin help children deal with parental (and in particular maternal) incarceration (Hanlon, Blatchley et al., 2005).

Resilience on the part of caregivers and ex-offenders contributes to family well-being as well. Caregiver resilience often involves the ability to locate, support, and connect with other families going through similar experiences (Nesmith & Ruhland, 2008). For example, it will be important for Tamika to find the necessary emotional support (which she may not be getting from her family, who look down on Mychal) regarding Mychal's incarceration so that she does not feel alone with her experience. Similarly, the more psychological capacity Mychal has to process any traumatic events associated with his incarceration, the more likely he can successfully reintegrate with his family. Central to Mychal's desistance process is the establishment of a new identity whereby he sheds his prisonized identity as a former inmate and embraces a new civic identity characterized by law-abiding behavior and positive social ties. The availability of fathering opportunities and other prosocial roles (such as employment) are crucial to help reconstruct a new life after confinement (Travis, 2005; Visher & Travis, 2003).

Reentry seems like a good time to equip families who are faced with the normal stressors of family life as well as all the risks that accompany incarceration (Foster & Hagan, 2009). Programs aimed at increasing parenting and family competence would help former offenders moderate their relationship expectations, reintegrate meaningfully into a community populated with risks, and improve intergenerational relationships. The quality of Mychal's family relationships and his ability to engage as a father are important protective factors with regard to successful reintegration. In the short term, intervention must center around strengthening these ties and helping the family adapt to Mychal's return.

The intergenerational risks we have documented necessitate intervention and reform strategies that are multipronged and involve a social policy agenda that focuses on reducing social and economic inequality, family risk reduction, and enhancing opportunity with the goal of promoting human capacity and agency (Arditti, 2012). Efforts to strengthen families can only be realized fully within the context of sweeping criminal justice reform. We are beginning to see the first glimmers of criminal justice reform with regard to a growing interest in parent offenders and their children, less punitive sentencing for nonviolent drug offenses, slight decreases in prison populations in some states, and movement away from retribution to a mounting emphasis on rehabilitation (Adelman, 2015; Travis, 2005). By enacting and implementing policy and interventions that target multiple ecological levels, we can begin to turn the tide of mass incarceration and promote more positive outcomes for at-risk families and youth.

References

Aaron, L., & Dallaire, D. (2010). Parental incarceration and multiple risk experiences: Effects on family processes and children's delinquency. *Journal of Youth and Adolescence, 39*, 1471–1484. doi: 10.1007/s10964-009-9458

Adelman, L. (2015). Criminal justice reform: The present moment. *Wisconsin Law Review, 2015*(2), 181–202. Retrieved from: wisconsinlawreview.org/wp . . . /Adelman-Final.pdf

Allen, S., & Hawkins, A. (1999). Maternal gatekeeping: Mothers' beliefs and behaviors that inhibit greater father involvement in family work. *Journal of Marriage and Family, 61*, 199–212. doi: 10.2307/353894

Arditti, J. A. (2003). Locked doors and glass walls: Family visiting at a local jail. *Journal of Loss & Trauma, 8*, 115–138. doi: 10.1080/15325020390168735

Arditti, J. A. (2012). *Parental incarceration and the family: Psychological and social effects of imprisonment on children, parents, and care-givers*. New York: NYU Press.

Arditti, J. A., Lambert-Shute, J., & Joest, K. (2003). Saturday morning at the jail: Implications of incarceration for families and children. *Family Relations, 52*, 195–204. doi: 10.1111/j.1741-3729.2003.00195.x

Arditti, J. A., & Savla, J. (2013). Parental incarceration and child trauma symptoms in single care-giver homes. *Journal of Child and Family Studies, 24*, 551–561. doi: 10.1007/s10826-013-9867-2

Arditti, J. A., Smock, S., & Parkman, T. (2005). "It's been hard to be a father": A qualitative exploration of incarcerated fatherhood. *Fathering, 3*, 267–288. doi: 10.3149/fth.0303.267

Arum, R., & LaFree, G. (2008). Educational attainment, teacher–student ratios, and the risk of adult incarceration among U.S. birth cohorts since 1910. *Sociology of Education, 81*(4), 397–421. doi: 10.1177/003804070808100404

Bahr, S. J., Armstrong, A., Gibbs, B., Harris, P., & Fisher, J. (2005). The reentry process: How parolees adjust to release from prison. *Fathering, 3*, 243–265. doi: 10.3149/fth.0303.243

Baker, J., McHale, J., Strozier, A., & Cecil, D. (2010). Mother-Grandmother coparenting relationships in families with incarcerated mothers: A pilot investigation. *Family Process, 49*, 165–184. doi: 10.1111/j.1545-5300.2010.01316.x

Beckmeyer, J., & Arditti, J. (2014). Implications of in-person visits for incarcerated parents' family relationships and parenting experience. *Journal of Offender Rehabilitation, 53*(2), 129–151. doi: 10.1080/10509674.2013.868390

Bogenschneider, K. (2002). *Family policy matters: How policymaking affects families.* Mahweh, NJ: LEA.

Boudin, C., Stutz, T., & Littman, A. (2013). Prison visitation policies: A fifty state survey. *Yale Law & Policy Review, 32*, 191–197. doi: 10.2139/ssrn.2171412

Bronfenbrenner, U. (1999). Growing chaos in the lives of children youth and families: How can we turn it around? In J. C. Westman & P. C. Gorman (Eds.), *Proceedings of the conference held in Madison, Wisconsin, April 19–21, 1998*. Published by the University of Wisconsin-Madison General Library System. Retrieved from: http://parenthood.library.wisc.edu/Bronfenbrenner/Bronfenbrenner.html

Browning, S., & Pasley, K. (2015). *Contemporary families: Translating research into practice*. New York, NY: Routledge.

Carlson, M. J., & Furstenberg, F. F. (2006). The prevalence and correlates of multipartnered fertility among urban U.S. parents. *Journal of Marriage and the Family, 68*, 718–732. doi: 10.1111/j.1741-3737.2006.00285.x

Cecil, D. K., McHale, J., Strozier, A., & Pietsch, J. (2008). Female inmates, family caregivers, and young children's adjustment: A research agenda and implications for corrections programming. *Journal of Criminal Justice, 36*, 513–521. doi: 10.1016/j.jcrimjus.2008.09.002

Christian, J. (2005). Riding the bus: Barriers to prison visitation and family management strategies. *Journal of Contemporary Criminal Justice, 21*, 31–48. doi: 10.1177/1043986204271618

Clemmer, D. (1940). *The prison community*. New York: Holt, Rinehart, and Winston.

Cochran, J., & Mears, D. (2013). Social isolation and inmate behavior: A conceptual framework for theorizing prison visitation and guiding and assessing research. *Journal of Criminal Justice, 41*, 252–261. doi: 10.1016/j.jcrimjus.2013.05.001

Comfort, M. (2007). Punishment beyond the legal offender. *Annual Review of Law and Social Science, 3*, 271–296. doi: 10.1146/annurev.lawsocsci.3.081806.112829

Comfort, M. (2008). *Doing time together: Love and family in the shadow of prison.* Chicago, IL: University of Chicago Press.

Cox, R., & Wallace, S. (2013). The impact of incarceration on food insecurity among households with children. *Fragile Families*. Working Paper 13–05-FF, Princeton University, Princeton, NJ. Retrieved from: http://crcw.princeton.edu/workingpapers/WP13–05-FF.pdf

Dallaire, D. H., Zeman, J. L., & Thrash, T. (2014). Children's experiences of maternal incarceration-specific risks: Predictions to psychological maladaptation. *Journal of Clinical Child and Adolescent Psychology, 44*, 109–122. doi: 10.1080/15374416.2014.913248

Dallaire, D. H., Zeman, J. L., & Thrash, T. (2015). Children's experiences of maternal incarceration-specific risks: Predictions to psychological maladaptation. *Journal of Clinical Child and Adolescent Psychology, 44*, 109–122. doi: 10.1080/15374416.2014.913248

deVuono-powell, S., Schweidler, C., Walters, A., & Zohrabi, A. (2015). *Who pays? The true cost of incarceration on families*. Oakland, CA: Ella Baker Center, Forward Together, Research Action Design.

Durose, M., Cooper, A., & Snyder, H. (2014). *Recidivism of prisoners released in 30 states in 2005: Patterns from 2005 to 2010*. Special report from the Bureau of Justice Statistics, Washington. Retrieved from: http://ejournals.ebsco.com.ezproxy.stedwards.edu/Direct.asp?AccessToken=95DIIIM8X4P1D9DDMURE4P45EEZR811MD5&Show=Object

Dyer, W. J., Wardle, B., & Day, R. D. (2004). *Effects of incarceration on successful prisoner reentry: A symbolic interaction perspective*. Presentation for the Pacific Sociological Association. San Francisco, CA.

Edin, K., Nelson, T., & Paranal, R. (2004). Fatherhood and incarceration as potential turning points in the criminal careers of unskilled men. In M. Patillo, D. Weiman, & B. Western (Eds.), *Imprisoning America: The social effects of mass incarceration* (pp. 46–75). New York, NY: Russell Sage Foundation.

Enos, S. (1997). Managing motherhood in prison: The impact of race and ethnicity on child placements. *Women & Therapy*, *20*, 57–73. doi: 10.1300/J015v20n04_05

Federal Communications Commission. (2014). *Rates for interstate inmate calling services* (WC docket no. 12–375). Washington, DC: Federal Communications Commission.

Foster, H., & Hagan, J. (2007). Incarceration and intergenerational social exclusion. *Social Problems*, *54*, 399–433. doi: 10.1525/sp.2007.54.4.399

Foster, H., & Hagan, J. (2009). The mass incarceration of parents in America: Issues of race/ethnicity, collateral damage to children, and prisoner reentry. *Annals of the American Academy of Political & Social Science*, *623*, 179–194. doi: 10.1177/0002716208331123

Geller, A., Garfinkel, I., & Western, B. (2011). Paternal incarceration and support for children in fragile families. *Demography*, *48*, 25–47. doi: 10.1007/213524-010-0009-9

Glaze, L. E., & Herberman, E. J. (2013, December). *Correctional populations in the United States, 2012* (NCJ 243936). Washington, DC: U.S. Department of Justice, Office of Justice Programs. Retrieved from: http://www.bjs.gov/content/pub/pdf/cpus12.pdf

Glaze, L., & Maruschak, L. M. (2008, August). *Parents in prison and their minor children*. Bureau of Justice Statistics Special Report (NCJ222984). Washington, DC: U.S. Department of Justice, Office of Justice Programs.

Glaze, L. E., & Maruschak, L. M. (2010). *Parents in prison and their minor children*. Bureau of Justice Statistics Special Report (rev. ed.). Washington, DC: U.S. Department of Justice. Retrieved from: http://www.bjs.gov/content/pub/pdf/pptmc.pdf

Hagan, J., & Dinovitzer, R. (1999). Collateral consequences of imprisonment for children, communities, and prisoners. *Crime and Justice*, *26*, 121–142. doi: 10.1086/449296

Hagen, K. A., & Myers, B. (2003). The effect of secret keeping and social support on behavioral problems in children of incarcerated women. *Journal of Child and Family Studies*, *12*, 229–242. doi: 10.1023/A:1022866917415

Hairston, C. (2009). *Kinship care when parents are incarcerated: What we know, what we can do*. Baltimore, MD: Annie E. Casey Foundation.

Hairston, C., & Oliver, W. (2006). *Safe return: Domestic violence and prisoner reentry: Experiences of Black women and men*. New York, NY: Vera Institute of Justice. Retrieved from: http://www.vera.org/content/domestic-violence-and-prisoner-reentry-experiences-african-american-women-and-men

Haney, C. (2002, January). *The psychological impact of incarceration: Implications for post-prison adjustment*. Retrieved from: http://www.urban.org/CraigHaney

Hanlon, T., Blatchley, R., Bennett-Sears, T., O'Grady, K., Rose, M., & Callaman, J. M. (2005). Vulnerability of children of incarcerated addict mothers: Implications for preventive intervention. *Children and Youth Services Review, 27*, 67–84. doi: 10.1016/j.childyouth.2004.07.004

Hanlon, T., Carswell, S., & Rose, M. (2007). Research on caretaking of children of incarcerated parents: Findings and their service delivery implications. *Children and Youth Services Review, 29*, 348–362. doi: 10.1016/j.childyouth.2006.09.001

Hanlon, T., O'Grady, K., Bennett-Sears, T., & Callaman, J. (2005). Incarcerated drug-abusing mothers: Their characteristics and vulnerability. *American Journal of Drug and Alcohol Abuse, 1*, 59–77. doi: 10.1081/ADA-200037564

Haskins, A. R. (2014). Unintended consequences: Effects of paternal incarceration on child school readiness and later special education placement. *Sociological Science, 1*, 141–158. doi: 10.15195/v1.a11

Hoffmann, H. C., Byrd, A. L., & Kightlinger, A. M. (2010). Prison programs and services for incarcerated parents and their underage children: Results from a national survey of correctional facilities. *The Prison Journal, 90*, 1–20. doi: 10.1177/0032885510382087

Hoffmann, H. C., Dickinson, G. E., & Dunn, C. L. (2007). Communication policy changes in state adult correctional facilities from 1971 to 2005. *Criminal Justice Review, 32*, 47–64. doi: 10.1177/0734016806297646

Hungerford, G. (1996). Caregivers of children whose mothers are incarcerated: A study of the kinship placement system. *Children Today, 24*, 23–34.

Johnson, R. C. (2009). Ever-increasing levels of parental incarceration and the consequences for children. In S. Raphael & M. Stoll (Eds.), *Do prisons make us safer? The benefits and costs of the prison boom* (pp. 177–206). New York: Russell Sage Foundation.

Kalkan, G., & Smith, N. (2014). *Just visiting: Experiences of children visiting prisons*. Report published by Bernardos Strategy Unit. Retrieved from: http://www.barnardos.org.uk/

Kennington, M. V. (2013). *Ambiguous freedom: A grounded theoretical analysis of life outside prison* (Doctoral dissertation). Retrieved from: http://Vtechworks.lib.vt.edu. (10742)

King, R., Mauer, M., & Young, M. (2005). *Incarceration and crime: A complex relationship*. Retrieved from the Sentencing Project website: http://www.sentencingproject.org/doc/publications/inc_iandc_complex.pdf

Kjellstrand, J., & Eddy, J. M. (2011). Parental incarceration during childhood, family context, and youth problem behavior across adolescence. *Journal of Offender Rehabilitation, 50*, 18–36. doi: 10.1080/10509674.2011.536720

Langan, P. A., & Levin, D. J. (2002). *Recidivism of prisoners released in 1994*. (NCJ 193427). Washington, DC: U.S. Department of Justice, Bureau of Justice Statistics. Retrieved from: http://www.bjs.ojp.usdoj.gov/content/pub/pdf/rpr94.pdf

La Vigne, N. G., Naser, R. L., Brooks, L. E., & Castro, J. L. (2005). Examining the effect of incarceration and in-prison family contact on prisoners' family relationships. *Journal of Contemporary Criminal Justice, 21*, 314–335. doi: 10.1177/1043986205281727

Lee, R. D., Fang, X., & Luo, L. (2013). The impact of parental incarceration on the physical and mental health of young adults. *Pediatrics, 131*, 1188–1195. doi: 10.1542/peds.2012-0627

Loper, A. B., & Clarke, C. N. (2013). Attachment representations of imprisoned mothers as related to child contact and the caregiving alliance: The moderating effect of children's placement with maternal grandmothers. *Monographs of the Society for Research in Child Development, 78*, 41–56. doi: 10.1111/mono.12020

Loper, A. B., Phillips, V., Nichols, E. B., & Dallaire, D. H. (2014). Characteristics and effects of the coparenting alliance between incarcerated parents and child caregivers. *Journal of Child and Family Studies, 23*, 225–241. doi: 10.1007/s10826-012-9709-7

Lopez, M., & Light, M. (2009). *A rising share: Hispanics and federal crime*. Washington, DC: Pew Research Center. Retrieved from: http://pewhispanic.org

Lopoo, L., & Western, B. (2005). Incarceration and the formation and stability of marital unions. *Journal of Marriage and the Family, 67*, 721–734. doi: 10.1111/j.1741-3737.2005.00165.x

Maroto, M. (2015). The absorbing status of incarceration and its relationship with wealth accumulation. *Journal of Quantitative Criminology, 31*, 207–236. doi: 10.1007/s10940-014-9231-8.

Mauer, M., & Chesney-Lind, M. (2002). Introduction. In M. Mauer & M. Chesney-Lind (Eds.), *Invisible punishment: The collateral consequences of mass imprisonment* (pp. 1–12). New York, NY: The New Press.

McBride, B. A., Brown, G. L., Bost, K. K., Shin, N., Vaughn, B., & Korth, B. (2005). Paternal identity, maternal gatekeeping, and father involvement. *Family Relations, 54*, 360–372. doi: 10.1111/j.1741-3729.2005.00323.x

Miller, K. (2007). Risk and resilience among African American children of incarcerated parents. *Journal of Human Behavior in the Social Environment, 15*, 25–37. doi: 10.1300/J137v15n02_03

Minton, T. D. (2012, April). *Jail inmates at midyear 2011—Statistical tables*. Bureau of Justice Statistics (NCJ 237961). Washington, DC: U.S. Department of Justice, Office of Justice Programs. Retrieved from: http://www.bjs.gov/content/pub/pdf/jim11st.pdf

Morenoff, J., & Harding, D. (2011). *Final technical report: Neighborhoods, recidivism, and employment among returning prisoners. (Grant No. 2008-IJ-CX-0018)*. Washington, DC: National Institute of Justice.

Mowen, T., & Visher, C. (2015). Drug use and crime after incarceration: The role of family support and family conflict. *Justice Quarterly, 32*(2), 337–359. doi: 10.1080/07418825.2013.771207

Nesmith, A., & Ruhland, E. (2008). Children of incarcerated parents: Challenges and resiliency, in their own words. *Child and Youth Services Review, 30*, 1119–1130. doi: 10.1016/j.childyouth.2008.02.006

Ng, I. H., Sarri, R. C., & Stoffregen, E. (2013). Intergenerational incarceration: Risk factors and social exclusion. *Journal of Poverty, 17*(4), 437–459. doi: 10.1080/10875549.2013.833161

Nurse, A. M. (2002). *Fatherhood arrested: Parenting from within the juvenile justice system*. Nashville: Vanderbilt University Press.

O'Brien, P. (2001). Just like baking a cake: Women describe the successful ingredients for successful reentry after incarceration. *Families in Society, 82*, 287–295. doi: 10.1606/1044-3894.200

Pager, D., & Western, B. (2009). *Investigating prisoner reentry: The impact of conviction status on the employment prospects of young men*. Final report submitted to the U.S. Department of Justice (National Institute of Justice Grant 2005-IJ-CX-0019). Retrieved from: http://www.ncjrs.gov/pdffiles1/nij/grants/228584.pdf

Pettit, B., & Western, B. (2004). Mass imprisonment and the life course: Race and class inequality in U.S. incarceration. *American Sociological Review*, *69*, 151–169. doi: 10.1177/000312240406900021

Phillips, L. A., & Spencer, W. M. (2013). The challenges of reentry from prison to society. *Journal of Current Issues in Crime, Law & Law Enforcement*, *6*(2), 123–133.

Phillips, S., Erkanli, A., Keeler, G., Costello, J., & Angold, A. (2006). Disentangling the risks: Parent criminal justice involvement and children's exposure to family risks. *Criminology and Public Policy*, *5*, 677–702. doi: 10.1111/j.1745-9133.2006.00404.x

Poehlmann, J., Dallaire, D., Loper, A., & Shear, L. (2010). Children's contact with their incarcerated parents: Research findings and recommendations. *American Psychologist*, *65*, 575–598. doi: 10.1037/a0020279

Rodriguez, M., & Emsellen, M. (2011). 65 million "need not apply": The case for reforming criminal background checks for employment. *The National Employment Law Project*. Retrieved from: http://www.nelp.org/content/uploads/2015/03/65_Million_Need_Not_Apply.pdf

Roy, K. M., & Dyson, O. L. (2005). Gatekeeping in context: Babymama drama and the involvement of incarcerated fathers. *Fathering*, *3*, 289–310. doi: 10.3149/fth.0303.289

The Sentencing Project (n.d.). *Racial disparity*. Retrieved from: http://www.sentencingproject.org/template/page.cfm?id=122

Shanahan, R., & Agudelo, S. V. (2012). The family and recidivism. *American Jails*. Retrieved from: http://www.vera.org/files/the-family-and-recidivism.pdf

Shlafer, R. J., Loper, A. B., & Schillmoeller, L. (2015). Introduction and literature review: Is parent-child contact during parental incarceration beneficial? In J. Poehlmann-Tynan (Ed.), *Children's contact with incarcerated parents: Implications for policy and intervention* (Advances in child and family policy and practice) (pp. 1–22). New York: Springer.

Shlafer, R. J., & Poehlmann, J. (2010). Attachment and caregiving relationships in families affected by parental incarceration. *Attachment & Human Development*, *12*, 395–415. doi: 10.1080/ 14616730903417052

Sugie, N. (2012). Punishment and welfare: Paternal incarceration and families' receipt of public assistance. *Social Forces*, *90*, 1403–1427. doi: 10.1093/sf/sos055

Sykes, B., & Pettit, B. (2014). Mass incarceration, family complexity, and the reproduction of childhood disadvantage. *The Annals of the American Academy of Political Science and Social Science*, *654*, 127–149. doi: 10.1177/0002716214526345

Sykes, G. M. (1958). *The society of captives*. Princeton, NJ: Princeton University.

Tach, L., Mincy, R., & Edin, K. (2010). Parenting as a package deal: Relationships, fertility, and nonresident father involvement among unmarried parents. *Demography*, *47*, 181–204. doi: 10.1353/dem.0.0096

Travis, J. (2002). Invisible punishment: An instrument of social exclusion. In M. Mauer & M. Chesney-Lind (Eds.), *Invisible punishment: The collateral consequences of mass imprisonment* (pp. 15–36). New York, NY: W. W. Norton & Company, Inc.

Travis, J. (2005). *But they all come back: Facing the challenges of prisoner reentry*. Washington, DC: The Urban Institute Press.

Trice, A. D., & Brewster, J. (2004). The effects of maternal incarceration on adolescent children. *Journal of Policy and Criminal Psychology*, *19*, 27–35. doi: 10.1007/BF02802572

Turanovic, J. J., Rodriguez, N., & Pratt, T. C. (2012). The collateral consequences of incarceration revisited: A qualitative analysis of the effects on caregivers of children of incarcerated parents. *Criminology*, *50*, 913–959. doi: 10.1111/j.1745-9125.2012.00283.x

Turney, K., & Wildeman, C. (2014). Redefining relationships: Explaining the countervailing consequences of paternal incarceration for parenting. *American Sociological Review*, *78*, 949–979. doi: 10.1177/0003122413505589

Visher, C., & Travis, J. (2003). Transitions from prison to community: Understanding individual pathways. *Annual Review of Sociology*, *29*, 89–113. doi: 10.1146/annurev.soc.29.010202.095931

Wakefield, S., & Wildeman, C. (2014). *Children of the prison boom: Mass incarceration and the future of American inequality*. New York: Oxford University Press.

Western, B., Lopoo, L., & McLanahan, S. (2004). Incarceration and the bond between parents in fragile families. In M. Pattillo, D. Weiman, & B. Western (Eds.), *Imprisoning America: The social effects of mass incarceration* (pp. 21–45). New York, NY: Russell Sage Foundation.

Western, B., & Pettit, B. (2010a). Incarceration and social inequality. *Daedalus*, *139*(3), 8–19. doi: 10.1162/DAED_a_00019

Western, B., & Pettit, B. (2010b). Collateral costs: Incarceration's effect on economic mobility. *The Pew Charitable Trusts*. Retrieved from: http://www.pewcenteronthestate.org/report_detail.aspx?id=60919

Wildeman, C. (2010). Paternal incarceration and children's physically aggressive behaviors: Evidence from the fragile families and child wellbeing study. *Social Forces*, *89*, 285–309. doi: 10.1353/sof.2010.0055

Will, J., Whalen, M., & Loper, A. (2014). From one generation to the next: Childhood experiences of antisocial behavior and parental incarceration among adult inmates. *Journal of Offender Rehabilitation*, *53*, 190–210. doi: 10.1080/10509674.2014.887606

Clinical Theory and Intervention for Families of Incarceration

John R. Hart, Kevin M. Roy, and Lorig Charkoudian

Families of incarceration represent a dynamic and complicated family configuration, marked by the absence of adults who shift and move through residence over time. In this way, families with an incarcerated adult may have some similarities to military families with deployed parents, or even families who face ambiguous loss due to divorce or separation. Incarceration exacerbates absence through heightened stigma such as that discussed in the research section. This is particularly relevant when parents return from correctional facilities and families are again impacted by a number of new challenges. Many incarcerated parents and their families are ill prepared for transitions back into family and community life. Finally, the system of mass incarceration reaches beyond ex-offenders and affects new generations of family members by reducing opportunities in education, employment, housing, health, and political participation.

The process of incarceration challenges the way clinicians conceptualize family configurations and dynamics and pushes us to be much more systemic in our thinking. In this way, to account for the full range of effects on families of incarceration, we must examine relational aspects of incarceration across people and systems, rather than simply the characteristics of ex-offenders or the predictors of behavior.

A Theoretical Foundation for Treatment of Families of Incarceration

We present a range of frameworks that prioritize a familial context for treatment and clinical intervention. As Arditti (2012) notes, most research on incarceration found in criminology, sociology, or demography draws either on macro-level theories that focus on social structure, or on patterns of deviance based on micro-level theories of individual decision making, behavior, or traits. A family perspective identifies the relational middle ground, between macro and micro levels of analysis, as a process site for intervention.

Ecological Systems

An ecological systems perspective often informs clinical interventions with families of incarceration (Bronfenbrenner, 1995). From this well-recognized systems framework, we highlight proximal processes in how families play a key role in *meso-level interactions* between individuals as they navigate the demands of social systems, such as incarceration, courts and correctional facilities, law enforcement, social welfare, schools, and local political economies for employment. In the midst of treatment, families strive to locate and obtain *resources*, including social, emotional, and financial capital, each of which ultimately encourages *support and adaptation* of family members throughout incarceration and during reentry.

Through application of an ecological perspective, therapists note how employers and the labor market both ignore and mistreat members of families of incarceration as they try to seek full employment and appropriate wages. Therapists also recognize families' experiences of discrimination with obtaining adequate and affordable housing. These issues, if not adequately addressed through public policy and clinical interventions, create higher risks for recidivism. From an ecological perspective, even the use of therapeutic intervention, at its most basic, is another opportunity for resources through which families adapt and cope with the multi-generational challenges of mass incarceration.

Life Course Framework

Similarly, clinical interventions with families of incarceration must take into account how family dynamics shift over time (Bengston & Allen, 1993). This framework draws on four key concepts from the work of Glen Elder (1998). A focus on *human agency* highlights the decision making and adaptations of individual family members, and the concept of *linked lives* recognizes how the experiences of one generation of incarcerated parents ripples into the lives of succeeding generations of children in families of incarceration. Life course theory places families *in context*, regarding racial, ethnic, socioeconomic, gender, and related socio-structural statuses. Most importantly, the framework integrates dynamic generational relationships with *historical time*. For example, it identifies the unique impact of incarceration on each successive birth cohort—those who came of age and were imprisoned in the war on drugs in the 1980s, on through their children, who have been incarcerated in the early 2000s under new loitering ordinances against gang activity. Life course theory is an effective theoretical framework to link individuals and families to new forms of social change due to a system of mass incarceration, as well as historical patterns of inequality (Alexander, 2012; Roy, 2014).

Family Systems Theory

Family systems theory and structural family therapy hold that individuals are inseparable from their network of relationships (Titelman, 2014). In this particular model, *individual*, *spousal*, *parental*, and *sibling* subsystems in the family unit all play a critical role in the development and maintenance of presenting problems (Minuchin, 1974). This means that throughout the treatment plan, the therapist should provide intensive and critical attention to each of these subsystems in order to systemically address the common problems of families of incarceration. The treatment model involves (a) joining and accommodating, (b) mapping family structure, and (c) intervening.

Once informed consent has been established, the therapist enters the family system in a hierarchical stance as the "leader" and adapts and joins the system's rules, patterns, and worldview. Families of incarceration have many complexities, and the individuals and dynamics are important to assess. This is when using a family map is critical. Distinct from the family genogram, the family map identifies each family member's position in the family while highlighting interaction patterns, conflicts, and coalitions. In the process of mapping the systemic structure, the therapist devises an initial hypothesis, compiles diagnostic information, and begins initial goal-setting procedures (Minuchin, 1974). The therapist then intervenes with techniques that strengthen and clarify structure and boundaries. We also recommend treatment integrate cognitive and behavioral therapy approaches to address underlying cognitions, beliefs, and attributions that have maintained the problem in these families. Cognitive and behavioral approaches complement the family structural treatment plan with interventions that include psychoeducation and disputing irrational beliefs. We will also add that, if necessary, referrals for other issues revolving around substance abuse and case management are critical.

Common Vulnerabilities Experienced by Families of Incarceration

Some of the common vulnerabilities relevant for clinical intervention are parent-child separation, importance of emotion, general instability, and risk of recidivism. Additionally, the degree to which a child is affected by incarceration of a parent depends on a number of variables, including the age at which the child is separated from the parent, the length of the separation, the level of disruption, the number and result of previous separation experiences, and the availability of family or community support (Seymour, 1998).

The role parents play in the development of their children's lives and the potential impact of a parent-child separation as a result of incarceration highlights the need to find ways to assist families in keeping in touch during incarceration and reuniting upon release. However, maintaining relationships during a period of incarceration can be difficult, as Arditti and Kennington presented earlier. Studies have identified many factors shaping this dynamic (e.g., inadequate information on visiting procedures, little help from correctional facilities about visiting arrangements, the time and financial cost). Further, the implications of a parent's incarceration for a child's development are well documented. As noted in the first half of this chapter, children of incarcerated parents are more likely to exhibit low self-esteem, depression, emotional withdrawal, and inappropriate or disruptive behavior, all leading to a high risk of future delinquency and/or criminal behavior.

Families who are experiencing or who have experienced the incarceration of a family member have to manage a range of emotions. From a therapeutic standpoint, it is important that the therapist provides enough space for each family member in the system to express their emotions about the incarceration and how it has shaped their well-being. More specifically, there is significant value in utilizing the concept from Susan Johnson's idea of assisting families to speak from more of a vulnerable standpoint (primary emotions) than a reactive emotional standpoint (secondary emotions; Johnson & Whiffen, 2003). The rationale behind this notion is that the level of reactivity that comes with secondary emotions strains both communication and other interactional patterns. Rather, speaking from a vulnerable emotional standpoint allows the speaker's message to be fully heard and received and for the listener to be able to receive the message and process it in a clearer stance than a reactive/defensive stance. This is especially the case for families of incarceration in which issues such as shame, guilt, and hurt are so prominent.

There are critical questions to explore with families of incarceration when addressing the emotional climate of the family system. Is the incarcerated family member feeling shame and guilt for putting his or her family through this predicament? Is there any fear from the incarcerated family member that he or she may recidivate? How much hurt does the romantic partner feel about being alone in the relationship? How much disappointment and hurt does the romantic partner have about raising the kids during the incarceration? How has each kid managed the hurt that he or she feels towards the incarcerated parent for being away? What was the emotional climate before the incarceration, during the incarceration, and now during post-release?

Another common vulnerability includes general instability. There are situations where families are better off without a neglectful or abusive parent or partner in their lives. Family members may have been convicted of a crime of violence or abuse in the home, whereas others were convicted of different crimes but may exhibit a pattern of abuse. Similarly, some family members are better served by not returning to a family environment still characterized by substance abuse, criminal behavior, and other negative influences that could act as triggers of past behaviors and habits.

Recidivism is a critical vulnerability for families of incarceration. The notion that a family member could engage in criminal activity again or violate parole conditions and be sent back to prison creates much tension throughout the family system. Some families of incarceration can provide a level of "protective" support that may result in lower recidivism rates among released inmates. Alternatively, some families of incarceration struggle with complex dynamics such as balance of power between family members. For example, family members' knowledge that violations to the family member's parole sends him or her back to prison quickly provides them with an "instrumental" tool. Other structural issues such as substance abuse, mental health, lack of job opportunities, and inadequate housing have been associated with higher levels of recidivism, whereas familial dynamics shape the well-being of the family system and its members and, therefore, can be protective.

It is important that, although there may be common vulnerabilities and issues with families of incarceration, the therapist should pay even closer attention to the variations that may exist among these families. Experiences around race, ethnicity, culture, geographical location, family complexity, and socioeconomic status can shape the presenting problems experienced by the family. We highly recommend therapists should check their judgments and biases (i.e., self of therapist) on all of these various issues in order to provide effective therapy through respect and support for the family unit.

Foundational Clinical Interventions for Families of Incarceration

We have identified five critical interventions that can be applied to families of incarceration: psychoeducation, genogram, reframing and/or disputing irrational beliefs, challenging family assumptions, and circular questioning. Psychoeducation is a helpful intervention when working with families of incarceration. Here, the therapist can educate the incarcerated individual, the couple, and the whole family system on related topics that have shaped the presenting problem (e.g., parenting, communication). Any information, discussion, or activities that can help family members better understand and cope with the presenting problem and better understand the family unit as a whole is a valued addition to the pool of therapeutic interventions applied to families of incarceration.

For families of incarceration in which there has been an intergenerational experience of incarceration, a genogram is a particularly helpful clinical intervention. Genograms are used as an assessment tool and as a technique. Genograms can be used to map the nuclear and extended family processes and provide a means of identifying intergenerational patterns (e.g., incarceration) that might otherwise be difficult to see. Particular attention is given to patterns of conflict, distance, emotional cutoffs, fusion, and close relationships, as well as processes related to the presenting problem.

According to Minuchin and Fishman (1981), families tend to enter a therapeutic situation with "their framing of the problem and their framed solution" (p. 76). It is important that the therapist consider the family's framing of the problem. For example, families of incarceration tend to focus on the problems revolving around the individual who was incarcerated rather than recognizing that they themselves sometimes need to change. As such, an important intervention to use is to reframe or modify this perspective in relational terms. Each person must be helped to see his or her role in the way the family functions. And, each person's situation can be understood from multiple perspectives. Once the therapist is capable of understanding the various "realities" that each person faces, the better the therapist is at reframing some aspect of the family.

The returning spouse is both happy and confused. The remaining spouse is pleased but extremely nervous. All human interaction can be explained by more than a single perspective (Browning, 2015). Post-incarceration families feel oppressed and are often unable to break a negative loop. If the therapist can honestly reframe the situation to highlight a positive possibility, the family often benefits. Certainly the reframe must be possible; these families are not interested in "Pollyanna" explanations and will confront a therapist who is unrealistic. But, if the therapist can sincerely defend the alternate possibility, the families may see a way to repair the problems. For example, a spouse who had remained at home might want to support the returning spouse in regaining parental power, but honestly believes that "protecting" the post-imprisoned partner is compassionate, not insulting.

According to Minuchin and Fishman (1981), families enter therapy because "reality, as they have constructed it, is unworkable." For example, persistent negative behaviors of the "problematic person" such as repeated incarcerations and/or parole violations allow for the family unit to develop a schema or reality that this person and his or her actions are straining the progress of the family, and things are "just not working" because of this individual. Therefore, the family therapist can intervene by challenging the family reality, constructs, and assumptions by reframing and highlighting possibilities. Challenging family assumptions is an intervention that involves discovering the family's "narrowed perception of reality" and challenging their reality by educating the family on appropriate family structure (Minuchin & Fishman, 1981). The therapist may apply psychoeducation techniques to teach families about family structure. Moreover, this intervention can be applied in a straightforward or paradoxical manner. For example, the therapist can either directly confront the incarcerated parent on his or her inability to be sensitive towards family members or paradoxically describe the dilemma facing the mother who continues to seek the counsel of her own mother on childcare decisions even though she wants her husband more involved.

Circular questioning is an effective clinical intervention that focuses on family interactions and behavioral exchanges within the family system rather than the problem itself (e.g., the incarceration; Palazzoli, Boscolo, Cecchin, & Prata, 1980). The rationale behind using this intervention is that these types of questions assist the clinician in providing the family a systemic view of the problem. Circular questions can take many forms, but all serve to highlight systemic interaction patterns in the family. The circular questions include:

Relational and interaction pattern questions: "What does your mother do when you argue with your father?"

Future-oriented questions: "If your mother stopped worrying about you, what would your father do?"

Comparisons and rankings questions: "Who gets most upset when you get into fights with your siblings?"

Before-and-after change questions: "What were the fights like before versus after your father came home from prison?"

Applying Treatment Interventions to the Case Study (Mychal & Tamika)

In this section we present a treatment plan that is based on a systems-oriented approach, but that also implements a critical community service for families of incarceration. We focus on a detailed reentry mediation phase and how it may link to subsequent clinical phases.

Reentry mediation is a process that is similar only to a specific range of therapeutic approaches. In general, if therapy is a directive interaction in which therapists frame experience of clients with a model of change as a guide, mediation can be seen as less directive, with less framing and lacking a preassigned model of change. Instead, mediation is designed primarily to help participants have a difficult conversation with an opportunity to develop deeper understanding within a couple, group, or family; but it is never an individual exercise. It also includes a structured brainstorming session with a trained community member (the mediator) who is not viewed as an expert. It is a relatively low-cost, short-term intervention. In contrast, therapeutic interactions are often deep and long-term experiences, in which clients see therapists as experts or guides.

Both interventions can be helpful for the families of individuals being released from incarceration. Reentry mediation has the potential to be scaled up significantly with fewer resources, due to its heavy reliance on volunteers and the short-term nature of the intervention.

We use the case study family to demonstrate how community reentry mediation can improve relational strain between family members as effectively as a therapeutic approach. There are a few notable contextual issues with this family: Mychal has some important mental health concerns from his recent prison stint, Mychal and Tamika have significant issues surrounding both their romantic and coparenting relationship, and there are issues revolving around the well-being of their children. As you will see, while there are shared assumptions behind both community reentry mediation and the therapeutic process, community reentry mediation has unique assumptions that have made it such a promising service for these families in the state of Maryland.

Community Reentry Mediation

The innovative phase of a prisoner reentry mediation program can be conducted prior to clinical family therapeutic intervention. Reentry mediation was developed in Maryland by community mediation centers that brought their grassroots low-cost model for conflict resolution and relationship transformation into prisons to resolve issues prerelease. The approach was designed to respond to the needs identified in criminal justice literature for positive relationships and to reduce the likelihood of recidivism. Although incarcerated individuals may choose to mediate with any number of people, most people choose to mediate with family members.

Mediation helps people reach agreements, rebuild relationships, and find permanent solutions to their disputes. Mediation is a process that allows individuals to speak for themselves and make their own decisions. There are important values behind mediation—it is nonjudgmental, confidential, and voluntary. For example, in the state of Maryland, community mediation has served as a vital role for the reentry process of individuals leaving the prison system and has had effects such as lowering recidivism and reducing family conflict (Flowers, 2014). Below we summarize what this process looks like and how it could be applied to Mychal, Tamika, and their family.

Introducing Mediation to Incarcerated Individuals

In institutions where individuals are serving long sentences, mediation should be introduced 6–12 months before the release date. This provides sufficient time for screening of the outside individual, managing all of the logistics with the institution, and still accounting for time which may be taken off the sentence, shifting release dates, and possible transfers to other facilities towards the end of the sentence. In facilities where individuals are serving shorter sentences, mediation should be introduced as soon as possible.

Ideally, the community mediation center case manager should have access directly to all individuals who meet the criteria as eligible for the reentry mediation services. When establishing the structure for introducing reentry mediation to a group of incarcerated individuals, it is important to consider that some individuals may be hesitant to express a need for help in front of others. Therefore, whatever system is established, it should allow for individuals to request the service without necessarily doing so in a public way.

The case manager begins by asking the participants to speak in general about their plans as they prepare for release and who on the outside will be important to them during the period of release and transition into the community. Mychal may have been invited to the large group and then met one-on-one with the case manager. In that meeting, he may have identified his goals of reconnecting with Tamika and reengaging as a father. The mediation case manager listens and reflects back to the incarcerated individual, using strategic listening and focusing the reflections on feelings, values, and topics for resolution.

For example, Mychal may have said,

> *I think Tamika is going to be there for me and we're going to try to do this family thing, but sometimes I don't know where she's coming from. She'll be saying one thing about how we're a family and then she can't get here to see me. I know it's hard for her and I'm lucky that she is raising those kids as well as she is, but it's hard for me in here, too. I basically have no one else. And when she doesn't come or call for a minute, I just don't know where things are at and I start thinking maybe she's not really about it.*

The case manager might reflect back,

> *It sounds like you feel confused and torn—you feel grateful for Tamika's role as the children's mother and you feel alone in here. It also sounds like you are looking for clarity about your relationships and consistency in terms of your time together and your communication with each other. Is that right?*

After Mychal confirms, the case manager can explain how those things might be worked on in mediation.

Once the incarcerated individual determines he or she wants to use mediation, the case manager completes an intake form, screens for fear of retaliation, and completes all of the preservice forms necessary. The prison staff also will check to make sure there are no stay-away orders and the person the incarcerated individual wants to mediate with is not on the individual's victim notification list.

The mediation ethic of *self-determination* requires that an incarcerated individual select the person with whom he or she wishes to mediate and that this not be restricted to blood relatives or any specific category (other than prohibiting mediation when there is a stay-away order or with someone on the victim notification list). Further, sometimes it may be best for incarcerated individuals not to reconnect with immediate family members (due to abusive situations), but they may need to reconnect with another person who has been important and helpful in their life.

Introducing Mediation to Outside Participants

The mediation case manager sends a letter to the outside participants, inviting them to participate in the prerelease mediation. The mediation case manager then follows up with a telephone call. All principles of good mediation intake processes are important here. Some especially important principles are to ensure confidentiality by not disclosing to the outside participant what the inside participant wants to talk about. It is best to give a brief overview of reentry mediation, inform the outside participant that the inside participant wishes to mediate, and ask the outside participant to speak about the relationship. As the outside participant describes the relationship and his or her feelings, the case manager uses strategic listening to reflect back feelings, values, and topics, with open-ended questions.

In the call with Tamika, she may have commented,

> *You know, I'm going to let him come back to the house. We're going to try to be a family, but I don't know how it's going to work because he just never changes. You know, he talks a good talk, but then he's kind of self-centered. I mean, while I'm out here killing myself to raise his kids and keep the lights on, he's complaining about "how come I don't come see him and bring the kids to see him?" Like, he doesn't get it, and I'm scared if he doesn't change things up, he's going to go right back in there, too.*

The case manager would reflect the feelings, values, and topics and connect the conversation to a possible mediation,

> *What I'm hearing you say is that you've felt overwhelmed with the responsibilities you've had on the outside and you're looking for understanding of what that's been like for you. It also sounds like you are looking for more consideration and follow-through on commitments. I'm also hearing that you are feeling scared for the future. Is that right?*

It is important the outside participant understands mediation is nonjudgmental and neutral, and that it is not an advocacy process. When outside participants recognize that they will have sufficient opportunity to express themselves in the mediation and that the mediators will be opening up dialogue for everyone, they are more likely to want to participate. Listening to them during the intake call is the best way to model that this is what will occur in the mediation.

Conversations with the outside participants include a range from gratitude to hostility. Often the relationships have been strained and the outside participants may want nothing to do with the incarcerated individual. Other times, they feel relieved at the idea of having a chance to have a prerelease conversation to address issues. The mediation case manager plays the same role of listening, reflecting, asking questions, and explaining the process in any of these scenarios. Often, individuals who begin the conversation with hostility open up once they experience feeling heard and not feeling judged. They may even decide they want to use mediation because of the positive experience on the call.

Mediation Logistics

The prerelease mediation logistics represent a balance honoring facility security and the privacy necessary for the mediation to address deep and complex issues. The institution screens outside participants in advance. The room in which the mediation occurs is private, and no one on the outside can hear the conversation. This privacy is crucial to ensure that participants feel comfortable discussing a range of issues that often make them feel vulnerable. These in-depth conversations often are critical to the mediation process, as they allow for new connections to be made between participants and they allow for underlying issues to be identified. There is generally a window that allows the corrections staff to see in as often as they wish. Mediators generally ask outside participants to sit on the opposite side of the table from the incarcerated individual. This further minimizes the possibility of any items being passed.

Mediations should not occur with glass between participants, by phone, or by videoconference. Mediation through any of these mediums will be compromised for several reasons. First, these systems may not be confidential, as a third party could listen in to a call or videoconference. Even if a third party is not listening, the mediation participants may not be able to trust that a third party is not listening and, therefore, may not be willing to open up and be as vulnerable as necessary for mediation to be successful. Second, in rebuilding the trust and relationship, the concept of body language and human energy that is only possible to read when people are in the same room is crucial. Mediators take cues from body language and need to be able to see everyone together. Finally, these mediums would generally require that the mediator be in one space with the outside participants and the incarcerated individual be in the other space alone. This compromises the mediators' neutrality and the participants' equal access to the mediation process. Even though it may take time to work out a plan that allows for all participants to be in the same private room, it is a worthwhile process.

Mediation Model and Key Components

In Maryland, the Inclusive Mediation Framework is used for reentry mediation. In the framework, the mediator's role is to strategically engage in deep, reflective listening. The role is not analytical, nor is the goal to provide the mediator's observations about the conversation. Mediators should use open-ended questions judiciously for the purposes of deepening the conversation. The dialogue that occurs should enhance the opportunity for participants to begin healing difficult relationships shaped by outdated assumptions and expectations. These types of conversations offer participants the opportunity to acquire an "in the moment" understanding of the thoughts and feelings of others. Participants also may become clearer about what is important to them as they attempt to express it to the other participant. Further, as understanding is built, the mediator assists participants in the process of becoming clearer about particular areas in which continued efforts toward resolution would be most beneficial for reentry. A portion of Tamika and Mychal's conversation may sound like the following:

TAMIKA: *You know how you get . . . You can talk a good talk now and all like, "Baby, this time it's going to be different," and for a few weeks it will be, but then, it will be back to how it always is.*

MEDIATOR: *Tamika, it sounds like you're looking for follow-through on commitments made and feel worried about things returning to how they were. Can you talk about what you mean when you say "How it always is"?*

MYCHAL: *This time it is going to be different. I've been taking classes in here, working my recovery, everything. I know stuff now I didn't know before. You don't even listen to who I am now, you just assume I'm how I've always been.*

MEDIATOR: *Mychal, it sounds like you feel proud and confident about the changes you've made and you are looking for recognition of those changes. It sounds like in terms of communication, you are looking for openness to those changes. Can you talk about some of the new stuff you know now that you didn't know before?*

As the participants acquire an understanding of each other's current thoughts and feelings, the mediator will work with them to identify the topics they want to resolve. With each topic, the mediator will identify the value or goal each participant has related to the topic. For example, in terms of communication, Mychal's value might be identified as "openness" and Tamika's might be "consistency and follow-through."

A second important component to the reentry mediation process is a chance to explore a range of options to the issues at hand, and to collaborate to develop solutions to unresolved concerns. In the Inclusive Mediation model, this is done through a formal brainstorming process. The process begins by focusing on one topic at a time and begins by clarifying the goals participants have for resolution. (For Tamika and Mychal, the question might be, "In terms of communication, what ideas can you think of that could give you the openness you are looking for and the consistency and follow-through you are looking for?") Then the mediators facilitate a more formal brainstorming procedure that encourages participants to consider all of the options. Leading this brainstorming process takes significant skills and patience on the part of the mediator. These include listening for and listing (on an easel paper in a public way) only ideas that come from the participants themselves, without the mediator offering any ideas or edits.

Often, people preparing for release are keenly aware of the limited options and limited resources at their disposal. The brainstorming process encourages considering all possibilities (even unattainable or undesirable), which allows for a thorough assessment of all options. This often leads to participants tapping into their indigenous community resources that they may not have previously considered. Experiencing this kind of brainstorming has a long-term effect on how participants handle future conflicts. Follow-up surveys conducted 3–6 months after release found that 84% of respondents agreed that "when a conflict arises, they try to think things through before responding" (Flowers, 2015).

Reentry mediation is a neutral process, meaning the process itself is not based on a sense that one person caused harm to another. During the process, either the incarcerated individual, the outside participant, or both often express remorse at harm they have caused themselves or others as well as expressing their experiences of being victims. This conversation is supported through the deep dialogue that is made possible during the reentry mediation, but the discussion of experiencing and/or causing harm would only become part of the conversation if the participants initiate that dialogue.

Post-Release Services

The best practice for post-release services is that within two weeks of release, the mediation case manager makes contact with the released individual and outside participant to offer additional mediation services. If participants choose to participate in additional sessions, they will be provided at a location determined to be convenient to the participants. If they choose not to mediate, they are informed that they can return to mediation for additional sessions on the outside whenever they think it is necessary.

A key component of the reentry mediation approach is self-determination and mediator neutrality. This is manifested in many ways, one of which is a restriction on the mediator to never offer advice or suggestions. Referrals are rarely made, and they are made only when both mediation participants have identified a specific outside service they want to pursue. They may ask the mediation center for assistance identifying outside agencies that provide such a service. This means that a mediator would never suggest or refer clients to therapy based on the mediator's observation of the participants' interaction or description of their challenges. However, it is not unusual for participants to reach the conclusion on their own that either individual or family therapy could be beneficial. If both agree, they may include this in their final mediation agreement. If participants request support identifying therapy services, the community mediation center may provide them with a set of referrals or a connection to an agency that has the ability to make such referrals.

From a general therapeutic treatment plan (i.e., without an identified therapeutic model selected), three important phases will need to occur with Mychal and Tamika. First, the therapist will engage in the early phase, through (a) the development of the therapeutic relationship, (b) problem assessment, and (c) goal setting. Second, the therapist will move the family into the middle phase, considered the "working phase" of therapy, in which presenting and/or assessed problems are addressed more specifically. Finally, the family moves into the late phase of therapy, which includes (a) addressing long-term issues, (b) solidifying gains, (c) strategies for handling future issues, and (d) referrals (if necessary).

In conclusion, this clinical application details both the promise and challenges of criminal justice reform for intergenerational families, as presented by Arditti and Kennington. A commitment to policy reform must be complemented by a commitment to craft effective and meaningful clinical interventions. Interventions like mediation would help to redress years of harmful effects of incarceration on family dynamics, including coparenting relationships and family competence.

References

Alexander, M. (2012). *The new Jim Crow: Mass incarceration in an age of colorblindness*. New York: The New Press.

Arditti, J. A. (2012). *Parental incarceration and the family: Psychological and social effects of imprisonment on children, parents, and caregivers*. New York, NY: NYU Press.

Bengston, V., & Allen, K. (1993). The life course perspective applied to families over time. In P. Boss, W. Doherty, R. LaRossa, W. Schumm, & S. Steinmetz (Eds.), *Sourcebook of family theories and methods: A contextual approach* (pp. 469–498). New York: Plenum Press.

Bronfenbrenner, U. (1995). Developmental ecology through space and time: A future perspective. In P. Moen, G. H. Elder, Jr., & K. Luscher (Eds.), *Examining lives in context: Perspectives on the ecology of human development* (pp. 619–647). Washington, DC: American Psychological Association.

Elder, G. H., Jr. (1998). The life course as developmental theory. *Child Development, 69*, 1–12.

Flowers, S. (2014). Maryland Public Safety Compact Recidivism Analysis Final Brief, Baltimore's Safe & Sound Campaign. Baltimore, MD.

Flowers, S. (2015). Snapshot of Re-entry Mediation Statistics: February 2009–June 2015. Choice Research Associates. Greenbelt, MD.

Johnson, S. M., & Whiffen, V. E. (Eds.). (2003). *Attachment processes in couple and family therapy*. New York, NY: Guilford Press.

Minuchin, S. (1974). *Families & family therapy*. Cambridge, MA: Harvard University Press.

Minuchin, S., & Fishman, H. C. (1981). *Techniques of family therapy*. Cambridge, MA: Harvard University Press.

Palazzoli, M. S., Boscolo, L., Cecchin, G., & Prata, G. (1980). The Problem of the Referring Person. *Journal of Marital and Family Therapy, 6*(1), 3–9. doi: 10.1111/j.1752-0606.1980.tb01699.x

Roy, K. (2014). Fathering from the long view: Framing personal and social change through life course theory. *Journal of Family Theory and Review*, *6*, 319–335. doi: 10.1111/jftr.12050

Seymour, C. B. (1998). Children with parents in prison: Child welfare policy, program, and practice issues. *Child Welfare New York*, *77*, 469–494.

Titelman, P. (2014). *Clinical applications of Bowen family systems theory*. New York, NY: Routledge.

8

CYBERBULLYING AND THE FAMILY

Case Study

Katherine M. Hertlein

Emily, a 15-year-old sophomore, attended a local high school. Her grades had been above average as a freshman, but as a sophomore, her grades dropped to average. Socially, she was active in the yearbook staff and the theatre group, and had a close circle of friends with whom she would spend an extended amount of time. As Emily became involved with this group of friends, she would consistently spend more time with her friends, was less conscientious about her schoolwork, and was very interested in adapting and molding to her emerging peer group. Her mother Katherine described this as a time where Emily stopped telling her about the specifics of her day-to-day life and seemed more isolated. Both Katherine and Emily's father, Henri, believed Emily's movement toward more isolation and greater autonomy was developmentally appropriate, but they were still concerned about making sure they had enough information about her life so that they could still protect her.

Two months ago, Emily began receiving odd emails from various organizations thanking her for registering for their newsletters. Emily initially wrote these off as spam and did not discuss the matter with her parents. Emily took no precautions with her email other than to delete these acknowledgements as they came into her inbox. After about a month of this, Emily began receiving messages to her phone via text message. These text messages listed the sender as an email address unrecognizable to Emily and contained vague messages about work opportunities and requested that she email them. She received these messages daily for a couple of weeks, and each time she received a message, the email address from which the text message originated was a different address. Again, Emily did not notify her parents to the messages she was receiving on her phone. She again deleted the messages she received.

Next, Emily began receiving texts from an anonymous texting service. The messages were crafted in a threatening way, stating the boy that she was interested in at school was in fact interested in someone else, just messing with her, and warning her to stay away from him as he was "dangerous." Again, Emily did not disclose having received such a message to her parents. She also did not block the address from where the text originated, reasoning that an anonymous text service would be difficult to block. Emily ignored the text and a few days later received another, more threatening in nature. The sender insulted Emily and told her she was "stupid" for not listening to the advice given earlier to stay away from that individual. Within another few days she received yet another anonymous text declaring she had "no self-esteem" if she was going to pursue this relationship and she was "dumber than I thought."

Emily was ashamed that she was receiving these messages and showed them to her best friend and one of their other close friends. Neither friend indicated receiving these messages and reported no knowledge of who the sender might be. Her best friend surmised that the person sending them might be a former partner of Emily's latest romantic interest, but neither girl was aware of how the former partner might have gotten Emily's phone number and/or email address (if in fact she was also being registered for various electronic newsletters at the hands of this same individual). In addition, the messages were sent at times that were not consistent with when the former partner was available due to her work schedule, as Emily discovered when querying her romantic interest. The messages kept coming in regularly (nearly daily), with more demeaning comments each time.

Emily's parents became aware of the cyberbullying when they sent an invitation via Facebook to a select and small group of friends to Emily's birthday party. It was at this point that Emily's mother Katherine received a text message to her phone stating that she shouldn't plan a party for Emily given that she was hiding things from them and lying, with specific reference to intimate details only shared on the invitation. Katherine confronted Emily about the text, and at this point, Emily shared with her mother the texts and messages she had been receiving. Katherine began to ask others to whom she sent the invite who they shared it with; each person denied sharing the invitation, leading the family to the conclusion that there must be some monitoring of the Facebook page going on by this individual as well. Emily went back to her circle of friends and tried to see if anyone in her peer group had an idea who this was, only to find out that several of her friends had received email messages from someone claiming to be Emily and stating she was using a new email address and to contact her at that address. This was the first Emily had heard about it, and she was now concerned someone had stolen her identity.

The effects on the family were quite pronounced. Emily's parents experienced a division in how they approached the punishment. Emily's father Henri was quicker to anger and blamed Katherine for being more permissive toward Emily. Katherine believed that Henri's anger served to further separate them from Emily and that she would rebel in other ways. In addition, neither Katherine nor Henri believed that Emily could be trusted to manage a cell phone and as a result made her turn in her phone every night to her parents. Emily's perception of this reaction was that it was draconian and would only serve to set her up for future isolation from peers and parents. Emily told her older sister Johanna, who was currently in college, about the matter, and Johanna stood firmly on Emily's side, suggesting that what was happening was a prank and nothing more. Johanna also blamed Katherine and Henri for isolating Johanna herself from the family through tracking her via her cell phone when she was in high school and negatively impacting her ability to trust her parents after that incident.

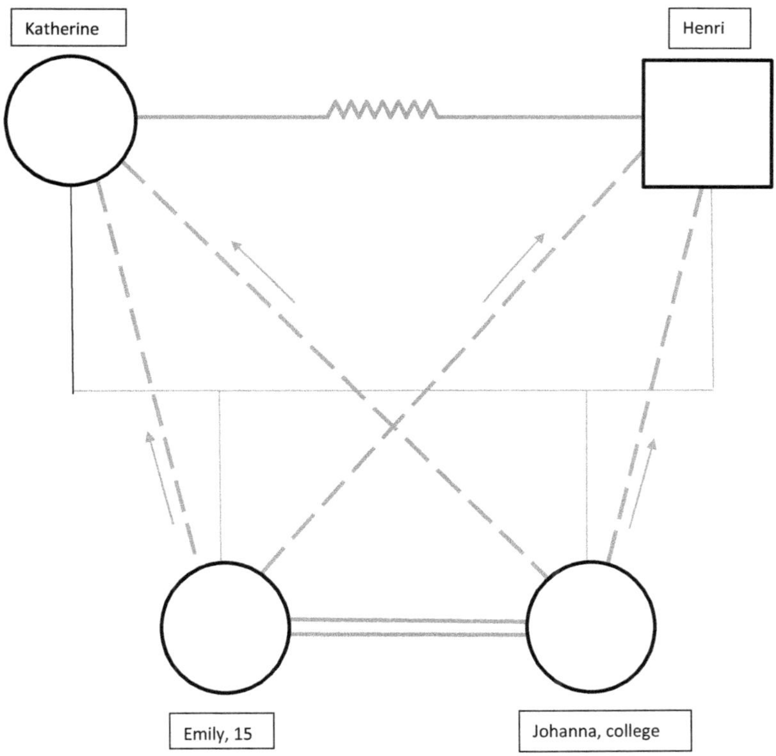

Figure 8.1 Families and Cyberbullying Genogram: Emily, Katherine, and Henri

Research on Family Experiences With Cyberbullying

Tracy E. Waasdorp, Krista R. Mehari, and Catherine P. Bradshaw

The vast majority of adolescents in the United States use technology to interact with their peers, through instant messaging, social media, texting, email, and the like. The data are striking, as findings from a recent study using a nationally representative sample of adolescents (aged 13–17) indicated that 92% of adolescents use the Internet daily, of which 24% reported going online "almost constantly" and 56% reported several times a day. Further, 81% reported using social networking sites (Lenhart, 2015). In a follow-up study using the same data, Lenhart, Smith, Anderson, Duggan, and Perrin (2015) found that 83% of adolescents used technology, such as social media and online gaming, to feel more connected with their friends. In fact, the vast majority (95%) of youth reported text messaging with friends occasionally, with 55% of them texting daily. Moreover, 68% reported that they use social media to find people to support them through difficult times. Another nationally representative survey of over 2000 youth found that adolescents (aged 13–18) averaged nine hours a day of electronic media use (excluding time spent at school or for homework), whereas those who were aged 8–12 averaged six (Common Sense Media, 2016). The use of electronic media (e.g., computers, tablets, cell phones) among children under the age of 8 is steadily increasing. For example, one study found that over a two-year period (2011 to 2013), technology access increased from 52% to 75% in children under age 8 (Rideout, 2013). Moreover, the amount of time spent per day on these devices to interact with others tripled among youth ages 5–8 (Rideout, 2013).

Given the amount of time youth spend using technology to interact with peers (Lenhart et al., 2015), it is not surprising that some of this time may include inappropriate or problematic interactions, such as cyberbullying (Ybarra et al., 2008). Also known as electronic aggression, cyberbullying is the use of technology (e.g., texts, social media) to harm another individual. Cyberbullying usually involves verbal aggression (e.g., threatening, insulting, and name-calling) and relational aggression (e.g., spreading rumors or negative text/images electronically to harm someone's reputation; Gladden, Vivolo-Kantor, Hamburger, & Lumpkin, 2014). Cyber victimization refers to situations in which a person is a target of these aggressive behaviors. This chapter discusses issues related to cyberbullying with a focus on the role parents play in preventing and responding to cyberbullying. Specifically, we present definitions and forms of cyberbullying, consider adolescents' difficulty in disclosing cyber victimization experiences, review common risk factors for and consequences of cyber victimization, and explore the important role parents play in preventing and responding to cyber victimization.

Defining Cyberbullying

Bullying is defined as (1) intentionally aggressive behavior that (2) occurs repeatedly against a victim, when there is (3) an "observed or perceived" power imbalance, whether it be physical, verbal, or relational in nature (Gladden et al., 2014). Cyberbullying is a specific form of bullying behavior that occurs through electronic media; therefore, the same three broad bullying criteria apply. However, cyberbullying has some distinctions as well. For example, with regard to repetition, the victim can repeatedly experience a single harmful cyber experience without the incident actually reoccurring, such as an email or text being forwarded to multiple people or posted online and subsequently viewed by many. Accordingly, although in-person bullying is defined by two or more experiences a month (e.g., Olweus, 1993), cyberbullying research has not suggested a finite frequency level from which to infer harm, as a one-time event viewed by many can be extremely harmful (Williford et al., 2013). With regard to power imbalance, youth who bully in person often have more physical power or higher social status (e.g., more friends, greater popularity) than the victim. However, this is not necessarily the case for youth who cyberbully, as the ability for the perpetrator to remain anonymous (e.g., creating a fake online persona) and having advanced technological skills can afford power in the cyber realm that would not be possible in person (Dempsey, Sulkowski, Dempsey, & Storch, 2011; Law, Shapka, Hymel, Olson, & Waterhouse, 2012). In the case study of Emily, this is a clear case of cyberbullying (i.e., she received frequent threatening and demeaning text messages over time from someone who was more technologically savvy; Emily felt powerless to deal with the situation). Further, the perpetrator was able to threaten and harass Emily anonymously, monitor Emily's online and in-person activities, and impersonate her.

As illustrated in the case example, cyberbullying can take many forms. Cyberbullying behaviors include electronic sending, posting, or sharing of words or pictures using these harmful behaviors: flaming (messages containing overt hostile, callous language), denigration/defamation (messages containing harmful rumors, lies, or gossip to ruin a person's reputation), outing (messages containing secrets or embarrassing information), trickery (tricking someone into revealing secrets publicly), exclusion (spitefully excluding someone), harassment (frequent, serious, and threatening messages), and stalking (harassment of an individual across multiple electronic communication platforms; Calvete,

Orue, Estévez, Villardón, & Padilla, 2010; Nucciteill, 2012; Willard, 2007). Cyberbullying also might involve impersonation, in which an individual pretends to be someone else by hacking, using someone else's account, or creating a false account. Emily experienced harassment, stalking, and impersonation.

As the case study illustrated, research suggests that cyberbullying often occurs outside of school hours (Agatston, Kowalski, & Limber, 2007). Although parents should be involved regardless of when and where the cyberbullying takes place, parents often play an important role in monitoring and detecting cyberbullying, given that cyberbullying may occur outside of school hours. Yet, parents often are puzzled about what to do in response to adolescents' use of technologies, particularly when it comes to problematic situations online. Even more concerning, parents may be unaware of their child's experience of cyber victimization (Dehue, Bolman, & Völlink, 2008), which obviously hinders their ability to respond.

Disclosure of Cyberbullying

As illustrated in the case study of Emily, many youth struggle with experiences of cyber victimization without informing adults. In fact, Emily did not seek help from her parents until the situation had escalated, and research suggests this is a common pattern. She did, however, go to her friends for support and help. Studies show that middle and high school aged youth typically do not go to parents or other adults when they are victims of in-person bullying (Waasdorp & Bradshaw, 2011) or cyberbullying (Waasdorp & Bradshaw, 2015). Interestingly, elementary school students do appear to disclose bullying to their parents at a higher rate than their older peers, suggesting some developmental differences in the way youth seek help (Waasdorp & Bradshaw, 2011). For example, research suggests that just 9% to 27% of youth who are cyber victimized report it to their parents (Huang & Chou, 2010; Smith et al., 2008). In fact, one study found that only about half of the parents were aware of their child's victimization (Dehue et al., 2008). There are many factors related to a child's willingness to disclose (Spears, Taddeo, Daly, Stretton, & Karklins, 2015). In most cases, youth do not tell parents about their victimization experiences because they believe their parents would restrict their Internet use or take away their phone. Youth also are concerned that their parents would not understand the problem or simply that their parents would not be able to do anything to stop it (Agatston et al., 2007; Bauman, 2009). In Emily's case, her reasons for not disclosing to her parents were unclear. It is possible that she could predict their reaction of further restricting her cell phone use, and she wanted to avoid that consequence.

Despite some youths' reluctance to talk to their parents about cyber victimization, parents can play a significant role in preventing and helping to intervene in cyberbullying situations due to their direct influence over youths' use of electronic devices (Bradshaw, 2014). Perhaps the first step is working to create a line of communication such that the child feels safe in sharing experiences. Specifically, parents are more likely to know about their children's cyber victimization if they have had discussions about risks of online behavior with their adolescents and worked jointly with their children to create rules about spending time online (Byrne, Katz, Lee, Linz, & McIlrath, 2014; Navarro, Serna, Martínez, & Ruiz-Oliva, 2013). One disconcerting factor in Emily's relationship with her parents was the lack of open communication, even prior to the cyber victimization experiences. As discussed in the subsequent section, open parent-child communication is associated with a reduced risk of being cyberbullied (Lereya, Samara, & Wolke, 2013).

Effects of Cyberbullying on Adolescent Adjustment

Although many of the risk factors for experiencing cyber victimization may overlap with in-person peer bullying, there is some research to suggest that the effects of cyber victimization may be more harmful. Some scholars suggest perhaps this is because the victim may not know the identity of the perpetrator. Whereas one study found that up to half of children who experience cyberbullying do not know the identity of the perpetrator (Bauman, 2009), other studies suggest that most cyber victims know the perpetrator (Bryce & Fraser, 2013; Tokunaga, 2010). Regardless of how often the attacks occur (Hamm et al., 2015), the ability of the perpetrator to remain anonymous appears to produce more harm than when the perpetrator is known (Sticca & Perren, 2013). For example, studies have shown that not knowing the identity of the perpetrator is associated with increased negative emotions such as feelings of loneliness, fear, and concern that the perpetrator could be a friend or someone close to them (Bryce & Fraser, 2013; Dredge, Gleeson, & de la Piedad Garcia, 2014; Nocentini et al., 2010; Sticca & Perren, 2013). In the case study, Emily appeared to be distressed by not knowing the identity of the perpetrator, and despite her efforts, she was unable to identify the perpetrator. A second factor that may make cyberbullying more harmful than in-person bullying is the potential for widespread dissemination of harmful content, which often is difficult to remove from the cyber world (e.g., Smith et al., 2008; Suzuki, Asaga, Sourander, Hoven, & Mandell, 2012).

Regardless of anonymity, there are myriad adjustment problems associated with cyber victimization. A recent meta-analytic review found that across correlational studies, youth who were cyber victimized had lower self-esteem, life satisfaction, and academic achievement compared to youth who were not cyber victimized. Similarly, they displayed other mental and behavioral health problems, such as a higher risk for drug and alcohol use, loneliness, depressive symptoms, anger, and anxiety (Kowalski, Giumetti, Schroeder, & Lattanner, 2014). Another rigorous review found a strong and consistent association between cyberbullying and depressive symptoms (Hamm et al., 2015). It is important to note, however, that most studies of the effects of cyberbullying are cross-sectional or short-term (e.g., six months apart, Sticca, Ruggieri, Alsaker, & Perren, 2013); therefore, it is difficult to draw conclusions regarding the order in which adjustment problems occur (i.e., which behaviors are causal). In fact, it is possible that youth who experience these problems may become targets for cyber victimization (Kowalski et al., 2014). Despite this limitation, these factors are clearly important to discuss and address in order to prevent cyberbullying and understand its effects on youth.

Predictors of Cyber Victimization Among Adolescents

Although research on cyberbullying, particularly longitudinal studies, is in its infancy (Livingstone & Smith, 2014), a recent meta-analytic review of the risk factors for cyber victimization indicated that there are individual-level, family, and environmental or situational factors associated with increased risk for this particular form of victimization (Kowalski et al., 2014). Of note, this meta-analysis included only cross-sectional data, so it is not possible to conclude whether these factors are potential causes or effects of the cyber victimization. Despite these limitations, we discuss these factors below.

Individual-Level Factors

A consistent predictor of cyber victimization across studies appears to be in-person victimization (Kowalski et al., 2014). For example, Hinduja and Patchin (2008) found that youth who were bullied in person were more than twice as likely to be bullied online compared to youth who were not bullied in person. A recent study of high school youth found that 75% of those who reported being a victim of bullying in person had not experienced cyberbullying; however, 95% of youth who were cyberbullied also experienced at least one other in-person form of bullying (Waasdorp & Bradshaw, 2015). This high level of overlap between in-person and online victimization among those who experienced cyberbullying (but not among those who were in-person bullied) was the same conclusion drawn in another recent review of the literature in which Mehari et al. (2014) provided compelling evidence that cyberbullying overlaps considerably with other forms of bullying. This further corroborates discussions by Olweus (2012, 2013) and others (Patchin & Hinduja, 2012) that suggest youth who are involved in cyberbullying (perpetrators and victims) are also predominantly the same individuals who are involved with in-person bullying. Therefore, it is important when parents become aware that their child is involved in cyberbullying, they should also inquire about other forms of peer victimization that may be affecting the child. Similarly, if a child is experiencing victimization in person (e.g., called mean names, having rumors spread about him or her), the parents should question whether any of that behavior is happening via electronic communication technologies as well. Interestingly, it appears that Emily was not experiencing victimization in person, indicating that she was possibly in one of those rare cases in which a youth is only bullied online.

Another consistent risk factor observed across studies is that youth who bully others in person are more likely to experience cyber victimization (Kowalski et al., 2014). Along the same lines, normative beliefs about aggression (believing that aggression is normal or acceptable) and moral disengagement were strongly associated with being cyber victimized (Kowalski et al., 2014). In contrast, youth with higher social intelligence and empathy, and who behave in prosocial ways, are less likely to be victimized (Kowalski et al., 2014). This suggests that treating others with kindness and empathy actually reduces youths' risk of experiencing victimization, thus making this skill a potentially important target for intervention. Moreover, youth with better adjustment in general, such as with higher academic achievement, greater satisfaction with life, less drug and alcohol use, and less loneliness, are less likely to be victimized online (Kowalski et al., 2014). From the case study, we know that Emily's academic achievement was suffering, which is associated with a greater risk for cyber victimization.

Other individual-level risk factors include more frequent use of the Internet and risky online behavior, such as sharing personal information and requesting or agreeing to meet up with someone they met online (Casas, del Rey, & Ortega-Ruiz, 2013; Kowalski et al., 2014; Navarro et al., 2013). In fact, such risky online behavior is consistently associated with cyber victimization (Kowalski et al., 2014). Although Emily's frequency of Internet use was unclear, it is possible that she could have used better protection online. For example, spam filters possibly could have screened out the job advertisements she received early on, and privacy settings on Facebook could have prevented others from viewing the invitation to her birthday party. Parents and educators should work to teach youth basic online safety (e.g., explanation of the risk of sharing personal information) as well as technologically based strategies for protection (e.g., privacy settings, blocking, and reporting).

Family-Level Factors

Specific family characteristics also appear to predict cyber victimization. In general, parent-child relationships that are supportive and have open communication protect children from victimization (Lereya et al., 2013). This also may be true for cyber victimization. In a review of the literature, Ang (2015) suggested having an open and supportive relationship is an important factor in predicting healthy Internet use. More specifically, one study of children in sixth through tenth grades found that parental support was related to lower rates of cyber victimization (Wang, Iannotti, & Nansel, 2009). Another study of sixth graders found that child-rated closeness of the parent-child relationship was associated with lower frequency of cyber victimization (Accordino & Accordino, 2011).

As with other forms of aggression and delinquent behavior, parental monitoring is associated with cyberbullying. In the Kowalski et al. (2014) meta-analysis, parental monitoring was strongly and consistently associated with lower frequency of cyber victimization. Parental engagement in online activities with their child is also protective. For example, children who are "friends" with their parents on Facebook are less likely to be victimized (Kanter, Afifi, & Robbins, 2012). In contrast, lack of monitoring and supervision were associated with increased risk for being cyber victimized. Byrne et al. (2014) found that parents who allowed their adolescent (aged 10–16) to use the Internet privately were less aware of their adolescent's victimization experiences. Another study found that boys (but not girls) were less likely to be victimized if their parents monitored the websites they visited and had rules about information-sharing online (Mesch, 2009).

Parenting strategies around adolescents' use of the Internet, also called *parental mediation*, can be active or restrictive (Ang, 2015). Active mediation involves open discussion and teaching around safe Internet use, whereas restrictive parental mediation involves limiting time on electronic communication devices or placing restrictions around where adolescents can go on the Internet. In general, there is more empirical support for *active parental mediation* as a protective factor than for *restrictive parental mediation* (Ang, 2015). In the case study, the parents' first instinct was to further restrict Emily's use of electronic communications technology. This is completely understandable, but research suggests that restriction alone will not necessarily reduce her risk of cyber victimization, and might even make the situation worse. It is important to note that monitoring, supervision, and engagement, rather than restriction alone, are associated with a decreased risk of cyber victimization. For example, one study found that youth whose parents were aware of and monitored their activities in general (i.e., the extent to which adolescents believed their parents knew about their whereabouts and activities) were 26 times less likely to be victimized than youth whose parents used Internet restriction methods only, such as blocking certain websites or restricting the amount of time youth were online (Khurana, Bleakley, Jordan, & Romer, 2015). Similarly, a study of youth in Canada found that having parents who used blocking software actually was related to higher likelihood of both cyberbullying and being cyber victimized at approximately the same time (Mishna, Khoury-Kassabri, Gadalla, & Daciuk, 2012).

Notably, although blocking adolescents' use of the Internet and cell phones is generally not helpful, some parental restriction may help to keep children safe. For example, research suggests that youth whose parents prevent them from using the Internet in their bedroom are less likely to be victimized online (Khurana et al., 2015). There is also some evidence that restrictive parental mediation can reduce adolescents' risky behaviors online (Ang, 2015). Taken together, the research seems to suggest that although there may be some benefit to restricting or blocking adolescents' use of the Internet and cell phones, proactive approaches such as parental involvement, monitoring, and communication are much more successful in reducing risk of being victimized.

Parental Responses to Cyberbullying

Given research on the relation between family factors and cyber victimization, it is clear that parents are in a crucial position for stemming cyberbullying involvement (Bradshaw, 2014). Through involvement, monitoring, and communication, parents can employ a number of strategies that reduce their child's likelihood of victimization online and increase their child's likelihood of disclosing problematic online experiences. In general, establishing warm, supportive relationships with open lines of communication protects adolescents from victimization (e.g., Lereya et al., 2013). This is a vital first step, and parental restriction and monitoring related to technologies should be rooted in that relationship. Specific to technologies, recommended strategies include parents communicating about the risks of online behavior, involving their adolescents in establishing rules for online behaviors, and having their adolescents use the Internet in public areas of the home rather than in their bedrooms as a method to increase parents' ability to monitor online activity. There is a growing interest in strategies that may reduce cyberbullying by helping parents to increase their monitoring of technology. For example, installing monitoring software appears to be a promising approach for reducing the risk of victimization (Navarro et al., 2013). Parents should also "friend" their child on Facebook and follow them on other social networking sites, which simultaneously increases involvement with their child and the ability to monitor their child's online behaviors (e.g., Kanter et al., 2012).

Ideally, these parenting behaviors will prevent cyber victimization before it happens. However, as in the case of Emily, sometimes youth are victimized despite parents' best efforts, and parents are put in the position of responding to their child's victimization experiences as well as guiding their child's responses. Parents need to create open channels of communication with their children in order to help them cope and try to stop the bullying. For example, parents should talk to their child about saving harmful texts, posts, and emails in order to have documentation of the bullying. As seen in the case study, Emily consistently deleted the harmful emails and texts without mentioning them to her parents, and without the documentation of the cyberbullying it can be harder to go to the school administration or legal authorities. Rather, she should have saved the threatening materials and turned them over to the authorities.

Research suggests that cyberbullied adolescents are more likely to believe that it is okay to retaliate. In fact, cyber victimization has been shown to predict later cyber aggression, thereby leading to mutually aggressive, escalating interactions and cycles of victimization (Wright & Li, 2013). Although some adolescents who are cyber victimized may respond with aggression online, most adolescents believe that the best way to deal with cyberbullying is to ignore it (Agatston et al., 2007; Tokunaga, 2010). There is cross-sectional evidence to support this notion, as ignoring the situation has been found to be associated with lower internalizing and externalizing symptoms. However, it is quite possible that youth who have better emotion regulation and fewer emotional problems are less likely to be affected or harmed by the bullying, thus making the event "easier" to ignore (Waasdorp & Bradshaw, 2011). Regardless, it will likely be helpful for parents to encourage their children not to respond to the person who is perpetrating the bullying.

Although it may be most helpful for the youth not to respond, research suggests parents should take a more proactive approach. However, most parents do not know how to help their children cope with victimization or lack information on how to respond effectively to try to stop the bullying (Mishna, Pepler, & Wiener, 2006). Instead, most parents only talk to their child about the bullying rather than engage in more proactive behaviors such as contacting the school (Waasdorp, Bradshaw, & Duong, 2011). Although it might be a parent's instinct to block their adolescents' use of the Internet and/or take away their cell phones, these reactive forms of restriction tend to be unhelpful and can even increase cyber victimization, as discussed previously (Sasson & Mesch, 2014). This may be due, in part, to the possibility of adolescents being cyber victimized even if they themselves are not online (Bauman, 2009). For example, a person could humiliate an adolescent online by spreading rumors, embarrassing pictures, or participating in polling sites; those behaviors would affect how an adolescent is treated at school or in other physical settings, regardless of whether or not the adolescent is online.

Alternatively, some parents engage directly with the bully or the bully's parents, which is not an effective response, as it may result in a "he-said, she-said" debate or conflict. Such behavior also could escalate the situation if parents take sides or try to protect their child physically or with threats. It is clear that parents should become more aware of ways in which to respond, such as notifying the school and working collaboratively to effectively resolve the situation and stop the bullying (e.g., Christenson & Havsy, 2004; Espelage & Swearer, 2004), reporting bullying behaviors to websites, such as social networking websites (Agatston et al., 2007), and blocking email addresses and/or certain phone numbers from contacting the youth.

Cyberbullying is unusual in that it does not occur in a physical space, raising the question of whose responsibility it is to monitor electronic interactions and enforce consequences for adolescents who are perpetrating electronic aggression. Some situations of cyber victimization may warrant a report of harassment or other criminal behavior to legal authorities—this response would likely be initiated by the parent rather than the child. In some cases, threatening language online is illegal, and thus should be reported to the police. In cases where the perpetrator's identity is unknown, it may be especially important to report the situation to the police. Each state determines what constitutes cyber harassment; every state has either laws or policy regarding bullying. Stopbullying.gov is an excellent resource and has a page that guides users to state-specific law and policy. There currently are no federal laws regarding bullying, but sometimes bullying overlaps with federal law regarding discrimination.

In other cases, most researchers suggest that parents reach out to the school to help mitigate the situation when the perpetrator is known and is a student in the same school (Hinduja & Patchin, 2015; Shariff, 2009; Willard, 2007). Yet, these situations can be challenging for schools to navigate, as they must balance concerns about students' freedom of speech, particularly when that speech is occurring off school grounds, with the potential liability if the school "effectively caused, encouraged, accepted, tolerated, or failed to correct" a hostile environment that impairs a student's ability to learn (Willard, 2007, p. S65). The school has to walk a fine line, making sure that any intervention taken was necessary because the electronic interactions were interfering with the work of the school, students' rights to safety, or students' rights to education (Willard, 2007). Schools have been punished for interfering with off-campus activities, but the Supreme Court ruled that schools have the responsibility to protect students from "tortious acts" of third parties (Hinduja & Patchin, 2009, p. 108). Specifically, schools can intervene when off-campus behavior impairs the ability of students to learn, creates an unsafe atmosphere, violates students' civil rights, or is perpetrated via school devices (Hinduja & Patchin, 2009).

Because of schools' somewhat nebulous position as monitor and enforcer, it is also important for parents to be involved and advocate for their children's rights. Schools are only responsible to intervene when they are aware of the situation and can demonstrate that it is interfering with the learning process or causing a disruption in the learning environment. If there is no school policy regarding cyberbullying, Emily's parents should advocate with the school to create policy and due process for cyberbullying. In fact, there is an urgent need for schools to establish and set clear expectations for electronic behavior and to identify and implement procedures for when those expectations are not met (Hertz & David-Ferdon, 2008). It is vital that those procedures do not unintentionally punish victims by intensifying the aggression directed at them or reducing their access to and freedom in communication technologies. Further, it is important that the consequences for the perpetrator help to identify prosocial strategies for reaching goals, managing anger, controlling impulsivity, and resolving conflict. Doing this will avoid vilifying adolescents who may also have experienced victimization. Specific ways to accomplish these goals may include peer or adult mediation and perspective-taking training.

Parents can advocate for changes in school policy and government regulations, as well as draw media attention to areas of concern (Shariff, 2009). In Emily's case, her parents should connect with the school to learn more about the school policy regarding cyberbullying situations and reach out to the police if the situation continues to escalate. Schools need clear and equitable policies for reporting cyber victimization that result in action by school officials.

Parents can advocate for anonymous methods for students to report bullying to the school, as research suggests youth prefer anonymous ways to report bullying due to fears that they would be called a "snitch" or that the bully would find out and retaliate (Cassidy, Jackson, & Brown, 2009). There are also some software applications and websites that allow students to anonymously report incidents of bullying. This level of anonymity may help youth feel more comfortable serving as reporters on their own bullying, as well as a peer's bullying.

Conclusions

Parents have a strong desire to protect their children and keep them safe. As a result, learning that their child is being cyberbullied can be scary for parents. The desire to protect their child may lead parents to take extreme and somewhat punitive measures, such as blocking cell phone and Internet use or lashing out against the parents of the perpetrator of the cyberbullying. However, research generally suggests that parents should avoid these types of responses, and instead should communicate, monitor, and remain highly involved in their adolescents' Internet use (e.g., Bauman, 2009; Navarro et al., 2013; Waasdorp et al., 2011). They should engage in frank discussions of risk, form mutual agreements regarding expectations of online behavior, and monitor their Internet use with software, as well as "friending" and "following" their children (e.g., Byrne et al., 2014; Kanter et al., 2012). Parents should stay up-to-date on their school's policy regarding cyberbullying behavior and be willing to advocate for policy at the school level (Shariff, 2009). Parents should also work with the parents of their children's friends to create a critical mass of parents who are providing a high level of parental monitoring of online behavior and are in agreement about the use of appropriate behavior online. In addition, parents should model respectful online behavior for others and make sure that they are supportive and fostering open channels of communication with their children.

References

Accordino, D. B., & Accordino, M. P. (2011). An exploratory study of face-to-face and cyberbullying in sixth grade students. *American Secondary Education, 40*(1), 14–30.

Agatston, P. W., Kowalski, R., & Limber, S. (2007). Students' perspectives on cyber bullying. *Journal of Adolescent Health, 41*(6, Supplement 1), S59–S60. doi: 10.1016/j.jadohealth.2007.09.003

Ang, R. P. (2015). Adolescent cyberbullying: A review of characteristics, prevention and intervention strategies. *Aggression and Violent Behavior, 25*, 35–42. doi: 10.1016/j.avb.2015.07.011

Bauman, S. (2009). Cyberbullying in a rural intermediate school: An exploratory study. *The Journal of Early Adolescence, 30*, 803–833. doi: 10.1177/0272431609350927

Bradshaw, C. P. (2014). The role of families in preventing and buffering the effects of bullying. *JAMA Pediatrics, 168*, 991–993. doi: 10.1001/jamapediatrics.2014.1627

Bryce, J., & Fraser, J. (2013). 'It's common sense that it's wrong': Young people's perceptions and experiences of cyberbullying. *Cyberpsychology, Behavior, and Social Networking, 16*, 783–787. doi: 10.1089/cyber.2012.0275

Byrne, S., Katz, S. J., Lee, T., Linz, D., & McIlrath, M. (2014). Peers, predators, and porn: Predicting parental underestimation of children's risky online experiences. *Journal of Computer-Mediated Communication, 19*, 215–231. doi: 10.1111/jcc4.12040

Calvete, E., Orue, I., Estévez, A., Villardón, L., & Padilla, P. (2010). Cyberbullying in adolescents: Modalities and aggressors' profile. *Computers in Human Behavior, 26*, 1128–1135. doi: 10.1016/j.chb.2010.03.017

Casas, J. A., del Rey, R., & Ortega-Ruiz, R. (2013). Bullying and cyberbullying: Convergent and divergent predictor variables. *Computers in Human Behavior, 29*, 580–587. doi: 10.1016/j.chb.2012.11.015

Cassidy, W., Jackson, M., & Brown, K. N. (2009). Sticks and stones can break my bones, but how can pixels hurt me?: Students' experiences with cyber-bullying. *School Psychology International, 30*, 383–402. doi: 10.1177/0143034309106948

Christenson, S. L., & Havsy, L. H. (2004). Family-school-peer relationships: Significance for social, emotional, and academic learning. In J. E. Zins, R. P. Weissberg, M. C. Wang, & H. J. Walberg (Eds.), *Building academic success on social and emotional learning: What does the research say?* (pp. 59–75). New York, NY, US: Teachers College Press.

Common Sense Media. (2016). *Media use by tweens and teens*. Retrieved on February 12, 2016 from: https://www.commonsensemedia.org/sites/default/files/uploads/research/census_researchreport.pdf

Dehue, F., Bolman, C., & Völlink, T. (2008). Cyberbullying: Youngsters' experiences and parental perception. *Cyberpsychology & Behavior, 11*, 217–223. doi: 10.1089/cpb.2007.0008

Dempsey, A. G., Sulkowski, M. L., Dempsey, J., & Storch, E. A. (2011). Has cyber technology produced a new group of peer aggressors? *Cyberpsychology, Behavior and Social Networking, 14*, 297–302. doi: 10.1089/cyber.2010.0108

Dredge, R., Gleeson, J. F. M., & de la Piedad Garcia, X. (2014). Risk factors associated with impact of severity of cyberbullying victimization: A qualitative study of adolescent online social networking. *Cyberpsychology, Behavior, and Social Networking, 17*, 287–291. doi: 10.1089/cyber.2013.0541

Espelage, D. L., & Swearer, S. M. (2004). *Bullying in American schools: A social-ecological perspective on prevention and intervention*. Mahwah, NJ: Erlbaum.

Gladden, R. M., Vivolo-Kantor, A. M., Hamburger, M. E., & Lumpkin, C. D. (2014). *Bullying surveillance among youths: Uniform definitions for public health and recommended data elements, version 1.0*. Atlanta, GA: National Center for Injury Prevention and Control, Centers for Disease Control and Prevention, U.S. Department of Education.

Hamm, M. P., Newton, A. S., Chisholm, A., Shulhan, J., Milne, A., Sundar, P., . . . Hartling, L. (2015). Prevalence and effect of cyberbullying on children and young people: A scoping review of social media studies. *JAMA Pediatrics, 169*, 770–777. doi: 10.1001/jamapediatrics.2015.0944

Hertz, M. F., & David-Ferdon, C. (2008). *Electronic media and youth violence: A CDC issue brief for educators and caregivers*. Atlanta, GA: Centers for Disease Control.

Hinduja, S., & Patchin, J. W. (2008). Cyberbullying: An exploratory analysis of factors related to offending and victimization. *Deviant Behavior, 29*, 129–156. doi: 10.1080/01639620701457816

Hinduja, S., & Patchin, J. W. (2009). *Bullying beyond the schoolyard: Preventing and responding to cyberbullying*. Thousand Oaks, CA: Corwin Press.

Hinduja, S., & Patchin, J. W. (2015). *Bullying beyond the schoolyard: Preventing and responding to cyberbullying* (2nd ed.). Thousand Oaks, CA, US: Corwin Press.

Huang, Y.-Y., & Chou, C. (2010). An analysis of multiple factors of cyberbullying among junior high school students in Taiwan. *Computers in Human Behavior, 26*, 1581–1590. doi: 10.1016/j.chb.2010.06.005

Kanter, M., Afifi, T., & Robbins, S. (2012). The impact of parents "friending" their young adult child on Facebook on perceptions of parental privacy invasions and parent—child relationship quality. *Journal of Communication, 62*, 900–917. doi: 10.1111/j.1460-2466.2012.01669.x

Khurana, A., Bleakley, A., Jordan, A. B., & Romer, D. (2015). The protective effects of parental monitoring and Internet restriction on adolescents' risk of online harassment. *Journal of Youth and Adolescence, 44*, 1039–1047. doi: 10.1007/s10964-014-0242-4

Kowalski, R. M., Giumetti, G. W., Schroeder, A. N., & Lattanner, M. R. (2014). Bullying in the digital age: A critical review and meta-analysis of cyberbullying research among youth. *Psychological Bulletin, 140*, 1073–1137.

Law, D. M., Shapka, J. D., Hymel, S., Olson, B. F., & Waterhouse, T. (2012). The changing face of bullying: An empirical comparison between traditional and Internet bullying and victimization. *Computers in Human Behavior, 28*, 226–232. doi: 10.1016/j.chb.2011.09.004

Lenhart, A. (2015). *Teen social media and technology overview 2015*. Pew Research Center. Retrieved on January 11, 2016 from: http://www.pewinternet.org/files/2015/04/PI_TeensandTech_Update2015_0409151.pdf

Lenhart, A., Smith, A., Anderson, M., Duggan, M., & Perrin, A. (2015). *Teens, technology, and friendships*. Retrieved on January 11, 2016 from: http://www.pewinternet.org/2015/08/06/teens-technology-and-friendships/

Lereya, S. T., Samara, M., & Wolke, D. (2013). Parenting behavior and the risk of becoming a victim and a bully/victim: A meta-analysis study. *Child Abuse & Neglect, 37*, 1091–1108. doi: 10.1016/j.chiabu.2013.03.001

Livingstone, S., & Smith, P. K. (2014). Annual research review: Harms experienced by child users of online and mobile technologies: The nature, prevalence and management of sexual and aggressive risks in the digital age. *Journal of Child Psychology & Psychiatry, 55*, 635–654. doi: 10.1111/jcpp.12197

Mehari, K. R., Farrell, A. D., & Le, A.-T. H. (2014). Cyberbullying among adolescents: Measures in search of a construct. *Psychology of Violence, 4*, 399–415. doi: 10.1037/a0037521.supp (Supplemental)

Mesch, G. S. (2009). Parental mediation, online activities, and cyberbullying. *Cyberpsychology & Behavior, 12*, 387–393. doi: 10.1089/cpb.2009.0068

Mishna, F., Khoury-Kassabri, M., Gadalla, T., & Daciuk, J. (2012). Risk factors for involvement in cyber bullying: Victims, bullies and bully–victims. *Children & Youth Services Review, 34*(1), 63–70. doi: 10.1016/j.childyouth.2011.08.032

Mishna, F., Pepler, D., & Wiener, J. (2006). Factors associated with perceptions and responses to bullying situations by children, parents, teachers, and principals. *Victims & Offenders, 1*, 255–288. https://doi.org/10.1080/15564880600626163

Navarro, R., Serna, C., Martínez, V., & Ruiz-Oliva, R. (2013). The role of Internet use and parental mediation on cyberbullying victimization among Spanish children from rural public schools. *European Journal of Psychology of Education, 28*, 725–745. doi: 10.1007/s10212-012-0137-2

Nocentini, A., Calmaestra, J., Schultze-Krumbholz, A., Scheithauer, H., Ortega, R., & Menesini, E. (2010). Cyberbullying: Labels, behaviours and definition in three European countries. *Australian Journal of Guidance and Counselling, 20*, 129–142. doi: 10.1375/ajgc.20.2.129

Nucciteill, M. (2012). 2012 cyber bullying tactics. *Forensic Examiner, 21*(3), 24–28.

Olweus, D. (1993). *Bullying at school*. Oxford, England: Blackwell.

Olweus, D. (2012). Cyberbullying: An overrated phenomenon? *European Journal of Developmental Psychology, 9*, 520–538. doi: 10.1080/17405629.2012.682358

Olweus, D. (2013). School bullying: Development and some important challenges. *Annual Review of Clinical Psychology, 9*, 751–780. doi: 10.1146/annurev-clinpsy-050212-185516

Patchin, J. W., & Hinduja, S. (2012). Cyberbullying: An update and synthesis of the research. In J. W. Patchin, S. Hinduja, J. W. Patchin, & S. Hinduja (Eds.), *Cyberbullying prevention and response: Expert perspectives* (pp. 13–35). New York, NY, US: Routledge/Taylor & Francis Group.

Rideout, V. (2013). *Zero to eight: Children's media use in America 2013*. Retrieved on January 11, 2016 from: https://www.commonsensemedia.org/research/zero-to-eight-childrens-media-use-in-america-2013

Sasson, H., & Mesch, G. (2014). Parental mediation, peer norms and risky online behavior among adolescents. *Computers in Human Behavior, 33*, 32–38. doi: 10.1016/j.chb.2013.12.025

Shariff, S. (2009). Confronting cyber-bullying: What schools need to know to control misconduct and avoid legal consequences. Montreal, Canada: Cambridge University Press. doi:10.1017/cbo9780511551260

Smith, P. K., Mahdavi, J., Carvalho, M., Fisher, S., Russell, S., & Tippett, N. (2008). Cyberbullying: Its nature and impact in secondary school pupils. *Journal of Child Psychology and Psychiatry and Allied Disciplines, 49*, 376–385. doi: 10.1111/j.1469-7610.2007.01846.x

Spears, B. A., Taddeo, C. M., Daly, A. L., Stretton, A., & Karklins, L. T. (2015). Cyberbullying, help-seeking and mental health in young Australians: Implications for public health. *International Journal of Public Health, 60*, 219–226. doi: 10.1007/s00038-014-0642-y

Sticca, F., & Perren, S. (2013). Is cyberbullying worse than traditional bullying? Examining the differential roles of medium, publicity, and anonymity for the perceived severity of bullying. *Journal of Youth and Adolescence, 42*, 739–750. doi: 10.1007/s10964-012-9867-3

Sticca, F., Ruggieri, S., Alsaker, F., & Perren, S. (2013). Longitudinal risk factors for cyberbullying in adolescence. *Journal of Community & Applied Social Psychology, 23*, 52–67. doi: 10.1002/casp.2136

Suzuki, K., Asaga, R., Sourander, A., Hoven, C. W., & Mandell, D. (2012). Cyberbullying and adolescent mental health. *International Journal of Adolescent Medicine and Health, 24*, 27–35.

Tokunaga, R. S. (2010). Following you home from school: A critical review and synthesis of research on cyberbullying victimization. *Computers in Human Behavior, 26*, 277–287. doi: 10.1016/j.chb.2009.11.014

Waasdorp, T. E., & Bradshaw, C. P. (2011). Examining student responses to frequent bullying: A latent class approach. *Journal of Educational Psychology, 103*, 336–352. doi: 10.1037/a0022747

Waasdorp, T. E., & Bradshaw, C. P. (2015). The overlap between cyberbullying and traditional bullying. *Journal of Adolescent Health, 56*, 483–488. doi: 10.1016/j.jadohealth.2014.12.002

Waasdorp, T. E., Bradshaw, C. P., & Duong, J. (2011). The link between parents' perceptions of the school and their responses to school bullying: Variation by child characteristics and the forms of victimization. *Journal of Educational Psychology, 103*, 324–335. doi: 10.1037/a0022748

Wang, J., Iannotti, R. J., & Nansel, T. R. (2009). School bullying among adolescents in the united states: Physical, verbal, relational, and cyber. *Journal of Adolescent Health, 45*, 368–375. doi: 10.1016/j.jadohealth.2009.03.021

Willard, N. E. (2007). The authority and responsibility of school officials in responding to cyberbullying. *The Journal of Adolescent Health: Official Publication of the Society for Adolescent Medicine, 41*(6 Supplement 1), S64–S65. doi: 10.1016/j.jadohealth.2007.08.013

Williford, A., Elledge, L. C., Boulton, A. J., DePaolis, K. J., Little, T. D., & Salmivalli, C. (2013). Effects of the kiva antibullying program on cyberbullying and cybervictimization frequency among Finnish youth. *Journal of Clinical Child and Adolescent Psychology, 42*, 820–833. doi: 10.1080/15374416.2013.787623

Wright, M. F., & Li, Y. (2013). The association between cyber victimization and subsequent cyber aggression: The moderating effect of peer rejection. *Journal of Youth and Adolescence, 42*, 662–674. doi: 10.1007/s10964-012-9903-3

Ybarra, M. L., Diener-West, M., Markow, D., Leaf, P. J., Hamburger, M., & Boxer, P. (2008). Linkages between Internet and other media violence with seriously violent behavior by youth. *Pediatrics, 122*, 929–937.

Clinical Practice in Families of Cyberbullying

Katherine M. Hertlein

Cyberbullying has received little attention as a clinical topic (Hertlein, Blumer, & Smith, 2014). This is surprising given the consequences of cyberbullying on the victim and family, including declines in academic or work performance, trouble with family and peers, and in severe cases, self-harm. Although these topics are all common in a family therapist's practice, situating cyberbullying as the origin of these issues is a relatively new phenomenon. This section reviews the theories used to address cyberbullying in clinical practice, highlights how the couple and family technology framework assists therapists in conceptualizing these cases, discusses how safety is created in cyberbullying cases, and presents the trajectory of treatment. This chapter also reviews these concepts via a clinical application.

Overview of Theories

The theories underlying my approach to working with these cases originate from three general areas: communication and new media studies, human development and technology, and technology's impact on broader society. The theories on communication and new media generally reference the specific technological characteristic of innovative technologies that effect communication, such as how visually and auditorally rich certain technologies are and the circumstances in which those technologies would be most appropriate. Such theories include *Media Richness Theory* (Daft & Lengel, 1984) and *Hyperpersonal Computer-Mediated Communication Theory* (Jiang, Bazarova, & Hancock, 2013; Rabby & Walther, 2002). In short, these theories describe how the structure of new media contributes to relationships.

Likewise, relational development theories (*Social Presence Theory*, Short, Williams, & Christie, 1993) highlight the impact of self-disclosure and immediacy on the development of intimacy processes in relationships, with specific attention to the reciprocal nature of exchanges. Finally, a family's stage in the human developmental life cycle has implications for how technology is understood, responded to, and used in relationship systems (e.g., Haddon, 2006).

Couple and Family Technology Framework

There are several other frameworks that attempt to explain the interaction between the technology user and the computer (e.g., the *Technology Acceptance Model, TAM*; Davis, 1989; *Uses and Gratifications Theory, UGT*; Blumler & Katz, 1974; and the *Sociotechnological Model*, Lanigan, 2009). Yet, these models fail to articulate specific ways in which families interact with, and how relationship processes are affected by, technology. As such, the *Couple and Family Technology Framework* (i.e., CFT) represents one of the most comprehensive treatment approaches grounded in theory and empirical findings (Hertlein, 2012). CFT is grounded in the theories mentioned above as well as three prominent theories in family studies: *Family Ecology Theory* (Granic, Dishion, & Hollenstein, 2003), *Structural Functionalism Theory* (Johnson, 1971), and *Interaction-Constructionist Theory* (Berger & Kellner, 1970). The family-ecology perspective posits that factors in the external environment affect people. In the CFT framework, we operationalize such factors as the *ecological elements*, or the seven elements specific to computers and new media that have transformative effects on relationships. The structural-functionalist perspective (Johnson, 1971) posits how one organizes oneself and how aspects in one's life influence one's organization.

As conceptualized within the CFT framework, ecological elements drive changes to how families organize and function. In many cases, changes to structure encourage positive and adaptive changes in family functioning; in other cases, structural changes can be detrimental. As discussed by Hertlein and Blumer (2013), "The determination as to whether technology and new media provides distance or closeness is best expressed as a function of (a) the type of activity (physical, psychological, or both) and (b) the target of the behavior (i.e., another person or an object?)" (p. 108). The third and final perspective is the interaction-constructionist perspective (Berger & Kellner, 1970), which states our communication with others is composed of rituals, behaviors, and gestures, which are interpreted by others.

Description of the Couple and Family Therapy Framework Applied to Cyberbullying

The CFT framework is organized into three concepts: characteristics of new technologies, the structure of relationships, and the processes of relationships (See Figure 8.2). What follows below is a description of the CFT framework as applied to cyberbullying in families.

Ecological Elements

The ecological elements refer to seven specific characteristics of the Internet that have both direct and indirect effects on family process and structure. These

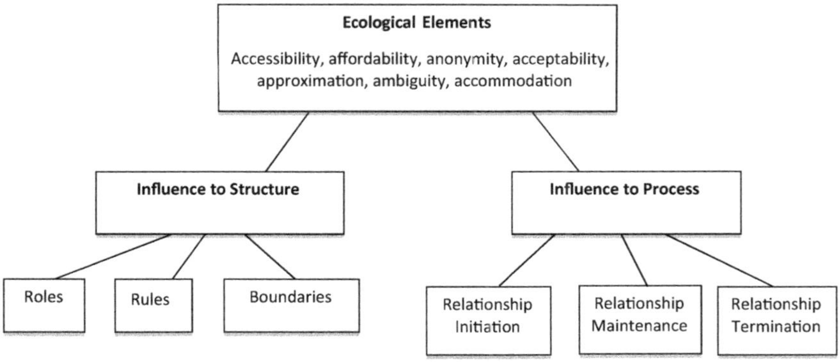

Figure 8.2 Couple and Family Technology Framework

include affordability, accessibility, acceptability, anonymity, approximation, accommodation, and ambiguity.

Affordability, Acceptability, and Accessibility

Cyberbullying cannot happen without access to mobile phones, smartphones, and other electronic devices. Part of accessibility hinges on the fact that these devices be affordable to consumers at nearly every level. Owning a cell phone is associated with a higher status among one's peers (Blair & Fletcher, 2011). Accessibility also hinges on the widespread acceptability of having and using these modes of communication constantly. The acceptability of having such tools at increasingly younger ages also pushes companies to continue making them affordable. In addition, many of the applications for communicating with others with a high degree of security, such as Confide, ChatSecure, and Wickr, can be downloaded and installed for free.

Once both hardware and software are affordable, accessibility increases. Accessibility affects family structure because it increases parents' difficulty in monitoring who contacts their children via these devices. New media and accessibility to virtual connections introduces people known and unknown into one's daily life. Adults have a better developmental ability to screen and monitor those who have access to them, whereas adolescents lack the ability to successfully regulate such relationships consistently. Further, accessibility also influences who has more technological literacy in a family. Adolescents are much better at adopting new technologies than parents and, consequently, may have more power in their relationship with their parents where technology is concerned (Marshall & Reday, 2007).

Finally, affordability, acceptability, and accessibility influence family processes. Adolescents have to balance being able to afford these services and using them to connect with others with the inherent risk of being accessible to others who may abuse the privilege. Parents may also feel pressured to allow the adolescent to use such technologies because they enjoy the access they, as parents, now have to their teen and see such owning of and using a device as a culturally acceptable form of communication.

Anonymity and Ambiguity

Cyberbullying also can be facilitated because of the anonymity associated with our online world. In some circumstances, such as the case described in the beginning of the chapter, some of the attacks come from an unknown entity. Likewise, it can be unclear whether something one is receiving is an attack or benign. Those who cyberbully others can hide behind anonymity. The anonymity can be highly destructive to one's emotional life because the victims become hypervigilant about future online interactions and text messaging. Ambiguity can create a problem for parents in that they may have less technological knowledge than their children and, therefore, experience more technological ambiguity when it comes to cyberbullying.

Approximation and Accommodation

Approximation and accommodation are distinct but related constructs. Approximation refers to the Internet's ability to approximate offline life and environment. Accommodation refers to one's use of the Internet to participate in behaviors one typically would not do offline. Accommodation plays a role in cyberbullying, both for the victim and the perpetrator. From a psychosocial developmental perspective, adolescents in Western culture try different roles in search of their individual identities. From the perpetrator perspective, there is an ability to gain control over someone and/or some situation in ways they would not be able to do offline, and in many cases would not be able to do without the advent of the Internet. Alternatively, victims may use technology to message statements/photos about themselves or others that they would not do in person because of fear of rejection, and these statements/photos may come back to be used by the cyberbully.

Creating Safety

Because cyberbullying is an issue involving adolescents, part of creating safety in the therapy room is making sure that one can adequately join with teens. Gaining trust is key given that victims of cyberbullying are not likely to advertise that information because they fear: (1) being perceived as adopting a victim mentality, and (2) the risk that the therapist may mention the cyberbullying to their parents. Cyberbullying can take many forms, including harassment, as presented in the research section of this chapter. Part of what contributes to a lack of safety and an inability to disclose to one's parents are the circumstances surrounding the topic of the bullying. For example, what may be threatening to the adolescent is the threat of having behavior not condoned by parents (sexting, photos, etc.) revealed to parents if bullying is discussed. Therefore, creating safety is predicated on the therapist operating from a nonjudgmental stance in order to gain the information needed to best protect the adolescent.

Cultural Issues

One of the benefits to using the CFT framework is its ability to be applied to couples and families of diverse backgrounds. At its core, the CFT framework does not advocate for one way or another of using the Internet and new media. The framework simply makes reference to the notion that technology affects process and structure—in some ways the effect is positive and in other ways it is negative. In this model, the therapist reserves judgment about how the family should proceed with technology in their lives and instead assists the family with the implications and interventions congruent with their own beliefs and value system. In some families, for example, appropriate interventions may center on increasing boundaries between parents and their teens; in other cultures or family systems, it may be more appropriate to decrease the boundaries.

Power is another culturally bound issue. In some cultures parents have more power within a family system than in others. In at least one study on emotional intelligence and parenting practices, those from an authoritarian and hierarchical parenting perspective tended to raise children who were less emotionally intelligent because discipline relied on shame and guilt and was punitive. It also relied on seeking approval of others (Sung, 2010). In families using technology, the power may shift among different subsystems. For example, adolescents are referred to as digital natives and have more expertise using technology than their parents (Thomas, 2011). In this way, adolescents may have more power in the parent-child relationship. These adolescents may be more prone to cyberbullying victimization because their parents may be unaware of what is happening to them or how to stop it.

Secrecy is another issue that manifests differently depending on the culture. Because cell phones are independent (as opposed to shared) devices, users have a certain amount of privacy regarding how they use the phone. Adolescents may opt to use the phone as one method of interacting with their peers in secret. For example, Sumon and Anamika (a brother and sister from a Bangladesh family) struggled with their relationship with their parents. Their parents had a habit of checking both teens' phones. Their parents reported that phone checking was a way to ensure the teens were not lying to them about where they were going and with whom. The teens, feeling violated and not agreeing with their parents' decision to check their phones, became even more secretive with their phones. As the teens became more secretive, however, they were using the Internet more frequently and engaging in more risky behavior online, which are two conditions associated with greater likelihood of being victims of cyberbullying (Kowalski, Giumetti, Schroeder, & Lattanner, 2014).

Milestones in Treatment

The treatment of cyberbullying systemically is composed of several family developmental milestones. The first milestone reached is the revelation of the bullying to other family members. This milestone may happen before the family comes to treatment; in other cases, cyberbullying is revealed after joining with the therapist, and that information may need to be revealed to others. A second milestone is the decision as a family to intervene against the bullying. In many cases, this milestone is initiated in the parental subsystem, but it is critical that the adolescent gain a sense of empowerment, as many who are victims of cyberbullying often experience symptoms associated with trauma such as anxiety and fear.

A final milestone is the reorganization of the family with regard to roles, rules, and boundaries that protect the adolescent and encourage family development. This is a milestone wherein the nature and severity of the cyberbullying is considered along with the family's goals. Altering of the boundaries may contribute to more communication among family members or more communication with the outside world, depending on how the boundaries have shifted. The reorganization also can prompt changes in communication among family members and levels of closeness and support.

Predictable Vulnerabilities

The pervasive nature of Internet/cell phone communication is the greatest vulnerability for these families. In some cases, protection from a cyberbully requires that one remove one's online presence, a strategy that may be close to impossible in today's current social climate. Additionally, the way many young people interact with each other relies on these technologies, so it is not realistic to have the adolescent limit accessibility drastically. Another vulnerability is the ability to delete and remove threatening messages without an ability on a parent's end to retrieve them. This increases the likelihood that both the bully and the individual being bullied can delete potentially incriminating messages and manage the perceived degree of involvement. A teen's ability to delete messages can also compromise parents' ability to trust their teen because it is hard to prove the presence of nothing, lending one to a sort of "Russell's teapot" argument and, consequently, relational stalemate.

Typical Interventions

Conducting a thorough assessment is key to intervention in families affected by cyberbullying. Because CFT is essentially a vulnerability framework, the therapist needs to conduct an assessment among the areas listed in the framework; namely, the extent to which affordability, acceptability, accessibility, approximation, anonymity, accommodation, and ambiguity are contributing to the problem. The therapist inquires how much access each family member has to the Internet, the circumstances of the access, and the extent to which each reveals their true selves online. This assessment leads to the second primary intervention—education. The therapist presents the general CFT framework to help the family understand how each factor—characteristics of the Internet/ new media, family structure, and family process—interact with one another. This stage also includes research on cyberbullying, in general, as a way to normalize the experience of both the victim and the family.

The therapist applies the information provided in the assessment phase by the family to how it interacts with their present concerns. The therapist and family then work to develop interventions to manage the ecological elements and restructure family roles to improve processes. For example, in what circumstances is accessibility creating more difficulty for the adolescent? Are there ways in which the family can make structural or process changes in order to manage that vulnerability? For some families the solution may be limiting accessibility. Another family member may identify the solution as increasing accessibility for all family members. This might include a shared email address, Facebook account, or shared smartphones for several members of the family. In this way, cyberbullying is more likely to be discovered.

Cognitive interventions are also critical for treatment. Once bullied, the client may feel ashamed, disempowered, anxious, and afraid to respond for fear of retribution. Such feelings can affect the ways in which the victim interacts with family members, which may result in changes to structure. Although education about cyberbullying can help normalize and reduce shame around the victim's response, it also can help the victim avoid internalizing messages that might contribute to an impaired self-esteem. Cognitive interventions also assist the family in supporting the victim with self-care strategies to manage depression, anxiety, and/or other trauma-related symptoms.

Another intervention to assist those being bullied and their families is encouraging development of appropriate coping skills. Depressive, emotionally focused, and avoidant coping skills are more likely to promote depression and future symptoms than other empowerment-based strategies (with emotionally focused strategies more likely to be employed by the victim; Vollink, Bolman, Dehue, & Jacobs, 2012). The implementation of positive coping skills may help to reestablish closer relationships in the family and assist in maintaining boundaries helpful to healing and the reestablishment of safety.

Case Example: Application of the CFT Framework

In the case study, Emily was receiving text messages of a threatening nature from an anonymous person directed at her and her romantic partner. In the first session, the therapist conducted an assessment to determine the extent to which the vulnerabilities related to the Internet and new media contributed to the experienced cyberbullying. The therapist began with an assessment of the ecological elements. Specifically, accessibility that Emily had to others via email and instant messaging was highlighted. It was this accessibility that prompted her parents to limit Emily's access to these devices. Additionally, her parents' lack of understanding and ambiguity around Internet technologies impaired their ability to respond in any other way than to take away the devices. Therapy around this topic would assist parents with asking questions that assess and clarify any ambiguity. It also includes psychoeducation around different technologies. Acceptability played a part in that it prevented Emily from telling her peers about what was happening to her because she wanted to be accepted by her peers.

One of the first issues addressed was Emily's deleting of messages and hiding what was happening from her parents, in part to resolve the ambiguity her parents experienced related to understanding what was happening. This led to a conversation about how each of the characteristics of new media affected how they parented Emily with regard to both roles and communication with her.

EMILY: *I hid the messages because I didn't think they were a big deal at first. And then I knew they (looking at her parents) would be mad.*

KATHERINE: *This is why we asked you to tell us what was happening.*

EMILY: *Mom, the messages were mine and none of your business and I could handle it.*

KATHERINE: *Obviously not.*

THERAPIST: *So how do you think that Emily's being the only person to have access to the phone and that access being rather unlimited affected how you parent her?*

HENRI: *I think we just need to be more strict.*

EMILY: *But it wasn't my fault!*

THERAPIST: *So the accessibility creates a sense of distrust for the two of you and creates more rules for Emily. Are the rules around the phone specifically, or around other areas in her life?*

EMILY: *They stopped letting me go out.*

KATHERINE: *We just didn't want anything bad to happen to you.*

THERAPIST: *Emily, do you feel like you lost some independence as a result?*

EMILY: *Definitely. I don't feel as if they think they can trust me.*

KATHERINE: *Well, part of that was we had no idea who was doing it.*

THERAPIST: *So how did the anonymity of who was behind it all contribute to your parenting?*

KATHERINE: *We don't feel that we could trust any of her friends. Not knowing who was behind it . . . we had to question and wonder about everyone.*

EMILY: *I feel like I am the one getting punished and I wasn't the one who was behind this all.*

THERAPIST: *When did you first start feeling that way? How do you think your parents' concerns and response about accessibility and the anonymity play out between you?*

EMILY: *It feels like I'm the one they don't trust, and I wasn't the one who did anything.*

HENRI: *You didn't keep us informed.*

THERAPIST: *Given that it is pretty acceptable in today's world to have teens with their own cell phones, what do you think you could do in terms for negotiating a different role for Emily to increase the likelihood that she will bring these issues to you and feel she can be trusted?*

HENRI: *She can bring us her cell phone every day.*

EMILY: *That isn't fair.*

THERAPIST: *I'm not sure that communicates trust. I think Emily loses some autonomy in that arrangement.*

The therapist facilitated a conversation regarding how the limiting of access might be construed as avoidance and contraindicated in treatment.

THERAPIST: *What other solutions are available?*

KATHERINE: *I think it starts with her being able to be able to talk to us. Just as much as she can talk to her friends online, it might be easy for her to screenshot what she is receiving so we can take a look and see if it's appropriate—not to yell at her, but to just make sure we are accounting for her welfare.*

EMILY: *You're just going to get mad.*

KATHERINE: *I don't think that's always true. I think if we find a way that you can start to trust that we are looking out for you, we can be a resource. I think the accessibility works in your favor.*

THERAPIST: *Another aspect of that is that when your parents feel more involved in your life, their ambiguity about what is really going on with you is reduced, which ultimately makes communication better. Would it be something you would be willing to try? Working on screen-shooting things that your friends send and asking either your mom, dad, or sister for advice?*

EMILY: *I can try it.*

The therapist used this opportunity to develop empowering strategies relying on accessibility. For example, Emily identified people with whom she could establish relationships as a way to begin to make decisions about who she could trust. She also used the cell phone to engage in more access with her parents and develop closer relationships with them. As a result, her parents (and sister Johanna) were better able to advise her on decisions related to interactions with others online.

After several family sessions discussing ways in which the family could support empowerment through better communication, the therapist met with

Emily individually to review strategies where she could incorporate different aspects of her personality in a way to both protect herself and use the anonymity provided to implement new assertiveness skills. She was able to practice these skills with her family in real-time situations. The therapist worked with the family to identify when to use technology and for what circumstances. For example, asynchronous methods of communication (email, texting with time delays) are used for when individuals want to solve problems and synchronous methods (real-time messaging/texting) are best for when one wants support. For example, when she wants support from her sister, Emily has to be thoughtful about contacting her at times and through a mechanism such as text that allows her sister to respond immediately. In the cases where she was trying to solve problems regarding how to respond to her friends, Emily used the screenshots of messages her friends sent as a way to start a conversion about how to solve it with her parents. She learned that she should refrain from responding to a friend's text until she was sure how she wanted to handle things. Such strategies can be applied to assist Emily in using anonymity to her advantage in terms of her revelations to others and assisting her in being suspicious of others because of anonymity.

References

Berger, P. L., & Kellner, H. (1970). Marriage and the construction of reality. In H. Dreitzel (Ed.), *Recent sociology* (Vol. 2, pp. 50–72). New York: Macmillan.

Blair, B. L., & Fletcher, H. C. (2011). "The only 13-year old on Planet Earth without a cell phone": Meanings of cell phones in early adolescents' everyday lives. *Journal of Adolescent Research, 26*, 155–177. doi: 10.1177/074355841037112

Blumler, J. G., & Katz, E. (1974). *The uses of mass communications: Current perspectives on gratifications research.* Beverly Hills, CA: Sage Publications.

Daft, R. L., & Lengel, R. H. (1984). Information richness: A new approach to managerial behavior and organizational design. In L. L. Cummings & B. M. Staw (Eds.), *Research in organizational behavior* (pp. 191–233). Homewood, IL: JAI Press.

Davis, F. D. (1989). Perceived usefulness, perceived ease of use, and user acceptance of information technology. *MIS Quarterly, 13*(3), 319–340. doi: 10.2307/249008

Granic, I., Dishion, T. J., & Hollenstein, T. (2003). The family ecology of adolescence: A dynamic systems perspective on normative development. In G. R. Adams and M. D. Berzonsky's (Eds.), *Blackwell handbook of adolescence* (pp. 60–91). New York: Wiley.

Haddon, L. (2006). The contribution of domestication research to in-home computing and media consumption. *The Information Society, 22*, 195–203. doi: 10.1080/01972240600791325

Hertlein, K. M. (2012). Digital dwelling: Technology in couple and family relationships. *Family Relations, 61*(3), 374–387. doi: 10.2307/4149521

Hertlein, K. M., & Blumer, M. L. C. (2013). *The couple and family technology framework: Intimate relationships in a digital age*. New York: Routledge.

Hertlein, K. M., & Blumer, M. L. C., & Smith, J. (2014). Marriage and family therapists' use and comfort with online communication with clients. *Contemporary Family Therapy, 36*, 58–69. doi: 10.1007/s10591-013-9284-0

Jiang, C., Bazarova, N. N., & Hancock, J. T. (2013). From perception to behavior: Disclosure reciprocity and the intensification of intimacy in computer-mediated relationships. *Communication Research, 40*, 125–143. doi: 10.1177/0093650211405313

Johnson, H. (1971). The structural-functional theory of family and kinship. *Journal of Comparative Studies, 2*, 133–144.

Kowalski, R. M., Giumetti, G. W., Schroeder, A. N., & Lattanner, M. R. (2014). Bullying in the digital age: A critical review and meta-analysis of cyberbullying research among youth. *Psychological Bulletin, 140*(4), 1073–1137. doi: 10.1037/a0035618

Lanigan, J. D. (2009). A sociotechnological model for family research and intervention: How information and communication technologies affect family life. *Marriage & Family Review, 45*(6–8), 587–609. doi: 10.1080/01494920903224194.

Marshall, R., & Reday, P. A. (2007). Internet-enabled youth and power in family decisions. *Young Consumers: Insight and Ideas for Responsible Marketers, 8*(3), 177–183. doi: 10.1108/17473610710780927

Rabby, M., & Walther, J. B. (2002). Computer-mediated communication impacts on relationship formation and maintenance. In D. Canary & M. Dainton (Eds.), *Maintaining relationships through communication: Relational, contextual, and cultural variations* (pp. 141–162). Mahwah, NJ: Lawrence Erlbaum Associates.

Short, J., Williams, E., & Christie, B. (1993). Visual communication and social interaction. In R. M. Baecker (Ed.), *Readings in groupware and computer-supported cooperative work: Assisting human–human collaboration* (pp. 153–164). Palo Alto, CA: Morgan Kaufmann.

Sung, H. Y. (2010). The influence of culture on parenting practices of East Asian families and emotional intelligence of older adolescents: A qualitative study. *School Psychology International, 31*(2), 199–214. doi: 10.1177/0143034309352268

Thomas, M. (2011). *Deconstructing digital natives: Young people, technology, and the new literacies*. New York: Routledge.

Vollink, T., Bolman, C., Dehue, F., & Jacobs, N. (2012). Coping with cyberbullying: Differences between victims, bully-victims, and children not involved in bullying. *Journal of Community and Applied Social Psychology, 23*(1), 7–24. doi: 10.1002/casp.2142

9

CONCLUSION

Scott W. Browning and Brad van Eeden-Moorefield

When we set out on the journey to produce this volume, our main goal was to establish additional pathways by which research and practice could be integrated. We hoped the end result would produce a strong knowledge base that ultimately could be used to support the well-being of various family types and their experiences through: (a) enhanced knowledge of the empirical literature, (b) the translation of that knowledge along with clinical theory into EBPs (or evidence-supported practices), and (c) that were grounded in an actual case study thereby adding a level of practicality. A particularly unique focus was the inclusion of both common family types that tend to experience periodic vulnerabilities (divorce, stepfamilies, fragile families, families with a member struggling with addiction) as well as some emerging, less common family experiences (homicide, imprisonment/reentry, cyberbullying) that contribute a heightened level of risk to well-being in many cases, and for which we have little empirical and or clinical literature.

We recognized integration across research and practice was a lofty goal, as there are many factors that make building such a bridge challenging (Horsfall, Cleary, & Hunt, 2010; Kazdin, 2008; Small, 2005). Additionally, the questions of "what exactly is integration" and "what balance of integration is optimal" continue to be elusive (Dattilio, 2002), and were issues we had to discuss before embarking on this journey. It is difficult to begin identifying pathways for integration without answering the preceding questions, especially when no one answer exists. Luckily, we firmly believe in iterative approaches and embracing *the gray areas* of life. Now at the end of this particular journey, we cannot say we have definitions or answers to provide. However, we believe this volume does represent some important progress toward these ends.

Over the past decade, more researchers, and universities in which many work, have become increasingly interested in applied research and less interested in basic research (notwithstanding many of the hard science fields). Part of this may be a result of stronger public and state interest in accountability, as measured in part by the community impact of our work (the measurement of this is an entirely different debate that we will leave for a different volume).

Related, many universities also seem to desire to be more research-focused, thereby leading to a heavier emphasis on research training in most graduate programs, including clinical programs. Essentially, one could argue a paradigm shift is occurring that will make it easier to bridge the research-practice gap in the coming years. However, we do not believe such a transition will be easy, nor its value recognized easily by many.

We also realize multiple barriers exist, especially those that would prevent collaboration—a key aspect of bridging research and practice. For university researchers, institutions tend to require generalized measures of impact such as number of publications, journal rankings, impact factors, and the like. Unfortunately, no metrics exist that could capture the extent to which research findings can be/are used to inform practice or activities related to informing practice. Accordingly, we expect researchers to spend little to no time engaged in such activities as they focus primarily on those activities that make tenure and promotion more likely. For community clinicians, time spent reading research, meeting with teams of researchers, or working on evaluation studies are not billable hours, and enough non-billable time is spent on paperwork. So, we have a less than ideal system, and families who deserve the best treatment are caught in the middle. In an ideal world, we would have teams of researchers and clinicians, among others family and healthcare practitioners, who would work together with families to develop comprehensive, holistic assessments that lead to evidence-supported treatments. From a more practice perspective, training research and clinical graduate students in a way that socializes them into thinking from both research and clinical perspectives is a cost-effective step, though, and one that is gaining momentum (Hershenberg, Drabick, & Vivian, 2012). Approaches to books such as the one we used are another step. We also suggest more continuing education unit (CEU) trainings focus on bringing researchers and clinicians together to develop EBPs in vivo. The most important element across these steps is opening the dialogue, and for that to happen time and space must be created with intent.

Several scholars before us have provided important points of entry (i.e., strategies) for establishing cross-communication between research and clinical scholars. The most prominent include fostering collaborative partnerships (Kazdin, 2008), use of theory (Southern & Devlin, 2010), and using evidence-based practice (EBP) frameworks (Hershenberg et al., 2012). Others identify several similar and additional strategies (e.g., see Small, 2005). For our purposes, we focused on the three most prominent strategies, although they were not implemented equally across research and clinical authors. For example, research authors were not required to use theory, but clinical authors were, whereas the reverse was true for EBPs.

As we conclude our work on this volume and reflect back, we are proud of the product produced and are in awe of the many contributing authors, who shared a commitment to bridging research and practice that was inspiring. Through this process we made important progress toward achieving our goal and gained valuable new insights that we hope will guide future efforts to bridge research and practice. To highlight some of this progress, we briefly discuss how theory, collaborative partnerships, and evidence-based frameworks were used to produce this text. Finally, we provide some examples of intervention techniques that resulted from collaborations within the preceding chapters and discuss some of the clinical highlights garnered. Throughout we provide some suggested next steps to continue bridging research and practice.

Strategies for Building Bridges

As stated above, the most prominent strategies that promote the integration of research and practice include fostering collaborative partnerships (Kazdin, 2008; Small, 2005), use of theory (Small, 2005; Southern & Devlin, 2010), and using evidence-based practice (EBP) frameworks (Hershenberg et al., 2012). Each was incorporated throughout the development of this volume. The first (and ongoing) focus was fostering collaboration across research and clinical scholars. Once authors were identified for each chapter, and connected to one another, clinical scholars prepared a case study that was an actual case they worked on and that represented a fairly typical family. Case studies were shared with research scholars, and all authors were asked to "consult" on the case. During this period they were to identify additional pieces of information relevant to the case and that might need to be incorporated into the written case summary, eventually placed at the beginning of each chapter along with the genogram.

Authors then were asked to discuss a basic outline of sorts for the research chapter to ensure findings that are clinically relevant were included along with some additional general research pertinent to family types and experiences included in this volume (e.g., demographic profiles, prevalence rates, typical developmental patterns). Clinical scholars also were asked to pose several questions to research scholars that represented types of clinical questions they often encountered when working with families and about which they wondered if research evidence existed that could answer them. Research scholars were asked specifically to incorporate that *evidence*, if available, into their chapters. All authors received and commented on each other's sections of the chapter at least once and were encouraged to communicate throughout the process as well.

As editors, we tried to encourage this in each of our communications with authors. We believe that our own backgrounds as researchers and clinicians aided this process. That said, we, too, had many conversations to ensure we were translating and using terminology with shared meanings across research and practice. In this way, integration became more of an encouraged process rather than a directive. In many cases, some incredibly strong collaboration developed, resulting in well-integrated chapters.

Southern and Devlin (2010) suggested that theory development holds great promise to bridge research and practice, although they discuss this as a technique in which clinicians engage individually. Small (2005) also discussed the importance of theory in bridging research and practice with a focus on only practitioners engaging in such work. Similarly, clinical scholars in this volume were asked to present the theoretical foundation of their work with case study families. In some instances theories used were prominent frameworks in the field (e.g., Wagner & Diamond, this volume) and in other cases they represented a clinician's own developed framework (e.g., Hertlein, this volume). This is important conceptual work and has implications for integration not used elsewhere to our knowledge. As we complete this volume, we believe that theory is an underused tool to foster integration.

Theory often is shared between researchers and clinicians and is included in graduate training for both. Further, in many cases theories are used for both research and practice (e.g., systems and feminist theories), and in other cases theories are more specific to one or the other realm. We believe there are several ways in which we can harness theory for integration. First, each theory comes with its own terminology, assumptions, perspective, and so forth. This means theory can provide researchers and clinicians with a shared language that should foster enhanced communication and shared meaning. Theories also help categorize and connect research findings using concepts and propositions, differentiate between typical and atypical functioning/development, explain problems, and identify potential intervention sites. Essentially, these all are pieces of one larger puzzle. By working together, researchers and clinicians are positioned to complete the same puzzle. We suggest the completed puzzle is a sophisticated clinical approach that may involve EBP, common factors, basic science research, and ongoing outcome assessment. To maximize this potential, it may be that future work should have researchers and clinicians identify a core theoretical framework that, along with the case study, can ground each chapter thereby resulting in a stronger integration.

If we return to the bridge idea, what we have are the major components of bridges: design, materials, and construction workers. We would argue that theory provides the design, research provides materials (i.e., evidence), and construction workers (researchers and clinicians) are able to correctly place and stabilize (i.e., collaboration) the various materials that create the bridge. In this case, then, the bridge is an EBP or ESP. From this it should be clear that researchers and clinicians offer important strengths unique to them, but it is through their collaboration enhanced by the creation of shared meaning that families truly can be supported and strengthened.

Intervention Techniques Developed Through Collaboration

Psychoeducation

Psychoeducation is one of the great benefits from the collaboration between researchers and clinicians. The clinician needs to see parallels between specific issues facing his or her case and the relevant literature. When it is clear that a research finding would be useful for the family, the clinician often simply reports it as research. The clinician need not feel compelled to align with a research finding. In fact, clinical neutrality, in these situations, can occasionally be better for the therapeutic alliance. On other occasions, the clinician may support the research findings by having anecdotal data from clinical practice. Thus, the clinician can advocate for a certain clinical direction by referring to both research data and clinical experience.

Validation

Research findings are very helpful to validate the work of the clinician. One is either more empathic due to being more knowledgeable, or one is reading research that specifically supports her or his clinical directions.

Intervention

Some specific interventions, such as reframing, are directly supported in the research literature. Research has taken an area that clinicians knew worked (in their hearts) and provided it with empirical support.

Clinical Highlights of EBPs

True clinical writing, preferred by clinicians, is not loaded with citations. While appropriate reference to the supporting research is critical, the flow of the writing must assist the reader in understanding the process of therapy (or in the case of the Families of Incarceration clinical section, mediation). When considering the clinical sections of this book, it is interesting to see how the clinical scholars considered their task. Two primary patterns occurred in the clinical sections, either a specific model (already established in the field) was illustrated in depth, or the author(s) laid out the necessary steps to provide an evidence-supported treatment. Again, it is important to remember that the creation of a fully validated evidence-based treatment is impossible following the standing criteria. The aim of this book is to identify therapy that is theoretically sound, takes the specific family types into account, and involves common factors of outcome success.

Certainly, all models shared one common thread; the complexity of these families must be understood by the families themselves. With greater structural complexity and increased emotional expression, some clinical tools must be used that create a calmer, more reasoned environment. Interestingly, certain interventions seemed more tailored to specific family types, and these clinical steps are supported by the reported research. Since this book represents the second in the Contemporary Families series, one can go to the earlier version (Browning & Pasley, 2015) for highlighted interventions for the original seven types: adoption, autism, interracial, grandparent-run, LGBTQ, medically challenged, and foster. Below, we provide some of the more important evidence-based intervention considerations for families included in this volume.

Families of Divorce

Therapeutic Alliance Needs to Exist With Both Parents

In divorce, it is critical that the parents achieve collegial status with one another. Anger and resentment that makes it impossible to coparent guarantees that the child(ren) will be placed in an untenable position. Meeting with parents together, even for a single session, is often appropriate to convey the necessity of keeping some channels of communication open.

Warn Against Triangulating a Child

Research on this topic is clear in that children suffer more if they are required to convey messages back and forth between warring parents. The clinician needs to be clear that other options exist that greatly benefit the children in these situations.

The Effect of Transitions Will Be Understood

Children often find transitions between homes, schools, and neighborhoods difficult; however, with reduced pressure, these transitions can be less disruptive. Part of what makes a transition difficult is a parent assuming that the child feeling "down" is because the child is not happy to be "home," whereas most kids simply are unable to immediately readjust when in a new setting.

The Inalienable Right to a Parent

Children have the right to know and see both parents. Certainly there can be a parent who has legally lost this right due to significant abuse, but otherwise, one parent should avoid believing that he or she is "protecting" a child by keeping the child from the other parent.

The Binuclear Family Replaces the Original Family

The family is not broken; it has two centers, each parent. This new reality needs to be respected by the therapist. While the occasional meeting between the parents may be necessary (since they remain co-parents), the model of recognizing this new structure is important.

Stepfamilies

The Clinician Needs Permission to Share Certain Information

Within a stepfamily, there are multiple subsystems. Treatment usually focuses on these subsystems. Thus, information is shared in one session that would greatly clarify actions and attitudes. Continued secrecy often erodes the stepfamily that does not have enough history to buffer against misperceptions.

Psychoeducation Is Critical

Stepfamilies usually have no point of reference as to what actions and feelings are typical. Most have not lived in a stepfamily before. Therefore, they use the first-union family as a point of reference, and this is frequently not an apt comparison. The clinician needs to know the research literature on this family type to offer a perspective that will assist the stepfamily to feel less out of control.

Misperceptions Can Be Corrected

Although misperceptions and misinterpretations occur in all families, they have a particularly insidious effect on stepfamilies. Without the relational history found in other families, members of a stepfamily may make a single mistake that results in a significant strain on tenuous family connections. The clinician needs to be highly alert for errors and find a way to shed light on the mistake as not intending to be as harmful as it is perceived.

Reality Is Contextual

A parent's perspective on her or his child and a stepparent's perception regarding this same child will often be significantly different. This is not just because of love. Perspectives are shaped by various factors, among them, the depth of knowledge that comes from years together. The stepparent may, in fact, be more objective. But couples in a stepfamily should refrain from acting as though all problems would cease if they could just convince their partner about how wrong the other is about a child.

Relationships Should Be Emotionally Matched

If a stepchild is reluctant to bond with a stepparent, that intention is best respected. In other words, no matter the direction of the relationship (stepparent toward stepchild or stepchild toward stepparent), trying to "win" the other over and have a more fulfilling relationship is difficult and can backfire. It is often preferable to build a slow and steady bond with people who do not seem open to rapid increases in closeness.

Fragile Families

Understanding Which Families Constitute This Label Is Crucial

These families have significant troubles both economically and relationally. Little is secure in these homes, so even the slightest "bump in the road" can become a major crisis. Thus, clinicians need to address multiple areas of the family at the same time.

Multiple Approaches Must Be Offered Simultaneously

Parent education, service coordination, crisis intervention, family support, and case management are all necessary. Without some type of team, these families are simply too chaotic to benefit fully from typical family therapy.

Communication Is Challenging Under This Pressure

Communication is difficult in these homes because the pressure to find money, keep shelter, and avoid negative interactions with the outside society makes the home an emotional pressure cooker. The clinician must be aware of how to lessen the emotional arousal while increasing familial support.

Strengthen the Co-Caregiver Alliance

The primary parents must experience some sense of being able to work together and help each other. Assignments and clear discussions are often necessary.

The Emotional Connection Between the Parent(s) and Each Child Must Be Improved

This relationship is inherently satisfying, so the clinician should continue to assert that this relationship can be made more emotionally satisfying for each party.

Supports Outside the Family Must Be Increased

These families need to have more stability, and healthy community involvement will invariably increase stability. There are people to offer some assistance, and following this support these "fragile families" become contributors to the community again.

Families and Addiction

Prevention Is an Overarching Goal

Due to the genetic predisposition for addiction to be passed from parent to child, clinicians need to avoid using hyperbole but be honest that young people need to be highly attuned to the presence of addicted behaviors.

Sometimes the Addicted Member Is Not in the Family Therapy

Treatment for addiction is developmental. At times the addict needs rehabilitation in which the family is only modestly involved. But the family can always benefit from some treatment, even if it is largely psychoeducational.

Solution-Focused Brief Treatment Is Well Established for Addiction

The "paradigm shift" aspect of solution-focused work pushes the idea of a preferred future, which is the appropriate focus for addiction. This work can exist in parallel with the 12-step approach.

Focusing on Female Clients Is Important

Women have been found to have more co-occurring conditions and have historically received less attention from the helping professions. Women also may feel more stigmatized than men by addiction due to the pressures placed on them by society to be good mothers. Thus, clinicians need to be sensitive to issues particularly difficult for women and addiction.

Family Strengths Need to Be Highlighted

Often the family has become defeated due to the insidious effect of addiction. Accordingly, looking for strengths is an important intervention. Any method to lessen the effect of addiction on the family is advised.

Families That Experience Homicide

Communication Patterns Are Permanently Altered Due to Loss of One Member

Families have specific communication patterns. With one family member missing, all the communication that used to involve that person is now different. This is not always a problem, but it needs to be pointed out to avoid frequent miscommunication.

Grief, Trauma, and Legal Issues May Be Present Simultaneously

Even one of these issues can be challenging in clinical practice, but these families often will have all three, to varying degrees. The clinician needs to be able to comment on the neurological processes in play for this individual trying to adapt these issues. Trauma, if present, makes the emotional intensity challenging.

The Term "Co-Victim" Is Purposeful

Each member of the family is a co-victim; she or he has fallen victim to the homicide of a family member. Systemic dynamics will occur in which the stigma of this crime will present predictable problems.

Play Therapy Is a Common Adjunct Treatment

When children are in these families, the topics are so scary and overwhelming that play is the most humane treatment. Play is the language of children. As children play, important themes can start in an unconscious way and slowly emerge as a point of discussion.

The Clinician Holds a Nonjudgmental Perspective

In general, clinicians are advised to be nonjudgmental. Given how likely one feels the bubbling up of judgment in these situations, it is critical to be diligent. Clinicians must be "partial" to every single family member, including those not in the therapy.

Families of Incarceration and Reentry

Prison Has an Intergenerational Component

The clinician needs to increase the seriousness of improvement. Too many people get caught in a pattern that does not have to be so repetitive. This does not imply that the clinician begins preaching to the family, but making them aware that resilience can be increased is an important clinical tool.

"Prisonization" Occurs

Returning citizens are usually burdened with interactional problems that affect family life. Trust and authenticity are dropped in prison; to be too trusting, or too honest, simply makes one weaker. Thus, this interactional style needs to be affirmed, understood, and then altered. Family members basically must trust each other and be authentic. We have to be our real selves to love and be loveable.

Mediation Precedes Family Therapy

There needs to be preparatory work that occurs before being released from prison that makes it clear things can be improved. Future family therapy should be desired by the family members and not forced.

Coparent Work Is Crucial

Much like the "Fragile Family," these families are so tense that even the parental relationship does not feel safe and supportive. No one knows his or her role in this revised family. The old family has been changed by the emotional world of the returning citizen.

Cyberbullying and the Family

Blaming Is Not Useful

Even in the case where an adolescent does something embarrassing that makes cyberbullying more likely, the person is still the victim, and blaming the victim is not a useful strategy.

Restriction of Technology Use by Itself Is Not Helpful

Parents may be tempted to place blanket restrictions on cell phones and Internet use as a way to ameliorate cyberbullying and protect their children. On the contrary, restriction by itself may lead to the adolescent engaging in more secretive online behaviors. Since adolescents are "digital natives," their power in gaining access to technology even when placed on restriction should not be underestimated.

A Thorough Assessment Is Key

It is important for the therapist to thoroughly assess the framework and context for technology use among family members. How specifically is technology contributing to the problem?

Psychoeducation About Cyberbullying

Because the victim of cyberbullying likely experiences negative emotions like shame and anxiety, and may experience them in secret (due to hiding the bullying from his or her family), open discussion about the incidence of cyberbullying can help normalize the experience for the victim.

Concluding Thoughts

Both research and practice benefit from a collaborative effort. The contemporary family, with its complexity and structural differences, provides the perfect laboratory to examine how this collaboration provides information that assists these families as they negotiate the world and proceed to live happy and healthy existences. We truly hope that you find the research on these families and their daily experiences as fascinating and informative as we do, and equally so, that you find the clinical theory and EBPs useful and effective in expanding your clinical efforts. Ultimately, we hope this work helps researchers and clinicians recognize what we have to learn from one another, offers some strategies to do this, and provides a foundation that serves to strengthen more families for years to come. We thank all readers for their commitment, dedication, and work in supporting families!

References

Browning, S., & Pasley, K. (2015). *Contemporary families: Translating research into practice*. New York, NY: Routledge.

Dattilio, F. M. (2002). A bridge and a couple of fences: A response to Silverman. *Psychotherapy*, *39*(3), 261–263.

Hershenberg, R., Drabick, D., & Vivian, D. (2012). An opportunity to bridge the gap between clinical research and clinical practice: Implications for clinical training. *Psychotherapy*, *49*, 123–134. doi: 10.1037/a0027648

Horsfall, J., Cleary, M., & Hunt, G. (2010). Developing partnerships in mental health to bridge the research-practitioner gap. *Perspectives in Psychiatric Care*, *47*, 6–12. doi: 10.1111/j.1744-6163.2010.00265.x

Kazdin, K. (2008). Evidence-based treatment and practice. *American Psychologist*, *63*, 146–159. doi: 10.1037/0003-066X.63.3.146

Small, S. (2005). Bridging research and practice in the family and human sciences. *Family Relations*, *54*, 320–334. https://doi.org/10.1111/j.0197-6664.2005.00024.x

Southern, S., & Devlin, J. (2010). Theory development: A bridge between practice and research. *The Family Journal: Counseling and Therapy for Couples and Families*, *18*, 84–87. doi: 10.1177/1066-480709358422

INDEX

For Product Safety Concerns and Information please contact our EU
representative GPSR@taylorandfrancis.com
Taylor & Francis Verlag GmbH, Kaufingerstraße 24, 80331 München, Germany

www.ingramcontent.com/pod-product-compliance
Ingram Content Group UK Ltd.
Pitfield, Milton Keynes, MK11 3LW, UK
UKHW021502240926
475702UK00035B/215
9781138950726